CW00545111

Nationalism w...

PAKISTAN

Nationalism without a Nation?

Edited by
CHRISTOPHE JAFFRELOT

MANOHAR

CENTRE DE SCIENCES HUMAINES

ZED BOOKS LTD
2002

First published 2002

© Individual contributors, 2002

All rights reserved. No part of this publication may be
reproduced or transmitted, in any form or by any means,
without prior permission of the editor and the publisher

ISBN 81-7304-407-4

Published by
Ajay Kumar Jain for
Manohar Publishers & Distributors
4753/23 Ansari Road, Daryaganj
New Delhi 110002

Published in the Rest of the World by
Zed Books Ltd
7 Cynthia Street
London N1 9JF, UK
and
Room 400, 175 Fifth Avenue,
New York
NY 10010, USA

ISBN 1 84277 116 7 Hb
ISBN 1 84277 117 5 Pb

Distributed in the USA exclusively by
Palgrave, a division of St. Martin's Press, LLC
175 Fifth Avenue, New York, NY 10010

A catalogue record for this book is available from the British Library
US CIP data is available from the Library of Congress

Typeset by
A J Software Publishing Co. Pvt. Ltd.
New Delhi 110005

Printed at
Rajkamal Electric Press
Delhi 110033

Contents

Nationalism without a Nation: Pakistan Searching for its Identity

CHRISTOPHE JAFFRELOT

> Since its inception, Pakistan has faced the monumental task to spell out an identity different from the Indian identity. Born from the division of the old civilisation of India, Pakistan has struggled for constructing its own culture, a culture which would not only be different from the Indian culture but that the whole world would acknowledge.[1]

ORE THAN HALF a century after its creation, Pakistan is still searching for its identity, as if Partition, instead of solving the problem of the Muslims of the Indian subcontinent, had generated new ones.

This book focuses on the contrast between the lack of a positive national identity—something different from the Indian culture, as suggested by the excerpt of *Dawn* cited above—and the prevalence in Pakistan of a strong nationalism directed against India. This distinction between nationalism and nation is not a rhetorical one. Nationalism is an ideology, be it based on territorial or ethnic notions.[2] On the other hand, a nation is a social construction, as evident from the definition of the French sociologist Marcel Mauss.

> We regard as forming a nation a society materially and morally integrated, with a stable and permanent centralised political power, well established borders, *a relative moral, mental and cultural unity of its inhabitants who consciously adhere to the state and its laws.*[3]

This definition rules out the presence of any intermediary bodies, be they linguistic groups or religious communities. Pakistan appears to be an unachieved nation precisely because of the persistence of ethnic identities which may even be described as 'nationalities'. The 'two-nation theory' gave the country a *nationalist* ideology—it has even been described as an 'ideological state'[4]—which has been formulated *against* India, the 'other nation'. But it did not endow Pakistan with the sociological qualities of a nation. Professor Khalid Bin Sayeed asked in the late 1990s: 'Pakistan, with all its weaknesses, has a state, but does it have a nation?'[5] The question primarily arose from the fissiparous tendencies that ethnic groups have developed right from the beginning. Lately, sectarian conflicts between Shias and Sunnis have further challenged the notion that Islam provided Pakistan with a common platform. However, one must take a nuanced view of this national integration issue because several separatist trends have been defused in the course of time. Besides, one needs to analyse to what extent the strength of Pakistani nationalism may make up for the weaknesses of the nation.

PAKISTAN BEFORE PAKISTAN?
NATIONALISTS IN QUEST OF A NATION

Mohammad Ali Jinnah wanted to build a strong state relying on the threefold principle 'one nation, one culture, one language'.[6] Pakistan was intended to be the homeland of the Muslims of British India, and its language could be nothing else but Urdu. Jinnah had the ideology but he missed the social and the geographical base. He represented the Muslims of the provinces of the Raj where they were in a minority and who, partly for this demographic reason, faced the threat of social decline. The Muslims of the United Provinces (today Uttar Pradesh) were a case in point. As early as the turn of the twentieth century, they prepared the ground for the Pakistan project.[7] They had been greatly affected by the British policy after the 1857 'Revolt'. Landlords had been deprived of some of their properties for having taken part in it and the intelligentsia—whose members often came from the same aristocratic milieu—were discriminated against in terms of administrative recruitment. This Muslim elite which had already been affected by the replacement of Persian by 'Indian vernaculars' for judicial and fiscal proceedings in 1837, was further weakened in 1899 by the recognition of Hindi as the other official language of the United Provinces, on the same footing as Urdu.[8] On top of it, the democratization process that the British initiated in the late nineteenth century made the Muslims fear that they would even lose the left-over influence since they were in a minority. In 1882, the Local Self-Government Act enabled the Indians who were enfranchised to elect some of their local representatives. In 1909, the provinces of the Raj were granted partly elected Legislative Councils. The introduction of the elective principle enhanced the fears of marginalization among the Muslims, who represented only one-fifth of the population according to the 1881 Census. While all the Muslims of British India were affected by these measures, those of the provinces where they were in a minority were naturally the most concerned, and, among them, those of the United Provinces, because in this region, the Muslim elite had more to lose. While the Muslims formed only 13.4 per cent of the local population, they occupied 45 per cent of the uncovenanted civil service in 1886, a clear indication of their still privileged position.[9]

In the late nineteenth century, the UP Muslims mobilized under the aegis of Syed Ahmed Khan. Khan was first eager to improve the education of his community. In 1869, he founded in Aligarh the Mohammedan Anglo-Oriental College, that was to provide the basis for the creation of the Aligarh Muslim University in 1911.[10] The MAO College trained the first generations of opponents to the Indian National Congress. The Congress claimed that it represented all the communities of the Indian nation, but Muslim Congressmen accounted for only 6.6 per cent of the total number of the delegates who took part in the annual sessions of the Congress between 1892 and 1909.[11] The 1882 Local Self-Government Act had already been a cause of great concern for Syed Ahmed Khan. His followers mobilized on a more overtly political platform in 1906 when the British announced the establishment of the Legislative Councils. Muhsin al-Mulk, the Secretary of the MAO College, led a delegation to the Viceroy, Lord Minto, in order to demand a separate electorate, a concession that Minto granted in a spirit of 'divide and rule'. With 11 members, the UP Muslims were largely over-represented in a delegation which comprised only 7 Punjabis and 1 Bengali!

The key role of alumni from Aligarh in the creation of the Muslim League, which was founded in late 1906, and then in the Khilafat movement, in which Mohammad Ali and Shaukat Ali were, for instance, very active,[12] reflects the importance of the UP Muslim in the genesis of Muslim separatism in India. Francis Robinson has explained this phenomenon by arguing that these Muslims 'had, in fact, a sense of Muslim identity'.[13] Such an analysis harks back to the primordialist interpretation of nationalism and nation-building.[14] Clifford Geertz, for instance, tended to explain nationalism as stemming from 'givens' such as religion or language.[15] This reading of nationalism appears to be simplistic and largely irrelevant in the case of Muslim separatism.

Interpreting Muslim Separatism[16]

The primordialist viewpoint has been strongly criticized by Ernest Gellner, for whom 'Men do not become nationalists from sentiment or sentimentality, atavistic or not, well-based or myth-founded: they become nationalists through genuine, objective, practical necessity, however obscurely recognised'.[17] In his theory of nationalism, Gellner assumes that there is always an unequal distribution of economic resources across the territory of a state. People, 'B', originating from a deprived region, ask for its share but another ethnic group, 'A', which is relatively more prosperous resists this demand to retain the monopoly of its privileged situation. Therefore, it exercises discrimination towards 'B', putting forward as a pretext its racial or cultural inferiority. Then the members of group 'B' are bound to revolt and '. . . their discontent can find "national" expression: the privileged are manifestly different from themselves, even if the shared "nationality" of the under-privileged men from B starts off from a purely negative trait, i.e. shared exclusion from privilege and from the "nation" of the privileged'.[18] For Gellner, it is in these situations that 'culture, pigmentation, etc., become important: they provide means of exclusion for the benefit of the privileged, and a means of identification, etc., for the under-privileged [. . .] Nationalism is not the awakening of nations to self-consciousness: it invents nations where they do not exist—but it does need some pre-existing differentiating marks to work on, even if, as indicated, they are purely negative.'[19]

This approach of nationalism provides us with a very useful framework to analyse the case of Muslim separatism in British India. Here, separatist feelings certainly did not develop among a group which had been discriminated against, but, all the same, the touchstone of the nationalist mobilization laid in social and economic factors since they derived from the fear of decline and marginalization that developed in the midst of the Muslim intelligentsia of UP. The first Muslim separatist movement resulted from the reaction of the Muslim elite from northern India, whose privileged position came to be challenged by the rise of the Hindu intelligentsia, a group which benefited from its more rapid assimilition into the English-medium education system and the anti-Muslim bias of the British till the late nineteenth century. The Muslim elite then used identity markers, through political organizations such as the Muslim League, to shape a nationalist Muslim identity. This manipulation of cultural symbols focused not only on Islam, but also on Urdu. The command of this language by the Muslims would have helped them to preserve their privileged positions, had not Hindi become an official language too. While it was almost indistinguishable from Hindi as a spoken language—both were the two faces of the same coin, Hindustani—and while it was used by many literate Hindus, the ideologues of Aligarh and the Muslim League, like the zealots of Hindi at the same time, tried hard to present it as *the* language of the Muslims. This is one more indication that Muslim nationalism did not derive from 'primordial' identity markers, but was an ideological construction.

The instrumentalization of these identity symbols helped Muslim separatism to crystallize, like the manipulation of Hindu symbols such as the sacred cow, contributed to the emergence of Hindu nationalism almost at the same time. In the case of Muslim separatism, however, this movement was weakened by the unevenness of the social frustrations felt by the 'victims' in question: while the Muslims of the provinces where they were in a minority—mainly those of UP, but also those of Bombay Presidency Jinnah's native region—were eager to emancipate themselves from the growing influence of the Hindus, the Muslims of the provinces where they were in a majority did not identify themselves with the ideology of separatism, since they often ruled their own region, like in Punjab and Bengal. The task Jinnah assigned himself in the 1940s was precisely to convert these 'majoritarian Muslims' to the 'two-nation theory'.

The Unachieved Conversion of the 'Majoritarian Muslims' to the Two-Nation Theory

Ayesha Jalal has shown that Jinnah was not only a rather unorthodox Muslim, but also a 'sole spokesman',[20] a nationalist in quest of his nation. For him, Islam provided the cultural basis for an ideology of ethnic nationalism that was intended to mobilize the Muslim community in order to defend the 'minoritarian Muslims'. The fact that he represented the 'minoritarian Muslims' was obvious in 1928, during the All Parties Muslim Conference, when he declared that he was prepared to exchange the advantages of separate electorates against a quota of 33 per cent of the seats at the Centre. He stuck to such views during the Round Table Conferences, while the Muslim representatives of Punjab and Bengal were more interested in promoting a further decentralized political set-up. The 1935 Government of India Act, which prepared the ground for a federal India, met many of their demands. Jinnah's Muslim League, at that time, played a very marginal role. In 1937, it could only win 5 per cent of the Muslim vote. However, Jinnah went ahead with his separatist agenda. He coined the formula, 'two-nation theory', on which he elaborated the following terms during the famous Lahore session of the Muslim League in March 1940.

Islam and Hinduism are not religions in the strict sense of the word, but are, in fact, different and distinct social orders [. . .]. The Hindus and the Muslims belong to two different religious philosophies, social customs, and literatures [. . .]. To yoke together two such nations under a single State, one as a numerical minority and the other as a majority, must lead to growing discontent and the final destruction of any fabric that may be so built up for the government of such a State.[21]

In accordance with this 'two-nation theory', he asked for a separate state—a state that the 'minoritarian Muslims' could govern. This project had been suggested first by Iqbal in his speech as President of the Muslim League in December 1930. Interestingly, the state he had envisioned then comprised only Punjab, Sindh, the North-West Frontier Province (NWFP) and Baluchistan. Three years later, a Cambridge student, Chaudhri Rehmat Ali, had taken up the idea and named this country to be born 'Pakistan', an anagram in which 'P' stood for 'Punjab', 'A' for 'Afghan' (in fact, the Pathans of the NWFP), 'K' for 'Kashmir', 'S' for 'Sindh', and 'Tan' for 'Baluchistan'. Once again, this project did not include Bengal in the proposed state. In March 1940, its name remained unacknowledged in the Lahore Resolution and its frontiers so uncertain that it was not even clear whether the Resolution envisaged one or two states. It demanded 'that the areas in which the Muslims are numerically in a majority, as in the north-western and eastern zones of India should be grouped to constitute independent states in which the constituent units shall be autonomous and sovereign'.[22]

The fact that the Lahore Resolution presented the states to be as loose groupings of the provinces where the Muslims were in a majority was part of the strategy of Jinnah for wooing the leaders of those provinces who remained hostile to the plans of the Muslim League. The 1937 elections, however, were the first turning point. The Congress party had won in seven of the provinces of British India and this achievement worried the Muslims, including those of the regions where they were in a majority. Jinnah re-launched his propaganda in this context by arguing that once the British would be gone, the Muslims would inevitably be subjected to some Hindu government, including in the provinces where they were in majority. He argued that the 'Hindu Congress' was putting 'Islam in danger'. This was a pretty efficient ploy in Punjab where the Muslim League was confronting not only the Congress—whose main supporters were to be found in the cities among Hindus—but also the Unionist Party that had been founded in 1922 by peasant leaders Fazl-i-Husain (a Muslim) and Chhotu Ram (a Hindu). The party had won all the elections between 1923 and 1937 (leaving very little political space to the Muslim League)[23] but in 1937 the new party leader, Sikander Hayat Khan, agreed to sign a pact with Jinnah. According to this pact, Hayat Khan committed himself to have the unionists to join the Muslim League. His motivations are still unclear. Was he nursing the idea of taking over the Muslim League? Was he concerned about the growing popularity of the Congress party and the rise to power of a 'Hindu party' which would deprive the Punjabi Muslims of their over-representation in the army?[24] Anyway, he helped the Muslim League to take roots in Punjab and during the 1946 election campaign, the party was able to propagate its views at length. The Muslim League openly used Islam by claiming that their religion was threatened by the Congress. It received the help of *pirs* and *sajjada nashin* who were able to attract Muslim voters towards the Muslim League.[25] The party won 75 seats, whereas the Unionist Party got only 10.

In Sindh also the Muslim League remained a marginal player till the mid-1940s. As in Punjab, he faced two other parties, the Congress and the Sindh United Party, which, founded in 1936 (at the same time as the Sindh province) was fashioned after the Punjab Unionist Party. However, the Muslim League made inroads in Sindh in the 1930s in the wake of the Muslim mobilization about the Manzilgarh issue, named after a very controversial site that the League wanted to be officially declared to be a mosque.[26] The Muslim League of Sindh, however, was probably more interested in defending the Sindhi culture than the idea of an Islamic State for the Muslims of British India, as is evident from the discourse of its leader in the 1940s, G.M. Syed. Syed had left the Congress in 1938 to become the real architect of the Muslim League in Sindh. However, he was a Sindhi nationalist more than anything else, as indicated by the zeal with which he advocated the cause of regional self-determination before the Cabinet Mission in 1946.[27] He had been expelled from the Muslim League just before, but the Sindhi branch of the party remained imbued with Sindhi nation-alism. In fact, many Sindhis might well have regarded the creation of

Pakistan as much a device for emancipating their region from the British tutelage, as a valuable project in itself.

In Bengal, the League had traditionally been stronger than in most of the other 'majoritarian' provinces, but here again, it gained momentum rather late in the day. Besides, it owed its popularity partly because of its capacity to endorse the separatist tendency of the Muslims of East Bengal, the area where they were concentrated most.[28] As in Punjab and Sindh, the Muslim League of Bengal was facing two parties in the 1930s, the Congress and a peasant party, the Krishak Proja Party, founded by A.K. Fazlul Haq in 1936. This party came first in the 1937 elections with 31 per cent of the valid votes, compared to 27 per cent for the Muslim League. However, the League swept the poll in 1946 when it won 104 seats out of 111, once again largely due to the threat that the rising 'Hindu Congress' was 'posing to Islam'. But the growing popularity of the 'two-nation theory' was superimposed on strong regional feelings. In 1944, the President of the Bengal Muslim League, Abdul Mansur Ahmed, declared in his presidential address, that:

Religion and culture are not the same thing. Religion transgresses the geographical boundary but *tamaddum* (culture) cannot go beyond the geographical boundary [. . .]. For this reason the people of Purba [Eastern] Pakistan are a different nation from the people of the other provinces of India and from the 'religious brothers' of Pakistan.[29]

In the NWFP, the Muslim League could hardly compete with the movement of Abdul Ghaffar Khan, a Pathan leader who was known as the 'Frontier Gandhi' because of his attempts at emulating the Mahatma. The Muslim League did not only face difficulties because of the Congress popularity, but also because of the strong Pakhtun identity that Ghaffar Khan articulated in the cultural as well as in the political arena. He launched a monthly in Pashto, the *Pakhtun*, in 1928 and, the following year, a movement called Khudai Khidmatgar, which was better known as 'the Red Shirts' because of its uniform. Supported by Ghaffar Khan, the Congress confined the political influence of the Muslim League to the non-Pakhtun area, specially the Hazara region. In 1946, the party won only 17 seats, against 30 to the Congress.

Thus, Muslim separatism developed primarily among the Muslims of the British provinces where they were in a minority and faced social as well as political marginalization. The intelligentsia of these regions evolved a nationalist ideology that was over-determined by its socio-economic and political interests—a good illustration of the Gellner thesis. From Syed Ahmed Khan to Jinnah, this elite shaped an ethnic variety of nationalism based on Islam. However, the nation that was supposed to embody this new identity remained rather elusive till the last moment, since the areas where the Indian Muslims were in the largest numbers did not adhere to the idea of Pakistan till the mid-1940s. In 1946, they did so as a reaction to the rise to power of the Congress that Jinnah depicted as a 'Hindu party'. That was 'a brief moment of political unity', to use the phrase of Yunas Samad[30] since the Muslim League had not fully taken roots in the regions where Muslims were in a majority. The leading role of the Muslims of UP in the Muslim League was evident from the over-representation of the leaders hailing from this province among 'the Council', the governing body of the party. Before 1938, Bengal, in spite of its 33 million Muslims inhabitants, had only 10 representatives, not more than the United Provinces where the Muslims were only 7 million.[31] The domination of the 'nationalists' over a nation that was still to be mobilized—or whose mobilization had to be sustained—became clear immediately after Independence in 1947.

ISLAM AND URDU, SYMBOLS OF UNITY OR DOMINATION?

A Migrant State

As mentioned above, the Lahore resolution had emphasized that the 'constituent units [of the states to come] shall be autonomous and sovereign', but soon after it turned out that this clause (like the idea that the League might ask for two states)[32] had been included for reassuring the regions where Muslims were in a majority. In practice, Pakistan was conceived as a centralized state dominated by the Mohajirs (lit. 'the migrants'), nationalists who wanted a nation state to govern. According to the 1951 Census, the Mohajirs were 7 million in the newly created Pakistan, including 7,00,000 in East Pakistan. In West Pakistan, they were 6.3 million out of 33.7 million, one-fifth of the total population. A majority of them remained in the same cultural environment, since most of the Punjabis from East Punjab crossed the border to settle down in West Punjab. But the situation was quite different for a vast minority: 1,00,000 Urdu-speaking Biharis went to East Bengal and also 1 million largely Urdu-speaking Muslims from the United Provinces, Bombay Presidency, Hyderabad, etc., migrated to West Pakistan. The latter gradually formed a single group and came to be known as *the* Mohajirs.

Their influence was immediately without any proportion to their number, not only because the architect of Pakistan came from the same milieu, but also because they formed an intellectual and commercial elite. Moreover, they settled down in towns and cities where they often replaced Hindus, mainly professionals, traders and civil servants who had fled to India.[33] They were especially nume-rous in Karachi, the state capital, which grew from 3,60,000 inhabitants in 1941 to 1.1 million in 1951. The Mohajirs, who accounted for one-fifth of the population of Sindh, represented 57 per cent of the city's population.[34] To begin with, they enjoyed a certain prestige due to the fact that they had played a leading role in the making of Pakistan and had often suffered severe hardships for migrating to the new state.

The Mohajirs also dominated Pakistan because of the personality of the two topmost leaders, Jinnah, the Governor-General and Liaquat Ali Khan, his Prime Minister. Besides, the Muslim League was their creation, and, on top of it, they exerted a strong influence over the bureaucracy. Out of the 101 Muslims of the Indian Civil Service, 95 had migrated to Pakistan in 1947—among them, only one-third came from East Punjab and one or two from West Bengal.[35] Pakistan being, to a large extent, the creation of the Mohajirs, Urdu was given the status of an official language in 1952. In order to promote this language the budget of the Anjuman-e-Taraqqi-e-Urdu was doubled between 1948-9 and 1950-1 and the courts and provincial assemblies were requested to use it.

Punjab was the most active province in advocating the cause of Urdu. The Official Language Committee that the regional government set up in the early 1950s established a list of Urdu synonyms of English and Punjabi words for promoting the use of this language in different fields.[36] The promptitude of the Punjabis to join the mainstream ideology went hand in hand with their endeavours to conquer the state apparatus.

The Punjabization of Pakistan or the Making of a Hegemony

The Punjabis represented only one-fourth of the Pakistani population according to the 1951 Census but they occupied 80 per cent of the posts in the army,[37] and this stronghold proved beneficial for their eventual rise to power in the 1950s.[38] However, the Punjabis were also very numerous in the administration. In 1947, they represented 55 per cent of the bureaucrats, much more than the Mohajirs.[39] The Punjabis also drew their growing influence from their agricultural activities. They had benefited from the irrigation works laid down by the British more than any other community. This relative prosperity prepared the ground for the Green Revolution of the 1960s.

Therefore, in the early years of Pakistan, the country was dominated by two communities, the Punjabis, who were over-represented in the army and in the administration, and the Mohajirs, who were also over-represented in the bureaucracy and controlled the political decision centres. For instance, a majority of the members of the Government of Liaquat Ali Khan were from his community.[40] However, this con-dominium was not tension-free since the Mohajirs and the Punjabis do not share the same political culture nor the same socio-economic interests. The Mohajirs tend to regard Islam as the foundation of their national identity, as a secularized cultural feature.[41] In contrast, the Punjabis, who rallied around the idea of Pakistan when they felt that the 'Hindu Congress' was posing a threat to Islam, continue to propagate a more conservative social and religious ethos. This opposition has also much to do with the fact that the Mohajirs are more urban whereas the Punjabis are more rural. Hence, another bone of contention: the Mohajirs tend to work more in the private sector, as professionals or businessmen, whereas the Punjabis depend on the state, not only for employment (in the army or the bureaucracy), but also as agriculturists who depend on the state for land reform, irrigation work or administered agricultural prices. The liberal mindset of the Mohajirs provides a stark contrast to the state-oriented mentality of the Punjabis.[42]

After the demise of Jinnah in 1948 and Liaquat Ali Khan in 1951, the Mohajirs gradually lost ground to the Punjabis. The rise to power of the latter was total in 1958 with the military coup of Ayub Khan, a Pathan who initiated a new Pathan–Punjabi axis, since an over-whelmingly Punjab-dominated army was now in command. The Punjabis who had come to Pakistan from East Punjab in 1947 (in large numbers among them Ayub Khan's lieutenants) and those from the west formed a single group, all the more so as Ayub Khan catered to the need of the Punjabi refugees who still needed land. The Mohajirs simply did not weild the influence they used to have anymore. This shift was materialized by the transfer of the capital from Karachi to Rawalpindi, and then Islamabad. In 10 years, those who regarded themselves as the makers of Pakistan had begun to recede to the background. But their ideology remained the official doctrine of the state since the Punjabis identified themselves with the Pakistan project, as evident from their adoption of Urdu. This identification prepared the ground for what Yunas Samad has called the making of 'Punjabistan', a process that was bound to alienate the other communities.[43]

From East Pakistan to Bangladesh: The Cost of Over-Centralization

The most obvious indication of a chasm between the ideology and the sociology of Pakistan lay in the failure of the State to integrate the Bengalis who formed a majority of the population. According to the 1951 Census, there were 41.9 million inhabitants in East Pakistan and 33.7 million in West Pakistan. This demographic balance was a good reason for the Bengalis to ask for the establishment of a democratic regime in which the 'one man, one vote' principle would have enabled them to rule the country.[44] They were in a position to push their point since Bengali representatives were in a majority in the Constituent Assembly (an assembly that had been designated by the legislative assemblies of British India in 1946), with 44 members, against 22 Punjabis, 5 Sindhis, 3 representatives from the NWFP and 1 from Baluchistan. In March 1949, the Constituent Assembly appointed a Basic Principles Committee which submitted its report in September 1950. It recommended the establishment of a federal democracy. The Punjabi representatives immediately objected that East Pakistan should not be allowed to be in a position to dominate West Pakistan simply because the Bengalis were in a larger number. For them, certain citizens were more equal than others.

Besides, the Pakistani Government created the right context for the crystallization of Bengali nationalism by elevating Urdu to the status of a national language. Bengalis, who were especially anxious to defend their language and literature, organized demonstrations. The repressive measures of the Centre were responsible for several deaths, and this event was to be commemorated every year by Bengali nationalists. Instead of accommodating the linguistic demands of the Bengalis, the Pakistan Government further alienated them by resorting to purely repressive measures. Unsurprisingly, the Muslim League badly lost the provincial elections in March 1954. The Centre decided then to recognize Bengali as an official language on the same footing as Urdu. But its basic strategy did not change.

The Constituent Assembly was about to vote on the formula evolved by the BPC in October 1954 when Governor-General Ghulam Muhammad (a Pathan born in Punjab), decided to dissolve the assembly, declared a state of emergency and established, in March 1955, the 'One Unit Scheme': Punjab, Sindh, Baluchistan and the NWFP now formed a single province, called West Pakistan, that was in a position to balance East Pakistan. The Punjabis had forced the other minority provinces of West Pakistan into an alliance that enabled them to counter the claims of East Pakistan. This decision was not only resented by the Bengalis, but also by the minority provinces of West Pakistan. The 1956 Constitution mentioned in its first article that 'Pakistan shall be a Federal Republic to be known as the Islamic Republic of Pakistan', but, in practice, the Punjabi-dominated political establishment orchestrated the centralization of the State.

The political marginalization of the Bengalis was aggravated by their under-representation in the administration. There were not more than a couple of Bengalis among the 95 ICS cadres who went to Pakistan in 1947. In 1949, East Pakistan got a quota of 40 per cent of the posts in the bureaucracy (against 23 per cent for the Punjabis). This quota was not sufficient for enabling the Bengalis to make up for their socio-economic backwardness. Among the 17 top civil servants in 1964, there were only 2 Bengalis. The situation was even worse in the army: in 1955, out of 58 Generals, there was only one Bengali. The contrast between East Pakistan and the other provinces was especially

TABLE 1.1: POPULATION GDP AND PER CAPITA GDP
IN 1951, PROVINCE-WISE

Provinces	Population (in '000s)	Per cent	Ann. Rev. Rs. mil.	Rev. Per capita Rs.
Punjab	18, 815	24.9	246,2	12
Sindh	4, 606	6.1	97	21.1
NWFP	5,865*	7.8*	65	20.1
Bahawalpur	1,822	2.4	50,5	27.7
Khairpur	319	0.4	12	37.6
Baluchistan States Union	552	0.7	5.8	10.5
Baluchistan	602	0.8	N.A.	N.A.
Karachi	1,123	1.5	N.A.	N.A.
Total West Pakistan	33,704	44.6	N.A.	N.A.
Total East Pakistan	41,932	55.4	234,5	5.6
Total	75,636	100	—	—

Source: Keith Callard, *Pakistan, a Political Study,* London: Allen and Unwin, 1957, p. 156.
Note: *Including the North West Frontier Agencies.

striking in terms of GDP per capita, as evident from Table 1.1.

The Bengalis suffered from an 'inner colonialism' kind of economic exploitation in the sense that West Pakistan utilized the income generated by their exports to finance its development. The Bengalis' resentment was further aggravated by the fact that the growth rate of the per capita GDP remained very low in East Pakistan, compared to the situation prevailing in West Pakistan (17 per cent against 42 per cent between 1959-60 and 1969-70).[45] Bengali economists began to oppose the 'two-nation theory' and the 'two-nation economy', a notion which substantiated the Gellner thesis once again.

Fazlul Haq, who had already left the Muslim League and founded the Krishak Sramik Party soon after Independence, and H.S. Suhrawardy who had launched the Awami League in 1950 joined hands in 1954, at the time of local elections. Their coalition, the United Front, formed the government but the Centre dismissed it after two months, claiming that Haq had made separatist declarations to the Indian media. The repressive methods of the Central Government fostered a radicalization process which is well illustrated by the career of Mujibur Rahman. A militant nationalist, Rahman established his Awami League as the main Bengali party after the demise of Suhrawardy in 1963 and then formulated, in 1966, a Six-Point Programme in which he asked for democracy and a loose federal system. The Centre would only retain the portfolios of Defence and Foreign Affairs. Each 'wing' of Pakistan would have its own reserve bank and be in charge of its monetary policy. Besides, each 'wing' would also be in command of its foreign trade, a claim that was a clear reconfirmation of the economic dimension of Bengali nationalism.

The only reply Ayub Khan gave to Mujibur Rahman was repression. Rahman was arrested and accused of receiving arms from India. This episode further strengthened Bengali separatism, a phenomenon which, therefore, did not only result from cultural and socio-economic differences, but also from the authoritarian methods of West Pakistani leaders who were simply unwilling to share power. Access to socio-economic resources was not the only issue; exclusion from power-centres and the non-accommodating attitude of these centres of power also rankled.

In a recent article Atul Kohli argues that in contrast to India, Pakistan cannot accommodate centrifugal movements (as those of Tamil Nadu and Punjab in India) because it does not have a federal framework and the democratic culture to do so.[46] These two characteristics enable (or oblige) India to make concessions in such a way that, finally, ethnic movements eventually become more moderate—hence Kohli's metaphor of the inverse 'U' curve—whereas in Pakistan authoritarian attitudes generate nationalist radicalization. This hypothesis, which supplements Gellner's theory, is well illustrated by the case of East Pakistan.

Ayub Khan realized the strength of the Bengali movement for self-determination in the late 1960s, but by then it was too late. He convened a round table conference in February 1969 to propose that the 1962 Constitution be amended in a truly federal perspective. This meeting, in which Rahman agreed to take part in March 1969 bore no fruit, largely because it was boycotted by Zulfikar Ali Bhutto who had just founded the Pakistan People's Party (PPP). Ayub Khan withdrew and Yahya Khan, who took over from him, immediately decided to declare a state of martial rule and to abrogate the Constitution, but also to hold general elections and to prepare a new, more federal-oriented Constitution. The Legal Framework Order that was promulgated in early 1970 prepared the ground for such an evolution. This order acknowledged the importance of East Pakistan since it gave 169 seats out of 313 to this province in the National Assembly.

The December 1970 elections marked a triumph for the Awami League which won 160 seats against 81 of the PPP, but it sealed the imminent divorce between both wings of the country since the League had not contested any seat in West Pakistan and the PPP none in East Pakistan. In fact, the performance of the PPP suggested that the provinces of West Pakistan found this party to be an instrument for resisting the Bengalis' rise to power. (Even though it was founded by a Sindhi, the PPP won 62 of its 81 seats in Punjab.) Interpreting his new mandate in these terms, Bhutto tried to present himself as the true embodiment of the real Pakistan, claiming that 'Punjab and Sindh [were] the bastions of power in Pakistan. [And that] Majority alone does not count in national politics.'[47] He shared the same concern as the Punjabis so far as the new, all round Bengali domination was concerned. He rejected the proposal of Yahya Khan regarding the meeting of a new Constituent Assembly in Dhaka. The postponement *sine die* of this meeting led Mujibur Rahman to launch a general strike and convinced him that East Pakistan and West Pakistan should only form a loose confederation, each unit having its own constitution. Once again, Islamabad resorted to repressive measures which were out of proportion by launching a military operation on 25 March. Thousands of innocents were killed and 10 million East Pakistanis fled to India. The fact that India had come to the rescue of these Bengalis and decided to 'free Bangladesh' by launching its own military operation in November 1971 gave an highly symbolic dimension to the second partition of South Asia: those against whom the 'two-nation theory' had been built were directly involved in the dramatic negation of this very notion. The history of Bengali separatism shows once again that cultural features do not explain nationalism alone: obviously, Islam did not provide a cementing force that was likely to hold Pakistan together and the language issue was not alone responsible for the rise of Bengali separatism. Socio-economic conflicts and access to power were also at stake. Besides, the elite of West Pakistan preferred to resort to authori-tarian methods instead of sharing power; they were unable to accommodate centrifugal forces.

THE INTEGRATIVE CAPACITY OF POWER:
THE CASE OF SINDH

While exclusion from power fostered separatist tendencies in the case of the Bengalis, symmetrically, access to power made the national integration of the Sindhis easier in the 1970s. After the creation of Bangladesh, the Punjabis became the majority community of Pakistan, but a Sindhi, Zulfikar Ali Bhutto took over from Yahya Khan as head of State.

At that point of time, the Sindhi nationalist movement remained rather strong under the aegis of G.M. Syed, who continued to cash in on the sensitivity of the local population to the language issue and used the Golden Age of the Indus civilization as a source of Sindhi national pride.[48] Since 1947, Syed had continuously protested against the domination of the Mohajirs and the Punjabis over Pakistan, especially Sindh. He strongly resented the development of Urdu at the expense of the Sindhi language in Karachi and other cities of the region. Even though most of the Sindhis did not share Syed's militancy, they appreciated his nationalist views.

The rise to power of the PPP in the early 1970s made a change. In 1972, the party formed the Government of Sindh and took up some of the issues which Syed and others had pointed out. It protested against the under-representation of the Sindhis in the army—they counted for only 2.2 per cent of the total force and none of the 48 topmost officers were from Sindh[49] and took exception to the marginal role of Sindhis in the administration compared to the Punjabis and Mohajirs. In 1973, the latter occupied 33.5 per cent of the posts in the bureaucracy, whereas they only formed 7 per cent of the population. The local Sindhis (who came to be known as the 'rural Sindhis' in contrast to the Mohajirs who were the 'urban Sindhis') represented only 2.7 per cent of the administration. In order to reverse this trend, the Government of Sindh decided to question the monopoly of Urdu in the education system. The Teaching Promotion and Use of Sindhi Language Bill became a law in July 1972. The introduction of the Sindhi language in the schools of the province was immediately resented by the Mohajirs who triggered off communal riots in Karachi, Hyderabad and Larkana, but Bhutto supported this move. Taking side against the Mohajirs, he made a speech replete with Sindhi nationalist connotations before the National Assembly in July 1972. He said, for instance:

We have given our lands; we have given our homes; we have given our lives [. . .] to people from all parts, to the Pathans, Punjabis, to the Mohajirs living in Sindh [. . .]. What else can we do to show our loyalty, our love and our respect for Pakistan and for our Mohajir brothers?[50]

In addition, the rural Sindhis were granted a quota of 11.4 per cent in the administration. The nationalization programme of Bhutto's government affected the Mohajirs too since they were over-represented in business, specially in Karachi.

The promotion of the Sindhis (at the expense of the Mohajirs)

TABLE 1.2:   QUOTAS INTRODUCED IN 1973 AND REPRESENTATION OF THE PROVINCES OF PAKISTAN IN THE FEDERAL BUREAUCRACY: 1973–83 (percentage-wise)

Provinces	Quota	General administration (1973)	Senior civil servants (1973)	General administration (1983)	Senior civil servants (1983)
Punjab	50.0	49.2	53.5	54.9	55.7
NWFP	11.5	10.5	7.0	13.4	11.6
Urban Sindh	7.6	30.2	33.5	17.4	20.2
Rural Sindh	11.4	3.2	2.7	5.4	5.1
Baluchistan	3.5	2.5	1.5	3.4	3.1
Northern Areas and FATA	4.0	2.6	1.3	3.6	3.4
Azad Kashmir	2.0	1.8	0.5	1.9	0.9
Total	90.0	100.0 N = 84,749	100.0 N = 6,011	100.0 N = 1,34,310	100.0 N = 11,816

Source: Adapted from Charles H. Kennedy, Bureaucracy in Pakistan, Karachi: Oxford University Press, 1987, p. 194.

helped spread nationalist feelings amongst them. Such a feeling was further strengthened when they realized that the topmost leader of the country came from their own province. Sindh's political trajectory shows that, contrary to Kohli's interpretation, Pakistan could experience with an inverted U curve, a trajectory ending with the defusing of ethnic tensions.

This interpretation is further substantiated by the fact that a wave of Sindhi nationalism gained momentum once again after Bhutto was dislodged from power by Zia, a Punjabi, and then condemned to death by a jury in which Punjabis were in a majority.[51] After his execution in 1979, Bhutto became a Sindhi martyr. The Sindhis also rejected Zia because of his policies affecting them in socio-economic terms. In February 1978, for instance, 1,746 Sindhi civil servants were dismissed from the province's administration. As a result, the Movement for the Restoration of Democracy was especially popular in Sindh where it benefited also from the infrastructure of the PPP, the party endowed with the largest network of cadres and activists. Once again, the Centre resorted to massive repression. For six months, 45,000 soldiers were deployed in the province. About 300 opponents were killed. The underground literature which was then in circulation often mentioned the demand for a 'Sindhi Desh'. One of the leaders, Mumtaz Bhutto, a former Governor of Sindh and a relative of Zulfikar Ali Bhutto, articulated a programme which recalled Mujibur Rahman's Six Points. He asked for the establishment of a loose confederation in which Sindh would enjoy wide autonomy.[52] However, the daughter of Z.A. Bhutto, Benazir, who was back after years of exile abroad, expressed reservations vis-à-vis such a programme.[53] The electoral success of her father had probably contributed in convincing her that a Sindhi could rise to power and govern Pakistan. Why should the Sindhis question their links with a country they may dominate once again? Benazir Bhutto preferred to play the national, Pakistan political game. She took over the PPP and led it to victory in 1988 when elections were organized for the first time after 11 years, as a result of Zia's death. This achievement was interpreted as a Sindhi success in the province. Certainly, the PPP had won 52 seats out of 113 in Punjab, but it had won all the seats of rural Sindh and two-thirds of those of the provincial assembly, whereas it had only wrested 94 of the 240 seats of the Punjab Assembly. The PPP was, therefore, perceived as a Sindhi party and the fact that a Sindhi once again became Prime Minister played a role in defusing the nationalist feelings in the province. The integrative impact of power was also evident from the steady decline of Pakhtun nationalism.

THE PATHANS, FROM PAKHTUNISTAN TO PAKHTUNKHWA

In 1947, the Pakhtuns engaged in the Red Shirts movement of Ghaffar Khan, opposed their integration with Pakistan and asked, instead, for the formation of a 'Pakhtunistan' that would cover the Afghan Pakhtuns and the Pakhtuns (or Pathans) of the NWFP. Ghaffar Khan and his supporters boycotted the referendum by which NWFP was finally merged into Pakistan[54] and later demanded in the Constituent Assembly (since he was a member) that the province be named 'Pakhtunistan'. He was arrested soon after and his brother, Khan Sahib, the then Chief Minister of the NWFP, was dismissed by Jinnah.

Yet, the heirs of the Red Shirts movement played the political game of the new regime. In 1957, the son of Ghaffar Khan, Wali Khan, was involved in the creation of the National Awami Party, which became part of the new party system. The steady integration of the Pathans was also due to sociological factors. First, in contrast to the Bengali or Sindhi elite, their intelligentsia had been trained in Aligarh or Lahore. Second, they were already well represented within the Pakistani state because of their role in the army (a legacy of the colonial period, since they had been classified among the martial races by the British), of which they comprised 19.5 per cent of the personnel in 1948.[55] By the late 1960s, there were 19 Pathans out of the 48 topmost military officers. The rise to power of Ayub Khan 10 years earlier had already testified to their presence upto the highest levels of the State. Right from the beginning, the intensity of Pakhtun nationalism turns out to decline in proportion to the possibilities of upward social (and political) mobility opened by the new State.

These factors of integration partly explained why the NAP remained below 20 per cent of the valid votes in the general as well as provincial elections. In 1970, it got 18 per cent of the votes against 14 per cent to the PPP and 23 per cent to the Jamiyat-i-Ulama-e-Islam (JUI). The limitations of the NAP's appeal were a strong incentive to dilute its programme. In 1969, the party accepted the official borders between the NWFP and Baluchistan, a province of which the NAP claimed a part till then. After the victory of his party (the NAP) in the 1972 election and the formation of a government coalition over which he exerted a strong influence, Wali Khan tried to acquire a national stature. He put his Pakhtun nationalism on the backburner, to the point of forgetting his promises about the renaming of the province—the only one in Pakistan with a name that did not reflect any ethnic identity—and to elevate Urdu to the rank of the official language of the NWFP, a decision which was also taken to avoid confrontation with the local Hindko speakers.

The Pakhtuns embraced a more radical form of nationalism as a reaction to the authoritarian methods of Zulfikar Ali Bhutto. When Bhutto dismissed the NAP-led Government of Baluchistan in 1973 (see below), the Government of NWFP resigned immediately as a sign of solidarity and Wali Khan returned to Pakhtun nationalism. Two years later, Bhutto got him arrested and dissolved the NAP under the pretext of his implication in the murder of a minister of the NWFP, H.M. Sherpao. The trial of Wali Khan lasted right till the dismissal of Bhutto in 1977.

After his release from prison in 1978, Wali Khan relaunched his party under almost the same name, the Awami National Party (ANP), but downplayed his Pakhtun nationalism again. One of the reasons for their change was that the Afghan war attenuated Pakhtun irredentism. Out of the 3 million Afghan refugees (four-fifths of whom were Pakhtuns), 80 per cent settled down in the NWFP, so much so the population of the province rose by 20 per cent, exceeding that of Afghanistan (16 million people against 14 million). As a result, Pathan leaders considered—or at least declared—that Pakhtunistan existed de facto. Wali Khan himself said that the Durand Line had disappeared because of the war.[56] The ANP also diluted its nationalist programme because its top priority was to support the war effort of Islamabad against the Soviets. The party showed solidarity with Zia (during the Movement for the Restoration of Democracy in 1983, for example), and the Pathan leaders who were still exiled in Afghanistan returned to Pakistan in 1986. In this context, Zia promoted Pathans in the state apparatus and the army.[57] Besides, the Pakhtuns who joined the army and the bureaucracy in great numbers came primarily from the districts which had traditionally been strongholds of the Pakhtunistan movement. The influx of Afghan refugees was also unlikely to relaunch Pakhtun irredentism because the newcomers soon became rivals to the local businessmen and artisans, specially in Peshawar.[58] The ANP protested in the 1980s against the cost of the war and asked for the return of the refugees after the Soviets began to withdraw in 1989. The victory of the Taliban in Afghanistan then opened new perspectives. In this process, an Islamist ideology and Pakhtun ethnicity tended to coincide: while the Taliban presented themselves as militant Sunnis, the sub-text of the movement was ethnic. As a result, this new ideology tended to prevail over Pakhtun nationalism.

In addition to the impact of the Afghan war, other socio-economic factors contributed to the decline of Pakhtun nationalism. After Punjab, it was without doubt the NWFP that profited most from the rural exodus towards Karachi and the emigration to the Gulf countries: the Pakhtuns represented 35 per cent of the Pakistanis who went abroad during 1976-81, which is about 3,00,000 persons.

The process of democratization started in 1988 did not result in the revival of Pakhtun nationalism, largely because the elections then showed that the national parties had made significant inroads in the NWFP and that the local parties had to make alliances with them. In 1988 the ANP and the JUI won 3 seats each, against 7 to the PPP and 8 to the Islami Jamhoori Ittehad (IJI). Soon after, in the spring of 1989, Wali Khan decided to enter into a new alliance with Nawaz Sharif against their common enemy, the Bhutto family. This coalition, which enabled both parties to govern in Peshawar, consummated the rapprochement between Punjabis and Pathans. For Sharif, it was a good means for defusing Pakhtun nationalism. This understanding lasted for 10 years.

In the 1997 regional elections, the ANP won only 28 seats out of 83 of the NWFP assembly, against 31 to the PML(N). Both parties formed a new coalition government. However, this arrangement broke down in 1998 when the Government of Nawaz Sharif refused that the NWFP be renamed 'Pakhtunkhwa'. This marked, apparently, the return of the ANP to some ethnic mobilization. Begum Naseem Wali (the wife of Wali Khan) declared in an interview: 'I want an identity [. . .] I want a name change so that the Pakhtuns may be identified on the map of Pakistan.'[59] And she emphasized that Pakhtunkhwa was 'the 3,000-year-old name of this area', the name used by Ahmed Shah Abdali who said he forgot everything including the throne of Delhi, but not Pakhtunkhwa. This kind of emotional rewriting of history is inherent in nationalist discourse. The primordialists take it at face value, but such a discourse is only resorted to when it serves some purpose. In which case, Nawaz Sharif had probably antagonized the ANP less with the renaming issue than with the famous Kalabagh Dam project whose royalties were bound to go into Punjabi pockets, whereas the NWFP could be affected by it (the risk of floods would have allegedly been greater on the frontier's side). Once more, the real motives behind this resurgent nationalism were socio-economic, but they were presented in the garb of national sentiments.

The trajectory of Pakhtun nationalism has more or less been in the form of an inverted 'U' curve. It got exacerbated in the 1970s because of the over-centralization of a repressive State, but then receded when Pathans benefited from some upward social mobility and got access to power, either through the army, the administration, or the making of alliances with national parties. Certainly, Pakhtun nationalist feelings are still articulated by the ANP but they have lost their separatist overtone, as evident from the demand of the renaming of the NWFP not in Pakhtunistan, but Pakhtunkhwa. The Pathan case comes as a confirmation that Pakistan can defuse separatist movements, like India, even though it does not have the same culture of democracy and federalism: access to power—socio-economic as well as political—are powerful factor of integration.

Rise and Decline of the Baluch Movement for Self-determination

The trajectory of the Baluch nationalist movement is rather similar to that of the Pathan movement. Like the Pakhtuns, the Baluchis are spread over several countries, not only Pakistan and Iran, but also Afghanistan and Turkmenistan. Hence, the irredentist dimension of Baluch nationalism. This ideology is a political construct which hardly relies on linguistic features since the Baluch speak two languages, Baluchi and Brahui, a Dravidian idiom that was the mother tongue of the Kalat dynasty. Now Baluch nationalism draws most of its inspiration from the kingdom of Kalat, a principality of the Afghan State whose frontiers almost coincided with the Baluch area in the eighteenth century. During the colonial period, the part of the Kalat kingdom which belonged to the Raj became one of the princely states recognized by the British, who, in fact, did not impose their direct rule on most of Baluchistan. In 1947, the Khan of Kalat Abdul Karim tried to achieve independence for his kingdom but the Pakistan Army decided otherwise and it was integrated with the new state in March 1948. The former ruler eventually entered the political arena by forming the People's Party.

Baluch nationalism really crystallized as a reaction to the over-centralization of the Pakistani State. In 1972, the provincial elections, the first elections ever organized in Baluchistan on the basis of universal suffrage, were won by the alliance of two regional parties, the National Awami Party of Wali Khan whose stronghold was in the NWFP but with which the People Party had merged, and the Jamiat-i-Ulama-e-Islam, an Islamic party that was supported by the Sardars of Baluchistan. The new government immediately attempted to indigenize the administration by replacing the non-Baluchi bureaucrats by 'sons of the soil'. Islamabad strongly reacted to this 'spoils system' which was about to deprive the other provinces (specially Punjab) of traditional sinecures. The other bone of contention was related to the unevenness of socio-economic development that was due, according to the Government of Quetta, to the concentration of the investments in Punjab, at the expense of the other provinces, including Baluchistan.

Z.A. Bhutto accused the Baluch Government of separatism and dismissed it in February 1973, after the police had found arms with an Iraqi diplomat which were allegedly destined for the Baluch nationalists. Most of the Baluch leaders having been put behind bars, a second rank of leadership, mostly students, took over the nationalist movement and launched a guerrilla war with Marxist overtones. The Baluch People's Liberation Front (BPLF) and the Baluch Students' Organisation (BSO) mobilized about 10,000 militants. The Pakistan Army, which received the support of the Shah of Iran who feared that 'his' Baluch citizens too would be attracted towards a separatist movement, had to deploy 80,000 soldiers in the province. In 1973-7 about 5,300 Baluchis and 3,300 soldiers were killed.[60] The scenario of this crisis is somewhat similar to that of East Pakistan, in the sense that the over-reaction by the Centre transformed a movement for autonomy into proper separatist nationalism.[61] To begin with, the Baluch

were not fighting for independence but rather for regional autonomy within a radically restructured, confederal Pakistani constitutional framework. [. . .] By the time the shooting subsided in 1977, however, separatist feeling had greatly intensified. The wanton use of superior fire-power by the Pakistani and Iranian forces, especially the indiscriminate air attacks on Baluch villages, had left a legacy of bitter and enduring hatred. Since nearly all Baluchis felt the impact of Pakistani repression, the Baluch populace has been politicized to an unprecedented degree.[62]

Soon after he took over from Bhutto, Gen. Zia appeased a section of the Baluch nationalists by liberating thousands of prisoners. Some of them took the path of exile, like Attaullah Khan Mengal, who left for London. He founded there the Sindh Baluch and Pakhtun Front with the help of Mumtaz Bhutto. Mengal still did not want anything short of a confederal regime in which Baluchistan would have been an inde-pendent country. Similarly, Khair Bux Mari established himself in Afghanistan with about 3,000 armed activists. But most of the other

Baluch leaders showed greater moderation, partly because of Zia's ability to co-opt them. The former BSO president and guerrilla militant, Khair Jan Baluch, for instance, gave up the fight and former Governor Bizenjo created the Pakistan National Party in order to put pressure on the regime from inside, for promoting a better functioning of the federal structure enshrined in the Constitution of 1973. Many of the Sardars preferred to collaborate with the Centre, which was most willing to co-opt them.[63]

From 1988 onwards, the democratization process gave even more room for manoeuvre to the Baluch notables in the political arena, and the more they took part competitive elections, the more they got divided. In November 1988, Sardar Akhtar Mengal formed the Baluchistan National Movement which played a pivotal role in the new governmental coalition, the Baluchistan National Alliance of Nawab Akbar Bugti. However, factional conflicts became more acute when the 1990 interim elections approached. Bugti broke away from the BNA and launched the Jamhoori Watan Party (JWP) which made an alliance with the Pakistan Muslim League of Nawaz Sharif. That was a clear indication of an interesting change in the strategy of the Baluch politicians: their factional rivalries led them to make alliances with national parties which could help them in getting access to power. Similarly, in 1996 Zulfikar Ali Khan Magsi formed a government with the support of the PPP, of the PML(N) and the JUI!

In December 1996, the factions of Mengal and Bizenjo formed a new party, the Baluchistan National Party. But none of the contenders won a majority of the seats to the provincial assembly in the February 1997 elections. With 10 seats out of 43, the BNP was the largest single party and Sardar Attaullah Khan Mengal therefore formed a coalition government with the support of the PPP. Simultaneously, the BNP supported the PML(N) in the National Assembly,[64] another indication of the increasingly pragmatic relationships between the Baluch leaders and the national, mainstream parties.

Mengal resigned in 1998 in protest against the conduct of the nuclear tests in Baluchistan because, he claimed, they had been decided without consulting him and the honour of the Baluchis was at stake. After he resigned, Mengal reverted back to his traditional Baluch nationalist discourse. In an interview to *The Muslim* he declared, for instance: 'We are forced to look for our identity.'[65] However, the main bones of contention between his government and Nawaz Sharif were not related to the identity question alone. Mengal resented the way the Centre kept for itself an unwarranted share of the royalties generated by the gas of Baluchistan. He was also very critical of the decisions of the National Finance Commission which, according to him were highly detrimental to Baluchistan.

The trajectory of the Baluch nationalist movement comes as a reconfirmation of three key features of the ethnic issues in Pakistan. First, self-determination movements crystallize in reaction to the overcentralized and authoritarian methods of the State (as already noticed in the case of the movement for Bangladesh and Pakhtunistan, or Pakhtunkhwa). Second, the co-option of the ethnic leaders or the making of alliances between their parties and national parties tend to defuse the centrifugal tendencies: this process reflects the integrative capacity of power that we have already underlined in the case of rural Sindh and the NWFP. Third, the intensity of the nationalist feelings also depends upon the distribution of power and the socio-economic situation: this political economy of separatism, a notion which has obvious affinities with the theory that Ernest Gellner developed on the basis of other case studies, was already evident from the Pakistan movement before 1947 and from all the ethnic separatist movements we have studied so far.

To sum up, national integration has made significant progress in Pakistan, compared to the early 1970s when Bengalis, Sindhis, Baluchis and Pathans were attracted to separatist movements. At that time, the ideology of Pakistan remained identified with the 'minority Muslims' of British India who had searched for a state to govern and even more with the Punjabis who had gradually dislodged the Mohajirs from political power. While the Bengalis were further alienated by the over-centralization of the Pakistani State, and seceded in 1971, the Sindhis, the Baluchis and the Pathans, who had to suffer from the Punjabi domination too, eventually got more integrated when they secured some power or achieved upward mobility. The Punjabi domination is still very much resented, as evident from the protests against the second Sharif Government (1997-9) when not only the Prime Minister and 85 per cent of his ministers were from Punjab,[66] but also the President, Tarar, and for some time the Chief of the Army Staff, Jahangir Karamat. The domination of Punjab is almost inevitable during the democratization periods since more than half of the constituencies of the National Assembly (115 out of 207) are located in Punjab (against 46 in Sindh, 26 in the NWFP and 11 Baluchistan).[67] But it is also inevitable as the Army which rules the country is Punjabi-dominated.

In October 1998, the opposition to the Punjabi 'hegemony' found a new expression in the establishment of the Pakistan Oppressed Nationalities Movement (PONM). This anti-Punjab front, which has been initiated by ANP leaders, has no separatist overtones and, furthermore, all its components, be they Pakhtun, Baluch or Sindhi, play the electoral game. It asks for a truly federal system, a proportional representation of all the provinces in the army as well as the administration and the creation of a Sraiki province.[68] The Sraiki movement took shape in the 1970s when the speakers of Riasti (in Bahawalpur), Multani (in Multan) and Derajati (in Dera Ghazi Khan) came to consider that they spoke the same language, an idiom called Sraiki. This local identity came to undermine the regional, Punjabi identity.

NATIONALISM WITHOUT A NATION: THE ARGUMENT OF THE BOOK

The Sraiki movement suggests that one must look at the Punjabization issue as a complex phenomenon. Ian Talbot argues in Chapter 1 of this volume that, though the Punjab can be seen 'both as the cornerstone of the state and as a major hindrance to national integration', we must take a nuanced view of the Punjabi domination precisely because Punjab is not a monolith but a province divided into different linguistic groups and along socio-economic lines. Taking all these criteria into account, Talbot identifies four distinct economic and cultural regions within Punjab. He also points out that the province is now divided along sectarian lines (between Sunnis and Shias) as well. But he admits that 'The perception in the minority provinces is, however, of a unified Punjabi political interest', resting largely with the army, hence their feeling of vulnerability.

While the Punjabization of Pakistan, and, correlatively, the integration of smaller provinces may not be such an insuperable problem, two other issues are affecting the nation-building process today, the one posed by the Mohajir movement and the 'sectarian' conflict, which are not confined to Punjab alone.

The case of the Mohajirs is very revealing of the malleability of political identity. As mentioned earlier, to begin with, the Mohajirs identified themselves with the new State of Pakistan which was largely their creation. But the more they *felt* threatened, the more they projected themselves as an oppressed minority with a distinct identity. In Chapter 2 Yunas Samad points out that 'As their hegemony was challenged by various administrations their enthusiasm for Pakistan nationalism diminishes and is replaced by Mohajir identification.' This new identity is in itself a construction since, for instance, it merged into a new synthesis two linguistic groups, the Urdu-speakers and the Gujarati-speakers. They really started to raise their voice under Bhutto as a reaction to the policies pursued in the early 1970s by the Central Government and the Government at Karachi, two sets of policies that we have examined above. But, as Samad points out, 'Their alienation was further exacerbated during Gen. Zia's rule as Pakhtun and Punjabi business houses became generally more influential, particularly in their respective provinces and began to make inroads into Karachi.' The Green Revolution, of which Punjab was the first beneficiary, reinforced the domination of this province and permitted its natives to invest in industry, including in Karachi. Besides, migrants poured into this city and benefited from its dynamism: in 1984, Karachi was inhabited by 3.3 million Mohajirs apart from 1 million Punjabis, 1.1 million Baluchis, 7,00,000 Pakhtuns (including a large number of refugees from Afghanistan) and a few hundred thousand Sindhis.

While the Mohajirs approved of Zia's policy of Islamization since it echoed their initial ideology, even before 1947, they resented the introduction of new quotas in the administration: 10 per cent of the posts in the public service were reserved for retired military personnel, who benefited also from additional commercial and industrial licences. The army being dominated by the Punjabis, it was an indirect bonus to the dominant community. Samad also emphasized the impact of the Afghan war which strengthened the hold of the Punjabis and the Pathans over the army, at the expense of the Mohajirs.

The Mohajir Qaumi Mahaz (Mohajir National Movement) was born in this context in 1984. Its cadre and even its chief, Altaf Hussain, came from the middle class and, above all, recruited its members amongst the students frustrated in their aspirations for social mobility. The MQM demanded that only persons settled in Sindh at least since 20 years should enjoy the right to vote; that the foreigners could not acquire properties in Sindh; that the Mohajirs should be recognized as the 'fifth nationality' of Pakistan; last, that Karachi should become a province (Karachi suba).[69] Altaf Hussain occasionally claimed that he wanted to partition Sindh the same way as Bangladesh was carved out if Islamabad continued to ignore his demands.[70] Yet, his strategies of contesting elections and allying the MQM with other national parties, a modus operandi that Samad examines in detail, suggest that he is more interested in exerting power in the institutional framework of Pakistan than anything else:'the main thrust of his political agenda was the reincorporation of Mohajirs by the Pakistan Establishment'. Another reason why one need not exaggerate the separatist potential of the MQM lies in the fact that, according to Samad, there is 'increasing disillusionment with the confrontational approach that had been taken up'.Violence assumed its height in the mid-1990s (1,500 dead in 1995). It came partly from vendettas between the MQM(A) and the Haqiqi fractions, which fought for controlling the drug and arms traffic.[71] The unleashing of violence was all the more difficult to contain as the two MQMs often turn out to benefit from police complicity. But, according to Samad, 'the violence was aliena-ting Mohajirs themselves'.

Samad's interpretation of the Mohajir issue offers a relevant illustration of the pattern that has emerged from other case-studies above: far from sticking to their original pro-state identity, the Mohajirs developed separatist tendencies as soon as they started losing ground in the administration as well as in socio-economic terms.[72] The state apparatus reacted harshly to their demands, so much so that the MQM radicalized its position, following a repressive scenario which had already been observed in the early 1970s in East Pakistan, Baluchistan, and, to a lesser extent, the NWFP. However, the Mohajirs continue to play the electoral game, precisely because they remain primarily interested in pragmatic gains in terms of political power or socio-economic benefits. Therefore, Karachi, may, at one point of time experienced an inverse U curve too.

In addition to the Mohajir problem, the Sunni-Shia issue probably remains the most difficult one in terms of nation-building, as the rising graph of this sectarian violence suggests.The roots of the matter hark back to Zia's Islamization policy which, as Vali Nasr shows in Chapter 3 of this volume,'claimed to manifest a universal Islamic vision, but in reality was based on narrow Sunni interpretations of Islamic theology and law, and. was therefore unacceptable to Shias . . .'. In areas where the Shias were the more militant,'the state used madrasas to strengthen Sunnism'. This policy was mainly implemented by the army and the Inter-Services Intelligence (ISI), which were hopeful that they could use these groups for their own purposes. However, besides the strategies of state agencies, the sectarian conflicts also resulted from socio-economic rivalries between the Sunni urban middle class and the Shia landed elite, for instance, in Jhang district and in other parts of Punjab. Once again, ethnic identities partly crystallized because of socio-economic tensions. The notion of ethnicity may sound out of place here, but Nasr convincingly argues that the Shia-Sunni relationship 'has metamorphosed from religious schism into political conflict around mobilization of communal identity'. For him, 'at its core, sectarianism is a form of religio-political nationalism'. The political dimension of this issue is evident from the ever-increasing number of Shia and Sunni organizations which are canvassing and contesting elections. In the last section of his Chapter, 'Sectarianism in Domestic Politics', Nasr shows that, like the MQM, the sectarian parties play the election game, a modus operandi which may integrate them in mainstream politics in the long run.

However, sectarianism has ramifications outside Pakistan as well, as Nasr himself points out. In Chapter 4 Mariam Abou Zahab shows that while Zia's Islamization policy prepared the ground for such developments, 'the Iranian revolution, the Iran-Iraq war and the Afghan jihad were the enabling factors which gave scale and sustenance to the sectarian tensions, so far latent, and led to the internationalization of sectarian politics'. The Iranian revolution fostered the politicization of the Pakistani Shias, to which Saudi Arabia, Iraq (at war with Iran) and Kuwait reacted by supporting Sunni movements: Pakistan became the battlefield of a new proxy war fuelled by foreign money. This war gained momentum also because of the Afghan war, during which Pakistani Sunni movements supported the Taliban, whose overt anti-Shiaism upset Iran a great deal. The links between these Sunni movements and the Taliban have become so strong that, according to Abou Zahab, 'Talibanism has started spreading across the border', specially in the NWFP.

The growth of sectarian conflicts poses an obvious threat to the nation-building process. It puts the very notion of Pakistan into question since it demonstrates that Islam cannot be the only cementing ideological force behind the nation. This development is more challenging than ethnic separatist movements because it takes place in the heartland of Pakistan—the NWFP and Punjab—and amounts to a kind of ethnicization of Islam. As mentioned above, Nasr describes sectarianism 'as a form of "ethnic" posturing, one that combines Islamist and ethnic discourses of power'. If Islam does not form a valid reference, on which basis can the ideology of Pakistan establish itself ? How can Pakistan articulate a nationalist ideology and how much can this ideology borrow from Islam? This is the main focus of the second part of the book.

In Chapter 5, Saeed Shafqat recalls that all the Pakistani leaders have referred to Islam as the bedrock for building the nation. He points out that even Z.A. Bhutto, who presented himself as a socialist, had written in the 1973 Constitution that Islam was the religion of the state, but immediately underlines that there was some contradiction between this attitude and its pan-Islamic implications: Bhutto organized the Islamic Summit in Pakistan in 1974 to make 'a passionate appeal before the heads of Islamic states to work for evolving a regional block of Muslim states, a "Muslim Commonwealth"'. How could he reconcile this orientation and the promotion of the Pakistani nation state? This question is even more acute in the case of the Islamic movements which are gaining so much momentum in Pakistan today. Shafqat argues that the Tablighi Jamaat's annual congregation, with two million participants, is the second largest congregation of Muslims after the Haj and that the Lashkar-e-Taiba's annual congregation is attended by a million people. These groups tend to promote the concept of the Muslim *Ummah* and, therefore, 'regard territoriality as manifested through the State, superficial and transient for a community of believers'. As a result, 'Islamic sentiment in Pakistan is instrumentalized by organizing the jihad and Mujahideen for Kashmir, Afghanistan and other Islamic causes'. Shafqat makes this point clear by presenting a case study, the movement Dawat-ul-Irshad and 'its militant arm, the Lashkar-e-Taiba'. The paradox of these groups lies in the fact that, on the one hand, for them, 'Negating Islamic identity is equated with opposing Pakistan', and, on the other hand, they undermine the very foundations of Pakistan by promoting a transnational (instead of a nationalist) version of Islam.

This contradiction is most obvious in the case of the relation between Pakistan and Afghanistan. In Chapter 6, Olivier Roy shows that the decision of Gen. Zia to intervene in this country on account of Islamic solidarity was partly motivated by his will to defuse Pakhtun irredentism: 'the "Pakhtunistan" issue was superseded by Islamic solidarity'. However, he emphasizes that the Taliban remained more Pakhtun than anything else. They try to bypass this ethnic identity 'through the *shariah* and the reference to the Afghan State, as established from the early nineteenth century to the late 1970s by the monarchy. But that does not erase their ethnic background which heavily influences their attitude, through prejudice and discrimination.' As a result, the Taliban 'are not building a state' and 'to compare the present state of the Afghan administration to the situation at the time of the former King is nonsense'. Gilles Dorronsoro, in Chapter 7, argues, on the contrary, that the Taliban are 'sincerely committed to the reconstruction of a legal system in Afghanistan'.

While Olivier Roy and Gilles Dorronsoro differ on the situation in Afghanistan, they agree that Pakistan, under Zia, has considered the war as an opportunity for enlarging its influence in the region and even 'to establish a protectorate state in Kabul' (Dorronsoro). While 'the Taliban are by no means ISI puppets' (even though they have received military help from Pakistan), and while none of their leaders are Pakistanis, they are 'a by-product of the Pakistani policy', as Dorronsoro shows in detail. However, to what extent has this strategy strengthened or, on the contrary, weakened, the Pakistani nation state? It has provided it with some 'strategic depth', but, on the other hand, it has hindered its efforts for taking roots in Central Asia since most of the governments of this region are 'extremely worried about a fundamentalist destabilization'. More important, the promotion of a Pakhtun Islamist rule in Afghanistan has blurred the border between both states. The way Pakistan got involved in Afghan affairs has subsumed the nation state identity in a new, pan-Islamic dynamic, a process that harks back to congenital contradiction of Pakistan. As Olivier Roy emphasizes 'Contrary to many ideological states, Pakistan had little opportunity to develop as a mere nation state, based on territory, institutions and citizenship: it always stuck with its ideological and transnational claim of gathering all the Muslims of the area.'

The situation is somewhat similar regarding Kashmir. This region has always been a key issue for the making of the Pakistani nation, given the tenets of the 'two-nation theory'. As Sumit Ganguly recalls in Chapter 8, for Pakistan it was important 'to control Kashmir to bolster its self-image as a homeland for the Muslims of South Asia'. Pakistan regards the Kashmiris as the victims of an unachieved Partition: they have to join 'the land of the Pure' in order to complete the initial project nursed by Jinnah and the Muslim League. Once again, the Pakistanis' fight for their 'Kashmiri brothers' is expressed in terms of Islamic solidarity. After the insurgency started in 1989, Ganguly points out, 'Pakistani decision makers, sensing an Indian window of vulnerability in Kashmir, have sought to exploit a notion of Muslim confraternity to support the insurgents'. While Kashmiri Islam has traditionally not been of a very orthodox brand, the National Conference not a religious party, and the Jammu and Kashmir Liberation Front (JKLF) a secular organization, Islamism developed in the 1980s partly as a result of the communalization of the Indian political scene under the aegis of Rajiv Gandhi, and, more important, because of the influx of 'mehmaan Mujahideen', 'guest militants' who came from other Muslim countries to support the jihad in Kashmir. Most of them were from Pakistan and had some experience of the Afghan war. In fact, they strove for achieving the same result in Kashmir as the Taliban.

While the involvement of Pakistani jihadist militants and army men in Afghanistan had tended to blur the frontier between both countries and to dilute the Pakistani national identity, we cannot draw the same conclusion from the case of Kashmir. First, the Kashmiris do not form the same kind of ethnic group as the Pakhtuns—they do not speak the same language on both sides of the border, for instance. Second, and more important, in Kashmir, Pakistan and Pakistan-supported groups fight against Indians.

As Ganguly points out, Islam could not be the main driving force behind Pakistani nationalism and after the creation of Bangladesh Pakistan had to find a substitute for cementing the country. It, therefore, sought to hold on to Kashmir 'from the imperatives of statecraft and little else'. This is sheer anti-India based nationalism.

In fact, the brand of nationalism that Pakistan has been able to articulate most efficiently is not rooted in Islam but which targets India, using Islamic overtones. Pakistan's nationalism is primarily anti-Indian: this is the essence of the country's identity. As Jean-Luc Racine points out in Chapter 9, 'the paradox of Pakistan lies in this very basic fact: born out of a partition chosen by itself, it appears to have found in independence neither the peace, nor the security, nor the freedom of spirit that would enable it either to live in harmony with India, or to ignore it'. According to Racine, the 'India syndrome' of Pakistan stems from an obvious asymmetry between both countries. This balance of strength nurtures a feeling of insecurity but also 'Pakistan's eagerness to take to task a much larger neighbour', partly because of the assumption that India represents a 'large country but small people'. Kashmir is the symbol of this conflict and fuels anti-Indian feelings. As Racine points out, 'anti-Indian rhetoric always serves as an effective rallying point to consolidate national unity in times of crisis or of political difficulty'. Politicians and military rulers alike have always been adept at instrumentalizing the Kashmir issue for mobilizing supporters. This is how the Pakistani nation exists, through nationalist feelings which are articulated against the Indian Other. In a way, the situation that prevailed in the 1940s remains the same several decades later: Pakistanis feel as such when they regard themselves in opposition to the threatening Indian/Hindu Other.

Yet, the Indo-Pakistani conflict is proving more and more costly and both countries may even consider that they should collaborate in the economic field. For Frédéric Grare (Chapter 10), the geopolitics of energy supply in South Asia prepares the ground for such a rapprochement. Occupying a critical space between India and the 'greater Middle East', Pakistan could play a role in the regional projects for the development of trade in oil and natural gas, two sources of energy that South Asia needs in increasing quantities to match its growing consumption. The pipelines to India may cross Pakistan since they would either originate in the Middle East and the Gulf countries, or in Central Asia.[73] Grare emphasizes the common interests of both countries in this perspective:

Like Pakistan, India faces a chronic and growing shortage of energy. Like Pakistan, it considers the recourse to natural gas—a less expensive and cleaner alternative—as being one of the possible options if it wants to reduce its dependence on oil. Last, its potential suppliers also are the same as those of Pakistan, namely Iran and Central Asia. All studies, moreover, concur in the view that, from the strictly economic standpoint, cooperation between the two countries, more specifically for the utilization of joint pipelines for the import of natural gas, would enable vast economies of scale, resulting for each of them in a substantial decrease in the unit cost of gas.

Will these perspectives be sufficient for the two countries to overcome their differences? So far, all the projects have been aborted, partly because of the strong nationalist distrust that these two countries continue to feel for each other.

Part III of the book deals with the ways in which Pakistan tries to project its anti-Indian nationalist ideology. According to Mohammad Waseem (Chapter 12), this ideology is rooted in a strong national consensus between public opinion and the decision-makers. More precisely, the 'continuously unstable regional environment along the eastern, northern and now western borders' has generated 'a high level of general conformity to the official version of events in the backdrop of public commitment to national security'. The input from the public cannot be really substantive in the making of the foreign policy because the defence of the nation and the projection of its interests are at stake and the 'more an issue is understood to be national or civilizational rather than partisan and parochial, the more the Government has control over it as a symbol of the state'. There are minor 'ethno-spatial' differences in this consensus since the regions which dominate the state apparatus—Punjab and the NWFP—rally around the consensus in question, whereas East Pakistan, Sindh and Baluchistan have never felt the same concerns regarding the key issues defining the national consensus (like Kashmir or Afghanistan). There have been variations in the course of time too, but they were not very substantial either. In the first phase identified by Mohammad Waseem, as between 1947 and 1971, Pakistan's 'foreign policy largely remained a preserve of the Foreign Office bureaucracy', till 1965. At that time the India–Pakistan war initiated the first shift: the civilians lost ground compared to the military in the making of foreign policy. During the second phase, under Bhutto (1971-7), the civil government regained somewhat its power of initiative but 'Islamabad's threat perception vis-à-vis India continued to be at the centre of its security considerations along with its need to seek Western support', specially after the 1974 Indian nuclear test. The third period (1977-88) was dominated by 'a general consensus about the need to resist the Soviet move in official circles, Islamic parties and groups, industrial and landed elite as well as Afghan refugees'. Once again, the consensus was based on the defence of national interests as a response to a regional threat. The fourth phase (1988-99) was marked by a similar consensus on the official policy on Kashmir and Afghanistan and about the development of a nuclear capability. Therefore, since 1947, public opinion in Pakistan and the state agencies share the some perception of foreign policy, this common ground being based on the need to preserve and project national interest.

But who projects this nationalist ideology? The policy of Pakistan regarding the Kashmir issue is a case in point, given the highly symbolic meaning of this bone of contention. In Chapter 12, Amélie Blom shows that there is 'a plethora of agencies being in charge of Kashmir', ranging from the Parliamentary Kashmir Committee to the Army 'and its several divisions', the ISI, 'which is sometimes credited as having an autonomous policy', the President, the Prime Minister, the Foreign Office (and its Kashmir Directorate) and the Defence Secretary: the Kashmir policy of Pakistan suggests that it is truly 'a multi-vocal state'. While the army and the ISI tend to dominate—or even monopolize—the decision-making process regarding Kashmir, Blom argues that the government does have a say in the Indian policy of Pakistan, including the Kashmir issue. But focusing on the second

Government of Nawaz Sharif, she points out that the Prime Minister and the army were often at cross-purposes, as is evident from the contradiction between the 'Lahore process' initiated by Sharif and Vajpayee on the one hand and the infiltration of Pakistani soldiers in Kargil in 1999. However, she offers a very nuanced analysis showing that the Prime Minister himself was not explicitly in favour of a diplomatic settlement, for the simple reason that no Pakistani ruler can afford to be soft on India, especially on Kashmir; hence the inner contradictions of Sharif's policy vis-à-vis his big neighbour. Blom's chapter, therefore, even if it looks at Pakistan as a 'multi-vocal state', ultimately reinforces the interpretation of Waseem regarding Pakistan's nationalist consensus.

This viewpoint is even more evident from the last chapter (Chapter 13) where Ian Talbot, linking—unintentionally—the three chapters of Part III, argues that 'the political leaders' similarities of outlook with the army on key issues [of foreign policy] was the result not only of deference, but of a common stance based on realpolitik and response to popular opinion'. Talbot's reading of the situation lies on a sociological approach. He emphasizes that in the post-Zia era, 'the army [was] part of a wider establishment with which the politicians had to contend'. This included the civil bureaucracy, the President who wielded considerable autonomous power, and the intelligence agencies which were prone to act independently in pursuit of gains in their turf wars. Implicitly, Talbot refers here to a rather unidimensional 'multi-vocal state', in the sense that while different and more or less autonomous agencies are involved in the making of the foreign policy, their actions converge towards the same aim, the projection of the nation's interests, and the army plays a leading part in this. The army's upper hand does not simply stem from the fact that it has become a state within the state which is in a position to defend its interests, as a mere pressure group—an interpretation Ayesha Jalal has put forward. According to Talbot, it is not only due to a 'fragility syndrome' vis-à-vis India either, because, according to him, in that case 'alternative strategies of rapprochement with India [could have] been adopted to remove this fear'. For him, these factors need to be supplemented by two others. First, the belief that a 'strong army equates with a strong nation' was a key element in the growing importance of this institution within the Pakistani state. Second, the army has gained so much importance because it is a 'Punjabi-based force' and one needs to acknowledge 'the congruence between its interests and those of significant sections of Punjabi society'.

The first factor reflects the traditional consensus on the need of building a stro.g nation which is largely based on the apprehension of an Indian threat. This consensus explains that, as Talbot points out, 'civilian and martial law agencies possessed very similar conceptions of policy objectives'. For Talbot, this convergence reflected 'first and foremost overriding security anxieties'. According to him, 'direct army control through the curbing of the bureaucracy and the rise of the ISI was much greater in the Zia era than before', but he emphasizes that the military continued to exert considerable influence over 'those areas of foreign policy linked to its security concerns, i.e. Afghanistan and Kashmir during the 1998-9 period', while the democratization process was supposed to go on par with the re-establishment of civilian rule.

However, Talbot's reference to the overwhelming domination of the Punjabis over the army suggests that the 'security concerns' in question may not always be those of all Pakistanis, but primarily those of Punjab. We are back to Chapter 1, where Talbot has already put stress on the tension between the majority region and the minority provinces.

In the conclusion of the book, Pierre Lafrance deliberately offers an optimistic interpretation of the Pakistan nation-building process in terms of political and cultural integration. According to him, the 'Pakistanness' is rooted in the geographical cohesion resulting from 'the enormous Indus Valley along with the mountains and plateaux that bear its tributaries while also forming natural borders', the Indus Valley being also the main axis for infrastructures of communications. Besides this, geographical cohesion is reinforced by history since the Indus civilization and the Gandhara culture were spread over the same area. For Lafrance, therefore, Pakistan's national identity is well identified with a clear-cut historical territory. However, he admits that Pakistan has not been able to develop a positive national identity but 'finds itself trapped in anti-Indianness'. This concession is in tune with the general argument of this volume, viz., Pakistan, as a State, relies more on anti-Indian nationalism than on national integration. To put it in a nutshell, this is a case of *nationalism without a nation*.

This book draws from a series of colloquia which have been organized at the Centre d'Études et de Recherches Internationales (CERI-Paris) in 1997-9.

NOTES

1. M. Ali, 'In Search of Identity', *Dawn*, 7 May 2000.
2. For a discussion of the theories of nationalism and the distinction between ethnic and territorial nationalism, see A.D. Smith, *Theories of Nationalism*, London: Gerald Dukworth and Co., 1971, pp. 217-18.
3. M. Mauss, 'La nation' (1920), *Oeuvre*, Tome 3, Paris: Minuit, 1969, p. 584. My translation. Emphasis added.
4. A. Hussain, 'Ethnicity, National Identity and Praetorianism: The Case of Pakistan', *Asian Survey*, vol. 16, no. 10, October 1976, p. 919.
5. Khalid Bin Sayeed, 'The Heart of the Pakistan Crisis', *Dawn*, 14 August 1998.
6. T. Amin, *Ethno-national Movements of Pakistan: Domestic and International Factors*, Islamabad: Institute of Political Studies, 1993, p. 73.
7. F. Robinson, *Separatism Among Indian Muslims*, Cambridge: Cambridge University Press, 1974.
8. Tariq Rahman, *Language and Politics in Pakistan*, Karachi: Oxford University Press, 1998, pp. 37, 69.
9. On the rather privileged position of the UP Muslims, see P. Brass, *Language, Religion and Politics*, Cambridge: Cambridge University Press, 1974.
10. On the Aligarh movement, see D. Lelyveld, *Aligarh's First Generation: Muslim Solidarity in British India*, Princeton, Princeton University Press, 1978.
11. J. Brown, *Modern India. The Origins of an Asian Democracy*, Delhi: Oxford University Press, 1985, p. 178.
12. G. Minault, *The Khilafat Movement: Religious Symbolism and Political Mobilization in India*, New York: Columbia University Press, 1982.
13. F. Robinson, 'Nation Formation, the Brass Thesis and Muslim Separatism', *Journal of Commonwealth and Comparative Politics*, vol. 15, no. 3, Nov. 1977, p. 219. See also *Separatism Among Indian Muslims*, Cambridge University Press, 1974, p. 13, where the author partly explains the emergence of Muslim separatism as resulting from a relative incompatibility between Hindu and Muslim cultures.
14. For a short discussion on this theory of nationalism, see C. Jaffrelot, 'Of Nations and Nationalism', *Seminar*, no. 442, pp. 31-6.
15. C. Geertz, 'The Integrative Revolution—Primordial Sentiments and Civil Politics in the New States', in C. Geertz, ed., *Old Societies and New States*, London: The Free Press of Glencoe, 1963, p. 128.
16. For a more detailed account of my interpretation of nationalist movements in Pakistan, see my article, 'Interpreting Ethnic Movements in Pakistan', *The Pakistan Development Review*, vol. 37, no. 4, Part 1, Winter 1998, pp. 153-79.
17. E. Gellner, *Thought and Change*, London: Weidenfield and Nicholson, 1964, p. 160.
18. Ibid., p. 167.
19. Ibid., p. 168.
20. A. Jalal, *The Sole Spokesman: Jinnah, the Muslim League and the Demand for Pakistan*, Cambridge: Cambridge University Press, 1985.

21. I.A. Malik, ed., *Muslim League Session 1940 and the Lahore Resolution* (*Documents*), Islamabad: National Institute of Historical and Cultural Research, 1990, pp. 156-7.

22. Ibid., pp. 298-9.

23. I. Talbot, *Punjab and the Raj: 1849-1947*, Delhi: Manohar, 1988, p. 89.

24. Y. Samad, *A Nation in Turmoil: Nationalism and Ethnicity in Pakistan, 1937-1958*, Delhi: Sage, 1995, p. 72.

25. D. Gilmartin, *Empire and Islam: Punjab and the Making of Pakistan*, Berkeley: California University Press, 1988.

26. I. Talbot, *Pakistan: A Modern History*, London: Hurst, 1999, p. 78.

27. M.S. Korejo, *G.M. Syed: An Analysis of his Political Perspectives*, Karachi: Oxford University Press, 2000.

28. In 1905, the British had agreed to divide Bengal into two provinces, a decision that they had reversed in 1911 under pressure from the Congress.

29. Cited in I. Talbot, *Pakistan*, op. cit., p. 90.

30. Samad, *A Nation in Turmoil*, op. cit., p. 90.

31. After the 1938 reform, Bengal was given 100 representatives, Punjab 90, the United Provinces 70 and Bombay Presidency 30. The first two provinces accounted for only 40 per cent of the Council, whereas they were the largest Muslim-dominated provinces of British India.

32. The Muslim League began to explicitly demand one State during the negotiations with the Cabinet Mission in 1946.

33. Something the local Sindhis (who feared that services would be disrupted) greatly appreciated, to begin with. See the personal testimony of Afak Maydar, 'The Mohajirs in Sindh: A Critical Essay', in J. Henry Korson, ed., *Contemporary Problems of Pakistan*, Boulder: Westview Press, 1993, p. 117.

34. F. Ahmed, *Ethnicity and Politics in Pakistan*, Karachi: Oxford University Press, 1998, p. 95.

35. K.B. Sayeed, *The Political System of Pakistan*, Boston: Houghton Mifflin, 1967, p. 132. While they represented 3.5 per cent of the population, the Mohajirs occupied 21 per cent of the Pakistan Civil Service (R. Braibanti, *Asian Bureaucratic Traditions Emergent from the British Imperial Tradition*, Durham: Duke University Press, 1966, p. 263).

36. Rahman, op. cit., pp. 230-1.

37. S.P. Cohen, 'State Building in Pakistan', in A. Banuazizi and M. Weiner, eds., *The State, Religion and Ethnic Politics: Pakistan, Iran and Afghanistan*, Lahore: Vanguard, 1987, p. 318.

38. The British had granted many 'tribes' of Punjab the status of 'martial races' and had recruited them in large numbers for fighting in Afghanistan and Europe. See C. Dewey, 'The Rural Roots of Pakistani Militarism', in D.A. Low, ed., *Political Inheritance of Pakistan*, Houdmills, Barsingstoke: Macmillan, 1991, pp. 255-83.

39. C.H. Kennedy, *Bureaucracy in Pakistan*, Karachi: Oxford University Press, 1987, p. 194. During the British Raj, Fazl-i-Hussain, who wanted to reduce

the over-representation of the Hindus in the administration, had established a quota for the Muslims in different educational institutions (such as the Civil Service Academy) as soon as he had become Education Minister in the Punjab Government in 1921.

40. L. Binder, *Religion and Politics in Pakistan*, Berkeley: University of California Press, 1961, p. 205.

41. Liaquat Ali Khan emphasized that there was no question of establishing a theocracy in Pakistan: Liaquat Ali Khan, *Pakistan: The Heart of Asia*, Cambridge, Mass.: Harvard University Press, 1950, pp. 6, 10.

42. Shahid Javed Burki, *Pakistan, Fifty Years of Nationhood*, Boulder: Westview Press, 1999, p. 29.

43. Y. Samad, 'Pakistan or Punjabistan: Crisis of National Identity', *International Journal of Punjab Studies*, vol. 2, no. 1, 1995, p. 30.

44. R. Raza, 'Constitutional Development and Political Consequences', in R. Raza, ed., *Pakistan Perspective, 1947-1997*, Karachi: Oxford University Press, 1997, pp. 1-60.

45. M. Rashiduzzaman, 'East-West Conflicts in Pakistan: Bengali Regionalism, 1947-1970', in Jeyaratnam Wilson and D. Dalton, eds., *The States of South Asia—Problems of National Integration*, London: Hurst, 1982, p. 117.

46. A. Kohli, 'Can Democracies Accommodate Ethnic Nationalism? Rise and Decline of Self-Determination Movements in India', *Journal of Asian Studies*, vol. 56, no. 2, May 1997, pp. 325-44.

47. Cited in Raza, 'Constitutional Developments', op. cit., p. 18.

48. M.G. Chitkara, *Jiy-e Sindh G.M. Syed*, New Delhi: APH Publishing, 1996.

49. S.P. Cohen, *The Pakistani Army*, Karachi: Oxford University Press, 1998, p. 44; see also Khalid B. Sayeed, 'The Role of Military in Pakistan', in J.Van Doorn, ed., *Armed Forces and Society*, The Hague/Paris: Mouton, 1968.

50. Cited in S. Wolpert, *Zulfi Bhutto of Pakistan: His Life and Times*, New York: Oxford University Press, 1993, p. 139. However, in reaction to the mobilization of the Mohajirs, the new law was amended in order to elevate Urdu to the same rank as Sindhi, as an official language in the province.

51. Interestingly, all the four Punjabi judges were in favour of the death penalty whereas all the judges from minority provinces opted for a less extreme sentence: O. Noman, *Pakistan—Political and Economic History Since 1947*, London: Kegan Paul, 1992, p. 193.

52. Ibid., pp. 196-7. The 'states' (note that the word used is not 'provinces' any more) which were to form the basic units of this confederation would have their own flag and, more important, the post of Prime Minister would have been offered to each province in turn.

53. S.S. Harrison, 'Ethnicity and the Political Stalemate in Pakistan', in Bannazizi and Weiner, eds., *The State*, op. cit., pp. 281-2.

54. The fact that 99 per cent of the voters approved of the integration of the NWFP with Pakistan certainly reflects the popularity of this integration, even though Ghaffar Khan's call to boycott makes interpretations uneasy. As in

Punjab, Jinnah's discourse about the threat that the Congress was posing to Islam had led many Muslims of the NWFP to rally around him. See I. Talbot, *Provincial Politics and the Pakistan Movement: The Growth of the Muslim League in North-West and North-East India, 1937-1947,* Karachi: Oxford University Press, 1999, p. 110.

55. Cohen, *The Pakistan Army,* op. cit., p. 44.

56. *Frontier,* 21 February 1998.

57. Y. Samad, 'Pakistan or Punjabistan: Crisis of National Identity', *International Journal of Punjab Studies,* vol. 2, no. 1, 1995, p. 30.

58. M.G. Weinbaum, 'The Impact and Legacy of the Afghan Refugees in Pakistan', in J.H. Korson, ed., *Contemporary Problems of Pakistan,* Boulder, Colorado: Westview Press, 1993, pp. 133-9.

59. *The News,* 1 March 1998.

60. Phadnis, *Ethnicity,* op. cit., p. 183; Harrison, op. cit., p. 274.

61. K.B. Sayeed, *Politics in Pakistan—The Nature and Direction of Change,* [n.p., n.d.]. See Chap. 6 entitled 'Pakistan's Central Government Versus Balochi and Pakhtun Aspirations', pp. 113-38. Sayeed mentions that 'There is not much evidence that the Bhutto regime explored every possible avenue to reach a compromise with the Balochi provincial government whereby a central government with its legitimate concerns could coexist with a provincial government committed to increasing provincial autonomy. As in other cases, Bhutto was interested in the aggrandisement of power, not in its sharing.'

62. Harrison, op. cit., pp. 274-5.

63. Their rallying around the state apparatus was crucial given the influence they exerted at the grassroots level. Indeed, the middle class and the intelligentsia formed a microscopic minority: Baluchistan presented the lowest literacy rate of the country (8.5 per cent).

64. *The News,* 20 February 1997, p. 1.

65. *Muslim,* 31 July 1998.

66. *The News,* 24 October 1999.

67. Hence, the opposition of many Punjabis to the conduct of the census in the 1990s: they feared that the growth rate of the other provinces appeared to be higher and that their share of seats should be reduced accordingly. However, the 1998 census has shown a very limited erosion of the weight of Punjab (Table 1.3).

68. *Dawn,* 3 October 1998.

69. J. Rehman, 'Self-determination, State-building and the Mohajirs: An International Legal Perspective of the Role of the Indian Muslim Refugees in the Constitutional Development of Pakistan', *Contemporary South Asia,* vol. 3, no. 2, 1994, pp. 122-3.

70. Interview in *India Today,* 15 July 1995, p. 42.

71. The MQM, indeed, had split up in 1992, with the formation of the MQM (Haqiqi) which pretended to represent the 'real' MQM. This group appeared, in fact, to have been tempted by the offers of the Army a little after Operation

Clean Up. It counted in its ranks a number of militants that Altaf Hussain had alienated by his autocratic style of functioning. It was composed of militants as violent as those of the MQM(A)—whence the vendettas and other bloody confrontations—but may be more linked to the local mafia.

72. They may not be involved in a pauperization process as they feel, but they may well have reached a plateau and be under the impression of a decline because of this very stagnation.

73. For instance, the American oil company UNOCAL had proposed to build a pipeline for taking the oil of Central Asia to the Indian Ocean via Afghanistan and Pakistan—one more good reason for supporting the Taliban, the only force that was likely to promote political stability in the neighbouring country according to Islamabad.

APPENDIX 1.1: THE LINGUISTIC GROUPS OF PAKISTAN IN 1984 (IN %)

Language/ Province	Punjabi	Pashto	Sindhi	Saraiki	Urdu	Baluch	Other
Punjab	78.7	0.8	0.1	14.9	4.3	0.6	0.6
Sindh	7.7	3.1	52.4	2.3	22.6	4.5	7.4
NWFP	1.1	68.3	0.1	4	0.8	0.1	25.6
Baluchistan	2.2	25.1	8.3	3.1	1.4	36.3	23.6
Pakistan	48.2	13.1	11.8	9.8	7.6	3.0	6.5

Source: Government of Pakistan, Statistical Pocket Book of Pakistan, 1984, Islamabad: Federal Bureau of Statistics, 1984, p. 61.

APPENDIX 1.2: THE ETHNO-LINGUISTIC GROUPS OF PAKISTAN
            (AS ESTIMATED IN 1996)

Communities	Number	%
Punjabis	7,36,40,000	56
Sindhis	2,23,55,000	17
Pathans	2,10,40,000	16
Mohajirs	78,90,000	6
Baluch	39,45,000	3
Other	26,30,000	2
Total	13,15,00,000	100

Source: S. Ahmed 'Centralization, Authoritarianism and the Mismanagement of Ethnic Relations in Pakistan', in M.E. Brown and S. Ganguly, eds., Government, Politics and Ethnic Relations in Asia and the Pacific, Cambridge, Mass.; MIT Press, 1997, p. 88.

APPENDIX 1.3: EVOLUTION OF THE ETHNO-LINGUISTIC COMMUNITIES
            OF PAKISTAN (IN %)

Communities	1981	1998
Punjab	56.7	56
Sindh	22.6	23
NWFP	13.1	13.4
Baluchistan	5.1	5
FATA	2.6	2.3
Total	100	100

Source: Dawn, 9 July 1998.

PART I
The Failed (Islamic) State: Ethnic Conflicts and Sectarianism

1

The Punjabization of Pakistan: Myth or Reality?

IAN TALBOT

THE PHRASE THE 'Punjabization of Pakistan' has become well known amongst commentators and politicians of the minority provinces as cryptic criticism of Pakistan's domination by its most populous province. The Punjab can thus be seen both as the corner-stone of the country and as a major hindrance to national integration. The Punjabization thesis has previously been linked with the region's ties to the army, the foremost unelected institution of the nation. The emphasis during the first one hundred days of Gen. Pervez Musharraf's regime following the October 1999 coup was on restoring national cohesion through removing inter-provincial disharmony. This aim was to be achieved in part by depoliticizing State institutions and devolving power to the grass-roots level. In fact, this policy has added a further element to criticism of the Punjabi 'big brother', as a result of the Punjabi domination of major State offices, the concentration of development funds in the province and the decision on the controversial Kalabagh Dam project. The aim of this chapter is to explore the basis for Punjabi predominance in Pakistan's politics, and to uncover both the myths and realities surrounding the Punjabization claim.

In a bloodless coup on 12 October 1999, the Pakistan Army under the command of Gen. Pervez Musharraf removed the Government of Nawaz Sharif. This decisive action came in the wake of the Kargil episode, but its catalyst was the Punjabi Prime Minister's attempt to intervene in the army's leadership, following his earlier cowing down of the judiciary. Musharraf justified his action as ending the 'sham democracy' which had undermined national unity and witnessed the plundering of resources by 'corrupt' politicians. Although power had now fallen into the hands of a Punjabi-dominated institution, its commander was a Mohajir by background. Musharraf, in his calls for the restoration of a common national purpose, echoed some of the criticism of Sharif's opponents regarding the Punjabization of Pakistan. The evidence for this charge was cited in terms of Punjabi domination of major State offices, including those of the Prime Minister, President and Senate Chairman, along with Nawaz Sharif's concentration of development funds in the province in such grandiose projects as the new terminal at Lahore airport and the Islamabad to Peshawar motorway. Simultaneously, projects had been starved of funds in Sindh and Baluchistan. All development work was halted in the latter province early in 1998 because the Federal Government failed to pay its monthly revenue instalment. Existing programmes were in themselves totally insufficient in this sparsely populated and underdeveloped province where less than a quarter of its inhabitants have access to clean drinking water.

The claim that Pakistan has become 'Punjabistan' was strengthened by the particular circumstances of Nawaz Sharif's second administration, but the Punjab region has played a key role throughout post-Independence Pakistan history. It is the home of the Pakistan Army, which has wielded power directly for two and a half decades and indirectly for longer still. During periods of democratic rule, the region has also been of pivotal importance. During her first (1988-90) Ministry, Benazir Bhutto found to her cost that a national administration in Islamabad could be undermined by a hostile Provincial Government in Lahore. It was, in fact, during the civilianization of martial law during the latter part of the Zia era that her bitter rival Nawaz Sharif had established the Punjab as his power base. Despite the PML(N)'s unexpectedly strong showing in Sindh (where it won 12 seats) in the 1997 elections, the bulk of its landslide majority of 135 seats was secured in Punjab. This was repeated in the provincial assembly results where it captured 211 out of the 240 seats in the Lahore legislature.

The Punjab has not only played an important role in the elected and unelected institutions of the Pakistani State, but in its economy. Since the breakaway of Bangladesh in 1971, the Punjab has also maintained a demographic majority (around 56 per cent) of the total population. This situation (which is without parallel in India, but may be compared with the northern regions in Nigeria) has drawn much adverse comments. Anti-Punjabi sentiments are held quite widely in contemporary Pakistan.[1] Indeed, they play an important component of both Mohajir and Sindhi political identity. During the crucial opening decade of independence, the locus of conflict between Punjabis and the 'others' centred around the Pakhtun-Punjabi rivalries in the western wing, and the clash between a Punjabi-led West Pakistan and

the Bengali eastern wing. The denial of the Bengali majority's democratic urges climaxed in the human tragedy and national catastrophe of
the unleashing of the Punjabi-dominated Pakistan Army on the
civilian populace of East Pakistan in March 1971.

A quarter of a century later, the consequences of the civil war are
still working themselves out. Punjab, paradoxically, has to be seen as
both the bulwark of the rump Pakistan State and the major barrier
to national integration because of the use of Punjabi military and
paramilitary forces during civil unrest in Baluchistan and Sindh. Fears
were expressed in the mid-1990s of a Dhaka-like situation repeating
itself in the troubled port city of Karachi. Such scholars as Yunas Samad
have coined the phrase 'the Punjabization of Pakistan' to describe
the region's post-1971 predominance.[2] Despite the Punjabi-bashing
sentiments of some minority-province politicians, the issue arises,
however, whether Punjabi interests are as monolithic as they are sometimes portrayed. In other words, should the Punjabization concept be
problematized? Is it as much myth as reality?

In a number of respects, the Punjab's importance in Pakistan's
political economy cannot be gainsaid. We shall look successively at the
historical, economic, and demographic reasons for this. The region's
significance in post-Independence politics is not, interestingly, rooted
in its historical contribution to the Pakistan movement. Although the
Punjab finally and decisively swung behind the freedom struggle, the
Muslim League, because of the Unionist Party's predominance, was
very much a latecomer in the future 'cornerstone' of Pakistan.[3] Indeed,
the Muslim League had no experience of wielding power in the
Punjab before the departure of the British, unlike, for example in
Sindh, Bengal, and, albeit briefly, in the Frontier.[4]

The historical roots of the Punjab's subsequent importance for
Pakistan lie elsewhere in the colonial pattern of economic development,
military recruitment and administration. Clive Dewey's,[5] empirical
historical research has fruitfully traced the 'military-ethnic equation'
in Pakistan to the colonial legacy of recruitment from a handful of
'martial-caste' communities and regions of Punjab. This policy, based
largely on the perceived threat from Afghanistan and the need for
'reliable' non-nationalist recruits, was buttressed by the martial castes
ideology.

The continuation of colonial policies of making land available to
servicemen has created a nexus of interest between the Punjabi landowners and the military. Many servicemen acquired resumed land at
knockdown prices after the 1959 Land Reforms. Their entry into the

rural and industrial elite continued apace during the eleven years (1977-88) of the Zia martial law period. Punjabi support for the military is not only based on a community of economic interests, however, but by the presence of a large East Punjabi refugee population in many of the province's cities. Zia himself came from this background[6] and articulated its pro-Islamic and anti-India attitudes.

The continuation of the martial castes ideology since Independence has ensured a predominant role for Punjabis in both the officer corps and the ranks of the Pakistan Army. Punjab has thus been associated with the most important non-elected institution of the Pakistani State, one which has arrogated to itself the responsibility for defending the territorial and ideological boundaries of the State. The 'unrepresentative' character of the army has increased ethnic tensions. As Table 1.1 indicates, the Bengali majority of the pre-1971 Pakistani population was largely excluded from military service. This helped perpetuate racial stereotypes which had tragic consequences in the army crackdown on civil unrest in East Pakistan early in 1971. The Punjabi-dominated army has now become a Punjabi-Pakhtun combine, but both Sindhis and Mohajirs are marginalized, although in Generals Aslam Beg and Pervez Musharraf, Mohajirs have risen to be Chief of the Army Staff.

Less well known is the colonial inheritance of a Punjabi predominance in the bureaucracy. The Bengali pre-1971 marginalization is again brought out in Table 1.2.

Punjabi influence in the bureaucracy was shared in the early post-Independence period with the Mohajirs, but increased substantially following the Ayub (1958-69) and Zia (1977-88) martial laws. It originated not from deliberate colonial policy as with military recruit-

TABLE 1.1: MILITARY ELITE IN PAKISTAN: 1955

	East Bengal	West Pakistan
Lt. Gen.	0	3
Maj. Gen.	0	20
Brig.	1	34
Col.	1	49
Lt. Col.	2	198
Maj.	10	590
Naval officers	7	593
Air Force officers	40	640

Source: Dawn, 9 January 1956. Cited in Mizanar Rahman, 'The Emergence of Bangladesh as a Sovereign State', Institute of Commonwealth Studies, Ph.D. thesis, 1975, p. 67.

TABLE 1.2: CENTRAL SECRETARIAT ELITE POSTS: 1955

	East Bengal	West Pakistan
Secretary	0	19
Joint Secretary	3	38
Deputy Secretary	10	123
Under Secretary	38	510

Source: Pakistan Constituent Assembly Debates, vol. 1, 7 January 1956, p. 1844. Cited in Mizanar Rahman, 'The Emergence of Bangladesh as a Sovereign State', Institute of Commonwealth Studies, Ph.D. thesis, 1975, p. 68.

ment, but resulted from the Punjab's greater educational development than that of the other 'Pakistani' areas. Hindus, as elsewhere in India, entered the new colonial educational institutions of the Punjab in much greater numbers than Muslims. The devolution of responsibility for education following the introduction of dyarchy was, however, seized upon by the Unionist Mian Fazl-i-Husain to improve the Muslims' standing. During the period 1921-6 when he served as Education Minister, he ensured a 40 per cent reservation of posts for Muslims in such prestigious centres of learning as Government College, Lahore and Lahore Medical College which had previously been Hindu preserves.[7] Punjabi Muslims thus entered the independence era with a strong position in both the army and the bureaucracy—the future unelected centres of power in the Pakistani State.

Finally, the massive irrigation projects introduced by the British in the late 1880s ensured that West Punjab would be the breadbasket of Pakistan, just as it had been of British India. Before the advent of the 1880s canal colony development, the richest agricultural areas of West Punjab lay in the districts of Lahore Division (especially the Lahore, Gujranwala and Sheikhupura districts). These enjoyed the benefits of good rainfall supplemented by canal or well irrigation. The unirrigated zones to the north and south (Upper Sindh Sagar Doab and the Bar and Thal) were far less productive.[8] Army recruitment increasingly sustained the economy of the former region, whose population was crowded in small farms. The southern dry zone was sparsely populated by nomadic herders with settled agriculture restricted to the land inundated by the annual riverine floods. Tribal landholders controlled vast tracts of land. Still further to the west, there lay the even poorer trans-Indus Dera Ghazi Khan district. The canal colony development both increased the differentiation between the agriculturally poor and productive regions, and shifted the region's agricultural wealth south-westwards. It also ensured that the infra-structure was present in the region to take full advantage of the Green Revolution technology introduced in the 1960s. Pakistan's agricultural output grew from Rs. 7.7 billion in 1960-1 to Rs. 12.2 billion in 1969-70, a growth rate of over 5.5 per cent per annum.[9] Output moved ahead much faster in the Punjab than the other Pakistani provinces as a result of the concentration of the new technology in the region. In 1976-7, the Punjab was producing 72 per cent of the country's output of major crops and 67 per cent of the food grains' output.[10] By the time of the 1981 Census, 80 per cent of all tractors and 88 per cent of all tube-wells in Pakistan were situated in the Punjab.[11] There was not only a marked disparity in growth trends between Punjab and other regions, but within the province itself where a relatively few districts led the way. Agricultural growth increased at a rate of 8.9 per cent per annum in the Lyallpur, Multan and Montgomery districts during the peak 1959/60 to 1964/5 period. At its end, these three districts accounted for 46 per cent of the Punjab's gross production value, despite occupying only 29.8 per cent of the cultivated area and containing only 32.6 per cent of the population.[12]

Akmal Hussain has revealed the polarization in the size distribution of farms and increased landlessness which followed the adoption of the new technology. His field survey demonstrated, for example, that large farms of 150 acres or over increased their total area by 106 per cent during the years 1960-78. In the same period, the total area of farms of less than 8 acres and of 8-25 acres both declined by 28 per cent.[13] His estimates based on population census data from 1961 to 1973 reveal that 43 per cent of the total number of agricultural labourers in Pakistan had entered this category during these years.[14]

Akmal Hussain links the increase in the size of large farms to the attractions of owner cultivation following the introduction of new technology. In order to maximize their opportunities for profit, large landlords have resumed their rented out land from small- and medium-sized tenant farmers. This process was associated with the purchase of tractors. Hussain's 1960-78 field survey data revealed a 67 per cent increase in tractor possession by farmers of 150 acres and above. His finding is corroborated by the 1970 Report of the Farm Mechanisation Committee. This showed that 52 per cent of all the tractors at the all-Pakistan level were owned by landholders operating farms in the size class above 100 acres.[15]

The Green Revolution thus not only increased the differentiation between the Punjab and other Pakistani regions, but exacerbated the differences within it, between rain-fed and irrigated areas. The access to technology also further underpinned class divisions which were themselves historically rooted in the British bolstering the power of their landlord collaborators. Such differentiation within the Punjab on class and regional lines is sometimes overlooked by those who are keen to castigate the 'big brother' for Pakistan's ills.

Punjab's industrial importance cannot be traced to the colonial inheritance, which was limited, with the exception of the Sialkot sports goods industry and the establishment of the Ittefaq foundries by Nawaz Sharif's father in 1940. Far more important was the boost to industrialization provided by the influx of refugee capitalists at the time of Partition. This was further assisted by the State's encouragement of development in the region during the extensive martial law eras. The mushrooming of the province's industries can be seen in the figures in Table 1.3. Symbolic of these processes was the emergence of Faisalabad, rich in refugee capital and labour, as the 'Manchester' of Pakistan. Lahore itself also became an important industrial centre. The Punjab was, of course, always ranked second to Karachi in industrial development, although the balance tipped in its favour with the flight of capital to Punjab following the 1990 troubles in the port metropolis.

We turn, finally, from the historical and economic roots of Punjab's significance to its demographic basis. Numbers, of course, only count in a democracy. Much of Pakistan's pre-1971 history must be understood in terms of the ruling elite's efforts to deny the Bengalis of their demographic majority. This was achieved through such devices as the

TABLE 1.3: INDUSTRIAL DEVELOPMENT IN WEST PAKISTAN: 1969-70

Region	Reporting Est.	Value of Fixed Assets (Rs. in '000s)
W. Pakistan	3,587	48,52,949
Punjab	2,052	21,78,582
Sindh	1,419	20,99,535
NWFP	98	5,54,208
Baluchistan	18	19,624

Source: Adapted from Government of Pakistan, Ministry of Finance, Planning and Development, Census of Manufacturing Industries 1969-70, Karachi, 1973, p. 5. Cited in M. Waseem, Politics and the State in Pakistan, Islamabad, National Institute of Historical and Cultural Research, 1994, p. 194.

One Unit Scheme designed to give parity between a unified West Pakistan province and East Pakistan. It was also a factor in deciding the 1958 coup and thus pre-empt the possibility of a Bengali-dominated government at the Centre. No national elections were held during Pakistan's first decade of independence, although in the provincial elections of 1954 in East Pakistan, the ruling national party, the Muslim League, suffered a humiliating defeat. Significantly, soon after its election, the East Pakistan United Front provincial ministry was dismissed. This hammered another nail in the coffin not only of national unity, but of democracy.

While Pakistan suffered a dearth of elections before the 1980s, since the restoration of democracy in 1988 there has been a veritable plethora. Numbers now count and ensure that national power lies in the most populous province of Punjab. The region's demographic importance in the post-1971 Pakistan state is revealed by the figures in Table 1.4.

Table 1.5 gives a clear indication of the two consequences of demography for the regional distribution of seats in the National Assembly. First, to win national power, a party must possess a power base in Punjab. The PML(N)'s eclipse of the PPP in the 1997 elections was at least in part explained by the latter's declining institutional strength and electoral support in Punjab. Second, the Punjabi electorate's outlook is important in shaping the political culture at the Centre.

There were signs during Nawaz Sharif's second administration

TABLE 1.4: PAKISTAN'S POPULATION BY AREA: 1981 (IN '000s)

Area	Pop.	% change 1973-81	% total 1981	% urban 1981
Punjab	47,116	26.3	56.2	27.5
Islamabad	335	42.6	0.4	60.2
NWFP	10,885	29.8	13.0	15.2
FATA	2,175	- 12.7	2.6	—
Sindh (except Karachi)	13,863	30.3	16.5	22.5
Karachi	5,103	45.2	6.1	100.0
Baluchistan	4,305	77.2	5.1	15.6
Pakistan	83,782	28.3	100.0	28.3

Source: Adapted from Main Findings of the 1981 Census (1983) cited in C. Baxter et al., *Government and Politics in South Asia*, 3rd edn., Boulder, Westview, 1993, p. 169.

TABLE 1.5:   REGIONAL DISTRIBUTION OF CONTESTED SEATS
FOR THE 1988 NATIONAL ASSEMBLY

Province/Area	Seats
Punjab	115
Sindh	46
NWFP	26
Baluchistan	11
Islamabad	1
FATA	8
Total	207

Source: I.H. Malik, State and Civil Society in Pakistan: Politics of Authority, Ideology and Ethnicity, Basingstoke: Macmillan, 1997, p. 36.

(1997-9) that the growing Punjabi business class was a factor in different moves to improve Pakistan's relations with India. In the past, however, the large migrant community in Punjab adopted a more hardline attitude. The Kashmir dispute, for example, never carried the same resonance for Bengalis as for Punjabis in pre-1971 Pakistan, nor since then have Sindhis been as committed as Punjabis.

Does this Punjabi military, administrative, economic and demographic predominance add up to a Punjabization of the Pakistan State? The answer must be only a qualified yes. For the depiction of a monolithic and unified Punjabi interest is as much a myth as Punjabi economic and political dominance is a reality. It is, for example, simplistic to regard Punjabi interests and those of the army as synonymous. Clive Dewey's historical scholarship reveals that the Punjabi-dominated army of Pakistani journalistic and polemical rhetoric is in reality an army recruited from just three Punjab regions, the Attock, Rawalpindi and Jhelum districts, although it is true that the economic multiplier effects of military recruitment ripple out to other areas of the province. Moreover, the Punjab itself is not as culturally or economically homogeneous as detractors of its role in Pakistani politics would have us believe.

As we have noted earlier, while Punjab was more developed during colonial rule than the other future Pakistan areas, economic growth exerted a differential regional and class impact. The same has been true of the Green Revolution. Independence did not result in any significant land reform, so that large areas of the south-west Punjab were left under the domination of feudal landowners. According to government records, even after the 1959 and 1972 land reforms, large landholders (with a farm size of 50 acres and above) still owned 18 per cent of the area of the Punjab. This contrasts dramatically with the system of peasant proprietorship in the Indian Punjab, which has produced higher rates of agricultural productivity, despite the impact of the Green Revolution in the Pakistani Punjab.

In addition to class divisions, Punjab is differentiated into four distinct economic and cultural regions. The northern region which corresponds to the administrative boundaries of the Rawalpindi Division contains approximately 10 per cent of the province's population. From the colonial era onwards, the inhabitants of this hilly region have supplemented low agricultural earnings with army recruitment, and latterly with remittances from the Gulf. The central Punjab contains virtually half of the province's population and includes not only the industrialized region around Faisalabad, but also the fertile agricultural districts of the Lahore and Gujranwala districts. The concentration of population makes this the most politically important region of the province with 55 of the 115 National Assembly seats. The south-west Punjab, which contains around a fifth of the province's population, comprises the Multan and Bahawalpur Divisions. The Cholistan desert forms the boundary with India; the canal irrigation of the colonial era has transformed other previously barren tracts into major cotton growing areas. The poorest region of the Punjab remains its western districts including Jhang district and the Sargodha and Dera Ghazi Khan Divisions. In contrast with the central Punjab, its agrarian society and economy is organized on a feudal basis.

Cultural differences overlay these socio-economic and climatic variations. To the north of the Salt Range, Hindko and Pothwari are spoken alongside Punjabi as regional languages; in the south-western Punjab, Saraiki, which is closely related to Sindhi, is spoken as a mother tongue by a considerable section of the population. By the mid-1980s, its leading organization, the Saraiki Suba Mahaz, was calling for a Saraiki suba (province).[16] The regional variations in Punjab were reflected in the 1993 National Assembly election results. The PPP lost badly to the Muslim League in the northern Punjab, but captured 22 out of 36 seats in the Saraiki-speaking divisions of Multan, D.G. Khan, Rahimyar Khan and Bahawalpur. Significantly, charges of the Punjabization of Pakistan during Nawaz Sharif's last tenure of office relate to the diversion of development funds to the central Punjab and the influence of its political elite. This was represented at the apex of power by Rafiq Ahmed Tarar and by Nawaz Sharif's close friends and troubleshooters, Ishaq Dar and Senator Saifur Rehman. A further, increasingly important source of division in contemporary Punjab has been sectarian conflicts. At the same time as mainstream religious parties have failed dismally in electoral politics, heavily armed extremist sectarian groups such as Sipah-e-Sahaba Pakistan, Lashkar-e-Jhangvi and Sipah-e-Muhammad have been launching murderous assaults on each other. The Jhang district with its Shia landholding class has been the epicentre of this violence. The complex history of the rise of sectarian violence lies beyond the scope of this chapter, but it should be noted in passing that amongst its causes have been cited the legacies of the Zia Islamization programme and the Afghan war, the return of the Taliban militia to Pakistan, the sectarian indoctrination of the young in the widespread networks of *madrasas* and the sponsorship of a proxy war in Pakistan by the Saudis and Iranians.

Thus Punjab, it is clear, is by no means monolithic. The perception in the minority provinces is, however, of a unified Punjabi political interest. This stands in the way of cross-regional political linkages on a class basis. The MQM's attempt to reinvent itself from an ethnic to a United National Movement (Muttahida Qaumi Movement) fighting against feudalism and corruption will form an interesting experiment in this respect.

Institutional reform represents, perhaps, a more fruitful way to solve the 'problem' of Punjabi domination. By creating three new provinces comprising two divisions with their headquarters respectively at Multan, Rawalpindi and Lahore, the imbalances in power which have undermined the country's stability will be addressed.[17] Moreover, such a constitutional step would also accelerate the pace of development in the more backward parts of Punjab. Such experimentation would not be entirely out of keeping in a country whose post-Independence history has been marked by 'the casting aside of older political forms for newer political experiments'.[18]

NOTES

1. See, for example, I.A. Rehman, 'Big Brother vs the Rest', *Newsline*, October 1995, pp. 67-8.
2. Y. Samad, 'Pakistan or Punjabistan: Crisis of National Identity', in G. Singh and I. Talbot, eds., *Punjabi Identity: Continuity and Change*, Delhi: Manohar, 1996.

3. See I. Talbot, *Punjab and the Raj, 1847-1947*, Delhi: Manohar, 1988.

4. I. Talbot, *Provincial Politics and the Pakistan Movement: The Growth of the Muslim League in North-West and North-East India 1937-47*, Karachi: Oxford University Press, 1988.

5. See C. Dewey, 'The Rural Roots of Pakistani Militarism', in D.A. Low, ed., *The Political Inheritance of Pakistan*, Basingstoke: Macmillan, 1991, pp. 255-83.

6. Zia came from a middle-class Arain family which migrated from Jalandhar to Pakistan in 1947.

7. Talbot, op. cit., n. 3, p. 69.

8. The Potwar Plateau was an exception in that it received greater winter rainfall.

9. M.H. Khan, *Underdevelopment and Agrarian Structure in Pakistan*, Boulder: Westview Press, 1981, p. 3.

10. Ibid., p. 11.

11. Shahid Kardar, 'Notes on National Unity and Regional Imbalances', in Iqbal Khan, ed., *Fresh Perspectives on India and Pakistan*, Oxford: Bougainvillea Books, 1985, p. 228.

12. Carl Gotsch, 'Regional Agricultural Growth: The Case of West Pakistan', *Asian Survey*, vol. 8, March 1968, p. 190.

13. Calculated from Table 1, p. 211 in Akmal Husain, 'Land Reforms in Pakistan: A Reconsideration', in I. Khan, ed., *Fresh Perspectives*, op. cit.

14. Ibid., p. 212.

15. Cited in A. Hussain, 'Technical Change & Social Polarisation in Pakistan', *Viewpoint*, 30 September 1982, p. 27.

16. See C. Shackle, 'Saraiki: A Language Movement in Pakistan', *Modern Asian Studies*, vol. 11, no. 3, 1979, pp. 379-403.

17. The three new provinces would have roughly the same size of population as Sindh, the Frontier and Baluchistan respectively. The proposal for the creation of new provinces is not, in fact, as radical as it seems, as it was put forward by the Ansari Commission during the Zia era. On the anniversary of the dismissal of Benazir Bhutto's first Government, Rashid Ahmad, a retired additional secretary to the Government of Pakistan, argued strongly for such a proposal along with a fixed three-year life for the provincial and national assemblies and local bodies. See, *Dawn*, 9 August 1991.

18. L. Ziring, 'Public Policy Dilemmas and Pakistan's Nationality Problem: The Legacy of Zia-ul-Haq', *Asian Survey*, vol. 28, no. 8, August 1988, p. 797.

2

In and Out of Power but not Down and Out: Mohajir Identity Politics

YUNAS SAMAD

HE EMERGENCE OF Mohajir identity politics has been synonymous with ethnic conflict in Karachi, which since 1985 has left nearly 9,000 dead.[1] Theoretically, globalization and new ethnicity were two concepts which assisted in understanding the emergence of Mohajir identity politics. Since the early modern period, there had been a relationship between territory, political structures and notions of collectivities. The relationships between these three coordinates were crystallized with the emergence of nationalism and the nation state, which had become the most common form of political community. There was a delicate balance between the three coordinates that were articulated as the dominant discourse. The ability of the state to regulate the national territory declined with globalization, but was exacerbated by Pakistan's involvement in the dying stage of the Cold War. The use of Pakistan as a staging post for Afghan Mujahideen had a profound impact on the ethnic composition of the military-bureaucratic oligarchy. The shifts in the balance of power set the stage for a new ethnicity to emerge. New identification emerges when structural shifts open up new spaces. Spaces that simultaneously undermine old identifications allow for the construction of new ethnicities.[2] The role of the State in this process was crucial, and changes in the dominant discourse set the backdrop against which identity construction takes place. There were many parallels with post-Fordist debates, which associate the shift away from Fordist to post-Fordist forms of production with the decline of class organizations and the emergence of new social movements.[3]

Concomitant with these shifts, globalization had also questioned the efficacy of the nation state and national forms of identification. The nation state had been the main sustenance of political and cultural identity. Globalization had resulted in divergent trends that either transcend the nation state, or undermine the nation by establishing themselves in the locale. The proliferation of trends and processes that were planetary in their location bypasses the regulatory functions of the nation state. The classic examples of globalization were the world economy, or the media, or both, which were beyond the regulatory functions of individual nation states, forcing them to increase multilateral cooperation so that such issues can be addressed. The process of localization, the mirror image of globalization, undercuts the nation state by producing subnational forms of identification or ultra-nationalism, which undermine the ability of the nation state to maintain its legitimacy over the collectivity.[4] In extreme examples such as in Yugoslavia, the emergence of ultranationalism had resulted in the collapse of the State.

The emergence of Mohajir identification was an example of the global-local nexus that had produced a context for militant identity politics. The Mohajir Qaumi Mahaz's (Altaf) or MQM(A) leadership, particularly Altaf Hussain, who had been in exile in London since 1991, uses these global processes with great effect. Via contemporary communications systems, he has articulated a multimedia campaign from his London base, relentlessly urging his supporters to carry on the struggle, via the telephone, fax, internet, video and satellite television. By using modern media systems, he was able to command his party but escape the clutches of the law enforcement agencies.

Mohajir Identity Politics

The situation in Karachi was only one facet of the global-local nexus in Pakistan. The population of the city, as estimated by the fifth population census, was 9.269 million.[5] This census held in 1998 was originally scheduled for 1991 but was delayed due to instability in the country, a volatility that was increased by the census itself, as resource allocation both national and provincial was based on these figures. When finally conducted in 1998, it was only possible due to the direct involvement of the army in the exercise. Thus, the only reliable figures that give an idea of the ethnic mix of the city—other than estimates— are from the 1981 Census. They show that Mohajirs are the largest group in Karachi, and for that matter in urban Sindh, but the city is a multi-ethnic megacity, which no individual collectivity can claim as its own. The attempt to assert Mohajir dominance has led to rivalry, which has widened into a chasm, first with Sindhis, the original in-habitants of Karachi, and latter with Punjabis and Pakhtuns.

TABLE 2.1: ETHNIC COMPOSITION OF KARACHI: 1981 CENSUS (%)

	Total	Urban	Rural
Mohajir	61.0	64.1	5.1
Sindhi	7.1	3.8	67.8
Punjabi	15.8	16.3	5.1
Pakhtun	11.0	11.3	2.6
Baluch	5.3	4.4	24.4

Source: Charles H. Kennedy, 'The Politics of Ethnicity in Sindh', Asian Survey, vol. XXXI, no. 10, October 1991.

The story really begins with the invasion of Afghanistan by the Soviet Union and the millions of refugees that poured into parts of northern and western Pakistan. This resulted in the political reconfiguration of Pakistani politics and simultaneously in the weakening of the State's ability to enforce its authority. Playing a proxy role in the dying stages of the Cold War had a profound impact on the hegemonic discourse. The ethnic composition of the military-bureaucratic oligarchy shifted even further in favour of Punjabis, and increased the significance of Pakhtuns due to their presence in the military and to the presence of large numbers of Pakhtun refugees from Afghanistan. These developments, which were at the expense of Mohajirs, exacerbated age-old dissatisfaction and set the stage for the emergence of Mohajir identity politics. Mohajirs, from the earliest days of the establishment of Pakistan, have been the most enthusiastic supporters of Pakistani nationalism, and politically this was reflected in their support for the religious parties. Their enthusiasm for Pakistani nationalism was inextricably linked to their location in the State, dominating the administration, both provincial and national. As their hegemony was challenged by various administrations, their enthusiasm for Pakistani nationalism diminished and was replaced by Mohajir identification. There was, however, a need to differentiate between the MQM as a political entity and Mohajir identity politics. It was true that the MQM(A) played a crucial role in the emergence of the Mohajir movement, but analytically, there were two processes that were operating here. One was about construction of a community, which in Anderson's[6] terms was about imagination, and the other was the instrumental character of political organizations representing Mohajirs' interests, now reflected by two MQMs, one led by Altaf Hussain, and a breakaway faction led by Afaq Ahmed called Haqiqi MQM ('Real' MQM).

Mohajir identification represents a new ethnicity, as it does not fit the anthropological notion of ethnicity.[7] The two main factors that make Mohajir identification a form of new ethnicity was the multi-various origins of the different Urdu-speakers, and the second was the lack of a common language. In general terms, Urdu-speaking Mohajirs migrated mainly from Uttar Pradesh (UP), Bihar or Hyderabad (the Deccan), and the only commonality they had was the Urdu language and the courtly culture, which it was associated with. There were variations in their understanding of Urdu language and culture, and sectarian differences such as those of Sunnis and Shias, which in other circumstances would have become markers of differentiation. Mohajir identity politics subsumes Urdu-speakers as one component (the largest one), and includes Gujarati-speakers, which includes the trading communities that settled in Karachi after Partition. The shift away from Pakistani nationalism towards imagining Mohajir identity politics takes place through a process of relative deprivation and increasing competition for limited resources at both the national and local levels. In the 1950s, a number of factors assisted the absorption of Mohajirs, both Urdu- and Gujarati-speakers, into the Establishment, both administrative and industrial. Urdu-speakers found employment opportunities in the Karachi administration, the Sindh provincial administration, the national bureaucracy and the judiciary. Being mainly of professional backgrounds, the opportunities provided by the formation of a new State provided considerable opportunity for employment and promotion. In the 1960s, the Urdu-speaking Mohajirs represented only 3.5 per cent of the total population and occupied 21 per cent of jobs in the Pakistan Civil Service.[8] At this time, there was intense rivalry between Urdu-speakers along regional lines over the control of various institutions. Those having migrated from UP would favour their compatriots over other Urdu-speakers from the other parts of India. Despite their internal differences, they became the strongest advocates for a centralized state and were those who gained most from this development. With Ayub Khan's military rule, their position in the bureaucracy became even stronger and Urdu-speakers became even more influential. The domination by the military-bureaucratic oligarchy was concomitant with an ethnic domination by a Punjabi-Mohajir axis at the Centre.[9]

However, the Urdu-speaking Mohajirs' fortunes began to turn. The debacle in East Pakistan not only meant that Biharis were stranded there, but at a stroke the opportunities for Urdu-speakers were slashed as Bangladesh emerged as an independent State. Antagonism in Sindh against Urdu-speaking Mohajirs boiled over and fermented the rise of Sindhi nationalism. Their arrogance vis-à-vis Sindhis, the high-handed manner in which they took over urban Sindh, particularly how Karachi was separated from Sindh province, and how the Sindhi language was replaced by Urdu as the provincial language were all issues which came to the fore under Bhutto's Prime Ministership. The agitation by Sindhis led to Zulfikar Bhutto's recognition of the Sindhi language by the Provincial Government and imposition of a quota on the number of Urdu-speakers entering the Pakistan Civil Service. Any hope that Zia's regime would restore the Urdu-speakers' position was dashed. Not only did the quota remain, the increasing significance of Pakhtuns in the upper echelons of the military due to the intervention in Afghanistan meant that their increasing influence was at the expense of Urdu-speakers. Their influence in the Federal Government and administration of Sindh remained, but their influence was declining.[10]

The business communities also found considerable opportunities in the newly emerging industrial sector. The Government's industrial policy favoured the location of industry in West Pakistan (and primarily in Karachi) over East Pakistan, in spite of the fact that the latter was the main earner of foreign currency through jute exports. Federal development plans, based on the import substitution model, favoured industry over agriculture and concentrated industrial development in Karachi. Papaneck noted intense rivalry between different business communities over controlling different aspects of the industrial sector and these quite often pitted Gujarati-speakers against each other.[11] The concentration of development in Karachi resulted in rapid industrial and commercial growth that attracted migratory flows from upcountry to Karachi. These opportunities persisted even when the federal capital was moved from Karachi to Islamabad by Gen. Ayub Khan. As long as Karachi continued to grow and the hegemony of Mohajirs remained undisturbed, despite the fact that its infrastructure was never able to keep up with the increased demand imposed on it by the rapidly growing population, their loyalties remained within the bounds of nationalism. However, with the independence of Bangladesh and Zulfikar Bhutto's policy of nationalization, industrial growth stalled, particularly in Karachi, due to the collapse of business confidence. The Gujarati-speaking business communities had dominated the industrial landscape and were particularly alienated by the policy of nationalization. Their alienation was further exacerbated during Gen. Zia's rule as Pakhtun and Punjabi business houses became generally more influential, particularly in their respective provinces, and began to make inroads into Karachi. The Gujarati-speaking business communities were finding that industrial growth had slowed down and competition had increased, which further alienated them, facilitating the shift towards Mohajir identification.

It was in this context that Mohajir identity politics emerges. The religious parties disillusioned the younger generation of Mohajirs led by Altaf Hussain.[12] Altaf Hussain had initially been a member of the student wing of the Jamaat-i-Islami, and realizing that it was a Punjabi-dominated organization, he went on to form the MQM. The migratory flows to Karachi from upcountry which had increased significantly were now joined by Afghan refugees, and Punjabis and Pakhtuns had made major inroads not only in the business sectors but also in transport. The Mohajirs' relationship with Sindhis fell to a new low with resurgence in Sindhi nationalism. Sindhis became increasingly alienated from Mohajirs, whose settlement radically transformed the province turning them into strangers in their own lands. The quota system curtailed Mohajir expansion into the bureaucracy, and Karachi's infrastructure was strained to breaking point. This resulted in Urdu- and Gujarati-speakers suppressing their internal and inter-ethnic differences and reimagining themselves as Mohajirs. In the process, they reinvented their genealogy, so while there had been a Gujarati presence in Karachi for many hundreds of years (considered to be old Sindhis). In the process, Mohajirs distanced themselves from Pakistani nationalism. This was not to endorse the point of view articulated by the detractors of the MQM(A), who argue that they were anti-State. All it means was that while previously they championed Pakistani nationalism, today they articulate Mohajir identification within a Pakistani framework. Even though Altaf Hussain uses the Bangladesh metaphor in his rhetoric, implying that if Mohajirs were pushed too far they would go down the road of separatism, the main thrust of his political agenda was the reincorporation of Mohajirs by the Pakistani Establishment.

MQM AND THE POLITICS OF ALLIANCE

The MQM in 1988 suppressed its distaste for Sindhis and entered into an alliance with the PPP (Pakistan People's Party). This pact brought the MQM to power at the provincial level in return for supporting a PPP Government at the federal level. The accord broke down over the Federal Government's unwillingness to repatriate Biharis from Bangladesh and continuation of placement bureaux in recruiting candidates to the federal bureaucracy. The PPP Government used these bureaux to recruit candidates, all PPP and mainly Sindhis, into the Civil Service. When the PPP–MQM accord broke down in the autumn of 1989, it resulted in bitter ethnic conflict. A brutal power struggle ensued to control the city, and in this process ethnic cleansing took place, so linguistically homogeneous shanty towns were created. The military had a hand in the downfall of Benazir Bhutto's first administration by being instrumental in forging an alliance between the MQM(A) and the Pakistan Muslim League (Nawaz) or PML(N) leading to Nawaz Sharif becoming Prime Minister. The ethnic conflict, however, continued, and compounded by the general propensity for violence, eventually forced the military to act against the MQM(A). This decision was taken unilaterally while Nawaz Sharif was out of the country and the army moved into Karachi determined to cut the MQM(A) down to size in 1992. It should be noted that Altaf Hussain had already departed for London: he was tipped off that an army crackdown was impending, and was able to lead the party through this troubled period.

The decision to initiate military operations was taken due to the increasing concern in the Establishment that the MQM(A) was taking over the local state machinery and the federal authorities were in danger of losing control. The army deployed a dual strategy of giving support to the Haqiqi group, a breakaway faction of the MQM on one hand, and on the other arresting the leadership and militants and initiating a campaign to discredit the organization. The MQM's torture chambers were exposed to the glare of the media. This strategy failed because of the partiality of the military operation. Armed groups such as the Punjab-Pakhtun Ittehad (Punjab-Pakhtun Front), MQM (Haqiqi) and criminal gangs in rural Sindh were ignored while the MQM(A) was crushed.

Nawaz Sharif's departure and the election of Benazir Bhutto for her second term did not make any difference to the MQM(A). This dual strategy continued even though the army was withdrawn from direct involvement in maintaining law and order in the city. The policy pursued by the civilian government used various agencies including the police, the Rangers,[13] the intelligence agencies and various paramilitary organizations[14] that were sympathetic to the authorities, under the Interior Minister Gen. Naseerullah Babar's command. The

Rangers, police and various intelligence agencies worked in concert in the crackdown against the MQM(A) and it became clear that there was regular abuse of human rights. The Human Rights Commission of Pakistan called upon the government to investigate serious and numerous allegations of custodial torture, death and extrajudicial killings. The commission was also deeply disturbed by the practice of rounding up large numbers of people without any charges being registered against them. It was also horrified at the large number of mutilated bodies found dumped in the city 'stuffed in sacks'. There was an absence of any thorough inquiry into these incidents, and no attempt was made to investigate custodial killings or extrajudicial executions. Consequently, 'the law enforcing agencies failure to distinguish the innocent from the criminal had alienated the people from the administration'.[15] President Farooq Leghari's submission to the Supreme Court referred to the extrajudicial executions taking place in Karachi as an important reason that motivated him in dismissing Benazir Bhutto's administration.[16]

GLOBAL NETWORKS AND LOCAL INSTABILITY

The global arms and drug networks were additional factors which aggravated the political crisis in Karachi. The flow of arms into Karachi had widened the gap between the warring parties into a chasm. Zia-ul-Haq's military junta, with the support of the Western powers, in particular the USA, initiated a campaign against the Communist regime in Kabul. The funding, arming, training and provision of intelligence information was conducted through the Inter-Services Intelligence (ISI) in collaboration with Washington, Beijing, Cairo, Riyadh and London. The proclaiming of the struggle as a *jihad* not only resulted in the more conservative elements of Afghan groups such as Hekmatyar's receiving preferential military assistance, but it also led to Arab brigades participating in the struggle.[17] Arriving with them were Arab clerics who joined the Jamiyat-i-Ulama-e-Islam's network of *madrasas*. These *madrasas* were known to have influence over Pakhtun tribes and this network was expanded into the refugee camps with the assistance of Saudi funding. This network of *madrasas* became the nursery from where the Taliban was raised. Once the Taliban gained momentum in their campaign in Afghanistan, they became independent of the ISI. The impact on Pakistan was that its permeable borders could not isolate the contagion of religious sectarianism that Pakistan had nurtured in Afghanistan. There were several main areas that affected Pakistan particularly with the rise of the Taliban. The first was that the Taliban were acutely aware of the number of Afghan groups supported and then discarded by the Pakistan authorities, and they attempted to pre-empt this by developing contacts with Islamist groups based among the Pakhtun population in Peshawar, Charsadda, Swabi and Mardan as well as districts in northern and southern NWFP.[18] The other impact was that the strident anti-Shiaism of the Taliban found resonance with militant Sunni organizations such as the Sipah-e-Sahaba and Lashkar-e-Jhangvi. The Taliban-affiliated Harkat-ul Ansar provided sanctuaries in its camps in Afghanistan for these sectarian organizations when they came under pressure from the law enforcement agencies in Punjab. The link with the Harkat-ul Ansar made it difficult for the Pakistani authorities in dealing with religious sectarianism as it overlaps with key networks involved in the fighting in Kashmir. The Deobandi network in the Punjab recruits for the Harkat, but the side effect was that it whips up sectarian tensions in the province.[19]

For the purpose of this chapter, I will focus on two other side effects of this strategy which was pursued by the Pakistani authorities: drugs, and arms. Arms shipments mainly Chinese and Egyptian copies of the Kalashnikov and more exotic items such as Stinger missiles from the USA were transported by the National Logistics Cell, a front for the ISI, from Karachi to weapons dumps around Islamabad prior to distribution to Afghan guerrillas. There was substantial leakage of these weapons, and both the Afghan guerrillas and the ISI sold the weapons on the open market in Pakistan. Even sensitive equipment such as Stinger missiles, it had been claimed, were sold and ended up in Iranian hands. A plausible explanation given for the explosion of the Ojhri ammunition dump in 1988, which destroyed substantial stocks prior to the arrival of an audit team from Washington, was that it was done deliberately by the ISI to cover up unexplainable gaps in the inventory. With the ending of the war, vast quantities of weapons including light weaponry as well as anti-tank guns and artillery pieces were stockpiled and put up for sale in the Federally Administered Tribal Areas (FATA), particularly in those regions which were adjacent to territory controlled by the Mujahideen. The scale of the operation in areas such as Bajaur was described in the following manner. 'Nowhere else in the FATA have I seen such heavy weapons on display. In Darra Adamkhel the dealers cater to individuals and urban terrorists, but here they were taking care of the battlefield requirements of their clients.'[20] Weapons from these arms bazaars were supplying the Taliban, Kashmiri and Tajik groups, militants from Pakistan and also beyond. The consequence for Pakistan of these globalized arms trails was that it flooded Pakistan with weapons, prompting social scientists to coin the term 'Kalashnikov culture'. Today, it has been estimated that there are hundreds of thousands of weapons in Karachi alone.[21] These flows of weapons had a profound impact on the political configuration of Karachi. The armed wings of political parties, usually consisting of students and criminal elements, use their weaponry to stake territorial control of various localities. The fact that politicians patronize criminal gangs means that they carry out their nefarious activities with relative impunity. The chaos created then becomes the backdrop for other criminal elements such as drug and construction 'mafias' to operate with relative impunity.

The globalized flow of arms into Pakistan was concomitant with an outflow of drugs in the opposite direction. The flow of opium through Iran to the West had been disrupted by Khomeini's crackdown on drug trafficking, leading to its smuggling through Pakistan, a process reinforced by the Afghan Mujahideen's use of drugs to finance their military operations. This fact was known to Western intelligence agencies, but they ignored the problem during the campaign against the Russians. In the late 1980s, laboratories refining opium into heroin were set up in FATA by criminal elements from outside Pakistan, and heroin flowed into Pakistan using the same channels as the arms trade. It was also claimed in the Pakistani press that Gen. Habib-ur-Rahman, Governor of the North West Frontier Province during Zia's military rule, as well as other military commanders were profiting from the drug trade. Arms, drugs and the Pakistani establishment were brought together into a crucial nexus for conducting the intervention in Afghanistan. The impact of this policy on Pakistan was equally serious and from a position of where there was no registered heroin addict in Pakistan in 1980, the traditional drugs consumed were opium and cannabis, the figure reached 1.2 million by 1989, more than 2 million by 1991, mainly heroin users.[22] Inevitably, this had a profound impact on the social and political fabric of Pakistan. For our purposes, these drug networks were inextricably associated with the arms flows into Karachi. Criminal networks became extremely powerful and influential through this process and fed on the political and ethnic antagonism of the city. The original flashpoint between Mohajirs and Pakhtuns was over the issue of drugs being peddled in the city.

No serious attempt to curb the violence in Karachi and other parts of Pakistan was possible unless the flow of arms and drugs was regulated. With the withdrawal of the Russians from Afghanistan, the US Drug Enforcement Agency (DEA) became more concerned with the growing and refining of opium in Pakistan. Assisted by the United States Agency for International Development's opium poppy substitution programmes, the law enforcement agencies obliged the drug laboratories to relocate to Afghanistan. This developments merely concentrated production and refining of opium in Afghanistan, but had not slowed or interfered with the flows into Pakistan and on to the West. Similarly, the arms supplies originally intended for the Mujahideen leaked into the remoter areas of the NWFP and Baluchistan, where there was an old tradition in manufacturing and selling weapons, and from there shipped to the urban centres. Benazir's administration, during its crackdown on the MQM(A), attempted to intercept arms shipments to Karachi from these areas, but the Nawaz Sharif administration was reluctant to do so for several reasons. The law enforcement agencies had identified nine of the top gunrunners who were supplying weapons to various organizations for a number of years. Anonymous sources described them to the press as being 'very well connected and having links with various political, ethnic, and sectarian parties and groups. Besides, these gunrunners have many administration and police officials on their payroll',[23] and these connections have made it extremely difficult for the law enforcement agencies to apprehend them. The Sindh Governor, Lt. Gen. (retd.) Moinuddin Haider, and the Sindh Chief Minister, Liaquat Jatoi, were not only ready to arrest these individuals, but wanted the Federal Government to crack down on the arms bazaars upcountry. While the Prime Minister appeared to support such a plan, he was unwilling to agree until his coalition partners in the Awami National Party, who were in power in the NWFP, gave assent, and without their approval it would be difficult to launch this initiative.[24] There were several reasons why approval was not given. The individuals who were claimed to be the gunrunners were linked to powerful and influential people in NWFP and Baluchistan and there would be many political ramifications if they were arrested, which would have had an impact on Nawaz Sharif's coalition partners in the region. The other implication if the arms bazaars were shut down would be that it would effect the fighting capacity of the Taliban and the Kashmiri resistance movements, as these arm bazaars were their main suppliers.

TABLE 2.2: PARTY POSITIONS IN THE SINDH PROVINCIAL ASSEMBLY

Party	Seats
Pakistan Muslim League (N)	15
Pakistan People's Party	36
Haq Parast Group (MQM)	28
National People's Party	3
Pakistan People's Party (S–B)	2
Muslim Welfare Movement	2
National People's Party (Working Group)	1
United National Alliance	1
Independents	12

Source: Dawn, 6 February 1997.

THE MQM AND THE 1997 ELECTIONS

The President's dismissal of Benazir's administration in 1996 led to fresh elections being called for, and in February 1997 Nawaz Sharif's Muslim League won a clear majority of 134 seats out of 203 in the National Assembly and an overwhelming majority in the Punjab of 203 seats out of 228. The PML(N) then continued its policy of alliance with the ANP (Awami National Party) to secure its position in NWFP and entered into an alliance with the MQM(A).[25] In the 1993 elections, the MQM(A) had boycotted the National Assembly elections and the benefit had gone to the PPP and the PML(N). However, in the 1997 elections, which the MQM(A) contested, it won 12 seats in the National Assembly. In the 1993 provincial elections, the MQM(A) won 27 seats, and its tally in the 1997 elections increased to 28, with 21 seats from Karachi, 4 from Hyderabad, 1 each from Sukkur, Nawabshah and Mirpurpkhas.[26] The MQM(H) won no seats in the elections.

The results clearly showed that to form a ruling coalition, the MQM(A) had to be included. There was speculation in the press that the PPP was in touch with the MQM(A), but considering the policy of Benazir in 1995-6 of extrajudicial executions and harassment of MQM(A) workers, it beggared belief how such an alliance was conceivable. The only alternative was to form a coalition with the PML(N), which was also problematic as it was under Nawaz Sharif's administration that the first crackdown by the military against the MQM(A) took place. By March 1997, after intensive negotiations, the MQM(A) entered into an alliance with the PML(N) both at the centre and in Sindh province. The MQM–PML accord agreed that the Chief

Minister would be the PML(N) nominee but the Governor and Speaker of the House would be nominated by the MQM(A) and that the MQM(A) would receive one ministry in the federal cabinet; Chaudhry Nisar Ali was nominated the Petroleum Ministry, political prisoners would be released and charges dropped. Other points agreed to in the accord were that Biharis would be repatriated from Bangladesh; the quota for Mohajirs would be raised to 11.5 per cent; a judicial inquiry would be held into the PPP crackdown and Rs. 3,00,000 would be offered as compensation to each victim; a census would be held by December 1997 and terrorists identified by the MQM(A) would 'be finished and arrested terrorists disarmed and their patronage stopped'.[27] This accord led to the formation of the Sindh cabinet, which comprised 7 nominees from the MQM(A), 2 from the PML(N), 2 Independents and 1 from the NPP.[28]

The organization had faced a number of problems, which were making the transition from opposition to party in power difficult. Even during the crackdown ordered by Benazir, there was an internal struggle for power. Azim Tariq, Chairman of the MQM(A), who had reappeared after the army operation in 1992, was murdered on 1 May 1993 and this was generally believed to be an inside job. More recently, Ishtiaq Azhar, Convenor of the MQM(A), who had been running the organization ever since the first attempt by the military to clip the wings of the MQM(A), was sacked. He was a former Senator and front-line leader and he could have been asked to go quietly, but the organization, in an unprecedented action, accused him of corruption and sacked him. Irrespective of the details of this case, it had not gone down well with MQM(A) supporters.[29] There was clear evidence of tension appearing within the party between its political wing and the militants. During the crackdown, the political wing went underground, seeking protection from the armed wing. The result was that while the political leadership was hiding, the militant wing took over the party. 'The militant arm of the MQM(A) had about five to six thousand activists comprising of student leaders, belonging to APMSO, hitmen and notorious criminals.'[30] The MQM(A) leadership had no choice but to side with its armed wing, as it was the only one resisting the army and the Haqiqis. With the fall of Benazir's Government, the political leadership began to re-emerge and to reassert its control over the party. In July 1997, the MQM(A) held elaborate party elections for the reorganization of zonal committees, the first since 1992. Most of the powerful sector committees and units, however, were dominated by hardliners and most of the grass-roots supporters were with the militants. A screening mechanism was applied to allow moderates to succeed and to keep a tab on hardliners but there was considerable difficulty for the political leadership in reasserting its authority over the militant wing. In the case of the important Organizing committee, the moderates were able to establish their authority only after Altaf Hussain intervened personally.[31] Eventually, the political leadership reasserted control over the party by expelling a large number of activists. Some of the militants went on to form their own faction, such as the Goga Group, while others simply turned into hardened criminals involved in contract killings and land grabbing.[32]

In August, the organization changed its name to Muttahida Qaumi Mahaz (United National Movement). The acronym MQM, the tricolour flag (red, green and white), and student wing, the All-Pakistan Mohajir Students Organisation, all remained. When this proposal was first mooted in 1992, it did not win universal approval from the party ranks. In fact, Afaq Ahmed used this as a pretext to leave and form the breakaway Haqiqi faction.[33] The leadership claims that the MQM would continue to fight against the 'jagiradari, waderana and sardarana' system[34] but now would extend the struggle to include all other communities. Also, Altaf Hussain now claims that the MQM was a secular organization.[35] The MQM(A) was the third largest party in the country, and this may be seen as an attempt to expand its influence into other provinces. The Multan District of the Punjab, for example, had the largest concentration of Urdu-speakers outside of Sindh, but it failed to make any headway in these areas in the 1997 elections. The suddenness of the announcement suggests that the party was concerned that it needed to blunt criticism, mainly in the intelligence agencies, that it was an anti-state organization. By changing its explicitly ethnic nomenclature, it was going down the road already taken by other ethnic parties in Pakistan. An organization such as the ANP had a non-ethnic nomenclature, but was essentially a Pakhtun party. In this sense, it appears that the MQM(A) was trying to make itself, in appearance at least, more acceptable to the military.

The MQM(A) had found a number of difficulties in getting its partner, the PML(N), to implement all the clauses of their agreement. Political prisoners were released but charges against them remained, the foreign ministry made some tentative investigation on how they could repatriate the Biharis. However, Nawaz Sharif publicly came out against the quota system and there were now doubts whether the MQM was softening on this demand.[36] The law enforcement agencies, the Rangers, the police and the intelligence agencies have blocked, so far, demands that those who broke the law while harassing the party should be prosecuted. The MQM(A) claims that 500 of its activists were executed.[37] So far, no law enforcement personnel have been prosecuted, and instead the former Director General of the Rangers, Maj. Gen. Mohammad Akram, was awarded the Hilal-e-Shujaat for 'liberating [the city] from terrorism . . . and bringing peace to Karachi'. The demand for the removal of the Rangers from the city had been flatly rejected by the military who were the real decision makers in this matter and not the Prime Minister. On the MQM(A)'s insistence, an inquiry into the extrajudicial killings was convened, but it was a cover-up. The terms of reference of the commission were merely 'to inquire into and investigate the extra-judicial killings' and to make recommendations. Without the power to fix responsibility, as was the case in the Murtaza Bhutto tribunal, the finding of such a tribunal will simply gather dust. Also, its demand that the Haqiqi should be done away with fell on deaf ears. The MQM(A) was outraged that sections of Korangi, an industrial area of Karachi, were no-go areas for it activists, and that the Rangers and other law enforcement agencies protect the Haqiqis. However, the settling of scores between the MQM(A) and the MQM(H) led to gang wars, in which the blame was laid on the agencies, by both sides.[38]

There was a strong perception within the law enforcement agencies that the MQM(A) was an anti-state organization in cahoots with India's Research and Analysis Wing (RAW) agents and was a terrorist organization. Naseerullah Babar, former Interior Minister, claimed that they cracked the Indian's code, which demonstrated that the MQM was receiving training from Javed Langra in Lucknow.[39] Hence the agencies' concern of letting the MQM(A) into power. One of the main issues that prompted the military operation in 1992 was that the administration was being taken over by the MQM(A). This was one of the reasons why it was so keen to eliminate the Haqiqis so that it would have complete control over Karachi. It seems that the MQM(A) wanted to act as intermediaries between the people and the government, and that the state institutions should not act without its approval. This may simply mean accessing the MQM's provincial ministers to get something done. However, it can be more sinister in that the police have to seek permission from MQM(A) area organizers if they want to register cases against MQM activists, or in the case of property crimes, the area organizer assist in the recovery of stolen property in exchange for *chanda* (donation) for himself. It is not difficult for the area organizer to arrange to return the property, since most robberies and

kidnappings-for-ransom were done at the behest of the MQM(A).[40]
With the release of MQM(A) militants from jail, violence had spiralled
out of control in the city. In the first six months of 1996, there were
fewer than 400 murders in the city. The figure had remained the same
for the first six months of 1997 but with one crucial difference: in
1996, most of the deaths were of MQM(A) activists, and now they
were mainly Haqiqi members, informers, government officials, police
and members of the intelligence agencies. There have been some
spectacular contract killings such as the murder of Malik Shahid
Hamid, former Home Secretary and Managing Director of Karachi
Electric Supply Corporation, the two sons of Inspector Aslam Hyatt
and Hakim Saeed, former Governor of the province, which had
resulted in accusations by the law enforcement agencies that the
MQM(A) had a hit list of government officials. Besides this, there was
a series of bomb blasts and shootings that have become so characteristic
of the violence in Karachi. Altaf Hussain and the rest of the leadership cry wolf and claim that this was the work of the agencies,
specifically the Rangers and the ISI. But the law enforcement agencies
were convinced of MQM(A) involvement in the majority of the cases,
resulting in MQM(A) members of the provincial government being
excluded from meetings on law-and-order issues with the Prime
Minister wherein intelligence information was revealed.[41]

With violence escalating, the law-and-order issue went back to the
top of the agenda, and the MQM(A), since mid-1997, was anticipating
that there would again be a crackdown. It had been trying to make
direct contact with Gen. Karamat in order to dispel the negative
impressions of the MQM(A) held by the high command. The
leadership was fully aware that the first military operation was
conducted during Nawaz Sharif's premiership and the military simply
bypassed the civilian government. However, with Nawaz's triumph
over the Chief Justice, Sajjad Ali, the gagging of dissent in his party by
passing legislation that prevented cross-voting and finally dismissing
Chief of the Army Staff Gen. Karamat, his position had become
unassailable and his dependence on the MQM(A) was not so
important. Sharif's central objective of reviving the economy, which
was in tatters after the detonation of nuclear devices and subsequent
sanctions made it even more important that there was peace in
Karachi. Of Pakistan's revenues, 70 per cent originate from the city.[42]
Clearly, the spiralling violence deters investors and paralyses the city's
industrial, commercial and financial centres.

The real problem for the MQM was that it was in power but did not have the authority to deliver on any of its promises. Unable to translate any of its demands into public policy, the political leadership had few incentives to restrain militants. Under these conditions, the MQM was forced to reconsider its alliance with the PML(N). The alternative was to form an alliance with the hated PPP, which had been responsible for the deaths of so many party workers. Instead, they withdrew from the provincial government, but continued to support the PML(N) in the provincial assembly. The alliance between the MQM(A) and the PML(N) was in limbo until September 1998 when it appeared that Nawaz Sharif had persuaded the MQM to re-enter the Sindh provincial government. This process of reconciliation was brought to an abrupt halt by the cold-blooded murder of Hakim Saeed, a respected figure, ex-Governor of the province and a renowned practitioner of indigenous medicine. The response of Nawaz Sharif was to give an ultimatum to the MQM to hand over the men responsible. His incontrovertible proof of MQM involvement later turned out not to be so solid,[43] and the MQM responded by withdrawing its support for the PML(N) in the provincial legislature. Nawaz Sharif's response was to impose Governor's rule under the emergency provisions of the Constitution and re-arrest released MQM activists and try them in military courts. Human rights activists have criticized the implementation of Governor's rule, arguing that if the Government could not maintain a majority in the assembly without MQM support, it should have allowed other parties the opportunity to form a government.

The irony was that under authoritarian pressure from the federal authorities, it had pushed the MQM into the arms of its hated enemies, the PPP. Sharif's crude attempt to centralize power, in spite of his huge parliamentary majority, had brought together a diverse opposition on a single agenda: his removal from power. Antagonized by the concentration of power in the hands of the Lahori clique and the imposition of Governor's rule in Sindh have brought together the bitter rivals, the PPP, MQM and ANP into a 19-party political alliance. This brought recollections of the last days of Zulfikar Bhutto, whose government was brought down by mass agitation.[44] But Nawaz's downfall came when he attempted to extend his influence over the last institution in the land that remained independent: the army. Mindful that his dismissal earlier was due to the intervention of the military, he knew that if it was not neutralized the same fate could befall him again.

He pandered to Islamic populism to garner public support and legitimacy and wooed the Islamic faction within the army. Gen. Ziauddin, who was promoted to replace Gen. Musharraf, was head of the intelligence service. Working closely with the Taliban and other Islamic groups, he represented the Islamic faction in the army. Nawaz simply tried to buy the support of other Generals against their Commander-in-Chief. This last act brought Nawaz's regime down, as Gen. Musharraf carried out a coup, removing the elected government that tried to dismiss him.

In Karachi the violence was alienating Mohajirs themselves. There was increasing disillusionment with the confrontational approach that had been taken up by the MQM(A). Unpopularity with the organization was increasing as its supporters could not lead normal lives and go about their business. The continuous, random violence made leading a normal life or doing business or work near impossible. These cracks that were growing while they were in power had submerged with the latest crackdown. Differences were again being suppressed as Mohajirs presented a homogeneous and unified opposition to the central authorities and the gap between MQM and Mohajir identification had collapsed.

CONCLUSION

Mohajir identification emerges as a consequence of relative deprivation. There was a difference between this phenomenon and the MQM(A) in that the latter as a political organization simply reflects wider developments within the Mohajir movement. The MQM had found it difficult to make the transition from a militant organization in opposition to being the ruling party. This failure was partly due to the inability to deliver on any of its manifesto's pledges, which was due to the Central Government failing to honour its promises made to the MQM. The objective that the MQM(A) should be the only power in Karachi was anathema to the other legitimate political organizations as well as the institutions, both local and federal. The MQM had not accepted the fact that Karachi was a multi-ethnic, multicultural city in which it was only one of the players. It cannot make demands that exclude other ethnic groupings, in particular Sindhis, and it needs to forge a consensus over the future of the city, something it is only now trying to do with the latest crackdown.

What it had hoped was that Mohajirs could be reincorporated into the dominant hierarchy and regain their old favoured position.

However, this, at present, is unlikely as the military does not trust the MQM. The fear is that if the MQM(A) captures all sources of power in the locale then it would become extremely difficult to deal with it if it tries to follow a policy of separation. The MQM(A) had manifestly failed to win over the army, and this was primarily due to the fierce resistance it had put up against the military operations and the continuance of violence by its members. There was consternation also to be found among its Mohajir supporters who were equally unhappy that the violence continued. But the centralizing tendencies of Nawaz Sharif's Government meant that Mohajirs had again closed ranks.

If violence is the main concern of the federal administration then flows of arms need to be arrested, arms bazaars shut down (irrespective of the political impact in the NWFP), and drug flows curtailed. It needs to do this to rejuvenate the economy, which cannot function in an atmosphere of uncertainty created by violence. The State has to reassert control of its borders and prevent or minimize the global flows operating through Pakistan. The State, both local and federal, needs to operate justice in an even-handed manner. Its neutrality, which had been lacking of late, has to be reasserted if it is to win over the confidence of the citizens of Karachi. This would then allow for militants of all organizations to be disarmed and the police to clear the city of criminal gangs that have flourished. The State also has to address the substantive issues, which have been raised by the Mohajir movement, about jobs and opportunities. However, this also has to be done in an impartial manner so that other ethnic minorities don't suffer.

NOTES

1. Zaffar Abbas, 'Chasing the Elusive Dawn', *Herald*, November–December 1998, p. 41.
2. Stuart Hall, 'New Ethnicity', in James Donald and Ali Rattansi, eds., '*Race*', *Culture and Difference*, London: Sage Publications, 1992.
3. Ash Amin, ed., *Post-Fordism: A Reader*, Oxford: Blackwell Publishers, 1994.
4. Anthony D. King, ed., *Culture, Globalization and the World-System*, Basingstoke: Macmillan, 1991.
5. *Dawn*, 9 July 1988.
6. Benedict Anderson, *Imagined Communities: Reflections on the Origin and Spread of Nationalism*, London: Verso, 1983.
7. Stuart Hall, 'New Ethnicity', in James Donald and Ali Rattansi, eds., '*Race*', *Culture and Difference*, London: Sage Publications, 1992.
8. R. Braibanti, *Asian Bureaucratic Traditions: Emergent from the British Imperial Tradition*, Durham, 1996.

9. Yunas Samad,'Pakistan or Punjabistan: Crisis of National Identity', *International Journal of Punjab Studies*, vol. 4, no. 1, 1995.

10. Yunas Samad, 'Reflections on Partition: Pakistan Perspective', *International Journal of Punjab Studies*, vol. 4, no. 1, 1997.

11. Gustav F. Papanek, *Pakistan's Development: Social Goals and Private Incentives*, Cambridge, Mass., 1967.

12. Altaf Hussain, former pharmacy graduate from Karachi University and New York taxi driver, had initially been a member of the Islami Jamiat-i-Tulba, the student wing of the Jamaat-i-Islami. His experience led him to conclude that it was a Punjabi-dominated organization. He, along with Farooq Sattar and Azeem Tariq, formed the All-Pakistan Mohajir Student Organisation (APMSO), which was the first identity-based organization to emerge among Mohajirs. The MQM was officially formed in 1984 and Altaf Hussain was acclaimed as the spokesperson of the Mohajirs. The MQM's rise to power was facilitated by the patronage it received from Gen. Zia's regime, which was anxious to keep Mohajirs from participating in the pro-democracy campaigns led by the Pakistan People's Party. See Iftikhar Malik, 'Ethno-Nationalism in Pakistan: A Commentary on Muhajir Qaumi Mahaz (MQM) in Sindh', *South Asia*, vol. XVIII, no. 2, 1995.

13. The Rangers were directly under the control of the Federal Government and were trusted with sensitive tasks, unlike the police who were considered to be less reliable and were under the jurisdiction of the provincial government.

14. The Punjabi-Pakhtun Ittehad and the MQM(H) were examples of these phenomena: they received arms and support from intelligence agencies and were used as counterweights against the MQM(A).

15. Yunas Samad,'Pakistan or Punjabistan: Crisis of National Identity', *International Journal of Punjab Studies*, vol. 2, no. 1, 1995.

16. *Dawn*, 5 November 1996.

17. During the war, the CIA-Riyadh-ISI combine allowed a large network of Islamist cadres from countries as diverse as Algeria, Egypt and the Philippines to come to Afghanistan and participate in the armed struggle. These 'Afghanis' have come to haunt their former masters like Ramzi Yusaf, Aimal Kansi, Osama bin Laden and others. Osama bin Laden was declared by his former masters in Washington to be enemy number one for his suspected involvement in the bombing of the US embassies in Kenya and Tanzania. It was not difficult to target his bases with cruise missiles, as the US military had helped build them to resist Soviet attack. The 'Afghanis' use US Marines training manuals, translated into Arabic, to make booby traps, strip down weapons and commit acts of sabotage. These were supplied to them when they were anti-Soviet heroes of the 1980s and not terrorists of the 1990s. See John Sweeney, 'From the Bazaars to the Hillsides, They see a Long War Looming', *Observer*, 30 August 1998.

18. M. Illyas, 'Home to Roost?', *Herald*, July 1997.

19. Ejaz Haider, 'Pakistan's Afghan Policy and its Fallout', *Friday Times*, 20-6 November 1998.
20. Habibul Hasan Yaad, Khar-based member of the Human Rights Commission of Pakistan, cited in M.I. Khan, 'Explosive Truths', *Herald*, November 1997.
21. Salman Hussein, 'Government Plans Arms Recovery Operation in Karachi', *Friday Times*, 14-21 August 1997.
22. Peter Blood, ed., *Pakistan: A Country Study*, Washington: Federal Research Division, Library of Congress, 1995.
23. Salman Hussein, 'Agency Identifies Nine Top Gun-Runners in Karachi', *Friday Times*, 22-8 August 1997.
24. Ibid.
25. *Dawn*, 5 February 1997.
26. *Dawn*, 6 February 1997.
27. *Dawn*, 7 March 1997.
28. *Dawn*, 14 March 1997.
29. Idrees Bakhtiar, 'Fall from Grace', *Herald*, October 1997.
30. Muhammad Shan Gul, 'Mohajirs Say MQM has Tyrannised Karachi', *Friday Times*, 1-7 August 1997.
31. Ovais Subbani, 'Back to Square One?', *Newsline*, July 1997.
32. Ovais Subhani, 'Karachi's Phantom Killers', *Newsline*, November 1999, pp. 42-3.
33. When the MQM(A) changed its name to Muttahida Qaumi Mahaz, the Haqiqis changed theirs to Mohajir Qaumi Mahaz.
34. Large landholders, euphemistically called 'feudals'.
35. Idrees Bakhtiar, 'United they Stand', *Herald*, August 1997.
36. Rafaqat Ali, 'Quota Conundrum', *Herald*, February 1999, p. 48.
37. Mazhar Abbas, 'MQM Gears up for War with Agencies', *Friday Times*, 4-10 July 1997.
38. Idrees Bakhtiar, 'Death Squads', *Herald*, July 1997.
39. Intasham ul Haque, interview with Naseerullah Khan Babar, *Herald*, November-December 1998, pp. 44a–b.
40. Gul, op. cit.
41. Idrees Bakhtiar, 'Shock after Shock', *Herald*, August 1997.
42. *Newsline*, July 1998, p. 28. This reflects the narrowness of the Pakistani tax structure, and as Mahbub-ul Haq points out, if agricultural incomes were taxed then that would yield 40-60 billion rupees of revenue. Ali Faisal Zaidi, interview with Mahbub-ul Haq, *Herald*, September 1997.
43. 'Clueless in Karachi', *Herald*, November-December 1998, p. 31.
44. Zahid Hussain, 'Dead End?', *Newsline*, September 1999.

3

Islam, the State and the Rise of Sectarian Militancy in Pakistan

S.V.R. NASR

I N RECENT YEARS, Islamism in Pakistan has found a new face. Islamist parties and ideology that had for most of the country's history influenced its politics have given place to a new brand of militancy. This new trend is less concerned with ideology and those issues that preoccupied Islamism, and instead places emphasis on sectarian posturing and violence. The new face of Islamism is a manifestation of the resurgent militant conservatism that has emerged in the Afghanistan–Pakistan corridor, and is tied to the rise of the Taliban.[1] In Pakistan, it is embodied in sectarian militancy, whose advent has deeply impacted society and politics, and portends to have broad regional implications.

Sectarian violence in Pakistan has exploded over the course of the past two decades. The principal parties are: the Sunni Sipah-e-Sahaba Pakistan (Pakistan's 'Army of the Prophet's Companions' or SSP, established in 1984) and its allies, the Sunni Tahrik ('Sunni Movement', established in 1993), Tehrik Nifaz Shariat-i Muhammadi ('Movement for Protection of Muhammad's Religious Law', established in 1994), Lashkar-e-Jhangvi ('Jhangvi Army', established in 1990), Lashkar-e-Taiba ('The Army of the Pure', formed in 1997–8), and Tehrik-i Jafaria Pakistan ('Pakistan's Shia Movement' or TJP, formed in 1979) and its militant offshoot, Sipah-e-Muhammad ('Army of Muhammad' or SM, formed in 1991). They have been engaged in a violent campaign to safeguard the interests of their respective communities.[2] Assassinations, machine-gun attacks on mosques and explosions have claimed 581 lives and over 1,600 injured between 1990 and 1997 (100 between January and July 1997, and 70 in the first 10 days of August 1997).[3] One incident, a five-day 'war' involving mortars, rocket launchers, and anti-aircraft missiles in Pachinar, a small town in the North-West Frontier Province (NWFP) in 1996, alone claimed

hundreds of lives and many more injured.[4] The escalating violence cast
a sombre mood on the celebrations of the 50th anniversary of the
country's Independence, which took place hours after a heated debate
in the parliament over a new 'anti-terrorism' law that was introduced
to combat the problem. After a brief lull, the massacre of 25 Shia
mourners at Maninpura cemetery in Lahore in January 1998
reignited sectarian violence that left 78 people dead and some
80 wounded in Punjab, and an estimated 150 in all of Pakistan.[5]

The scope of sectarianism has extended beyond sporadic clashes
between Sunnis (75–85 per cent of Pakistanis) and Shias (15–25 per
cent of Pakistanis) over doctrinal issues, and has become a form of
politics of identity. Shia–Sunni conflict has a long history in South
Asia,[6] and on occasion has been a feature of Pakistan's politics. In
recent years, however, it has grown in scope, and more important,
changed in nature and direction.[7] It has metamorphosed from religious
schism into political conflict around mobilization of communal
identity.[8] It has found political function, and the militant forces that
represent it operate in the political rather than religious arena.

All this has eroded law and order in Pakistan, damaged civic
relations, and undermined the national ethos and the very sense of
community in many urban and rural areas. The violence has also
complicated democratic consolidation, for, in the least, it forced the
civilian government to look to the military and extrajudicial procedures
to restore order, and paved the way for the coup of 1999.[9]

The greater prominence of sectarianism in Pakistan's politics can
be seen as a new phase in Islamist ideology and politics[10]—specially
among the Sunnis—one which is more militant and combines the
demand for an Islamic State with a drive to disenfranchise Shias.
Sectarianism must, however, be understood as a form of 'ethnic'
posturing, one that combines Islamist and ethnic discourses of power.
It is tied to Islamism in that its foundational identity is defined in
Islamic terms, and the ideological world-view of Islamism also controls
the politics of sectarianism, although sectarianism places greater
emphasis on Sunni or shia purity as opposed to establishment of a
universal Islamic orthodoxy. Still, the sectarian discourse of power
and its underlying paradigm of politics are 'ethnic'. Hence, whereas
sectarianism in Pakistan displays far more concern for religious
orthodoxy than confessionalism does in Lebanon, or Protestant and
Catholic politics do in Northern Ireland, the fundamental directives of
their politics are not all that different. The Islamist veneer should not

obfuscate the fact that, at its core, sectarianism is a form of religio-political nationalism, and as such, our examination of its root causes are directly related to discussions of identity mobilization and ethnic conflict.

THE ORIGINS OF THE CURRENT SECTARIAN CONFLICT

The recent rise in sectarian conflict in Pakistan has its roots in the intensification of regional conflict after the Iranian revolution of 1979 and the start of the Afghan war in 1980, and in Pakistan's failure to contain the impact of these developments on its domestic politics.[11]

The Iranian revolution had a profound impact on the balance of power between Shias and the State, and more to the point, Shias and Sunnis in Pakistan. The revolution set in motion, first, a power struggle between the Pakistani State and its Shia community, and later a broader competition for power between Shias and Sunnis. These struggles for domination coincided with competition for influence in Pakistan between Saudi Arabia and Iraq on the one hand, and revolutionary Iran on the other—an extension of the Persian Gulf conflicts into Pakistan. The confluence of these struggles for power mobilized and radicalized sectarian identities.

The Iranian revolution changed the character of sectarian politics in Pakistan. Its impact on Shias was, however, more direct, and that in turn influenced the politics of Sunni activism as well.[12] The ideological force of the revolution, combined with the fact that the first successful Islamic revolution had been carried out by Shias, emboldened the Shia community and politicized its identity. Soon after the success of the revolution in Teheran, zealous emissaries of the revolutionary regime actively organized Pakistan's Shias,[13] which led to the rise of the TJP and its various wings and offshoots. The Iranians were no doubt eager to export their revolution to Pakistan. The leadership of the revolution was also unhappy with Gen. Muhammad Zia-ul-Haq (d.1988), the military ruler of Pakistan, for having travelled to Iran in 1977-8 to shore up the Shah's regime. In addition, after the Soviet invasion of Afghanistan in 1980, Gen. Zia's Government would become closely allied with the United States, with which Iran was increasingly at loggerheads.

More important, the Zia regime was then in the midst of an ambitious Islamization project which sought to transform government institutions, legal codes and policy-making apparatuses in accordance with Islamic teachings. Pakistan's Islamization initiative was different from Iran's Islamic experiment in many regards. In fact, it was this competition between the Iranian and Pakistani models that lay at the heart of Iran's posturing to Pakistan,[14] and also provided Pakistan's Shias with a cause to rally around.

Gen. Zia's Islamization initiative, set in motion in 1979,[15] claimed to manifest a universal Islamic vision, but in reality was based on narrow Sunni interpretations of Islamic theology and law, and was, therefore, unacceptable to the Shias, who, buoyed with pride from the Iranian revolution, asserted the validity of their own religious interpretations. In addition, Shias viewed Zia's Islamization as a threat to their social position in Pakistan. In fact, Islamization produced a siege mentality among Shias that lies at the heart of their political posturing. Consequently, Shias refused to submit to Sunni prescriptions in matters of religious conduct.

The Shias made their opposition known when the Zia regime sought to implement Sunni laws of inheritance and *zakat* (the obligatory Islamic alms tax).[16] Throughout 1979–80, Shia leaders mobilized their followers in opposition to the Zakat Ordinance and other Sunni laws that the state intended to implement. These protests culminated in a two-day siege of Islamabad by Shia demonstrators from across Pakistan on 5 July 1980, which openly defied the martial law ban on public gatherings, and virtually shut down the government.[17] Faced with the strong Shia protest and significant pressure brought to bear on Pakistan by revolutionary Iran, the Zia regime capitulated, granting Shias exemption from all those aspects of the Islamization package that contravened Shia law.

The Shia victory was a defeat for the ruling regime. The military was unhappy with the Shia show of force, specially because it had defied martial law rules and had effectively challenged the military's authority with impunity, and had done so owing to Iranian pressure. For the military, therefore, Shia activism was a threat to the martial law regime. It was also a strategic problem in that it tied domestic political issues to regional concerns and relations with Iran. Pakistan, at this time, was concerned with revolutionary Iran's regional ambitions and desire to export its ideology, revolution, and control of its neighbours.

The formation of the TJP and its militant student wing, the Ithna Ash'ariaya Student Organization (Twelver Shi'a Student Movement or ISO) in 1979, their assertive politics and emulation of the Iranian model, and the emergence of charismatic 'Khomeini-like' leaders among the Shias—notably Allamah Arif Husaini (d.1988)—were also instrumental in convincing the ruling establishment of the threat that Shias posed to government authority.[18]

Zia's capitulation to Shia demands was seen by his Sunni Islamist allies as nothing short of constricting their envisioned Islamic State and diluting the impact of Islamization. Shia protests had, in effect, reduced Zia's Islamization to 'Sunnification', undermining the universal Islamic claims of the entire process. Sunni Islamists were not prepared to accept in their Islamic order separate but equal status for Sunnis and Shias. They asserted that *Sunnism was Islam,* and by implication, *Shiaism—by refusing to submit to Sunni law—was outside the pale of Islam.* As such, Shiaism could not enjoy a status equal to that of the 'orthodoxy', i.e. Sunnism. Shiaism could at best be accepted as a minority, which in a Sunni State must live according to the norms and laws of the State—which closely parallels the Bharatiya Janata Party's ('Indian Peoples Party' or BJP) arguments against exemptions from civil laws that are afforded to Muslims in India.

The organizational prowess of the TJP and ISO, however, made it difficult for Sunni Islamists to reign in the Shias, and integrate them into their promised Islamic order. Consequently, Shia assertiveness was construed as proof of that community's disloyalty to Pakistan and its Islamic ideology, and, more important, as threat to veritable Islamization. In the mind of Sunni Islamizers, Shiaism thus gradually became a problem for their desired 'Islamic State'. That Pakistanis who were looking for exemption from Islamic laws began to declare themselves Shias—turning Shiaism into a haven from State-led Islamization—led Zia and his Islamist allies to develop a concerted strategy for containing Shia mobilization and limiting both Pakistani Shias and Iran's influence in Pakistan. Zia also sought to placate Shias and Iran when necessary, mainly through symbolic measures, for instance, between 1985 and 1988 the Speaker of the National Assembly, Syed Fakhr Imam, was a Shia, and throughout the 1980s Shia Generals held prominent positions in the military, albeit none were placed in charge of sensitive operations.

Pakistan initially sought to resolve the problem through diplomacy.[19] For the better part of 1980-1, Foreign Minister Agha Shahi (himself a Shia), who favoured conciliation with Teheran, sought to dissuade Iran from meddling in Pakistan's domestic affairs, and to enlist its support in pacifying the Shias.[20] Iran was, however, implacable. Perturbed by the failure of the diplomatic initiative, Zia dismissed Agha Shahi and looked for other ways of contending with Shia assertiveness and Iran's aggressive attitude towards Pakistan. Successful social resistance to the State's policy initiative, combined with the intrusion of outside forces into the body politic, thus led State leaders to look to mobilizing sectarian identities as a means of contending with the resultant challenges.

The Central Government began to invest in strengthening various Sunni institutions. In particular, it poured money into existing Sunni *madrasas* (seminaries) and established new ones.[21] Curriculum reforms in the *madrasas* allowed their graduates to enter the modern sectors of the economy and join government service.[22] The government believed that expansion of the role of the *madrasas* in national education would entrench Sunni identity in the public arena, just as *madrasa* graduates would help establish the place of Sunni identity in various government institutions. Furthermore, the *madrasas* and their students were viewed as important to the government's efforts to contain Shia activism. The Zia regime thus helped entrench Sunni Islamism in Pakistan in order to contend with the political and geostrategic threat of Shia Islamism.

The *madrasas* gradually grew in number and spread across Pakistan. They became a notable socio-political institution with roots in local communities and ties to vested political interests. In the process, their religious vocation too underwent change, producing a new political force, a new political phenomenon, in Pakistan. *Madrasas* are often situated in mosque complexes, provide education to boys between the ages of 6 and 16, who generally come from underprivileged backgrounds. Government estimates place the number of registered *madrasas* around 4,000; others cite a higher number, 8,000.[23] The number of unregistered *madrasas* is estimated to be far higher, close to 25,000. Some of them are very big: in Karachi alone at least 29 *madrasas* have more than 2,000 students each.[24] In 1975, there were 1,00,000 seminary students in Pakistan; in 1998 the number stood between 5,40,000 and 5,70,000, with about 2,20,000 in Punjab alone.[25]

These *madrasas* receive their funding from larger religio-political parties or outside donors, and instruct their students in accordance with the sectarian beliefs and agenda of those donors. Their focus is less on training ulema and more on producing sectarian activists, less on spiritual matters and more on sectarian hatred. Many *madrasas* provide military training to their students, combining sectarian vigilance with a jihadist outlook.[26] Students that come out of these seminaries have few skills that would encourage them to follow traditional careers in scholarship and religious services, or would allow them to join the mainstream economy. Many join the ranks of extremist Islamist parties and sectarian organizations. Those who find employment in the traditional religious offices, such as preacher or imam, impart their sectarian and extremist biases on their religious roles.

The madrasas, in addition, produce large amounts of religious literature. These books, journals, magazines and pamphlets all propagate sectarian hatred and violence. That much of this literature is distributed free of cost[27] makes it more widely available and with broader impact. The cost of the propaganda, which runs into millions of rupees, is financed by outside donors, the larger national parties, criminal activity, and advertisements from sympathetic or scared local merchants.[28] For instance, in Jhang district of Punjab, local merchants have responded positively to the SSP's strike calls and demonstrations, which often originate in the bazaar.[29]

The state used madrasas to strengthen Sunnism, particularly in areas where the threat was perceived to be greatest. Much of this effort was undertaken by Pakistan's military, and its elite intelligence wing, the ISI. The military's involvement in sectarianism would grow over time as Sunni militancy would develop organizational ties to the Islamist resistance in the Afghan war, and sectarianism would become relevant to the military's domestic political agenda after the return of democracy to Pakistan in 1988. It is argued by many in Pakistan that the military and ISI use the instability which is caused by sectarian violence to pressure democratically elected governments.[30]

Throughout the 1980s, the military Governors of Punjab and NWFP helped the ISI organize militant Sunni groups in their respective provinces to contend with the 'Shia problem'.[31] Similarly, the State diverted much of its funding for madrasas towards Baluchistan and NWFP—provinces that border Iran. As one observer remarked: 'If you look at where the most [Sunni] madrasas were constructed you will realize that they form a wall blocking Iran off from Pakistan.'[32]

As part of the new strategy, in 1988 the Central Government permitted marauding bands of Sunni activists to raid the town of Gilgit—the centre of the Northern Areas of Pakistan which has not as yet become a province, but should it ever become one it will be the only majority Shia province of Pakistan—killing some 150 Shias, burning shops and houses in the process.[33] The government then proceeded to build an imposing Sunni mosque in the centre of the predominantly Shia city. Sunnification of the Northern Areas was also part of the strategy of using Sunni sectarianism in the Kashmir civil war. The arrival of the SSP in Gilgit paved the way for the active role of its offshoot, the Harkat-ul Ansar ('Movement of the Companions of the Prophet' or HUA, recently renamed as the Harkat-ul Mujahideen or HUM) in Kashmir.

The State's efforts to contain Shia resurgence were complemented with those of Saudi Arabia and Iraq. The two Arab States were also concerned about Shia activism in Pakistan and Iran's growing influence there.[34] In 1980, Iraq began a war with Iran that would last eight years, and Saudi Arabia was wary of Iran's ideological and military threat, and was leading a bitter campaign to contain Iran's revolution and limit its power in the Persian Gulf. Since then, Saudi Arabia has sought to harden Sunni identity in countries around Iran, a policy which extends into Central Asia. Pakistan was an important prize in the struggle for the control of the Persian Gulf, as well as for erecting a 'Sunni wall' around Iran. Saudi Arabia and Iraq, therefore, developed a vested interest in preserving the Sunni character of Pakistan's Islamization and bolstering its effort to contain Shia assertiveness. The two States began to finance *madrasas* and militant Sunni organizations, the primary beneficiary of which was the SSP.[35]

The onset of the Afghan war would further deepen Saudi Arabia's commitment to its Sunni clients in Pakistan. In fact, the funding that Saudi Arabia provided Afghan fighters also subsidized militant Sunni organizations in Pakistan, often through the intermediary of Pakistan's military and the ISI. Afghanistan's Taliban, SSP and HUA/HUM all hail from the same *madrasas* and receive training in the same military camps in NWFP and southern Afghanistan. These camps operate under the supervision of the Pakistan military. The war that spanned the decade between 1979 and 1989 not only flooded Pakistan with weapons, but also embedded militancy in the country's Islamism. It also spawned several militant Islamist groups with international connections. According to one estimate, over 25,000 volunteers from 30 countries were trained in Pakistan and fought in Afghanistan.[36]

In addition, the Taliban's austere militancy and its drive to consolidate power over Afghanistan provide the sectarian forces with a model to follow.[37] For instance, the Tahrik-i Tulaba (Students Movement), a recent creation, as is indicated by its name, follows the example of the Taliban. It operates in the Orakzai Agency in the

Federally Administrated Tribal Areas (FATA) of north-western Pakistan. In December 1998, in an act that is reminiscent of the Taliban's rule over Kabul, a shariah court established by the Tahrik ordered the execution of a group that it found guilty of criminal activity. The executions were carried out in public, and the houses of the executed were burned to the ground.[38]

Similarly, Ramzi Ahmed Yusuf, convicted for bombing the World Trade Center in New York, was affiliated with a Saudi-financed *madrasa* in Baluchistan that was active in the Afghan war, but had also been prominent in anti-Shia activities in Pakistan. Yusuf is alleged to have been responsible for a bomb blast that killed 24 people in the Shia holy shrine of Mashad in Iran in June 1994.[39] Osama bin Laden's network too has close relations with the SSP and HUA/HUM, many of whose fighters have been trained at bases also used by bin Laden, such as the Al Badr camp that was destroyed during the US missile attack against bin Laden.

The Saudi and Iraqi involvement in effect imported the Iran-Iraq war into Pakistan as the SSP and its allies on the one hand, and the TJP and its offshoots on the other, began to do the bidding of their foreign patrons. The flow of funds from the Persian Gulf radicalized the Sunni groups as they sought to outdo one another in their use of vitriol and violence in order to get a larger share of the funding. Since 1990, Sunni sectarian groups have assassinated Iranian diplomats and military personnel and torched Iranian cultural centres in Lahore and Multan. Attacks on Iranian targets have been launched in retaliation for sectarian attacks on Sunni targets. By openly implicating Iran in attacks on Sunni targets and retaliating against its representatives and properties in Pakistan, Sunni sectarian groups have sought to complicate relations between Teheran and Islamabad, and to portray Pakistani Shias as agents of a foreign power.[40] When in September 1997 five Iranian military personnel were assassinated in Rawalpindi, the Iranian and Pakistani Governments depicted the attack as a deliberate attempt at damaging relations between the two countries.[41] The killing of 25 Shias in Lahore in January 1998 escalated tensions between the two countries further as Iran openly warned Pakistan about the spread of sectarian conflict.[42]

The regional dimension of the sectarian conflict, therefore, helped increase the scope of the violence which quickly went out of the control of the government in Pakistan. Hence, the State's use of sectarianism in contending with the impact of the Iranian revolution produced a wider struggle for power between Iran, Iraq and Saudi Arabia.

THE IMPACT OF THE AFGHAN AND KASHMIR CONFLICTS

The Afghan war and the Kashmir conflict, meanwhile, helped aggravate the situation. There has been a direct link between these regional conflicts and the use of militant Islamist forces as proxy soldiers in guerrilla campaigns and rise in sectarian violence in Pakistan. This trend was first evident in the Afghan war. There, to begin with, Saudi Arabia's role boosted Sunni militancy in Pakistan—often in conjunction with elements in Pakistan's military—and limited Pakistan's willingness (or ability) to contain the Saudi exercise of power within its borders.[43] In addition, the Afghan scene itself was wrought with sectarian tensions as Shias and Persian-speaking pro-Iranian factions vied for power and position with the Saudi and American-backed Mujahideen groups based in Pakistan.[44] The rivalry between these groups and the competition for control of Afghanistan ineluctably spilled over into Pakistan. Pakistan's sectarian conflict, therefore, quickly became a regional affair. As a result, Pakistan's response to sectarianism became entangled with its own Afghan policy. For instance, in the 1994-6 period while the government began to reign in Sunni militancy within Pakistan—which was by then deemed to be out of control—it was promoting it in Afghanistan and Kashmir. Pakistan's Minister of Interior at the time, Gen. Naseerullah Babar, was strongly in favour of closing religious madrasas to deny TJP and SSP recruits, and launched Operation Save Punjab which led to the arrest of some 40 sectarian activists.[45] Yet, he was also instrumental in organizing militant Sunni madrasa students into Taliban and HUA/HUM units for Pakistan-backed operations in Afghanistan and Kashmir. Strong links have existed between the HUA/HUM and the SSP and the violent sectarian force, Lashkar-i-Jhangvi. In the end, madrasas—and hence the SSP—thrived during Gen. Babar's tenure of office. In fact, since the advent of the Taliban and the HUA/HUM, Sunni militancy has become more prominent. These links have become increasingly entrenched, creating organizational ties as well as ideological ones. According to a Pakistan Government report, 800 SSP and Lashkar-e-Jhangvi fighters were receiving training at the HUA/HUM's Khalid Bin Waleed military training camp in Afghanistan in 1998-9.[46] It was reported that the Lashkar activists who were responsible for the Maninpura massacre as well as an attempt on Nawaz Sharif's life were trained in HUA/HUM camps.[47] Increasingly, young activists are looking to the Taliban as a model. During a recent demonstration in Karachi, young activists taunted government leaders, proclaiming, 'Do not think of us as weak. We have ousted Soviet troops and infidels from Afghanistan, we can do the same in Pakistan.'[48]

The Afghan war was also important in that it flooded Pakistan with weapons of all kinds, and imprint militancy on its political culture, specially among Islamist groups. The 'Kalashnikov culture' turned sectarian conflicts bloodier, and transformed militant organizations into paramilitary ones. In recent years, the Kashmir conflict has played the same role. The HUA/HUM and Lashkar-e-Taiba forces which have grown in prominence in Kashmir have also bolstered Sunni sectarianism in Pakistan. For instance, members of the Lashkar who were involved in the Kargil operation, were also involved in assassinations of Shias in September and October 1999 in Punjab.

The Afghan war also produced criminal networks that profit from trade in contraband and drugs. The collapse of the State in Afghanistan led to an increase in production of heroin, which finds its way to international markets via the Pakistani port city of Karachi.[49] The heroin production spawned formidable political relations that included Mujahideen fighters, tribal leaders, Pakistani military commanders, and criminal gangs in Pakistan. The drug trade thus gave rise to criminal networks whose reach extends through the length of the country, from the borders of Afghanistan in the north to the port city of Karachi in the south.

The relation between criminal networks and militant activists first surfaced in Afghanistan itself. Over time, the drug trade developed ties with sectarian organizations, reproducing in Pakistan relationships between militant groups and drug traffickers that had already developed in Afghanistan. Many of the Afghan Mujahideen fighters who were involved in the narcotics traffic have also been involved in sectarian conflict. The Mujahideen thus, helped forge linkages between their Pakistani sectarian allies and their partners among drug traffickers. The drug trade, in addition, found sectarian violence a useful cover for its criminal operations.[50] Sectarian organizations have accepted the pact with the devil for the most part because it has been financially beneficial, and has provided them with expertise and resources in perpetuating violence. There are also cases where criminals have actually set up sectarian organizations as fronts for criminal activity.[51] According to one report, when some 500 gunmen belonging to the Haqiqi fraction of the Mohajir party, the MQM, were abandoned by an intelligence agency, they turned to sectarianism in search of work, and helped forge an alliance between the MQM (Haqiqi) ('True MQM') and the SSP.[52] As a result, criminal networks have become deeply immersed in the politics of sectarianism, and their financial, political, and criminal interests, in good measure, control the ebbs and flows of sectarianism. The result is an 'Islamization of criminal activity', and criminalization of segments of Islamism in Pakistan. The growing influence of the drug trade has, therefore, promoted sectarianism.

The authorities in Pakistan are hard-pressed to contend with organizations that operate in the name of Islam and claim to be defending its interests: police action against criminals here is seen as harassment of the true servants of the faith, and, as such, faces resistance from local communities. There is evidence that sectarian organizations draw on entrenched support in Pakistani society.[53] According to one senior police official, 'a large number of people . . . collect information about the target before they [sectarian militants] arrive in the area. . . . [Their] refuge at a [local] madrasa . . . is arranged in advance, and they are given weapons and logistical support from a place near the target area.'[54] The availability of this kind of network and local support makes it very difficult for the authorities to prevent violent attacks, and then to effectively contend with the perpetrators.

In addition, since sectarianism is an 'Islamic' issue, sectarian activists have had the tacit support of some of the larger national parties—from the Pakistan People's Party (PPP) to the Pakistan Muslim League (PML) to ulema parties—which have routinely used their influence to protect sectarian activists from prosecution in order to placate the pro-Islamist constituency. Sectarian activists are often freed from jail with small bribes, and have received preferential treatment at the hands of the authorities. At the district administration level, even deputy commissioners and superintendents of the police have been known to curry favour with sectarian militants. In most localities, any arrest of a sectarian activist 'would have to be cleared from the top'.[55] Criminal organizations have benefited from the protection that is provided to sectarian forces, and have, therefore, sought to use it as a cover. The participation of criminals in sectarian conflict has escalated the violence, for hardened criminals have been more willing to attack mosques and people at prayer, and have generally been more willing to kill.

The consequence for the State has been that its control over both sectarian and criminal forces has been weakened, its ability to contend with violence has been restricted, and in many places in the country, the combined forces of sectarian and criminal organizations have eliminated government authority altogether, replacing it with local political control rooted in criminal activity and sectarian politics.

THE SPREAD OF SECTARIAN FORCES

The SSP was formed in the Jhang district of Punjab, and since 1986, the urban centres in the region of Jhang city, Sialkot, Sargodha, Gujranwala, Chiniot, and specially Faisalabad have been centres for militant *madrasas*, and the scene of most of the sectarian violence.

Jhang politics has long been dominated by Shia landed families whose constituencies have included both Shias and Sunnis. Rural politics here has largely worked through the clientelist ties between the landlords and the peasants, and has not (until recently) reflected sectarian identities. Throughout the late-1970s and the 1980s—owing to population pressure and labour-remittances from the Persian Gulf— the urban centres of Punjab grew in size, and also quasi-urban areas developed on the edge of agricultural lands. Urbanization has meant changing patterns of authority, specially because these urban developments have been dominated by the Sunni middle classes and bourgeoisie—traders and merchants who are tied to the agricultural economy but are not part of the rural power structure. The Sunni middle classes in the burgeoning urban centres in the region from the 1970s on (specially with the greater prominence of the post-Partition migrants from India)[56] who do not have the same ties with the landed elite have looked for a say in local politics. Whereas nationally the SSP fought for an Islamist cause, in Jhang it was posing as the vanguard force for the frustrated urban Sunni middle classes, which could see in sectarianism a powerful tool with which to break the hold of the Shia landed elite over local politics. The growth in the size of urban centres in and around Jhang by the mid-1980s had made the claim to power of the urban Sunni middle classes stronger.

In Jhang city, the SSP was able to win national and provincial elections. The organization was not, however, able to perform well in other Jhang constituencies. This showed that its influence has not spread beyond the urban centres. In 1993, the SSP received 46.8 per cent of the valid votes in Jhang city (NA-68) constituency that it won, but tallied 6.3 per cent, 4.9 per cent, and 3 per cent in other Jhang contests. In fact, the SSP has since done better in other urban centres in Punjab, and notably southern Punjab (where Sunni middle classes compete for power with Shia landlords) and has been able to show its presence in Peshawar and Karachi more than in rural Jhang.

The SSP's growing power in southern Punjab also followed greater pressure on the organization by the authorities. The SSP's activities in the late 1980s and early 1990s eventually elicited a response from the government. The organization then moved a great deal of its activities to the Bahawalpur district in southern Punjab.[57] There, it became closely associated with the two *madrasas* of Jam'iat'ul-Ulama of Idgah in Bahawalpur city and the Daru'l-'Ulum Faqirwali in Fort Abbas. From these *madrasas*, it organized sectarian activities in the neighbouring districts of Vehari and Khaniwal, thus spreading sectarianism to southern Punjab.

THE SPLINTERING OF SECTARIAN FORCES

Over the years, the SSP has spawned numerous splinter groups. Some, such as the Lashkar-e-Jhangvi, operate as proper organizations, whereas others are in essence 'more personal mafias of influential feudals, led by local mullahs, than organizations in the real sense of the word'.[58]

The SSP's splintering was due to pressure by the police, whenever the authorities decided to limit the organization's activities or eliminate the influence of some of its leaders. Also important has been the toll that assassinations by Shia rivals have taken on the organization. Violence has fractured the SSP's internal unity and eliminated leaders at key junctures. Another contributing factor has been finances. The size of the financial endowment of the SSP's *madrasas* has been so great that after the assassination of its first two leaders (Haqnawaz Jhangvi and Israr-ul-Haq Qasimi) in 1989 and 1991 respectively, factional conflicts over the control of the purse and the *madrasas* ensued. The losing faction then split, forming a new sectarian organization with its own *madrasa(s)*, and the hope that it would replicate the SSP's financial success and political power. The Lashkar-e-Jhangvi was, for instance, formed in such a manner in 1990 by Riaz Basra, and soon exceeded the SSP in assassinations and use of violence. Although the divisions have been real, they have not necessarily produced completely separate organizations. The SSP has continued to maintain close ties with its splinter groups, some of which have collapsed back into it, while others remain only nominally independent.

The rise of the Lashkar-e-Jhangvi is instructive in that it elucidates the working of these factors. The Lashkar is named after the SSP's founder and first leader, Haqnawaz Jhangvi. It split from the SSP in 1995-6 in protest to a possible dialogue between the SSP and militant Shia organizations.[59] Its leader, Riaz Basra, had come into prominence for the assassination of the Iranian Cultural Attache in Lahore in 1990. Basra quickly distinguished the Lashkar as the most violent Sunni sectarian force in Pakistan. Its campaign of terror included massacre of Shia civilians in mosques and other places of worship. It had also targeted Sunni officials, including Prime Minister Nawaz Sharif in Lahore in January 1999. The Lashkar has also repeatedly targeted Iranian diplomats, personnel and interests in Pakistan, a policy that was also followed by the Taliban after their capture of Mazar-e-Sharif in 1988. The organization has openly admitted to its acts of terror, informing newspapers by telephone. Its Urdu newspaper, *Intiqam-i-Haq* ('Revenge of Truth') openly discusses the organization's actions and provides justification for them.

The scope of the Lashkar's violence soon made it the focus of government reaction. The targets chosen by the organization along with the nature of its violent attacks on civilians go beyond the scope of other sectarian acts. The government, however, has found it difficult to crack down on it. This is partly due to the ambiguous relationship between the SSP and the Lashkar. Although the Lashkar claims to be separate from the SSP, and the SSP has viewed some of the Lashkar's campaigns as politically damaging to itself, the two operate still in the same sectarian circles and appeal to the same constituency. There is even the suggestion that as the SSP has sought to become a national party, it has found the Lashkar a useful cover for continuing acts of violence. In addition, the Lashkar proclaims fidelity to the founder of the SSP, and there is little that distinguishes between the ideological positions of the two organizations.

The Lashkar's close ties with the Taliban and the HUA/HUM are also important in providing it with support networks that allow it great latitude in carrying out its campaigns of terror, and in eluding police action. For instance, it is reported that following the assassination attempt against Nawaz Sharif, Riaz Basra and other Lashkar leaders took refuge in HUA/HUM camps in Afghanistan.[60] In addition, the Lashkar's decentralized organization gave it great resilience in the face of outside pressure. The Lashkar was organized into small cells of five to eight militants, who operated independently of one another.[61] The activists are mostly between 16 and 20 and have received extensive military training. The breakdown or elimination of any one cell had no bearing on the operations of the others, nor could it lead to their elimination. In fact, other cells had ample time to regroup, set up replacement cells, and plan new operations. After the Maninpura massacre, when the authorities began to turn on the Lashkar, they found it difficult to proceed beyond apprehending members of the cell that was responsible.[62]

It was only after the Lashkar's attempt against Nawaz Sharif's life—which was an act of revenge against the government crackdown against sectarian forces in 1998 and the arrest of Basra's right-hand man, Mazhar-ul-Haq—that the government began a concerted campaign to destroy the organization. In the following months, several Lashkar activists were apprehended. Others, including four of the organization's most wanted assassins and explosives experts, were killed in Langharwal in April 1999 by Special Forces units after a five-hour gun battle.[63] Putatively, Riaz Basra too was killed in another shootout with the police in Sargodha in April. The organization's capabilities have, for now, been greatly reduced. The crackdown against the Lashkar since 1999 has, in effect, highlighted the limits to government tolerance of sectarian violence.

SECTARIANISM IN DOMESTIC POLITICS

While intensification of regional conflicts was instrumental in promoting sectarianism in Pakistan, the vicissitudes of Pakistani politics have decided the direction that this form of politics of identity has taken, and the role that it has come to play in the country. Sectarianism has become prevalent in circumstances of weakening of the political centre in Pakistan. Throughout the 1980s, the ethnic war in Sindh escalated, adversely affecting life in the country's most populous city and princi-pal commercial centre, Karachi.[64] The conflict in Sindh has, since the Zia period, posed a serious threat to the territorial integrity and political stability of Pakistan.[65] The conflict has proved particularly problematic for democratic consolidation. The weakness of ruling coalitions in Islamabad and Karachi has limited the ability of the governments led by Benazir Bhutto (1988-90 and 1993-6) and Mian Nawaz Sharif (1990-3 and 1997-9) to end the conflict, reform the economy, restore law and order, maintain the legitimacy of the government, and manage its delicate relations with the military.[66]

All this has occurred as the levers of power have become increasingly ineffective. A case in point is of the police force, which is the instrument of force most directly involved with containing sectarian violence. The police in Pakistan is ineffective: it is corrupt, weak, badly organized, lacking in resources, and is deeply penetrated by political and criminal interests. There is even evidence that the police force has been infiltrated by sectarian groups.[67] The ineffectiveness of the police became apparent in October 1996 when it failed to gain entry into the village of Thokar Niaz Beig in Punjab, where the militant Shia SM is headquartered and maintains a large cache of arms. In May 1997, the police was dealt yet another blow when the officer investigating the torching of Iranian cultural centres in Lahore and Multan in January 1997 was assassinated. For a time after the assassination, the police actually appeared to fear confrontation with sectarian groups, and officers have apologized to sectarian groups for their past 'misdeeds', i.e. arrest and prosecution of activists.[68] The message of the assassination was also not lost on judges who have proved unwilling to convict sectarian activists for fear of reprisals.[69] The impunity with which sectarian forces contend with police authority (and the warning that the assassination delivered to vigilant police officials and judges) made it clear that the law enforcement system is not up to the task. In addition, since the police is controlled by provincial authorities, it is difficult for the Centre to rely on it to contend with sectarian violence.[70] The problem is compounded further when larger national parties, powerful politicians or landlords protect sectarian groups and interfere with police action. In these cases, governments at the Centre and in the provinces are compelled to restrain the police in the interests of maintaining parliamentary coalitions.

As a result, when violence reaches a critical stage, the military has stepped in to restore order. In 1992 in Peshawar, in 1995 in Pachinar, in August 1997—when in the first 10 days of the month, days before celebrations marking the 50th anniversary of the country's Independence, 70 died in Punjab in incidents of sectarian violence—and in March 1998 in NWFP, the military intervened to end the violence. These were, however, limited operations during which the army merely imposed a ceasefire and ended the bloodshed. If the military were to participate in disarming militant organizations and rooting out sectarianism (which some elements in the military had helped organize) it would need a broader mandate and be allowed to assume a greater political role. The army's critics argue that it has used sectarianism to gain exactly such a mandate. That would not be in the interests of democracy. At any rate, there is indication that the military is not prepared for such an undertaking. In August 1997, the government resorted to a draconian anti-terrorism Bill as the fulcrum for containing sectarian violence. The Bill gives broad powers to the government and police in arresting and trying suspects without due process and in contravention to civil rights that are stipulated in the Constitution.

In many ways, in Pakistan today State power exists only in pockets and regions and is absent in others. The limits to State power in the rural areas can translate into unmanageable sectarian conflict and criminal activity. Some among State leaders now go so far as to view it as a strategic problem: sectarianism and its challenge to the State could also provide for circumstances wherein Pakistan's perennial nemesis, India, may interfere in the country's domestic affairs.

Sectarianism began in earnest during the Zia period, for it was after 1979 that mobilization of Shia identity galvanized the Shias into a distinct political group in Pakistan's politics. Until that time, Shias had, on occasion, placed demands before the State, and had asserted their political importance by lending critical support to Z.A. Bhutto and the PPP in the 1970s. After 1979, however, taking note of Shia importance in the political arena gave place to using as well as contending with sectarianism as a political force.

In 1983, the principal Shia party, the TJP, joined Benazir Bhutto's Movement for Restoration of Democracy. The Shias had been favourably disposed to the PPP ever since the 1970s. The Bhutto family is Shia,[71] and, moreover, the PPP's avowed secular orientation (manifested in the party's socialist rhetoric and the secularism of its leadership) had appealed to Shia voters. By joining Benazir's anti-Zia coalition, the TJP tied Shia sectarian posturing vis-à-vis the Sunni State to the issue of democratization. The identification of the military regime with Sunnism, and conversely, Shiaism with the pro-democracy movement in broad brush gave sectarian identities new significance. The military regime began to look more favourably on Sunni sectarianism to constrict the TJP. This policy further alienated Shias, and in the end had the reverse effect. In the elections of 1988 the TJP did poorly, but the PPP carried the Shia vote. The military regime and Sunni activists allied with it had hoped to weaken the PPP's ties to the Shia community by constricting the TJP. They succeeded, instead, in pushing wary Shias into the PPP's camp. The

Shias responded to rising Sunni militancy not by voting for the Shia party, but for the secular one.

The identification of Shias with the PPP in the 1988 elections only further entrenched the linkage between sectarianism and the politics of democratization. The opposition to the PPP, which was cobbled together by the ISI, and enjoyed the strong backing of the military, coalesced around the PML and formed the Islamic Democratic Alliance (IDA)—which took control of Punjab—following Zia's strategy. It turned a blind eye to Sunni sectarian activities in Punjab, and sought to balance the PPP's Shia base of support with a Sunni one of its own. Much like Gen. Zia, the IDA assumed that if the PPP became identified with the Shias, then in an environment of heightened sectarianism the far more numerous Sunni community would probably vote against the PPP.

This has not been tantamount to the emergence of a Sunni vote bank. For Sunni sectarianism does not sit well with many Pakistani Sunnis who hold the family of the Prophet, the *ahl al-bayt* ('people of the house', including those whom Shias view as infallible imams), in high esteem. Still, Sunni sectarianism serves as a wedge issue, one that underscores communal differences between Shias and Sunnis, and problematizes the relations between the two even for those who do not condone the violence.

The IDA's strategy placed those among the Shia landed elite of Punjab who were opposed to the PPP in a difficult position. These Shia landlords were not tied to the TJP, but were threatened by sectarianism, specially if their constituencies contained both Shias and Sunnis. Sectarian tensions in such areas of Punjab as Jhang and Kabirwala (where sectarian tensions were most pronounced) could undermine the position of the landed elite as it divided the voting blocs that supported their power base. To prevent this from happening, with few exceptions these Shia landed elites began to gravitate towards the IDA. They concluded that if they were to have an influence in the IDA, they may be able to control its policy towards sectarianism. Since 1988, there has been a competition for influence between the Shia landed elite and the SSP and its allies within the IDA and the PML (after the IDA dissolved in 1993).

In addition, the Shia landed elite concluded that whereas traditional religious and feudal ties could keep their Shia peasants in check, association with the IDA (and later the PML) was necessary for placating their Sunni constituents. By 1997, many important Shia landlords had joined the PML. As they became more powerful within the PML and were able to somewhat limit the party's support for Sunni sectarianism, their positions within their constituencies were strengthened. In this regard, Shia landlords created sectarian bridges, and protected Shia interests in the PML.

An important consideration here was that both the PPP Government at the centre, and the IDA (and later the PML) in Punjab, were weak, and neither enjoyed a solid parliamentary majority. Three national elections in Pakistan in 1988, 1990 and 1993 had failed to produce stable majorities with the result of perpetuating the juggling for power and numbers in the assemblies. In addition, each party was hoping to exploit the weakness of the other to topple its government. In such circumstances, every vote and every member of the parliament counted, and the ruling parties and their challengers went to great lengths to curry favour with members of national and provincial assemblies. Fringe parties and independents benefited most from these circumstances, as they were able to exert power and influence beyond that which their numbers warranted.

Sectarian parties and their allies exploited these circumstances to pursue their activities. Since 1988, representatives associated with sectarian parties, and from 1990 on, when the SSP ran candidates of its own and won seats to national and provincial assemblies, members of sectarian parties were able to exert significant influence. For instance, the PPP had to give the SSP a provincial ministerial position in the Punjab provincial cabinet between 1993 and 1996 in order to get the party's support and deny it to the PML. The ruling parties turned a blind eye to sectarian activities, and, in essence, gave them immunity from prosecution for criminal and violent acts. For instance, owing to the SSP's pressure on the Punjab Government, in 1994 the authorities dragged their feet in charging the SSP leaders Azam Tariq and Zia-ul-Rahman with a crime after they were arrested during a crackdown on sectarian violence, although there were already over 30 cases of murder registered against them.[72] Similarly, the SSP's member of the Punjab Provincial Assembly and member of the Punjab Cabinet, Sheikh Hakim Ali, served in these positions between 1993 and 1996 despite eight cases of murder registered against him.[73] Azam Tariq and Zia-ul-Rahman were implicated in the murder of Shahnawaz Pirzada in November 1995. Pirzada was a prominent Shia leader of the Bahawalnagar district, and his son, Riaz Pirzada, served as a PPP member of parliament in 1993-6. Still, the PPP Government failed to charge the two SSP leaders. It was not before 1997 when the PML won comfortably in the general elections, and gained control at the Centre as well as in Punjab and NWFP—and was thus relieved of the considerations that had hitherto governed its position on sectarianism— that the government began to crackdown on sectarian forces in earnest, arresting 1,500 activists between February and May 1997, closing a Shia *madrasa* for sectarian activities in July, pushing through the parliament a new anti-terrorism law in August of that year, and rounding up more activists after the resumption of sectarian violence in 1998-9.[74]

THE PPP GOVERNMENT OF 1993-1996

In 1993 Benazir's party still enjoyed strong support among Shias. A large number of the country's Shias had voted for her, and the TJP was tacitly allied with her party. Confident of Shia support, Benazir began to explore the possibility of making inroads into the Sunni vote bank. Her main success in this regard was the 'Party of Ulama of Islam' (Jamiyat-i-Ulama-e-Islam or JUI). The JUI made a deal with the PPP as a result of which it was given access to important aspects of government policy making. The JUI has had close organizational and political ties with the SSP—in fact, the SSP candidates ran on JUI tickets in the 1993 elections. Its prominence in the government translated into protection for SSP activists.[75]

That Benazir was viewed as secular and lacked Islamic legitimacy, and her government was in dire need of such legitimacy, made her over-reliant on the JUI. Whereas initially Shias accepted Benazir's deal with the JUI in the hope that she would reign in the JUI and its sectarian allies, in practice the opposite happened. She was unable to control the JUI and its sectarian allies, and instead the JUI began using government resources to support sectarianism. This failure began to alienate the PPP's Shia supporters.

From 1994 onwards, it became increasingly evident that not only was the government incapable of reigning in the JUI and the SSP, but was actually fanning the flames of sectarianism. In that year in local elections in the Northern Areas—a predominantly Shia area—the TJP won six seats and the PPP came in second with five. The TJP proposed an alliance with the PPP that would be led by the TJP, and that the Vice-Chairmanship (the highest elected office) of the territories would be held by the TJP. The PPP refused, demanding that it lead the alliance and occupy the major administrative positions.[76]

The PPP eventually got its way, took over all the major offices, formed the ministry in the Northern Areas, and denied the TJP control in its stronghold. The PPP's victory, however, came at the cost of causing a breach between the TJP and the party. The TJP, and more generally, Shias, who were already perturbed by the PPP's alliance with the JUI, began to view Benazir as only nominally pro-Shia, but in reality unfavourably disposed towards their interests. The TJP was particularly disturbed by the tussle over control of the Northern Areas, because the victory there had been the party's only strong electoral showing and its first opportunity to exercise power. The TJP flatly refused to yield to the PPP's demand to be the representative of Shias, viewing such an outcome detrimental to its own interests. To make its point of view clear, the TJP held a large anti-PPP rally in Lahore which was the first open sign of unhappiness of the Shias with Benazir, and was, therefore, viewed with alarm by her government.

The government, however, preferred divide-and-rule strategies to addressing Shia concerns and accommodating the TJP. Benazir, therefore, turned to the more militant Sipah-e-Muhammad (SM), forming a tacit alliance with the most sectarian element among the Shias. Benazir's husband, Asif Zardari, who is a Shia, and PPP Governor of Punjab at the time, Altaf Husain, were instrumental in this regard.

Having lost the support of the TJP, and with Shia landlords gravitating toward the PML, the SM was the only Shia organization that the PPP could turn to in hope of maintaining its political position among Shias. Benazir was also hoping to use the SM to undermine the TJP's position within the Shia community. By 1995, the PPP Government found itself in the position of actively supporting the most militant sectarian forces on both sides: the SSP through the JUI, and the SM in order to weaken the TJP and maintain a foothold in Shia politics. Serving its immediate interests, Benazir's Government thus resorted to pulverizing civic order and promoting violence. It was for this reason that the TJP too began to move in the direction of the PML as well, and in March 1995 joined efforts by the National Reconciliation Council (Milli Yikjahati Council) to contain sectarian conflict, which for the TJP meant containing the SM as well as the SSP. The TJP even managed to bring one faction of the SM into the process.

The council was formed by the mainstream Sunni Islamist parties and Islamist elements in the PML in order to end sectarian conflict. It also enjoyed the support of the Shia landed elite and the TJP. The Islamist parties believed that the violence was damaging the cause of

Islam, and would eventually provide the government and the military with the excuse that they would need to crackdown on all Islamist parties. The council hoped to show that sectarian conflict did not enjoy the support of mainstream Islamist parties, and to dissociate Islamist politics from sectarianism. Since both the JUI and the TJP were on the council, it was hoped that they would cooperate in reigning in the SSP and the SM.

The council sought to defuse sectarian tensions by focusing attention on what all Islamist parties shared: the demand for an Islamic State. Benazir viewed such a consensus dangerous to her interests. If Islamist parties were able to cobble together a united front that would focus its energies on the demand for an Islamic State, they could pose a threat to her government and lay the grounds for a strong Islamic electoral alliance in the next elections.[77] Benazir concluded that it would be better for Islamist parties and their constituencies to be fighting each other, and spend their energies in sectarian conflict rather than challenge the existing political order. The PPP Government, therefore, actively worked to undermine the council. With the government's prodding, the JUI distanced itself from the council, and the SSP and SM resumed their violent attacks, effectively making the council defunct.[78] Murid Abbas Yazdani, the SM leader who had participated in the council, was among those who fell victim to the violence. He was denounced and later assassinated by the SM for the 'sin' of signing on compromises suggested by the council.[79]

This development was viewed with alarm in all circles, and especially among the Shias who began to view the PPP as detrimental to their interests. Benazir's brinkmanship between 1993 and 1996 alienated the Shia community, the TJP, and the Shia landed elite, all of whom went over to the PML. She was never in a position to control Sunni Islamist or sectarian parties, but in attempting to do so, she lost the one constituency that, since 1970, had been committed to the PPP. Benazir's strategy in turn provided the PML (which had been more closely associated with Sunni interests) with inroads into the Shia vote. Symbolic of the extent of Shia disgruntlement with the PPP was the defeat of Faisal Salih Hayat in the 1997 elections to the National Assembly. Hayat is a prominent Shia landlord in Jhang and a notable PPP leader. He had won his seat in the elections of 1988, 1990 and 1993, and his hold over his predominantly Shia peasants was once unchallenged. In the 1997 elections, Hayat's constituency abandoned him (along with the PPP) for the PML candidate.

THE PML GOVERNMENT: 1997-1999

Between 1997 and 1999, the PML enjoyed the support of both Sunni and Shia politicians and constituencies, and, as a result, developed a vested interest in ending sectarian conflict. The party thus moved away from the divisive sectarian policies that it inherited from the Zia regime. For the first time since then, the centre-right in Pakistan sees its political interests—a stable majority and marginalization of the PPP—as tied to sectarian peace rather than sectarian conflict.

In August 1997, the PML Government passed the Anti-Terrorism Act. The Act was designed to end all terrorism, which at the time was mostly sectarian in nature. It would give the police sweeping powers, would provide for speedy trials, and would resolve the problem of prosecution of militants owing to police and judicial inaction, fear, or political influence peddling. In 1998, the government began to crack down on the Lashkar-e-Jhangvi, and redoubled that effort after the organization's retaliation by placing a bomb on the path of Nawaz Sharif's car in early 1999. The PML Government also convinced Iran to help reign in Shia sectarian forces, pursuant to which Iran cut funding to the SM. In April 1999, as the government began its crackdown against the Laskhkar-e-Jhangvi, Nawaz Sharif met Shia and SSP leaders in Islamabad, as did his brother and Chief Minister of Punjab, Shahbaz Sharif, in Lahore.[80] The purpose of these meetings was to create a common ground for a negotiated truce between the two sides. After the meetings, Sharif announced the creation of a 'high-powered committee of ulema and religious scholars' to provide recommendations to the government for ending sectarian violence.[81] The committee put forward some recommendations, but its work was disrupted when Shia leaders withdrew from the committee accusing its head, Israr Ahmad (known for his anti-Shia tendencies) of bias in favour of Sunni militants.[82] Consequently, sectarian violence returned to Pakistan with the assassination of Shia leaders in September 1999, and assassination of 11 Lashkar-e-Taiba and HUM activists in Karachi in retaliation in early October 1999.[83] This precipitated the assassination of 45 Shias in the first 10 days of October 1999, a development which led the TJP to call on the army to intervene. It has become evident that the government's measures against sectarianism had only a short-term impact, for Pakistan has not contended with the sources of support for sectarianism in Afghanistan and Kashmir. In fact, the renewed violence followed the HUM's incursion into Kashmir through Kargil, which attested to the growing prominence of Sunni militancy, and its fecund ties with the Pakistan military.

CONCLUSION

The proliferation of militant sectarianism in Pakistan in recent years has produced an important fault line in the country's politics with broad ramifications for law and order, social cohesion, and, ultimately, government authority and democratic consolidation. The manner in which largely theological differences between Shias and Sunnis have been transformed into a full-fledged political conflict provides new insight into the root causes of identity mobilization in the context of State–Society relations and regional conflicts. It also sheds light on the manner in which the confluence of these factors have facilitated an interface between Islamism and ethnic politics in a State in which both discourses of power are prevalent. The result has been an explosive pattern of politics that combines ideological puritanism with communal exclusivism. As this pattern of politics has found ways to relate its demands to vested political, social and criminal interests, it has become both entrenched in the political process, and found new functions in society and politics. The powers-that-be have taken serious note of sectarianism only of late. Consequently, they have found it difficult to eradicate a religio-political force that has grown roots in society and a place in politics and now has a strong institutional base. The most important hurdle before the government, however, is its continued commitment to the Taliban and HUA/HUM, which will fuel militancy and the culture of sectarian violence in Pakistan. Elimination of any one organization or the work of any one committee will fall short of the intended goal, unless the foundations for sectarian militancy in Afghanistan and Kashmir are dealt with.

NOTES

* I would like to thank the John D. and Catherine T. MacArthur Foundation for a Research and Writing Grant that made this research work possible, and Mumtaz Ahmad, Christophe Jaffrelot, Gilles Kepel, and Muhammad Qasim Zaman for their suggestions and comments on earlier drafts of this chapter.

1. On this issue, see Olivier Roy, 'Changing Patterns Among Radical Islamic Movements', *The Brown Journal of World Affairs*, vol. 6, no. 1, Winter/Spring 1999, pp. 109-20.

2. The SSP was originally the Anjuman-i Sipah-i-Sahaba, Pakistan ('Organization of the Army of the Prophet's Companions'); and the TJP was initially the Tahrik Nifaz Fiqh-i Jafaria, Pakistan ('Pakistan Front for Protection of Shia Law').

3. Figures have been compiled based on reports in: the *Herald*, September 1996, p. 78, *The Economist*, 10 May 1997, p. 34; and the *International Herald Tribune*, 16-17 August 1997, p. 1.

4. *Newsline*, October 1996, pp. 71-2.

5. Figures are cited in *Human Rights Commission of Pakistan: State of Human Rights in 1998*, Lahore: HRCP, 1999.

6. For a discussion of this problem in India, see Theodore P. Wright, 'The Politics of Muslim Sectarian Conflict in India', *Journal of South Asian and Middle Eastern Studies*, vol. 3, 1980, pp. 67-73.

7. Samina Ahmad, 'Pakistan at Fifty: A Tenuous Democracy', *Current History*, vol. 96, no. 614, December 1997, p. 423.

8. Mobilization of identity in this article refers to 'the process by which . . . [a community defined in terms of identity] . . . becomes politicized on behalf of its collective interests and aspirations'; Milton J. Esman, *Ethnic Politics*, Ithaca, NY: Cornell University Press, 1994, p. 28.

9. In September 1997, the government gave law enforcement agencies six months to contend with violence before it would call on the military to do so: *Dawn*, 29 September 1997, p. 1. It has since that time employed special police units, the terrorism law, and special courts to clamp down on sectarianism.

10. On the history of Islamism in Pakistan, see Leonard Binder, *Religion and Politics in Pakistan*, Berkeley: University of California Press, 1961; Freeland Abbott, *Islam and Pakistan*, Ithaca: Cornell University Press, 1968; and S.V.R. Nasr, *The Vanguard of Islamic Revolution: The Jama'at-i Islami of Pakistan*, Berkeley: University of California Press, 1994.

11. Ahmed Rashid, 'Pakistan: Trouble Ahead, Trouble Behind', *Current History*, vol. 95, no. 600, April 1996, pp. 160-1.

12. On Sunni politics in Pakistan, see S.V.R. Nasr, 'The Rise of Sunni Militancy in Pakistan: The Changing Role of Islamism and the Ulama in Society and Politics', *Modern Asian Studies*, vol. 34, no. 1, January 2000, pp. 143-85, and Muhmmad Qasim Zaman, 'Sectarianism in Pakistan: The Radicalization of Shia and Sunni Identities', *Modern Asian Studies*, vol. 32, no. 3, 1998, pp. 687-716. On Shia politics in Pakistan, see Nikki Keddie, *The Shi'a of Pakistan: Reflections and Problems for Further Research*, Working Paper 23, Los Angeles: The G.E. von Grunebaum Center for Near Eastern Studies, University of California, Los Angeles, 1993; Saleem Qureshi, 'The Politics of the Shia Minority in Pakistan: Context and Developments', in D. Vajpeyi and Y. Malik, eds., *Religious and Ethnic Minority Politics in South Asia*, Delhi: Manohar, 1989, pp. 109-38; Afak Haydar, 'The Politicization of the Shias and the Development of the Tehrik-e-Nifaz-e-Fiqh-e-Jafaria in Pakistan', in Charles H. Kennedy,

ed., *Pakistan 1992*, Boulder: Westview Press, 1993, pp. 75-93; Maleeha Lodhi, 'Pakistan's Shia Movement: An Interview with Arif Hussaini', *Third World Quarterly*, 1988, pp. 806-17; and Munir D. Ahmad, 'The Shi'is of Pakistan', in Martin Kramer, ed., *Shi'ism: Resistance and Revolution*, Boulder: Westview Press, 1987, pp. 275-87.

13. Mushahid Hussain, 'Pakistan–Iran Relations in the Changing World Scenario: Challenges and Response', in Tariq Jan, ed., *Pakistan Foreign Policy Debate: The Years Ahead*, Islamabad: Institute of Policy Studies, 1993, pp. 211-22.

14. Olivier Roy, *The Failure of Political Islam*, Cambridge: Harvard University Press, 1994; Chibli Mallat, 'Religious Militancy in Contemporary Iraq: Muhammad Baqer as-Sadr and the Sunni-Shi'i Paradigm', *Third World Quarterly*, vol. 10, no. 2, April 1988, pp. 699-729.

15. On the Zia regime's Islamization policies, see S.V.R. Nasr, 'Islamic Opposition to the Islamic State: the Jama'at-i Islami 1977-1988', *International Journal of Middle East Studies*, vol. 25, no. 2, May 1993, pp. 261-83; Afzal Iqbal, *Islamisation in Pakistan*, Lahore: Vanguard Books, 1986; Shahid Javed Burki and Craig Baxter, *Pakistan Under the Military: Eleven Years of Zia ul-Haq*, Boulder, CO: Westview Press, 1991; Charles Kennedy, 'Islamization and Legal Reform in Pakistan, 1979-89', *Pacific Affairs*, vol. 63, no. 1, Spring 1990, pp. 62-77; Mumtaz Ahmad, 'Islam and the State: The Case of Pakistan', in Matthew Moen and L. Gustafson, eds., *Religious Challenge to the State*, Philadelphia: Temple University Press, 1992, pp. 239-67; and Anita Weiss, ed., *Islamic Reassertion in Pakistan: Application of Islamic Laws in a Modern State*, Syracuse: Syracuse University Press, 1986.

16. S. Jamal Malik, *Colonization of Islam: Dissolution of Traditional Institutions in Pakistan*, Delhi: Manohar, 1996, pp. 85-119.

17. Syed M. Zaidi, 'Shia Activism in Islam: An Overview', unpublished manuscript, p. 36.

18. Zaman, 'Sectarianism in Pakistan', pp. 687-716.

19. On relations between Iran and Pakistan at the time, see Musha-hid Hussain, 'Pakistan-Iran Relations in the Changing World Scenario: Challenges and Response', in Tariq Jan, ed., *Pakistan Foreign Policy Debate: The Years Ahead*, Islamabad: Institute of Policy Studies, 1993, pp. 211-22.

20. Interview with former Foreign Minister Agha Shahi.

21. S. Jamal Malik, 'Islamization in Pakistan 1977-1985: The Ulama and their Places of Learning', *Islamic Studies*, vol. 28, no. 1, Spring 1989, pp. 5-28.

22. S. Jamal Malik, 'Dynamics Among Traditional Religious Scholars and their Institutions in Contemporary South Asia', *Muslim World,* vol. 87, nos. 3-4, July-October 1997, pp. 216-17.

23. The figures are for 1997: *Herald*, December 1997, p. 64.

24. Ibid.

25. Figures are cited in *Jane's Intelligence Review*, vol. 11, no. 1, January 1999, p. 34; and *Human Rights Commission of Pakistan 1997*, Lahore: HRCP, 1998, p. 222.

26. *Human Rights Commission of Pakistan 1997*, p. 222.

27. *Herald*, June 1994, p. 31.
28. John Bray, 'Pakistan at 50: A State in Decline?' *International Affairs*, vol. 73, no. 2, 1997, pp. 329-30; Zaman, 'Sectarianism', no. 70; p. 710; *Herald*, June 1994, p. 30 and September 1998, p. 29.
29. Zaman, 'Sectarianism', pp. 706-7.
30. Samina Ahmed, 'Centralization, Authoritarianism, and the Mismanagement of Ethnic Relations in Pakistan', in Michael E. Brown and Sumit Ganguly, eds., *Government Policies and Ethnic Relations in Asia and the Pacific*, Cambridge: MIT Press, 1997, pp. 107-27.
31. *Herald*, August 1992, p. 67.
32. *Herald*, 1992, p. 34.
33. Tor H. Aase, 'The Theological Construction of Conflict: Gilgit, Northern Pakistan', in Leif Manger, ed., *Muslim Diversity: Local Islam in Global Contexts*, London: Curzon, 1999, p. 58-79; *Herald*, August 1992, p. 66.
34. Hussain, 'Pakistan-Iran Relations', pp. 217-18.
35. Rashid, 'Pakistan', p. 161. The Pakistani government has alleged that the SSP-receives funding from India as well as Iraq: *Herald*, June 1994, p. 35.
36. Rashid, 'Pakistan', p. 161.
37. On the Taliban, see William Maley, ed., *Fundamentalism Reborn? Afghanistan and the Taliban*, New York: New York University Press, 1998; Kamal Matinuddin, *The Taliban Phenomenon: Afghanistan 1994-1997*, Karachi: Oxford University Press, 1999; and Barnett Rubin, 'Afghanistan Under the Taliban', *Current History*, vol. 98, no. 625, February 1999, pp. 79-91.
38. *Herald*, February 1999, p. 60.
39. Mary Ann Weaver, 'Children of Jihad', *The New Yorker*, 12 June 1995, p. 46.
40. *Herald*, February 1998, p. 21.
41. *Dawn*, 20 September 1997.
42. *Dawn*, 16 January 1998.
43. On Pakistan's role in the Afghan war, see Marvin Weinbaum, *Pakistan and Afghanistan: Resistance and Reconstruction*, Boulder, CO: Westview Press, 1994.
44. Olivier Roy, *Islam and Resistance in Afghanistan*, New York: Cambridge University Press, 1990; and Barnett Rubin, *The Fragmentation of Afghanistan: State Formation and Collapse in the International System*, New Haven, CT: Yale University Press, 1995.
45. *Far Eastern Economic Review*, 9 March 1995, p. 24.
46. *News International*, 4 March 1999, pp. 1, 4.
47. Ibid.
48. *Herald*, December 1997, p. 64.
49. For more on this issue, see Ikramul Haq, 'Pak-Afghan Drug Trade in Historical Perspective', *Asian Survey*, vol. 36, no. 10, October 1996, pp. 945-63.
50. For the role of the Taliban in this regard, see Matinuddin, *The Taliban*, pp. 118-24.

51. *Herald*, June 1994, p. 29 and interviews with police officials in Karachi and Punjab.
52. *Human Rights Commission of Pakistan: State of Human Rights in 1997*, Lahore: HRCP, 1998, p. 87.
53. *Herald*, June 1997, p. 56; *Dawn*, 3 February 1999; and *Friday Times*, 21-7 November 1996, p. 7.
54. *Herald*, June 1997, p. 56.
55. Ibid.
56. Zaman, 'Sectarianism in Pakistan', p. 705.
57. *Friday Times*, 21-7 November 1996, p. 7.
58. *Herald*, June 1994, p. 29.
59. *Herald*, June 1997, p. 55.
60. *News International*, 4 March 1999, pp. 1, 4.
61. *Herald*, October 1997, p. 53 and September 1998, p. 18.
62. *Herald*, September 1998, p. 18.
63. *Herald*, May 1999, p. 49.
64. On this issue, see S.V.R. Nasr, 'The Negotiable State: Borders and Struggles of Power in Pakistan' forthcoming in Ian Lustick, Thomas Callaghy and Brendan O'Leary, eds., *Rightsizing the State: The Politics of Moving Borders*; Tahir Amin, *Ethno-National Movements in Pakistan: Domestic and International Factors*, Islamabad: Institute of Policy Studies, 1988; Astma Barlas, *Democracy, Nationalism, and Communalism: The Colonial Legacy in South Asia*, Boulder, CO: Westview Press, 1995; Theodore P. Wright, Jr., 'Center-Periphery Relations and Ethnic Conflict in Pakistan: Sindhis, Muhajirs, and Punjabis', *Comparative Politics*, vol. 23, no. 3, April 1991, pp. 299-312; and Moonis Ahmar, 'Ethnicity and State Power in Pakistan', *Asian Survey*, vol. 36, no. 10, October 1996, pp. 1031-48.
65. Samina Ahmed, 'Centralization, Authoritarianism and the Mismanagement of Ethnic Relations in Pakistan', in Michael E. Brown and Sumit Ganguly (eds.), *Government Politics and Ethnic Relations in Asia and the Pacific*, Cambridge: MIT Press, 1997, pp. 107-27.
66. *Nawa-i-Waqt*, 24 August 1997.
67. Interviews of former Minister of Interior, Gen. Naseerullah Babar.
68. *Herald*, June 1997, p. 53.
69. *Nawa-i-Waqt*, 27 August 1997 and 31 August 1997.
70. Ibid., 4 August 1997.
71. The Bhutto family has deliberately been vague regarding its sectarian affiliation. On occasion, Benazir Bhutto has hinted that she is a Sunni. However, the names of her father and grandfather—Zulfiqar Ali and Murtaza Ali—are distinctly Shia names, and Benazir's mother is an Iranian Shia. Regardless of the actual sectarian affiliation of the family, it is popularly believed that they are Shia.
72. *Friday Times*, 21-7 November 1996, p. 7.

73. *Herald*, September 1996, p. 78.
74. In that case, 200 students, 5 teachers and 13 other staff members were arrested: *Dawn*, 23 July 1997.
75. Rubin, 'Afghanistan Under the Taliban', p. 85; *Friday Times*, 14-20 August 1998, p. 1.
76. Interviews with TJP leaders.
77. Interviews with Qazi Husain Ahmad, S. Faisal Imam, and Mawlana Abdul-Sattar Niazi, who sat on the council.
78. *Herald*, October 1996, p. 53.
79. *Herald*, June 1997, pp. 54-5.
80. *Dawn*, 1 April 1999, p. 1.
81. *Dawn*, 4 April 1999, p. 1.
82. *Herald*, May 1999, pp. 48-9.
83. *Dawn*, 3 October 1999, p. 1.

4

The Regional Dimension of Sectarian Conflicts in Pakistan

MARIAM ABOU ZAHAB

UNNI-SHIA CONFLICTS were mostly unknown before Partition in the areas which now form Pakistan because of the influence of pirs and Sufis. After 1947 and despite the migration to Pakistan of Mohajirs belonging to areas with a strong tradition of sectarian conflicts,[1] relations between Sunnis and Shias remained normal except for occasional riots[2] or minor clashes during Muharram ceremonies. The State was neutral and had no sectarian agenda. In the late 1970s-early 1980s, Zia-ul-Haq attempted to implement the Sunni *Hanafi fiqh*; this became the starting point of Shia resistance. Zia used religion to acquire domestic legitimacy and counter Shia dissent, which implied economic and political patronage to Sunni extremists,[3] strengthening them vis-à-vis their Shia opponents, always viewed as 'troublesome'. The ground was fertile for proxy wars: the Iranian revolution, the Iran–Iraq war and the Afghan jihad were the enabling factors which gave scale and sustenance to the sectarian tensions so far latent and led to the internationalization of sectarian politics. Religious parties radicalized by foreign influences started receiving foreign funds which they used to launch campaigns in favour of their programmes. Mosques and *deeni madrasas* (religious schools) with sectarian affiliations were built everywhere, often on State lands, and a new kind of maulvi, the 'donor funded maulvi', appeared, moving around in a Pajero with armed bodyguards. Religious scholars started travelling to Saudi Arabia, Iraq and Kuwait and their influence with the local administration became tremendous. Successive governments ignored their activities because the donors were friendly Muslim countries.

The Iranian revolution inspired Pakistani Shias and contributed to their politicization, but it had a backlash: to counter this influence, Saudi Arabia, Iraq and Kuwait started patronizing Wahhabis and other non-Shias. Pakistan became a primary battlefield: it shares a border with Iran, has a sizeable Shia population (15-20 per cent) and Zia had made it the centre of US-sponsored Sunni Islamism. Sectarian divisions are now militarized in a way not previously seen. Sectarian violence as we experience it now[4] is the legacy of the Afghan war and the result of the rise of the Taliban which has exacerbated pre-existent rivalries and may seriously destabilize the country.

TRANSFORMATION OF THE SHIA COMMUNITY AFTER THE IRANIAN REVOLUTION

The Iranian revolution[5] brought about a complete change in the Shia community and in the shape of Shia leadership which was earlier in the hands of zakirs who had followers through their control of majlis. Shia organizations were apolitical and concerned with rituals and the organization of Muharram processions, which had become a competition for status. Their successful resistance to Zia's Islamization[6] and the Iranian revolution empowered Pakistani Shias: a new genera-tion 'saw a light coming from Iran'. After the revolution and during the Iran–Iraq war—which was seen in Pakistan as a war between Sunnis and Shias—Iran funnelled large sums of money to the Pakistani Shias and opened cultural centres in every major town. Members of the Imamia Students Organization (ISO),[7] most of whom belonged to the lower-middle class and came from a rural background, started studying Persian and got scholarships to study in Iran. They came back very impressed and saw Pakistan as 'the mirror of Iran'. They translated the works of Shariati, Muttahari and Beheshti into Urdu and gave a new interpretation to the paradigm of Karbala (kul yom Ashura, kul ardh Karbala [every day is Ashura, the whole earth is Karbala]). They wanted to rationalize religion and to be involved in politics in order to create justice and to empower the downtrodden (mustazafin). They introduced pan-Islamism in the Shia mosques.[8] The zakirs became irrelevant in the new atmosphere and a campaign was launched against them. At the same time, a new generation of clerics, belonging mostly to the Pakhtun tribal areas and the Northern Areas of Gilgit and Baltistan, studied in Najaf and in Qom[9] where they built up contacts with Shias from Middle Eastern countries and particularly Lebanese Shias. They came back to Pakistan in the early 1980s and opened madrasas with Iranian funding. These clerics soon took control of the community, they rationalized the rituals and utilized the old structure for political activism. The 'ISO-sponsored majlis', although very Iranian in style[10] and quite austere compared to the traditional Punjabi majlis, started attracting crowds and the speeches became more political. This created a rift between the 'old Shias' led by the traditional ulema educated in Najaf for whom involvement in politics was a sin, and the minority of 'new Shias' under the influence of these younger ulema educated in Qom who were soon accused by the conservative of being 'Wahhabi Shias' who wanted to destroy the religion.

Allama Arif Hussain al Hussaini, a Turi Pakhtun from Parachinar, who studied in Najaf and Qom was sent back to Pakistan after the Iranian revolution to organize the Shia community.[11] After the death of Mufti Jaafar in 1984, he became head of the Tehrik-e-Nifaz-e-Fiqh-e-Jaafria (TNFJ) created in Bhakkar in 1979. Shia leaders who felt threatened by Zia's policy of Sunni Islamization created this movement to assert their separate religious identity (Shia qaum), protect their rights and prevent the Sunni majority and the government from imposing an interpretation of the shariah contrary to *fiqh-e-jaafria*. This religious movement was radicalized after the Quetta incidents of 1985, and Allama Hussaini decided in July 1987 to transform it into a political party to fight 'American and Zionist imperialism' and to follow the path shown by Ayatollah Khomeini. The charter of the party ('Sabiluna'), inspired by Shariati's ideas, is very similar to the charter of Amal, the Lebanese movement.

The absence of *marja-e-taqlid* in Pakistan had traditionally meant close links with Najaf, which were now replaced with links with Iran where part of the money collected as *khoms* was sent. Shia leaders, who were boasting of their close contacts with Lebanese Shia clerics and political leaders, consistently denied receiving any funds from Iran despite evidence to the contrary. Iran stopped financing Pakistani Shias in 1996 because it was counterproductive and perhaps also because it feared a backlash of Sunni militancy fuelled by Pakistani Sunni extremists in Iranian Baluchistan.

THE SUNNI REACTION

Pakistan practised an open door religious policy to foreign countries and soon became a battlefield for a proxy war between Iran and Saudi Arabia. Iraq was also trying to mobilize Pakistani Sunnis in the context of its war with Iran, and it invested much to fuel anti-Shia feelings. Radical Sunni groups exploited every sign of Shia militancy to ask for more money. Funds came from the CIA and anti-Iran Arab States and from private donors for widening the gulf between Sunnis and Shias by promoting a narrow extremist interpretation of Sunni Islam.[12] Militant groups emerged, the Afghan jihad gave them easy access to arms and training and brought them into contact with Arab volunteers, some of them with Wahhabi persuasions. Madrasas—which were a recruiting ground for Sunni extremists and provided them material and moral support—were proliferating and became recipients of Arab money.

Shia radicalization caused a great deal of apprehension in Pakistan. After the creation of the TNFJ, two Ahl-e-Sunnat conferences were organized by the Jamiyat-i-Ulama-e-Pakistan (JUP) and Jamiat-e-Ulama-e-Islam (JUI) to counter the 'move by this tiny Shia minority to impose its will to Sawad-e-Azam' (i.e. the great Sunni majority).[13] The agencies sought out Haq Nawaz Jhangvi as a front to counter Shia militancy. This young Sunni extremist, who was naib amir (vice-chairman) of the JUI in the Punjab, created the Anjuman-e-Sipah-e-Sahaba (later Sipah-e-Sahaba Pakistan or SSP) in 1985 with a virulent anti-Shia programme. Haq Nawaz Jhangvi, who belonged to a poor Sunni family, launched a political campaign against the Shia feudals of Jhang. He wanted to defeat Syeda Abida Hussain in the elections and resorted to sectarian slogans. As his party gained popularity, he started receiving outside support to fight the Shias. The SSP remained associated with the JUI till 1989 when they split because of a completely different line of struggle.

AFTERMATH OF THE AFGHAN WAR

Sectarian conflicts acquired a new dimension from 1988, and particularly so when the jihad was 'brought home' after the Soviet withdrawal from Afghanistan. The assassination of Allama Hussaini in August 1988 (Iraq was most probably involved) was a turning point: it was the first of a long series of sectarian killings. Till 1995, killings were confined to leaders and activists of both sects; then symbols of State authority, main government functionaries, police officers and judges, were targeted. A change was seen in 1997 with indiscriminate gunfire on ordinary citizens who were not involved in sectarian activity and whose only fault was to be Sunni or Shia, and tit-for-tat killings targeting doctors, lawyers and traders.

The governments pretended for a long time that the sectarian organizations were a strictly local problem which could be dealt with at any time by arresting a few dozen extremists. The SSP and the TJP[14] both became mainstream parties: they entered into electoral alliances with the PPP or the PML; there was even an SSP minister in the Punjab Government (Sheikh Hakim Ali, Minister of Fisheries) of Sardar Arif Nakai in 1995 when the PPP needed the SSP's support to have a majority in the province. In return, the government freed the detained SSP leaders. Breakaway factions soon emerged either because some members disapproved of the 'moderation' of the party leaders, or just because they were expelled from their party. Some sources claim that the SSP and the TJP created the Lashkar-e-Jhangvi (LJ) and the Sipah-e-Muhammad (SMP) to have a militant wing independent of the political one. It would rather appear that the SMP was created for purely internal reasons, some Shia radicals thinking that the TJP politics of waging a political fight against the SSP had not brought anything to the Shias who were feeling more and more insecure and that an organization had to be created to safeguard the Shia sect.

Although it had a very weak organizational structure, the SMP soon acquired a political dimension of its own. The ambitions of Ghulam Raza Naqvi, founder of the SMP, were more global than just protecting the Shias: he wanted to form a Quds force comprising both Sunnis and Shias to liberate Jerusalem. The LJ always remained closely associated with the SSP (despite many statements of the SSP claiming that it had nothing to do with the LJ)[15] and was never political but purely terrorist. Almost the entire leadership of the LJ is made up of people who fought in Afghanistan. Riaz Basra,[16] who created the LJ in 1994 after he 'escaped' from a summary trial court, had been sentenced to death for the murder in 1990 of Sadiq Ganji, Director General of the Iranian Cultural Centre in Lahore.

The LJ rhetoric is much more anti-Iran than just anti-Shia: it keeps accusing the Pakistani Government of being under the influence of a foreign government (Iran), and has claimed responsibility for the assassination of Iranian diplomats and military cadets.[17] The fact that only Ithna Ashari Shias are killed while Ismailis and Bohras have so far been spared tends to prove that it is, in fact, Iran which is targeted. In January 1999, 17 Shias were killed in Karamdad Qureshi, a village situated some 60 km from Multan, which had never known Shia–Sunni conflict before. The timing of this attack is highly significant: Pakistan Foreign Secretary Shamshad Ahmad was in Teheran trying to mend fences with the Iranian authorities the very day it occurred.

Evidence of Arab private financing and of transfers of funds through American banks was disclosed after the arrest of several LJ activists responsible for the killing (in May 1997) of Ashraf Marth, a high-ranking police officer who had apprehended the killers of Agha Mohammad Ali Rahimi, Iran's cultural attaché in Multan. Ramzi Yusaf's alleged links with the SSP and the HUA are also documented as well as the links between the SSP and the Iranian Sunni Baluchis. The SMP, created in 1994 by Ghulam Raza Naqvi, was funded and armed by Iran whose aim was to protect the Shias. It may be argued that both the SMP and the LJ which are part of transnational networks are just tools for the perpetuation of a global war between Sunni fundamentalism and Shi'ism on Pakistani and Afghan soil.

Since the Soviet withdrawal from Afghanistan, about 10,000 Pakistanis have received military training in Afghanistan under the garb of the jihad in Kashmir or Afghanistan. Between 1990 and 1994, the camps in Afghanistan (Al Badr-1 and Al Badr-2 in Zawar, Paktia) and in the tribal areas of Pakistan were mostly training Jamaat-i-Islami and Lashkar-e-Taiba (LT or 'Army of the Pure')[18] members for the Kashmir jihad.

After the emergence of the Taliban, the camps which belonged to the Hizb-e-Islami and Jamaat-i-Islami were handed over to Harkat-ul-Ansar (HUA), a Deobandi anti-Shia movement fighting for the accession of Kashmir to Pakistan, which appeared in October 1993 in central Punjab after the merger of the Harkat-al-Jihad-al-Islami (formed in 1980) and the Harkat-al-Mujahideen, its splinter group which had separated in 1985. These two groups were getting CIA and Inter-Services Intelligence (ISI) backing to help the Afghan Mujahideen. The HUA is apparently supported, directly or indirectly, by rich businessmen from Saudi Arabia, Egypt and the Gulf and it collects donations from Pakistanis and Kashmiris settled in Britain. According to former members of Pakistan's Intelligence Services, the HUA is linked to Osama bin Laden and is provided 'training, expertise and funding' by the ISI.[19] The HUA's office in Peshawar was inaugurated in July 1997 by Maulana Mohammad Ajmal Qadri of the JUI in the presence of Maulana Sami-ul Haq, chief of his own faction of the JUI and head of the prestigious Dar-ul Uloom of Akora Khattak, often described as the centre of gravity of the Taliban. Although it claims to be a non-sectarian organization and insists on its affiliation with the Tablighi Jamaat,[20] the HUA is closely associated with the SSP/LJ. It was alleged in 1995 that activists of the SSP in Karachi had taken shelter with the HUA. One of the recruits was quoted as saying, 'Both [SSP and HUA] are working for the same goals, except Harakat-ul-Ansar does not believe in launching a militant movement against Shias and believes that the Hindus and Jews are their biggest enemies.'[21] The HUA provides training facilities and 'Islamic teaching' and also a safe haven to SSP and LJ activists.

Sanctuaries are provided to terrorists wanted in Pakistan, specially those who were involved in the attack on the Iranian cultural centre of Multan in March 1997 and escaped from Dera Ghazi Khan jail in December 1997 before perpetrating the Mominpura massacre[22] in Lahore in January 1998. Riaz Basra, absconding chief of the LJ, who carries a reward of Rs. 5 million, is believed to regularly take shelter in HUA camps in Afghanistan. After the US strikes, Maulana Fazlur Rehman Khalil, leader of the HUA, claimed during a press conference in Islamabad that 21 members of the group were killed in Khost.[23] A number of them belonged to south Punjab, namely Bahawalpur, Bahawalnagar and Leiah, cities which are strongholds of the SSP. Some sources claimed that the three LJ activists involved in the Raiwind bomb blast[24] were closely associated with the HUA and were trained at the HUA camps inside Afghanistan. According to intelligence reports, 'At Khalid bin Waleed camp in Afghanistan, 800 Pakistanis are under training, most of whom have linkages with SSP/LJ. The Mominpura massacre was also executed by [these] the HUA trained personnel.' It means that apart from its original objective of jihad in Kashmir, HUA is involved, though not directly but by providing an infrastructure, in sectarian activities and in *takfir*, i.e. purging the community of the Shias.[25] According to the same intelligence report, the 'HUA is expanding its agenda, which now besides jehad in Afghanistan and Kashmir, includes terrorist activities in Pakistan and abroad. HUA may attract more religious political parties within its fold and may attempt to initiate a Taliban like movement in Pakistan.' A large number of HUA militants attended the LT annual gathering in Muridke in November 1998. As early as 1995, an HUA militant was quoted as saying, 'Ours is a truly international network of genuine Muslims [and] holy warriors. We believe frontiers could never divide Muslims. They are one nation and they will remain a single entity.'[26]

The composition of the Mujahideen in Kashmir seems to have undergone a change since 1993 which witnessed an 'Afghanization' of the struggle. Experienced non-Kashmiri militants, mostly Punjabis but also Afghans and some Arabs, joined the insurgency in great numbers.

An Indian intelligence report released in August 1998 under the title 'Involvement of Foreign Muslim Mercenaries in Terrorism in Jammu & Kashmir' contains a list of 99 'foreign Muslim mercenaries' arrested by Indian forces with about 50 photographs and rather stereotyped profiles of some of them.[27] The report also gives a list of 520 militants killed, many of them just referred to as 'foreign national', and 500 other foreign militants 'identified' in Jammu & Kashmir—more than half of them are said to belong to the HUA. Apart from a few Arabs and British nationals of Kashmiri origin, most of the militants about whom details are given belong to Azad Kashmir or central and south Punjab, Pakistani Pakhtuns and Afghans[28] being rather surprisingly under-represented. The report also contains maps of training camps located in Afghanistan, Pakistan and 'Pakistan-occupied Kashmir'.

Maulana Fazlur Rehman, leader of the JUI, has been accused of trying to convert the Kashmir freedom movement into sectarianism.[29] It is undeniable that when Fazlur Rehman was chairman of the National Assembly Standing Committee on Foreign Affairs under the PPP Government, he was in a position to influence policy on Kashmir, and, under his influence, Afghan policy became more linked to militancy in Kashmir. Pan-Islamist movements, like the Lashkar-e-Taiba, have carried out killings of Hindus in the Jammu region in an effort to communalize the situation. According to Indian sources, over 130 Hindus were killed in Jammu & Kashmir between January and October 1998.[30] The HUA even tried to prevent the Amarnath *yatra*, a Hindu pilgrimage.

On 14 June 1999, Hafiz Mohammad Saeed, head of the LT, said during a meeting in Lahore that the Mujahideen were not working for the liberation of Kashmir alone: 'We'll also work for the independence of 200 million Indian Muslims. We'll take a revenge for the Babri Masjid.' He added that jihad would continue till the independence of Himachal Pradesh, Bihar, Hyderabad, Uttar Pradesh and Junagadh.[31]

Reuters press agency, quoting an interview with Abdullah Muntazir, information secretary of the LT, reported on 3 June 1999 that more than 200 Afghans from Nuristan[32] were helping Lashkar-e-Taiba militants in their 'struggle against India' in Kargil.

Azam Tariq, the jailed vice-chairman of the SSP, offered 'to provide 50,000 men if the government announces jehad in the held Kashmir'.[33] These militants believe that the example of Afghanistan can be replicate in Kashmir and that, after the nuclear tests which have made Pakistan's defence 'impregnable', the circumstances are right for liberating Kashmir from Indian occupation.

The Taliban, who have close links with Pakistani society, have 'one foot in Pakistan and one foot in Afghanistan'. They played an active role in September 1996 and in March 1998 in the clashes between the Sunni Orakzai and the Shia Bangash tribes in Parachinar and Hangu which claimed over 300 lives. Those tribes lived in relative peace and did not have heavy weaponry before the arrival of Sunni Afghan refugees. The Shias of Hangu have no complaint against the local Sunnis: they hold the Afghan refugees, many of whom have got Pakistani identity cards, and the Taliban administration responsible. Land disputes degenerated into sectarian clashes as Sunnis managed to get the support of Afghan refugees. In 1987 in the Kurram Agency, Mangal Sunni tribesmen occupied, with the help of Afghan refugees, lands claimed by Shia Turis. Orakzai Agency is run by mullahs exactly on the lines of the Taliban shariah in Afghanistan. The Sunni population has also become strongly anti-Shia; the ulema who were previously affiliated to the JUI and who have joined the SSP consider the Shias as non-Muslims.

The links between the SSP and the Taliban are well known. Since 1994, SSP activists have been trained in Afghanistan and thousands of them are fighting with the Taliban or administering the captured areas. They see the Taliban's victories as a victory of Sunni Islam, and preachers in Pakistani mosques say that once the Taliban control the whole of Afghanistan, they will transform Pakistan into a real Islamic State purged of the Shias and the Barelvis.[34]

After the capture of Mazar-e-Sharif by the Taliban in August 1998, hundreds of young Pakistanis went to Afghanistan to fight alongside the Taliban. Over 4,000 Pakistanis, most of them Punjabis, joined the Taliban after a meeting of representatives of 12 major *madrasas* which took place on 31 July 1998 in Akora Khattak.[35] Four hundred SSP members were apparently expelled from Kabul after the attack against UN personnel which caused the death of an Italian colonel in August 1998.[36] When relations between Pakistan and Iran were very strained after the killing of Iranian diplomats in Mazar-e-Sharif and the reported massacres of Afghan Shias, Maulana Azam Tariq, head of the SSP who was detained in Attock military jail at the time,[37] announced that his party was 'ready to send 20,000 militants to fight alongside the Taliban if Iran tried to impose a war on Afghanistan'.[38]

Dharb-e Momin, a weekly published from Karachi, Lahore and Rawalpindi by circles close to the Taliban, supports the HUA and LT. It also presents the Taliban as fighting for the survival of Pakistan. *Dharb-e Momin* regularly publishes reports about Pakistani Mujahideen, most of them Punjabis and often belonging to the HUA, having attained shahada (martyrdom) in Afghanistan or Kashmir.

Pakistani Sunni extremists are also active in Sinjiang and in Central Asia. The Chinese authorities regularly claim to have arrested suspected terrorists, who, according to them, have been trained in Pakistan. Pakistani missionaries were expelled in 1998 from Tajikistan and Kazakhstan because they were disseminating pro-Taliban and anti-Shia propaganda in the mosques. Uzbekistan has repeatedly accused religious groups in Pakistan of training young Uzbeks, Tajiks and Kyrgyz in camps situated near Peshawar. According to the Uzbek authorities, these militants are sent back through Afghanistan to carry out terrorist activities in Central Asia, their main motive being to establish Islamic governments in Central Asia.[39]

THE TALIBANIZATION OF PAKISTAN

The chicken are coming home to roost: Talibanism has started spreading across the border. The Afghan war has left an indelible imprint on Pakistan's cultural, economic and political life, specially in the tribal areas bordering Afghanistan and even in the adjacent settled districts. Sectarian hatred has reached unprecedented levels in NWFP: 21 Shias and 5 Sunnis were killed in Hangu in March 1998 and 7 people were killed in January 1999 in Orakzai Agency following a land dispute. In January 1999, the Tehrik-e-Taliban-e-Zargari launched a movement, on the Taliban model, in Hangu district for 'the removal of all prime sources of social evils' (i.e. television, dish antennae, music and unveiled women). The Tehrik-e-Nifaz-e-Shariat-e-Mohammadi (TNSM) led by Sufi Mohammad in Malakand Agency continues to challenge political institutions and to demand a shariah-based system: the government has yielded and a peculiar version of shariah laws has been implemented in December 1998 in Malakand and Kohistan Divisions. Baluchistan is also affected: a cinema was burnt down and video shops attacked in Quetta during the month of Ramadan in January 1999. The statements of the Prime Minister praising the Taliban system of swift justice can only give legitimacy to such movements.

The situation in Kashmir shows that some military circles in Pakistan thought that the method which was successful in Afghanistan could be used to compel the Indian Government to give up Kashmir under the pressure of militancy. There is obviously an Afghanization of the struggle: the tactics used by the militants against the Indian Army are those taught by the ISI in the 1980s for similar operations against Afghan Government facilities.

Political parties keep quiet on the sectarian issue and successive governments have routinely compromised with sectarian groups which feel immune because they fight in Kashmir. After announcing its intention of regulating the operations and funding of *deeni madrasas* in December 1998, the government had decided to 'go slow' because it was afraid of the reaction of religious parties and organizations.[40] More recently, the security agencies announced that 126 *deeni madrasas*, none of which were located in the NWFP, were involved in activities against national interests and were sending their students for training in Afghanistan.[41] The Federal Government announced once again its intention to clamp down on *madrasas* involved in fanning sectarianism and religious militancy. At the same time, as a warning to the government, the JUI organized a conference attended by more than 5,000 representatives of *deeni madrasas* and denied involvement in such activities.

Sectarian forces have the potential to shake the foundations of the state and the society. Most of the volunteers for jihad belong to social classes more and more alienated from the power structure. There is no dearth of unemployed young people who are looking for a solution to their economic problems and who think that an Islamic revolution is long overdue in Pakistan. While the society seems resigned to violence and has learnt to cope with it, the government reacts by adopting strict laws and creating more anti-terrorist and military courts. Such measures have no impact on militants who believe that they have a mission to complete and are ready to 'die in the path of Allah'. If the present government does not succeed in taking the country out of the economic, political and law-and-order crises, those frustrated young people might, out of despair, resort to violence in the name of religion to obtain social justice and their rightful share in national resources.

NOTES

1. Ambala, Rohtak, Karnal, Patiala, Hisar.
2. The only major anti-Shia riot took place in 1963 in Tahri, Khairpur district (Sind) during Muharram. Posters were published in 1970 which incited Sunnis to take over Pakistan with the slogan 'Jaag Sunni, jaag, Pakistan tera hai' ('Wake up Sunnis, Pakistan is yours').

3. Samina Ahmed, 'The (Un)holy Nexus?' *Newsline*, September 1998.

4. Between 1990 and April 1998, in the Punjab alone, 344 Shias and 212 Sunnis were killed in incidents of sectarian violence. The most violent year was 1997, with over 200 dead and 175 injured.

5. The analysis of the Shia community is based on personal observations and interviews with Shia intellectuals and office bearers of the ISO and TJP as well as dissidents of these movements conducted between August 1996 and September 1998.

6. Zia-ul-Haq introduced (in 1980) the deduction of *zakat* from all savings accounts. The Shias rebelled against this measure and were finally exempted after huge demonstrations in Islamabad in July 1980.

7. The ISO was founded in 1972 in the Engineering University of Lahore. In the beginning, it was just organizing rituals in the universities and taking care of the material problems of the students; cf. Taslim Raza Khan, *Safir-e-Inqilab* (biography of Dr Mohammad Ali Naqvi), Lahore: Al Arif Publications, February 1996.

8. Palestinian clerics made speeches in Shia mosques asking for moral support and the ISO started celebrating Yom al Quds. There was also a mobilization in favour of Bosnian Muslims. The 'new Shias' always emphasized the fact that neither Palestinians nor Bosnians were Shias, which, in their eyes, demonstrated their commitment to the cause of Islam rather than to Shi'ism.

9. Cf. Syed Hussain Arif Naqvi, *Tazkira-e-Ulama-e-Imamia Pakistan*, Islamabad, 1984; and *Tazkira-e-Ulama-e-Imamia Pakistan* (*Shumali Ilaqejat*), Islamabad, September 1994.

10. Zakirs started going to Iran for training in order to impress their audience. The Iranian influence was also visible in the adoption of a new style of dress: black cloaks and black turbans became commonplace.

11. According to his 'official' biography, he studied in Najaf from 1967 to 1973, then in Qom, and he was expelled from Iran in 1978.

12. Anti-Shia literature was promoted in Pakistan and the Iranian revolution was presented as a Zionist conspiracy to capture the holy places of Mecca and Medina. Allama Ahsan Elahi Zaheer, chief of the Jamiat Ulama-e-Ahl-e-Hadith, a Wahhabi movement closely associated with Saudi Arabia, wrote a book in 1980 entitled *Shias and Shi'ism*, which denounces Shia Islam as a heresy and accuses the Shias of being Zionist agents in Islamic countries. This book, translated into Arabic and English, was widely distributed by the Saudi Government.

13. Mumtaz Ahmad, 'Sectarianism and Zia', *News*, 15 April 1998. A Deobandi anti-Shia movement called Sawad-e-Azam was created in Karachi in the 1980s with the support of the intelligence agencies.

14. The TNFJ changed its name to Tehrik-e-Fiqh-e-Jaafria Pakistan (TJP) in 1993.

15. 'We parted ways because Lashkar-e-Jhangvi's way of pursuing its policies was different from the SSP's. The Lashkar does not like our moderate policies'.

Maulana Zia ul Haq Qasmi, Chairman of the Supreme Council of the SSP, *Nation*, 7 April 1999.

16. Riaz Basra contested elections to the provincial assembly in 1988 from Lahore on an SSP ticket.

17. Thirteen Iranians including two diplomats have been killed in Pakistan since 1988.

18. The Lashkar-e-Taiba (LT) is the militant arm of the Markaz-al-Dawat-wal-Irshad, a Salafi movement established in the early 1980s by the Palestinian Muslim Brother Abdullah Azam, Hafiz Muhammad Saeed and Dr. Zafar Iqbal and based since 1987 in Muridke, near Lahore. It aims at establishing the supremacy of Islam all over the world and is fighting a jihad against Hindus and Jews. It founded a camp in Kunar province in 1990 where both religious and military training were imparted. Along with the Punjab Governor and two Punjab ministers, Mushahid Hussain Sayed, Federal Information Minister, visited their headquarters in Muridke in April 1998 'to bring them out in the mainstream and make them an ally in our fight against sectarianism. . . . The idea was to neutralise the SSP and Lashkar-e-Jhangvi by getting them on our side.' He added: 'It is not a sectarian organisation and is not a source of domestic destabilisation.' *Friday Times*, 24-30 April 1998.

19. The ISI provides funds to radical terrorists, says a report: *Dawn*, 17 May 1999. This article refers to a report, parts of which were published by the *Sunday Telegraph*.

20. The Lizah camp near Khost was managed by Qari Saifullah (who succeeded Maulvi Irshad Ahmed killed in Afghanistan as Amir) who has been absconding since a plot for a military takeover was foiled in September 1995. The HUA was involved in the plot, and the existence of a faction of the Tablighi Jamaat advocating *jihad bil saif* was revealed at that time.

21. Mohammad Mirza, 'Afghan Jehad Reaches Karachi', *Friday Times*, 16-22 February 1995.

22. The LJ claimed responsibility for this massacre in which 25 Shias were killed and at least 50 injured in a graveyard in Lahore in January 1998.

23. According to the CIA, at least 7 members of the HUA and 8 members of the LT and Hizbul Mujahideen (linked to the Jamaat-i-Islami) were killed in the US attacks.

24. This targeted the Prime Minister on 3 January 1999.

25. Cf. Ejaz Haider, 'Price of Kashmir–Afghanistan Policies', *Friday Times*, 3-9 July 1998 and Ejaz Haider, 'Have Your Cake and Eat it too', *Friday Times*, 10-16 July 1998 for more details about an intelligence report on terrorist groups in Pakistan and their links with Afghanistan and Kashmir.

26. John Ward Anderson and Kamran Khan, 'Pakistan Shelters Islamic Radicals', *Washington Post*, 8 March 1995.

27. They are mostly described as semi-literate, drug peddlers or smugglers, belonging to very poor families and motivated by monetary considerations.

28. According to the report, eight Afghans from a village of Baghlan province,

arrested in October 1997, had left their homes and come to Muzaffarabad (Azad Kashmir) in search of better job prospects.

29. Al Faran organization, a brain-child of Fazl: *Observer*, 26 October 1995.
30. In January 1998, 23 Hindus were killed in Vandhama (Srinagar), 26 in Parankote (Udhampur) in April 1998 and 25 at Chapnari (Doda) in June 1998.
31. *Dawn*, 15 June 1999.
32. Hence probably Wahhabis.
33. *Frontier Post*, 7 June 1999. The SSP had already made exactly the same statement in February 1994.
34. Ejaz Haider, 'A Pyrrhic Victory?' *Friday Times*, 12–20 August 1998.
35. Frontier Post, 12 August 1998; *News*, 12 August 1998 and 14 August 1998.
36. *Le Monde*, 8 October 1998.
37. He was later transferred to Faisalabad jail.
38. *Pakistan Times*, 15 August 1998.
39. 'Pakistan's Islamists training Uzbeks?' *BBC News*, 17 February 1998.
40. 'Govt to "Go slow" on Regulating Religious Institutions', *Dawn*, 29 December 1998.
41. '126 Madaris Involved in Militant Activities', *News*, 17 May 1999.

PART II

At the Crossroad of Regional Tensions: How to Articulate a Nationalist-cum-Islamic Ideology?

5

From Official Islam to Islamism: The Rise of Dawat-ul-Irshad and Lashkar-e-Taiba

SAEED SHAFQAT

THIS STUDY VENTURES to highlight the relation between Islam and nationalism in Pakistan. These two notions may appear self-contradictory since Islam transcends the frontiers of nation states—including Pakistan. At the same time, the ideology of Pakistan has been built on the basis of the Muslim identity of the followers of Islam inhabiting the territories of British India. This paradox is even more evident from the discourse of the Islamist groups which are gaining momentum in Pakistan, especially in Punjab.

In the last decade or so, Lahore, Gujranwala (Murdike) and Multan have developed into a triangular circle of annual religious congregations and international conferences. Jhang is the other significant centre for similar congregations. According to credible newspaper reports and independent observers, the Tablighi Jamaat's annual congregation at Raiwind is considered the second largest congregation of Muslims after the Haj. It is attended by 2 million participants, while the Lashkar-e-Taiba's annual congregation is attended by 1 million participants. The Anjuman-e-Sipah-e-Sahaba and Lashkar-e-Jhangvi's congregation in Multan had an attendance of 5,00,000. Similarly, the Jamaat-i-Islami's annual congregation in Lahore is attended by 5,00,000 participants. In a country with a population of over 130 million, an annual turnover of 4 million people on religious congregations is not a large but significant number. It is interesting to note that the social class base of the Tablighi Jamaat's participants is most diverse. They come from all over the country, low- and middle-income groups are preponderant, but the rich and prosperous are also visible in the congregation. Punjabi, Pakhtun and Mohajir presence is conspicuous. The participants include traders, merchants, petty government officials, high-ranking public officials, professionals (engineers, doctors, educationists), businessmen and industrialists. By contrast, Dawat/

Lashkar-e-Taiba congregations are dominated by the lower-middle classes, peasants, traders, merchants, petty government employees and mostly young men from various parts of Punjab and some from NWFP. How should one interpret these congregations and the expansion of religio-political groups? These annual congregations perform several functions. First, they provide an opportunity of social networking and solidarity among the participants. Second, the leaders of these religious groups use it as a forum to send their political and religious messages across. Third, these annual congregations also serve as important indicators of the size and support base of each religious group and its organizational skills. Fourth, the Lashkar-e-Taiba uses these congregations to narrate success stories of the jihad (holy war) and for sharing experience of waging 'holy wars' in different parts of the world. They have a motivational purpose, because they explain the bravery, sacrifice and success of martyrs. Fifth, they promote the concept of the Muslim ummah, as a significant number of participants from other Muslim countries also attend these congregations. Last, these congregations are ranked as important international media events. This paper will first propose a definiton of the notion of religio-political groups, then it will examine the rise of such groups under Z.A. Bhutto and during the Afghan war and finally it will focus on the Dawat-ul-Irshad and Lashkar-e-Taiba. It will show that Pakistan's difficulties in establishing a national identity have remained the same while, since the 1970s, the country has experienced a shift from official islam to islamism.

Religio-political Groups—a Definitional Context

Religio-political groups are very much like any other interest group. In most cases their membership is open and encourages formal and informal association. They articulate the interests of those who are associated with them and aim to influence the public policy process and the government. However, a distinguishing characteristic of religio-political groups is that they are not restricted by the boundaries of interest or ethnicity alone, but also rely on cultural and ideological affinity among the members. Thus these are groups of *association, solidarity* and *belief.* The Pakistani case reveals that in their orientation, outlook and interpretation of religion and its role in society, they may have divergence and variation emanating from the philosophies of their respective schools of *fiqah*/sect. But their basic thrust is doctrinal.

Islam is presented as the panacea of all ills that confront Muslim societies in general and Pakistan in particular. Therefore, their broad goal is to establish the supremacy of the Koran and enforcement of the Shariah (Islamic law). Most Pakistani religio-political groups regard territoriality as manifested through the State, superficial and transient for a community of believers. At best, they see the State as an instrument to transform society according to their doctrine of Islam. They claim to promote fellow feeling and unity among believers, i.e. the ummah. Their primary target is society, and they aim at the transformation of society through imposition of Islam and the doctrinal world-view that they expound.

Religio-political groups are vehicles for social networking. They fulfil an important associational function. In them, besides practice and preaching of religion, individuals with shared interests and orientations band together. Like any other associational activity, membership within a religio-political group also produces awareness about one's identity. By function and association, they restrict the formation of a pluralistic society. One relates, interacts and reinforces one's identity not only within a group, but also in opposition to other groups.

Religio-political groups also influence the process of identity formation. Negating Islamic identity is equated with opposing Pakistan. Consequently, the liberal and progressive manifestations of Pakistani identity have remained underdeveloped and weak. Over the years, the religio-political groups have become not only militant in responding towards imagined or real enemies—the 'West' or 'India'— but have also become the champions of 'Pakistani ideology'. In this new sense, Islamic sentiment in Pakistan is instrumentalized by organizing the jihad and Mujahideen for Kashmir, Afghanistan and other 'Islamic causes'. A number of religious groups invoke the concept of jihad to show support and solidarity for the 'Kashmir freedom fighters'.

Religio-political groups and their existence is not a new phenomenon in Pakistan. They have been existing and playing a role in social and political life since 1947; what is certainly new is their political activism, in some cases militancy, and most important, their rapid expansion in the country. Currently, there are 58 registered religious political parties and 24 armed religious militias. Similarly, *deeni madrasas* (religious schools) have also been in existence for centuries, but what are new are their proliferation, sectarian overtones, expansion in support base, diverse and ambiguous sources of funding.

CAUSES OF RELIGIOUS ACTIVISM

What are the forces and factors that have triggered political activism among the religious groups? The immediate causes of religious political activism in contemporary Pakistan can be traced from three sources. First, the policies of the State towards religion and especially Zia's Islamization policy; second, extraneous factors, particularly the Iranian revolution (February 1979) and the Soviet intervention in Afghanistan (December 1979). Second, these events were turning points and had considerable influence in intensifying the demands and policies of Islamization in Pakistan, viz., enhancing the role of the State in giving direction to religious discourse in the country. Third, it was in the context of the Iranian revolution and Soviet intervention that in the West Islam began to be viewed largely through a 'security lens'. It was the American policy response to these events which fostered the perception that Pakistan was a 'frontline state'. It was in pursuance of this broad goal that America evolved a policy of 'dual containment', i.e. containing Iran and the Soviet Union. To attain this goal, it encouraged Pakistan to forge an alliance among various religious factions in Afghanistan. The result was the emergence of an 11-party coalition under the umbrella of the Hizb-e Islami, under the leadership of Gulbuddin Hekmatyar (Cooley). From its inception to degeneration (the Geneva peace process in 1987), this alliance worked in close association with religious organizations in Pakistan, particularly the Jamaat-i-Islami and the military regime of Zia-ul-Haq (Mushaid Hussain). In short, the collaboration between the US and Pakistan was instrumental in forging unity among various Afghan groups and religious groups in Pakistan. The American policy intellectuals promoted a favourable policy environment and gave legitimacy to these Afghan warriors by using the metaphor 'Mujahideen'—those who were fighting a holy war against the infidels. This metaphor had an effect not only on the popular consciousness of Afghans, but also gave a boost to the revival of Islamic sentiments among the religious groups in Pakistan. Thus, by the 1980s, Islam had come on centre stage as a powerful political as well as cultural and religious force, affecting the political thinking and feeling of virtually all elements of the population, not only in Pakistan, but in a large number of Muslim societies (Esposito).

These developments provided the military regime in Pakistan an opportunity to not only provide patronage to the religious groups, but also to develop an institutional linkage that lent legitimacy to their functioning.

Here, it may be useful to give a snapshot view of the interplay of religion and politics in Pakistan in the framework of the current Constitution (Shafqat). During the civilian government of Zulfikar Ali Bhutto (1971-7), religious groups developed into a potent opposition force. In his pronouncements and policy choices, Bhutto oscillated between socialist, developmentalist rhetoric and Islamic symbolism. These professions and policy outcomes produced contradictory trends: first, a compromise on the formulation of a Constitution. The 1973 Constitution declared Pakistan an Islamic Republic, with Islam as the religion of the State. Thus, foundations for enforcing the shariah and the potential of giving legitimacy to religious groups were laid. The size and representation of religious political parties in the parliament was insignificant, but given the nature of debate on ideology and dismemberment of Pakistan, they played a role larger than their size in the making of the Constitution. The 1973 Constitution has more Islamic clauses as compared to previous Constitutions. It carried references to the Islamic way of life, compulsory teaching of the Holy Koran, Islamiat, and encouraged learning of Arabic. It gave a commitment to promote the institution of zakat, organize mosques under the Auqaf department, and declared that no law repugnant to the Holy Koran and Sunna would be adopted.

Second, the social and cultural permissiveness of the Bhutto regime and a popular tilt towards 'folk Islam' rather than 'high Islam' prompted the religious groups to accelerate demands for Islamization (Gellner).

The third important element of the 1970s was the formation of JUI–NAP coalition governments in the NWFP and Baluchistan. Although the duration of these coalition governments was short (1972-3), the provincial governments were able to embark on symbolic policies of Islamization (e.g. respect for the Ramadan Ordinance). This encouraged other religious groups to demand greater Islamization of laws and policies. After its dismissal from the government, the JUI leadership played upon the idea that had their government been allowed to continue they would have introduced more Islamic laws. It is in this context that Jamaat-i-Islami continued to press for declaring the Ahmadiyas a minority, vociferously criticized the socialist policies of Bhutto, insisted on enforcement of the shariah, declared Bhutto a 'kafir' and demanded his ouster. Thus, during the Bhutto years, despite socialist rhetoric and social and cultural permissiveness, religious issues remained a potent political force.

Fourthly, Bhutto's holding of the Islamic Summit in 1974 brought Islam to centre stage, and gave a new life to religious groups and

Islamic political parties. The Bhutto regime's Islamic rhetoric, songs, symbols and calls for the ummah's unity created a euphoria for Islamic revival and unity of the ummah (the gathering of heads of Islamic States), captured the imagination of the people, and created an environment of expectancy for Islamic unity and possible Islamic social order. In his speech as Chairman of the Summit, Bhutto evoked images of Islamic glory, its great tradition, its principles of justice, equity, fairness in the comity of nations and a desire of unity among the Muslim States. He made a passionate appeal before the heads of Islamic States to work for evolving a regional block of Muslim States— a 'Muslim Commonwealth'.

In an age when no nation can sustain its insularity, at a time when communications and economic forces are serving to promote larger groupings of nations and countries, we owe no apology for the reassertion of the common affinities amongst the countries of the Muslim world. . . . It is time that we translate the sentiments of Islamic unity into concrete measures of cooperation and mutual benefit. (Bhutto 1980)

The speech, the gathering and its reportage by both the print and electronic media had a deep impact on popular consciousness. Last, in 1974, the religious groups succeeded in getting the Ahmadiyas declared as a minority. This declaration gave a new sense of confidence to religio-political groups. In subsequent years, they became more vociferous in demanding Islamization, while the PPP regime under Zulfikar Ali Bhutto slowly and gradually succumbed to these demands.

Despite these conciliatory gestures, Bhutto could not win the confidence of the religious groups, which perceived him as secular minded and not a practising Muslim. Therefore, between January and July 1977, the religious groups not only built an alliance against the Bhutto regime, but waged a one-point agenda of enforcing Nizam-e-Mustafa (i.e. enforcement of the shariah). As Bhutto announced holding of national elections in March 1977, the religio-political groups announced a coalition against his regime. They formed the Pakistan National Alliance (PNA). The coalition consisted of nine parties, but the Jamaat-i-Islami and Jamiat-ul-Ulama-e-Islam dominated it.

These elections were held in an atmosphere of distrust, hostility and political confrontation. The PPP emerged as the winner, but the opposition parties alleged that the elections were massively rigged. The government failed to prove its innocence of these charges, thus between March and July 1977, the PNA movement brought the demand of Islamization to the core of Pakistan politics. The movement paralysed the government—traders, merchants, the Tuleba of *deeni madrasas*, Jamaat-i-Islami workers and students, protested in the urban centres in Punjab and Karachi—the army intervened and dislodged the Bhutto Government (Richter).

Bhutto claimed that the PNA movement was not a 'desi' (indigenous) but 'an international conspiracy', implying that it had American support, because his government pursued an independent foreign policy. He had embarked Pakistan on a nuclear programme and worked for the unity of the Islamic ummah, therefore the US Government provided material and intellectual support to the movement. He alleged that the US, the army and the religious groups acted in concert to overthrow his government (Bhutto, 1979).

In subsequent years, the policies of the military regime under Zia, its close collaboration with the religious groups—particularly the Jamaat-i-Islami and the explicit US support to the military regime— were to give weight to Bhutto's argument. Additionally, as noted earlier, the Iranian revolution and Soviet intervention in Afghanistan changed the fortunes of the Zia regime and the religious groups, particularly the Jamaat-i-Islami, which showed eagerness in supporting the Afghan jihad under US patronage.

Zia's virulent de-Bhuttoization campaign in the post-1977 period weakened the liberal/socialist socio-political groups, which were in their infancy and had already suffered setbacks under Bhutto. To counter the perceived threat from the PPP, the Zia regime allowed exceptional scope to the religious groups, particularly to the Jamaat-i-Islami for a return to active politics in the universities, colleges, labour unions and other organizations (Nasr). This arrangement got a further boost with President Reagan assuming power in 1981, and the US policy towards the Soviet Union and using the Islamic groups to contain the Soviet Union became handy.

The US–Pakistan Recruitment and Training Connection

During the 1980s, the State expanded its patronage and coercive capacity through new techniques of manipulation. Involvement in the Afghan war made it imperative for the Zia regime to gain the support of Islamic groups. Therefore, through psychological warfare, the intelligence agencies manipulated public opinion to support the war effort (Muneer Ahmed). In the process, the State itself began to cultivate groups which could sustain Islamic fervour. Therefore, during the Zia years, demands for restoration of democracy and imposition of Islamic laws grew as parallel currents, growing simultaneously but not complementing each other.

A recent study provides graphic details of how the Central Intelligence Agency (CIA) of the US and the Inter-Services Intelligence Agency (ISI) in Pakistan developed a nexus with the religious groups to sustain a military and political war effort in Afghanistan (Cooley). This nexus was built around the concept of Islamic jihad against the 'infidel' Soviet forces. According to Ahmed Rashid, 'the effort of the two (CIA-ISI) was to turn Afghan jihad into a global war waged by all Muslim states against the Soviet Union' (Ahmed Rashid, 1999).

In fact, the Afghan war not only gave new life to the coercive capacity of the State, but also provided an incentive to expand its manipulative capacity. The ISI got deeply involved in the training and recruitment of Mujahideen: it had to devise strategies to motivate the Afghan groups to sustain the war. The collaborative arrangement between the US and Pakistan relied extensively on recruitment and training. According to Cooley, the US experts gave training to the ISI on a broad range of tangible and intangible areas, 'endurance, weapons, sabotage and killing techniques, communications and other skills'. It is estimated that the US experts (the Special Forces, Green Berets, etc.) provided over 60 skills, which in turn were imparted by the ISI to 'Afghan holy warriors'. The military regime under Zia performed this task ably, which further strengthened the coercive and manipulative capacity of the State.

The CIA–ISI collaboration in pursuit of the Afghan war had two consequences for religio-political groups. First, it led to factionalism and fragmentation of the religious parties, because religious groups began to jostle for procuring funds and training. This tension produced personality-centric factions among the religious groups. In 1980-8, the JUI got split into about 11 factions, while the JUP got divided into 5 factions (Fig. 5.1). Second, each of these factions began to centre around a religious leader, who aimed to create his own *madrasa*. Religious education and training for jihad became complementary.

The *madrasas* developed into sanctuaries of religious zealots and political power. The factional religious leaders began to encourage some form of military training, therefore, jihad was portrayed as a tool to achieve a higher goal for the glory of Islam. Thus, for motivation and mobilization, jihad was propounded as a legitimate concept to

	JUI			
SSP	JUI (Sami)	JUI (Fazl-ur Rehman	JUI (Darkha Wasti)	Lashkar-e-Jhangvi

	JUP			
(Sunni Tehrik (Maulana Saleem Qadri Karachi)	Dawat-i-Islami (Maulana Ilyas Qadri)	Punjab Sunni Tehrik	Minhajul Qurana (Tahir-ul Qadri)	Tehrik Tahag-i-Namoos-i-Risalat (Tahir-ul Qadri)

FIGURE 5.1: THE JUI AND JUP FACTIONS

wage war against infidels. Supporting the Afghan Mujahideen against Russia was portrayed as supporting Islam. Besides jihad, the other consequences of the Afghan war were proliferation of portable weapons, the drug trade and a scramble for donations for the madrasas. According to Ahmed Rashid, between 1947 and 1975, about 870 new madrasas were set up. He points out that in 1976-90 (14 years), 1,700 new madrasas emerged—most of these were established in 1977-88.

Factors like zakat funds, foreign donor support and Islamization policies facilitated the expansion and growth of seminaries. In 1997, there were 5,500 seminaries, half of them in Punjab. There is an almost equal split between Barelvi (1,200 seminaries) and Deobandi (1,000 seminaries), compared to some 200 Ahl-e-Hadith and 100 Shia seminaries. It is estimated that around 2,00,000 students study in these seminaries. Through zakat funds and foreign support, these schools have been able to procure millions of rupees as donations. These deeni madrasas impart religious teaching and memorization of the Koran. Those students who have middle level (eight years of education) are allowed to take the Daras-i-Nizami course, which leads to Saanvi-i-Allama (equivalent to Matric 10 years), Darja-i-Mutwast (Intermediate), Darja-i-Alia (B.A. level), Darja-i-Alaimia (M.A. in Arabic/Islamic Studies).

Each madrasa has its own curriculum, which also has a tilt towards its particular sect. The 1979 education policy through the University

Grants Commission (UGC) recognized these *madrasas* as degree awarding institutions. However, the UGC has no control over the curriculum of these schools. Besides religious education, the Daras-i-Nizami courses offer teachings on *fiqah* (interpretation of Islam), Hadith, Tafseer, philosophy, history and Islamic jurisprudence. Most children come from the lower-income groups of parents who cannot afford to send them to other government schools. *Deeni madrasas* provide free meals, give token stipends, provide some clothing, and during holidays give pocket money for travel home.

The overall effect of the Zia regime's education and other policies was: (1) they revived religious symbolism and lent legitimacy to religious groups; (2) they gave a new status to religious schools; which were allowed to award degrees; (3) and they provided funding to these schools. Thus, the religious groups made a transition from the periphery to the mainstream in education and politics.

THE GENEVA PEACE PROCESS AND PARTING OF WAYS

With the initiation of the Geneva peace process, the US began to disengage from the Afghan war, but it was a disengagement without dismantling the infrastructure that it had built for jihad against the Soviet Union. The religio-political groups involved in jihad were not fully convinced about disengagement, therefore the culmination of the Geneva peace process marked the parting of ways between the US policy makers and the 'holy warriors'. A new phase began in the development and orientation of the religio-political groups. These groups began to seek greater autonomy from the Pakistani State and the US experts. The US once again put on the 'security lens', now the religious groups were portrayed as 'terrorists' and 'engines of Islamic fundamentalism' (Mark). In this context, the 'clash of civilizations' was portrayed as being larger than its size (Huntington). Thus, the pattern of religion and politics in Pakistan underwent a paradigm shift. Religio-political groups began to take not only an anti-America, but also an anti-democracy position. The changing equation in the US–Pakistan strategic partnership brought the realization among the religio-political groups that in the post-Geneva period the US not only disengaged itself from the Afghan war and religious groups, but was also hostile to those which persisted in pursuing 'holy war'. It is in the light of this paradigm shift that one may analyse the emergence of the Taliban in Afghanistan (1994) and the Lashkar-e-Taiba (1987) in Pakistan. This changing equation has propped up and enlarged what are called jihadi organization militant militias; the Lashkar-e-Taiba makes an interesting case study of this phenomenon. There is considerable historical, religious and theoretical literature available on the Jamaat-i-Islami, Tablighi Jamaat, and various factions of the Ulema-e-Deoband. Some of these studies are rich in detail, description and analysis. They also provide a good overview of the interplay of religion and politics in Pakistani society (Mumtaz; Metcalf; Esposito; M.Z. Hussain; Shafqat). However, there is little literature that reviews the emergence of jihadi organizations. How and why do some religious groups consider jihad as an essential and integral component of Muslim renaissance? What tactics have they adopted to integrate jihad with modern education? How is military training imparted? There are at least four such groups that have ventured to synthesize religious and modern education. These religious groups have invested heavily in education, opened up schools, colleges and universities. They have even launched their own publications and developed their web sites. The distinguishing feature of these religious groups is that they have been able to use technology as an instrument for expansion of Islamic education. These groups are Minhaj-ul-Quran (Maulana Tahir-ul-Qadri), Tanzim-ul-Ikhwan, Lashkar-e-Jhangvi, and the Dawat-ul-Irshad, the group on which we shall now focus.

Dawat-ul-Irshad/Lashkar-e-Taiba

The Dawat-ul-Irshad Markaz was established in 1987 by two professors from the Engineering University, Lahore: Hafiz Saeed and Zafar Iqbal. The third founding father was Abdullah Azam, an Arab from the International Islamic University, Islamabad. However, Azam was killed two years after the creation of the new organization in a bomb blast in Peshawar.

The personal history and early life of Professor Hafiz Saeed who continues to be the principal architect of the Dawat educational system and its militant arm, the Lashkar-e-Taiba, is indicative of the imprint of religious education and how it may have influenced his world-view. Professor Hafiz Saeed's family migrated from Haryana (India). At the time of Independence, 36 members of the clan were killed while migrating to Pakistan. Along with his mother, he settled in Sargodha.

His mother taught him and his five brothers and sisters the Holy Koran. His maternal uncle Hafiz Muhammad Abdullah Bahawalpuri gave him religious education. He did his M.A. in Arabic and Islamic Studies from Punjab University. For two years, Hafiz Saeed taught in a Saudi university, at Ryadh. Later, he returned and joined as a research officer in the Islamic Ideology Council. Subsequently, he was appointed as lecturer in Islamic Studies at the Engineering University. He has recently retired from the university.

Markaz-e-Taiba, headquarters of the Dawat, is situated on the Grand Trunk Road at Murdike near Gujranwala. It covers an area of 200 acres. The compound was set up in 1990 with a 'rumored price of 18 crores rupees' (Khalid Ahmed). It is residential, provides trade skills and ensures observance of the Ahl-e-Hadith school of thought. The Markaz forbids TV, outlaws pictures, but cassettes of warrior songs are available. The religious philosophy of the group is Sunni–Ahl-e-Hadith—orthodox and puritanical. The Markaz publishes a magazine, *Aldawa* (Urdu), with a reported circulation of 80,000.

The Dawat-ul-Irshad propounds a clear educational philosophy and is vigorous in propounding its world-view. The twin principles of its educational philosophy are developing a jihadi culture by combining Islamic teaching, preaching with modern education, producing a reformed individual who is well versed in Islamic moral principles and the techniques of science and technology, to produce an alternate model of governance and development. Second, by relying on jihad as a skill for military training, inculcating a spirit of motivation for waging jihad. For this purpose, jihad mythology is used as an important tool to train the potential Mujahideens by narrating stories of bravery, sacrifice and success of martyrs and by building faith in martyrdom. Thus, the edifice of the Dawat/Lashkar reformist philosophy revolves around the 'twin fields of education and jihad'. There is a symbiotic relationship between the two: the one cannot be separated from the other. Based on this philosophy, a Dawat university is under construction at Markaz Dawat-ul-Irshad, Murdike. It is expected to have five faculties, which will include economics, languages, religious studies, computer science, and management. Boarding and lodging facilities would be available, and Muslims from all over the world would be encouraged to join the university.

Hafiz Saeed's religious and political philosophy is challenging and innovative.[1] It has been correctly observed that jihad has varied meanings and interpretation among Muslims from a 'spiritual, intellectual struggle' to a 'recourse to armed warfare'. Similarly, for Western observers, it also poses problems of interpretation and implications (Sivan). Hafiz Saeed provides yet another interpretation which is both problematic and challenging. He postulates a complementarity between holy war and education. According to Hafiz Saeed (*Takbeer*, August 1999):

Islam propounds both Dawa and Jihad. Both are equally important and inseparable. Since our life revolves around Islam, therefore both Dawa and Jihad are essential, we cannot prefer one over the other. This was also the practice of the Prophet (PBUH). If beliefs and morals are not reformed, Dawa alone develops into mysticism and Jihad alone may lead to anarchy. Therefore recognizing the salience of Dawa and Jihad, the need is to fuse the two together. This is the only way to bring about change among individuals, society and the world.

Thus, the distinguishing characteristic of the Lashkar is its emphasise on integrating *tabligh* with *jihad*. The two are portrayed and propounded as inseparable. Hafiz Saeed further contends that jihad and modern education are intertwined. He reminds Muslims that when they 'gave up Jihad, science and technology also went into the hands of others. This is natural. The one who possesses power also commands science, the economy and politics.'

So jihad is presented as a military skill and essential for political power. Among the religio-political groups, Dawat-ul-Irshad is clear in advocating that modern education does not conflict with religious education: the two need to be merged. It strongly propounds teaching of modern management, computer sciences and communication along with religious education. Modern technology should be used and adopted to pursue Islamic education and for providing military training. This concept of jihad on one hand gives a boost to training and education, and on the other declares armed warfare as a legitimate goal. It does have seeds of popular appeal and motivation.

Hafiz Saeed maintains an analytic distinction between 'Islamic politics' and 'democratic politics'. He maintains that politics is a vital component of Islam, but that the Western concept of democracy and elections is un-Islamic. Hafiz Saeed is clearly guided by considerations of power. To him, politics means control over people, 'harnessing their capabilities and evolving an efficient administrative machinery'. Dawa and jihad perform these tasks; this is Islamic politics; it enhances the potentialities of Muslims. It is in this framework that he rejects Western democracy and propounds that politics must lead to harnessing people's capability and administrative efficiency. Politics must have a purpose and a sense of direction. Obviously, he believes that Western democracy does not fulfil this basic purpose.

He calls for reviving Islamic spirit:

> Muslims should not change according to changing circumstances, instead they should revert the circumstances towards Islam. Those who have abandoned Islamic politics and adopted democratic politics and attempted to merge Islamic politics with the former, they changed themselves. They could not bring any change in society, they lost in the process. We are strict and rigid in our approach therefore we stand committed to our fundamentals.

Pursuing this logic, Hafiz Saeed defines *fundamentalism* and says: 'unless one strictly adheres to one's beliefs only than one can build faith in one's basic principles and convictions. We are convinced that without strictly adhering to our beliefs we cannot bring any meaningful change. Islam does not absorb unislamic ways, it reforms these. Our problem is that we keep on bringing unislamic ways into [the] Islamic system, therefore Islam becomes restricted.' He does have a puritanical approach and asserts that 'the need is to save the Ummah from this dangerous trend. We need to arrest this trend and instead of adopting other systems must restructure the entire system on Islamic principles.' It is in this spirit that he focuses on the 'twin fields of education and jihad' to bring about a transformation in Pakistani society in particular and Muslim societies in general. The basic direction of the Dawat/Lashkar is clear that without military training, education is meaningless. Therefore, training has a special place in the workings of the Lashkar.

Training of Mujahideen is done in two stages. The trainers are also divided into two categories: ordinary trainers and specialist trainers. The first stage of training of ordinary trainers comprises 21 days. But before this training, the trainees are asked to go in the society for 15 days on a Dawa tour, where they are expected to preach others. Then there is a three-month waiting period, after which a character evaluation and assessment of the trainees is made from the people of the area. After about four months of evaluation and assessment, the second phase of training starts. This training imparts skills in warfare and guerrilla tactics: how to throw a bomb, how to operate a rocket launcher, carry loads and march through mountainous areas, the tactics of guerrilla warfare. This training combines three months of religious and commando training.

The Lashkar-e-Taiba claims that the trainee-Mujahideen are recruited from all social classes. Some are rich and prosperous, others belong to the middle classes and a large number are of humble social origins. These people are genuinely motivated to fight against the infidels and create an Islamic order. Dawat does not regard Osama bin Laden as a criminal and does not support American and Saudi policy towards him.

In 1998, the Lashkar revealed that during 1993-7, 10 of its leaders were martyred in the Kashmir jihad (8 were from Punjab, 1 from Swat, 1 from Afghanistan). Punjabi recruits dominated the Mujahideen fighting in the Kashmir jihad. Upon return from various jihads, the Mujahideen narrate their stories in front of congregations, where these are received with respect and admiration.

CONCLUSION

The foregoing analysis indicates that the role and significance of religion has undergone radical transformation in Pakistan. The number of religious groups and *deeni madrasas* has multiplied. Their congregations and conferences have also become more regular and visible. Some of these groups are prolific in pamphleteering Islamic publications. The lower- and middle-income groups, particularly in Punjab, seem to be more vulnerable to Islamic causes, symbols and this jihadi culture. This transformation is visible and pronounced, but does not necessarily mean that it could be converted into an expandable support base or 'vote bank'.

The Lashkar-e-Taiba asserts that a return to the Islamic system is the only choice, and that it provides a fresh model of education and Muslim renaissance which will revive Islamic spirit. Through education and jihad, the Lashkar appears to be 'reconstructing' an Islamic identity. Hafiz Saeed argues that the Lashkar is playing a major role in transforming Pakistani society: through its educational institutions, it is producing a new breed of Pakistanis. These men are semi-educated but motivated to wage 'holy war'. The Lashkar leadership is correct in diagnosing that people are alienated with the present political system, but this alienation does not mean that they are eager to accept the alternative that the Lashkar-e-Taiba offers.

From the point of view of the Pakistani nation-building process, islamist movements such as the Dawat-ul-Irshad/Lashkar-e-Taiba play a rather ambivalent role. On the one hand they put a stress on the equation between Islam and Pakistan and on the other hand they promote transnational activities on behalf of Islam, an activity which is bound to blur the identity and the frontiers of the nation state.

Building bridges between the transnational aspirations of such islamist movements and the demands of nation-building is becoming a daunting task in Pakistan.

NOTE

1. I have translated freely from the following Urdu publications. For an extensive and wide-ranging discourse on Hafiz Saeed's world-view, see his interview in *Takbeer* (Urdu), Karachi, 12 August 1999, pp. 37-9. For reports on annual congregations, narration-of-martyrdom syndrome, see *Zindigi*, 15-21 November 1998, pp. 38-41. For information on university, educational philosophy, training, other aspects of organization of congregations, see *Aldawa*, October 1996, pp. 15-19; December 1996, pp. 17-40; March 1996, pp. 41-3; 1992, pp. 50-3; August 1995, pp. 47-8.

REFERENCES

Ahmed, Khalid, 'The Power of Lashkar-e-Taiba', *Friday Times*, 20 November 1998; 10 September 1999.

Ahmed, Mumtaz, 'Islamic Foundation in South Asia: The Jamaat-i-Islami and the Tablighi Jamaat of South Asia', in *Fundamentalisms Observed*, pp. 457-530.

Ahmed, Muneer, *The Role of Intelligence Agencies in the Politics of Pakistan*, (Urdu), Lahore: Jehangir Books, 1993.

Bhutto, Z.A., *New Directions*, London, New York, 1980.

————, *If I am Assassinated*, New Delhi: Vikas Publishing, 1979.

Clyde, Mark, *Islamic Reform Movements in Middle Eastern Countries*, Washington: Congressional Research Service, The Library of Congress, 15 March 1993.

Cooley, John L., *Unholy Wars, Afghanistan, America and International Terrorism*, London: Pleeto Press, 1999.

Esposito, John L., *Voices of Resurgent Islam*, New York: Oxford University Press, 1983.

————, *The Islamic Threat: Myth or Reality*, New York: Oxford University Press, 1992.

Gellener, Ernest, *Post-Modernism: Reason and Religion*, London, Rawalpindi: Routledge, 1992.

————, 'Allah's Army', *Herald*, January 1998, pp. 123-33.

Hussain, Mir Zohair, 'Islam in Pakistan Under Bhutto and Zia-ul-Haq', in Hussin Mutalib, et al., *Islam, Muslims and the Modern State*, pp. 47-79.

Hussain, Mushaid, 'Jamaat-i-Islami and Power Structure', *Nation*, 15 June 1992.

Metcalf, Barbara D., 'Living Hadith in the Tablighi Jamaat', *The Journal of Asian Studies*, vol. 52, no. 3, August 1993, pp. 584-604.

Nasr, Syyed Vali Reza, 'Students, Islam and Politics: Islami Jamiat-i-Tuleba in Pakistan', *Middle East Journal*, vol. 46, no. 1, Winter 1992, pp. 59-76.

P. Huntington, Samuel, 'The Clash of Civilizations', *Foreign Affairs*, 1993.

Rashid, Ahmed, 'The Taliban: Exporting Extremism', *Foreign Affairs*, vol. 78, no. 6, November/December 1999, pp. 22-35.

————, 'Raise the Crescent', *Far Eastern Economic Review*, 3 December 1998, pp. 20-3.

Richter, William, 'The Political Dynamics of Islamic Resurgence in Pakistan', *Asian Survey*, vol. XIX, no. 6, June 1979, pp. 547-57.

Shafqat, Saeed, *Political System of Pakistan and Public Policy*, Lahore: Progressive Publishers, 1989.

Sivan, Emanual, 'The Holy War Tradition in Islam', *Orbis*, vol. 42, no. 2, Spring 1998, pp. 171-94.

6

The Taliban: A Strategic Tool for Pakistan

OLIVIER ROY

THE PAKISTANI SUPPORT for the Taliban since 1994 can be explained at two levels: (1) a geo-strategic perspective, designed at the time of the Soviet invasion of Afghanistan, with the aim of asserting the regional influence of Pakistan by establishing a kind of control on Afghanistan through a fundamentalist, Pakhtun-dominated movement; (2) an ideological and religious connection provided by extending the informal networks of *madrasas* in Pakistan, which at the same time challenge the Islamic credentials of the Pakistan Government and provide it also with non-governmental tools of influence in the region. In using the second level in order to implement the first one, the various Pakistani Governments, or more precisely, the military establishment in charge of the regional policy of Pakistan, have been successful in pushing their interests with little direct involvement, in terms of both money and manpower. Pakistan has always been able to put forward a 'plausible deniability' of its role in Afghanistan, with little or no pressure from the international community. But the Taliban's failure to achieve a decisive victory and the perpetuation of the deadlock have entailed negative side effects for Pakistan: a growing radicalization and internationalization of the 'Islamic hub' (as embodied by the case of Osama bin Laden), the economic consequences of the transborder smuggling, and increasing hostility of the international community. Pakistan is now facing a choice: either to go on with its 'forward policy', or, as it did temporarily with Kashmir in May 1999, to defuse the tension by softening its support for the Taliban.

To a certain extent, the Afghan issue shares many common features with the Kashmir one: a disputed border (the Durand Line) and a territory whose status has been contested in the aftermath of the 1947 Partition (Pakhtunistan),[1] the use of radical Islamist movements to bypass ethno-nationalist affiliations, an indirect involvement of the

Pakistani military in supporting Islamist movements, and growing internationalization of the issue. In fact, the Pakistani policy embodies the predicament of the Pakistani State; since its founding.

Pakistan has been first established as an Islamic State, that is a State whose aim is to gather together all the Muslims of the Indian subcontinent, whatever their ethnic or linguistic background. Contrary to many ideological States, Pakistan had little opportunity to develop as a mere nation state, based on territory, institutions and citizenship: it always stuck to its ideological and transnational claim of gathering all the Muslims of the region. After the defeat of East Pakistan, the Islamic factor in foreign policy became more relevant at the time of the Soviet invasion of Afghanistan. In fact, the Islamic dimension of the regional policy of Pakistan is not an added ideological factor, but is closely interrelated to strategic constraints, as we shall see in the case of Afghanistan.

THE PAKISTANI GREAT DESIGN

Relations have been strained between Pakistan and Afghanistan since the Partition of the Indian empire in 1947. Afghanistan was the only country not to vote in favour of the admission of Pakistan into the UN. The bone of contention was the border separating the two countries: the Durand Line, established by the British at the end of the nineteenth century, was not (and is still not) seen by Afghanistan as an international border, but as a divide between the zones of influence of the two parties on the Pakhtun tribes. To undermine Pakistan, Prince Daoud, Prime Minister from 1954 to 1963, and President from 1973 to 1978, launched the 'Pakhtunistan' issue, that is a quest for autonomy, if not independence, of the North West Frontier Province of Pakistan, populated by Pakhtuns (or Pathans). Largely as a result from this Afghano-Pakistani antagonism, from 1947 to 1989, all Governments in Kabul have sided with New Delhi; Afghan officers were sent to India for training. The close military relations between both capitals and Moscow was also a concern for Islamabad.

Pakistan has adopted a defensive policy towards Afghanistan until 1978: the border was regularly closed, and Pakistan gave asylum, after Daoud's coup against his cousin, King Zahir, to an array of Islamist groups, headed by young militants like Hekmatyar and Massud, who became the leaders of the Islamist Mujahideen movements in the 1980s.[2] The main actors of the Pakistan–Afghan connection were already in place in the early 1970s: Afghan Islamist leaders, directly supervised by a Pakistani religious-political movement, the Jamaat-i-Islami (one of its leaders, Qazi Husseyn Ahmed, a Pakhtun, was in charge to advise, if not supervise, the fledgling Afghan movement, and was to become the Amir of the movement in 1987) and Pakistani intelligence officers, many of them Pakhtun, who gave training to the Afghan Islamists. As we shall see, other connections existed between Pakistan and Afghanistan, but without government support.[3]

The Soviet invasion of Afghanistan provided an opportunity for Pakistan to wage a more offensive policy. The great success of Gen. Zia was to make Washington endorse, in the name of the 'roll-back' policy against the Soviet Union, his own decision of playing the Islamic tool in the region.

The Afghan policy of Gen. Zia was manifold. First, the Islamic option and the ethnic issue have always been closely linked, although this connection was never acknowledged as such. Islamabad supported the Pakhtun 'Islamist' parties, mainly the Hizb-e-Islami of Gulbuddin Hekmatyar (and then the Taliban), in order to play the main ethnic group. Hence the 'Pakhtunistan' issue was superseded by Islamic solidarity, but a new importance and more room of manoeuvre was given to Pakistani Pakhtuns. In fact, instead of repressing their own 'Pathans', the Pakistani military establishment (dominated by the Punjabis, but wherein the Pakhtuns were over-represented in proportion to their demographic weight), chose to turn the Pakhtunistan issue the other way around, by blurring the contested borders and taking roots inside Afghanistan. Ethnic and religious policy are thus closely related: the Islamic issue, used to bypass the ethnic one, did in fact reinforce the dominant groups, both in Afghanistan and Pakistan. Another positive side effect of this 'Islamic' policy was to make use of the Islamist wave that has engulfed the Middle East during the 1980s, to turn it against Communism instead of the West, and to strengthen its Sunni component, undercutting the Iranian influence in the area. In fact, playing this card allowed Pakistan to enlist US support against all of its neighbours (Iran, India).

The second fold of the policy was to establish a friendly government in Afghanistan, or more exactly a 'junior partner', using ethnic and religious connections. Throughout the war, the Pakistani policy was to maintain a permanent tutelage on the Afghan Mujahideen movement through the distribution of weapons, the right to issue refugees' cards, the use of camps and facilities inside Pakistan. This patronizing policy was rather flexible and subtle: if some groups got the bulk of the help, none was left without any support.

The expected strategic benefits were multiple: to break the Kabul–New Delhi axis, to get strategic depth vis-à-vis India, to isolate Iran by strengthening the Sunni specificities of the Islamist movements, to carve out a corridor to Central Asia in case of a collapse of the USSR. Of course, the latter aim was not formulated in 1979, but it seems that very rapidly the Pakistani military, unlike the diplomats, understood the weakness of the Soviet empire (the ISI has encouraged if not organized armed incursions inside the territory of the USSR in 1987.[4] Pakistan was playing on US support and determination to get an almost free hand in devising the policy of support to the Mujahideen, while enjoying protection against a Soviet backlash. Washington and Riyadh gave a huge amount of money. In fact, the Pakistani policy was clever and risky, but seemed successful when the Soviet troops left Afghanistan in February 1989.

But the endeavours to put Hekmatyar in charge in Kabul failed: the Communist Najibullah regime stood in charge until 1992 and fell in March that year to Massud, not to Hekmatyar. Hekmatyar did not succeed in dislodging Massud from Kabul during four years of civil war and bombings. In the meantime, Hekmatyar's vocal support for Saddam Hussain during the Gulf war had antagonized the Saudis.

Pakistan had to find another Afghan, fundamentalist Pakhtun card.

THE ISLAMIC CONNECTION

The religious connection between Afghanistan and the Indian sub-continent is an old story.[5] The subcontinent had been the main source of religious training after Iran became Shia (in the sixteenth century) and Central Asia came under Russian rule. The connection was at two levels. On one hand, Afghan ulema used to go to the main madrasa of India (Deoband after 1867). One should be reminded here that Persian was the official language of the Mughal empire and remained one of the main vectors of Islamization, before being slowly replaced by Urdu. There was, thus, a linguistic (Persian) and religious community (Sunni Hanafi'ism). On the other hand, the frontier was the place of an almost missionary movement, launched by Indian reformist mullahs, who instigated jihad against either the Sikhs or the British. This militant frontier tradition was embodied in the building of countryside madrasas. As often in tribal areas, 'holy' men, sometimes rooted in the Sufi tradition, sometimes in a more fundamentalist and scripturalist conception of Islam (which the British political agents had already dubbed 'Wahhabism'), regularly provides a tool for uniting tribes against a common alien enemy.

Strangely enough, Afghanistan never developed a network of its own of high-level *madrasas*. Going to India was a common pattern of ulema wanting to achieve higher studies. After Partition in 1947, the Afghan mullahs stopped going to the 'infidel' State of India and went to Pakistan. Worried by this connection with the 'enemy' and haunted by the tradition of tribal revolts headed by charismatic religious leaders, the Afghan monarchy endeavoured to establish a 'State clergy', through the Faculty of Shariat created in 1951, whose first professors were sent for training to Cairo, in Al Azhar. Out of mistrust, Pakistan-trained ulema were not recruited by the Afghan Government in the newly established Faculty of Shariat. But the government policy to bypass the Pakistani connection did not work and even backfired: the ulema sent to Cairo came back with sympathy for the Muslim Brotherhood movement which was to become a close ally of the Pakistani Jamaat-i-Islami. On the other hand, the gap between government and 'private' mullahs increased. The fact that they were not allowed in the small official clergy did not matter for them: they were funded either by their local constituency or by the Pakistani *madrasa* they were trained in.

The consequence of this exclusion of State (and hence urban) clergy was that Afghanistan has been, with Pakistan, one of the few Muslim countries where a network of *madrasas* has developed in rural, and specifically tribal areas. More or less linked with Sufi *naqshbandi* connections, but developing a kind of scripturalist fundamentalism, these *madrasas* flourished in the south and to a lesser extent in the north, but not in the centre (Shia), west and east. These *madrasas* superseded tribal connections and brought together people from different clans and tribes.

Usually, the heads of *madrasas* were trained in a Pakistani *madrasa*, thus bringing to Afghanistan the brand of Islam taught in Pakistan. Two main networks seem to be at stake, but both are related to the nineteenth century Deobandi school. The smaller one is called the '*panjpiri*', from the place where the 'mother' *madrasa* is situated in the NWFP. Linked to the Ahl-e-Hadith movement, the '*panjpiri*' ulema are dubbed 'Wahhabi' in Afghanistan, for their strong anti-Sufi, or more exactly, anti-*zyarat* trend. They have rooted themselves mainly among Tajiks and Uzbeks in the Afghan province of Badakhshan. The *panjpiris* have recently joined the Taliban movement. The bulk of the *madrasas* of southern Afghanistan are linked with the Jamiyat-i-Ulama-e-Islam movement in Pakistan, itself the political expression of the Deobandi movement. The biggest 'mother' *madrasa* is the Haqqaniyah in Akora Khattak (NWFP) headed by Senator Sami-ul Haq. As usual, the Islamic connection had also something to do with the ethnic one. Although different languages were used in the Pakistani *madrasas* (Urdu, Pashto, Persian, Arabic), and despite the fact that most students were bi- or multi-lingual in schools deprived of ethnic prejudice, a sort of ethnic polarization did take place, mainly through language. For reasons too long to be dealt with in this article, a network of *madrasas* has developed in southern Afghanistan, along the Arghandab Valley and around Kandahar, bypassing both the traditional division between Pakhtun Durrani and Ghilzay. Although, as we said, many founders were members of the *tariqat*, it seems that a generation change, accelerated by the war, has brought the traditional *pir* to the margins: they were apparently not replaced by their '*khalifa*' but by a new generation of ulema having a dual legitimacy, religious through their education in Pakistan, and military, through their deeds during the war. Interestingly enough, this new generation shared many patterns with the Communist Pakhtuns: they were not born among the tribal aristocracy and were enlisted in schools at very young ages (military for the Communists and religious for the Taliban), whose recruitment cut across tribal affiliations, thus developing a relation both with a supra-national community (the world revolution for the Communists and the Muslim ummah for the Taliban) and an ethnic one (the Pakhtuns, whatever the tribal affiliations). It is not by chance that many former Communist officers joined the Taliban against Massud.

During the 1980s, these networks joined two of the main Mujahideen parties, the Harakat-i-Inqilab-i-Islami of Nabi Mohammedi, and the Hizb-e-Islami of Younous Khales (not Hekmatyar), two Pakhtun and fundamentalist parties. They did not appear, at that time, as a military and political movement, but were already known as 'the Taliban'.

PAKISTAN AND THE TALIBAN MOVEMENT

The present movement owes its characteristics to three elements: a sudden transformation, inside Afghanistan, of a loose local religious network into a political and military movement, under the charismatic leadership of Mullah Omar (August 1994); the Pakistani decision to endorse the movement and to use it as its new tool for serving the same 'great design'; the linking of the Taliban to the international Islamic hub, which has been established in Pakistan in the aftermath of the Afghan war.

In August 1994, Mullah Omar, himself a Pakhtun Ghilzay but enlisted in the *madrasa* of Panjway, located in Durrani area, launched an attack against former Mujahideen commanders-turned-highway robbers (Daro Khan).[6] He got the support of a Pakistani based association of Pakhtun traders and truck owners, who were upset by the tolls and bribes levied by the commanders. In some weeks, he took Kandahar. The Pakistani Minister of Interior, Gen. Babar, decided to rise to the occasion. (It is interesting to see that the Pakistani ministry in charge of Afghanistan is the Interior.) Gen. Babar endeavoured to sell the Taliban to the international community and organized a trip from Kandahar to Herat for Western ambassadors accredited in Islamabad, including the US ambassador (without any authorization of the legitimate Afghan Government, although it was recognized by the international community). A group of high-ranking ISI members was posted in Kandahar, while Pakistani agents, like Col. Iman in Herat, covertly worked to convince local commanders to join the Taliban. Financial, logistic and military help were provided to the Taliban.

At that time, a change was occurring among the Pakistani religious networks. The Jamaat-i-Islami, a staunch supporter of Gulbuddin Hekmatyar and a bridge between Pakistan and the Middle East Islamist milieus, began to lose some influence in favour of more conservative, traditional and clerical movements, like the Jamiyat-i-Ulama-Islam. At the same time, these conservative movements became more radical, with armed branches or splinter groups like Sipah-e-Sahaba, whose main activity is to fight the Shias. The shift from political Islamism to radical neo-fundamentalism occurred in tandem in both countries.[7]

Thousands of international Islamic activists came to be trained in Afghanistan. They used channels established during the 1980s by the ISI, where the Jamaat and the Hizb-e-Islami played a pivotal role, with a direct connection with the Middle East Muslim Brotherhood (as Abdullah Azam, who played the role of a middleman in Peshawar from 1983 till his assassination in September 1989). But after the Gulf war, these networks became more independent from their tutelary institutions. The role of Osama bin Laden is a good example of this radicalization and autonomization. While delivering some activists incriminated for terrorist actions on US territory (Ramzi Yusaf, Amal

Kansi) to the Americans, the Pakistani authorities turned a blind eye to the activities of these net-works, which provide volunteers to the ISI and the army to fight in Kashmir or to enlist in a poorly manned Taliban army. When the US cruise missiles hit a so-called 'terrorist base' in Paktia in August 1998, it appears that the Taliban were in charge, but that the activists in the camp belonged to the Harkat-ul-Ansar movement, and were trained to fight in Kashmir, where they were infiltrated during the winter of 1998-9.

The Pakistani support for the Taliban had also antagonized Iran, because of the strong anti-Shia bias of the latter, reinforced by the presence of Pakistani militant groups inside Afghanistan. It seems that the killing of the Iranian diplomats in August 1998 in Mazar-i-Sharif was perpetrated by an armed SS group.

Hence, the Pakistani support for the Taliban has to be framed in a broader picture: the training and use of an international network of activists in order to achieve a regional strategy. This has progressively antagonized countries which were not hostile to Pakistan as the USA, but also Uzbekistan, whose Foreign Minister, A. Kamalov, made an unusual, undiplomatic statement in February 1998 accusing Pakistan of harbouring and training many Uzbek Islamist militants.

The links between this Pakistani Islamic hub and the military establishment seems to be obvious, either because the latter thinks that it could handle them to its benefit, or because some of the officers promoted during Gen. Zia's leadership are themselves Islamist, like Gen. Hamid Gul, former head of the ISI towards the end of the Afghan war.

The problem for Pakistan is that its risky strategy did not work: the 'Islamic volunteers' had to withdraw from Kashmir, while the Taliban did not succeed in occupying the whole of Afghanistan and being recognized as the sole legitimate government by the international community (except by Pakistan, Saudi Arabia and the United Arab Emirates). Moreover, the Taliban became the target of international criticism for their treatment of women and their hosting of Osama bin Laden: they became subjected to international sanctions in October 1999.

In August 1999, they tried a last offensive against Massud, but failed. The Taliban suffer from the fact that they are seen as an army of occupation in the north (except Pakhtun and Wahhabi pockets, like Zardeyo in Badakhshan), and that they lack manpower. They have been affected by huge losses due to their inexperience in the field and their war tactics. The tribal levies who helped the Taliban to win from 1994 to 1996 are very reluctant to become enlisted as regular soldiers and to fight in the northern part of the country. Hence, the Taliban rely heavily on the volunteers coming from Pakistan. The military coup of October 1999 in Pakistan did not change the picture. On one hand, both Gen. Musharraf and Gen. Mohammed Aziz were involved in the offensive policy towards Kashmir and Afghanistan. The coup was greeted by the Islamist organizations which are pro-Taliban and anti-American. On the other hand, any reform of Pakistani domestic as well as foreign policy necessarily supposes at least a decrease in support to the Taliban. It will send a strong signal to Washington, but also to Teheran that Islamabad is not supporting radical movements any longer. It will also put an end to the Talibanization of Pakistan, which was pointed out by Nawaz Sharif in September 1998. It will also restore to some extent the border between Afghanistan and Pakistan as far as smuggling is concerned. (Smuggling through Afghanistan, a traditional activity, not only costs huge amounts of money in taxes and excise duties to the Pakistani budget, but is also one of the main sources of income for Afghan traders.) It will also play down the Pathan–Punjabi alliance and give a signal to the Baluchis, Mohajirs and Sindhis that a new ethnic balance might be considered in Pakistan. (Among all these ethnic groups, the radical religious parties are less influential, hence 'secularization' and ethnic balance are progressing hand in hand.) In a word, less support for the Taliban would mean not only a redefinition of the role of Pakistan in the region, but could also reopen the debate about the nature of the Pakistani nation. Apparently, the time has not come yet for an overall reassessment of the Pakistani foreign policy, largely based on the manipulation of Islamic militant groups as tools for covert action, influence and remote control. This strategy of the 'weak' against the 'strong', using proxies, proved to be very efficient against the Soviet Union and India, and allowed Pakistan to escape strong criticism and pressure from the West. Hence, there is no reason to see a weakening of Pakistani support for the Taliban. But the latters' weakness might be domestic and not linked with Pakistani support, or lack of support.

The Taliban movement could hardly be considered a revolutionary one, although they constitute an original movement. They are, in fact, the offspring of two different traditions: charismatic mullahs in tribal societies and the Deobandi *madrasas*' networks. The Taliban movement, although not tribal in itself, is the expression of the Pakhtun tribal society precisely to the extent it tries to bypass the tribal divisions by using the shariah, which is a regular pattern of charismatic religious leaders in tribal milieus. They recruit almost exclusively in the southern Pakhtun tribal society. The fact that members of other groups join them is not a sign of a occultation of ethnicity: the newcomers might be allowed to live in peace in their region, but are not associated with the power (that was the ruling pattern of the Afghan Pakhtun monarchy during the nineteenth century). Despite their tribal and Pakhtun constituency, the Taliban surely try to bypass both, through the shariah and the reference to the Afghan State, as established from the early nineteenth century to the late 1970s by the monarchy. In this sense, they are in line with the traditional Pakhtun perception of the State. But that does not erase their ethnic background which heavily influences their attitude, through prejudice and discrimination.

One cannot define the Taliban as the expression of the Afghan ulema either. They are in no way a clerical institution. There are many other ulema in Afghanistan who do not recognize the Taliban as ulema both because of the ethnic divide and second, because they are not 'ulema': they call themselves 'students' not 'ulema'. The opposition of intellectuals to clerics does not work: Massud is probably the only 'intellectual' in the Panjshir and his constituency could be explained purely in ethnic/regional terms and never in sociological terms. But there is definitely a conflict of generation between the Taliban and the former tribal aristocracy or ulema's establishments. The only modernity of the Taliban is that they are also a result of the crisis of the traditional Pakhtun society.

The predicament of the Taliban is that they use two contradictory sets of legitimacy (the shariah and Afghan/Pakhtun nationalism) and refuse to address the real issue, that of ethnicity, except in words. By doing that, they are in tune with the way the Afghan monarchs had built the State. But the problem of the Taliban, at least under the leadership of Mullah Omar, is that they are not building a State. There is no real administration (educational system, civil servants, state-organized courts, modern army). A taste for stamps, titles and paperwork should not be confused with state construction. They laid off half of the civil servants, for the right reason: these people were doing nothing. To compare the present State of the Afghan administration to the situation at the time of the former King is nonsense.

NOTES

1. In 1947, the Pakhtun Khudayi Khidmatgaran movement, headed by Khan Abdul Ghaffar Khan and based in the North West Frontier Province, joined hands with the Indian Congress and then opted for independence, or at least autonomy within Pakistan.
2. See Olivier Roy, *Islam and Resistance in Afghanistan*, Cambridge, UK: Cambridge University Press, 1990.
3. On the relations between Pakistan and the Taliban, see W. Maley, ed., *Fundamentalism Reborn? Afghanistan and the Taliban*, London: C. Hurst, 1998.
4. Mohammad Yousaf and Mark Adkin, *The Bear Trap*, Lahore: Jhang Publishers, 1992.
5. B. Metcalf, *Islamic Revival in British India*, Princeton: Princeton University Press, 1982.
6. I happen to have been the host of Daro Khan in Panjway in the summer of 1984 and thus was able to observe the proto-history of the Taliban movement.
7. See Olivier Roy, *The Failure of Political Islam*, Boston: Harvard University Press, 1994.

Pakistan and the Taliban: State Policy, Religious Networks and Political Connections

GILLES DORRONSORO

HE EMERGENCE of the Taliban in the autumn of 1994 dramatically changed the course of the Afghan civil war. By imposing a new clerical order, unknown in Afghanistan or in other Muslim countries, the Taliban has changed the course of power politics in the region.[1] Western media, however, which liked to portray the main opponent of the Taliban, Gen. Massud, as the new Che Guevara has projected the Taliban only in stereotypical terms. If we wish to comprehend the relationship between Pakistan and Afghanistan in the regional context we will have to understand the complex nature of the Taliban movement bereft of the stereotypes.

THE NATURE OF THE TALIBAN MOVEMENT

Between 1994 and 1996, the Taliban managed to control two-thirds of Afghanistan partly because it was able to garner strong popular support, mostly in Pakhtun and the rural areas. Actually, the emergence of the Taliban is directly related to the anarchic situation of southern Afghanistan in the 1990s. Because of social and political fragmentation, no political power could be stable for long and the fall of the Najib Government in 1992 did not help the law and order situation in the country. On the contrary, cities like Kandahar were split between different commanders, fighting futile battles in the centre of the town. Schools were closed, and administration was non-existent. The behaviour of the political parties after the Soviet withdrawal suggested that politics was purely instrumental. The growing distance between the Mujahideen and the population was perceptible in the vocabulary used: people talked of *jang-i dakheli* (civil war) and not of *jihad* (holy war). The Mujahideen were accused of racketeering and killing and the people waited for someone to stop the chaos provoked by the never-ending conflicts between local commanders. Some of these popular expectations were met by the Taliban, which was sincerely committed to the reconstruction of a legal system in Afghanistan. Mullah Omar, the leader of the movement, has a distinctively charismatic legitimacy born from this popular expectation: his dreams are said to be inspired by God.[2]

Resurgence of Tribal Power
or Clerical Organization?

According to Olivier Roy[3] that the Taliban represents the resurgence of the traditional model of mobilization in Pakhtun (Pathan) areas but there are strong arguments against such a point of view. Mullah Omar is not an isolated, charismatic *alim* who has emerged temporarily in a situation of social discord to unite the Pakhtun tribes.[4] He is, instead, the pre-eminent figure of a collective religious leadership with a general (although imprecise) vision of Afghan society. The Taliban has actually established a central government, largely on the pattern of what existed in the 1950s, as well as a legal system. Likewise, the fact that the Taliban has systematically collected weapons militates against it being a tribal phenomenon as well as the fact that its interpretation of the sharia is frequently contradictory to the Pakhtun tribal code (Pakhtunwali), for example, the ban on vendetta or the (limited) right of inheritance for women.[5]

In the long-term, the victory of the Taliban is the result of the changing position of the ulema in the Afghan society. Traditionally, the Afghan ulema were reluctant to get involved in politics, but in the last century, they gained political prominence because of their opposition to modernization.[6] Since the end of the nineteenth century the ulema have played a key role in all protests against the government: in the 1924 and 1929 rebellions, and, less successfully after the Second World War, against several modernist laws such as the abolition of the veil for women in 1959.

Their role in social mobilization can be interpreted as a by-product of their removal from power.[7] Before the war, the ulema did not come from the tribal aristocracy and they did not have enough resources to keep a clientele, but they were close to the rural population. In the Badakhshan province, for example, they were the spokesmen of the people.[8] The strong social influence of the ulema in the country-side explains why approximately a quarter of the MPs in the 1964

Parliament had some religious backing.[9] In the spring of 1971, the ulema and the mullahs managed to organize a demonstration with thousands of people, a congregation which was much larger than any political party could have mobilized at that time.

During the war, some ulema became local commanders with the help of their religious students (Taliban) and this direct and long-term participation in political power was a new phenomenon in Afghan society. The ulema-commanders were found in all of Afghanistan, but more so in south Ghazni (Helmand, Badghis and Logar). Furthermore, the leaders of the political parties in exile were almost exclusively ulema. Hekmatyar, the head of the Hizb-i-Islami, is the only notable exception. By the time of the revolt against Amanullah in 1929,[10] the ulema were no more just a force behind the scene that could organize a revolt against the state, yet not directly assume power.

The Taliban is, to a certain extent, the outcome of this process, but the leadership of the movement no longer comes from the old religious families—Mojaddidi[11] or Gaylani[12]—who were quite influential before the war. These families, deeply involved in political games since the beginning of the war, have lost much of their religious charisma. The Taliban represents a brutal change in the religious field with the promotion of young and relatively uneducated mullahs.[13]

The 'Shariatization' of Society

In comparison with the pre-war situation in Afghanistan, when different ideologies (Nationalist, Maoist, Islamist, Communist), competed with each other for supremacy in the field is now much more homogeneous since Islam has emerged as the dominant ideology and the idea of *jihad* defines the legitimate ideological field since 1978. Political parties appear to be less flexible on social issues in order to attract the rural and conservative population. Even if many of the ulema had a more open ideological stand before the war, it is evident that the majority of them have now changed their stand and actively support a fundamentalist orientation. On some issues ideological differences between Islamists and fundamentalists are disappearing (the rights of women, for example). However, Islamists are still calling for a political system in which the ulema have no special place. Consequently, there is now a growing *political* opposition between the two groups since the emergence of the Taliban.

The Taliban ideology, based on the Islamization of society at the grass roots level, is derived from the fundamentalist movement inspired by Shah Wallihullah (1703-62) and the Deoband school.[14] This movement is puritanical and reformist, opposing all unorthodox practices.[15] And although the Taliban is more puritanical and reactionary than the majority of the ulema before the war, it does not oppose traditional practices (like the cult of the Saints), and, therefore, it is acceptable to the rural population, as opposed to the Wahhabi movement that has failed to gain support in Afghanistan.

The enforcement of the sharia is the main point in the Taliban's political agenda. It aims at building a theocratic State in which the ulema have the power to designate and control the government. Furthermore, the Taliban does not permit the emergence of any political party; elections are said to be un-Islamic, and a source of *fitna* (division) within the Muslim community (*ummah*). The present leader, Mullah Omar, was recognized as Amir al-Mominin by a *shura* of ulema in Kandahar (20 March to 4 April 1996) and is currently the main source of legislative texts.[16] Clearly, the ultimate legitimacy of power is not political, but religious and charismatic. This is why Mullah Omar does not live in Kabul, the capital and political centre, but in Kandahar.

The Taliban's interpretation of the sharia is extremely conservative. It condemns any attempt at *ijtihad* (interpretation) and, perhaps because of its Pakhtun background, forbids any kind of public activity for women.[17] Adultery and male homosexuality are severely condemned, and stoning has been publicly conducted in such cases. Music is forbidden till the end of jihad and any kind of representation of living creatures is prohibited.

Political Legitimization

Like in any other State, the establishment of a new regime in Afghanistan is a complex process in which the question of legitimacy is crucial. Islam has been the source of legitimacy for every regime until 1978, and thereafter as well. In the case of Abdul Rahman Khan (1880-1901) and his successors Habibullah and Amanullah, the ulema had to recognize the divine source of the power of the Amir. This was a radical change because their predecessors had been *primus inter pares*. (The first Amir had been elected by a tribal assembly in Kandahar.) The Amir claimed Islamic legitimacy: the sermon (*khutba*) was read in his name, and this obligation was even referred to in the 1923 Constitution. (Today, the *khutba* is said in the name of Mullah Omar.) Therefore, when some mullah no longer preached the *khutba* (Friday sermon) in the name of Zahir Shah as in 1971[18] as a protest against some reform or the other, this omission had quite a political significance. The Taliban, thus, validates the return to a political legitimization of power in religious terms. For example, non-Muslims in Afghanistan, must from now on, wear some distinctive sign. This is reminiscent of the amendment of the 1923 Constitution by the Loya Jirga[19] which imposed heavier taxes and wearing of distinctive symbols by non-Muslims.

In accord with its religious discourse, the Taliban refuses a Pakhtun nationalist ideology, but the *qwam* (network of solidarity) plays a major part in the power structure. Most of the cadres are Pakhtun mullahs, originally from the Kandahar area. Mullah Omar's family is from Tarin Kot (Uruzgan province) and the ulema hailing from this place are found in positions of power (Mullah Mohammad Abbas, the Mayor of Kandahar, for example). Besides, Mullah Omar is a Hottak (a Pakhtun Ghilzay tribe) which is over represented in the Government in Kabul.[20]

Relationship with the Shi'ite Minority

Even if the Taliban is refusing a nationalist ideology,[21] its relationship with the non-Pakhtun ethnic groups and the Shia minority is not easy. The fact that its members have been educated (partly at least) in Pakistan often implies that they are no more part of the Persian cultural tradition. Being practically all Pakhtun, they are perceived by the other groups as epitomizing the return of the old domination of the Pakhtun on the State.

We would logically expect that, as Sunni fundamentalists, the Taliban should have an antagonistic relationship with the Shias who make up 10 to 15 per cent of the population. It is all the more so since they are Pakhtuns with an old tradition of feuding with Hazaras and 80 per cent of the Shia community is Hazara.[22] But, surprisingly, the Taliban has been conciliatory with the Shia minority during their advances in Uruzgan and Ghazni provinces, even if the death of the Hazara leader Mazari at the hands of the Taliban in March 1995 somewhat dented this initial attempt to establish a good relationship with the Shias. However, in the part of the country it controls, the Taliban has stopped armed robberies against Shia Hazaras which had been quite common, specially in the Ghazni province, and the Hazaras living there have come to an understanding with the Taliban.

After the fall of Mazar-i Sharif in August 1998, thousands of Hazaras were slaughtered by the victorious Taliban, to avenge the killing of their comrades the year before. None the less, in November 1998, Akbari, a key figure of the Hizb-i Wahdat, defected to the Taliban, offering cooperation and asking for a role in the government. The reason for this surrender, besides the fact that the military situation had become desperate for the Hizb-i Wahdat, was the hope that Shia ulema would find a place in a clerical state, even if dominated by Sunnis. What is at stake here is the Taliban's ability to enlarge the government to accomodate the ulema from different ethnic backgrounds. However, it is too early to assess the definitive position of the Taliban in this matter, while the popular feeling against the Shias, and even more the Hazaras, seems to be growing. The Shia minority in Pakistan sees the Taliban as extremely anti-Shia, but the actual situation in Afghanistan is more complex.

A THREE-LEVEL RELATIONSHIP WITH PAKISTAN

Since 1994, the relationship of the Taliban with Pakistan has become a controversial question. At first, the broad set of links between the Taliban and Pakistani suggests that the Taliban is a transnational movement. Most of the members of the Taliban originally came from the refugee camps in Pakistan, and many of them have Pakistani identity cards because they have lived there as refugees for years, but their 'real' nationality is sometimes difficult to ascertain. A number of Pakistani citizens (besides ISI officers) have participated in the fighting alongside the Taliban, specially in the conquest of Jalalabad and Kabul. But the leadership of the Taliban is exclusively Afghan, and the movement has no claim on the Pathan side of the border.

In fact, the Taliban is neither a pure Pakistani creation nor an Afghan phenomenon and the intermeshing of the two is a complex affair. That is why we must distinguish between the religious networks, the role of the political parties and State policy.

The Link between the Taliban and the Pakistani Deeni Madrasas

In the 1980s, there was a dramatic development in the network of the *deeni madrasas* in Pakistan. Between 1960 and 1983, the number of the Taliban studying in Pakistan had increased from 7,500 to 78,500 and the number of teachers from 227 to 321.[23] This trend continues to grow, since in 1988 there were 1,320 *deeni madrasas* in Punjab which rose to 2,521 in 1997, imparting education to 2,20,000 students.[24] In Karachi alone, there are 29 *madrasas* with an average of 2,000 students a year.[25] This situation is largely due to Zia ul-Haq's policy of Islamization (1977-88). The fact that a part of the compulsorily collected *zakat* was given to the *deeni madrasas*[26] and that the universities recognized the diplomas issued by the *madrasas* goes a long way to explain this phenomenon. Furthermore, Zia ul-Haq encouraged the building of *deeni madrasas* in the NWFP to help the Afghan *jihad*, which is why the number there is growing more rapidly than in the rest of the country.

These *madrasas* belong to different religious schools: Deobandi, Barelvi, Ahl e-Hadith. The syllabi of the Deobandi and Barelvi *madrasas* are generally very conservative. For example, the basic text is still the Dars i-Nizamiyya, from the eighteenth century. Aristotelian logic is taught in its classical form. Some of those *madrasas* wield a national influence, notably the Jamiyat ul Ulum ul-Islamiyah, created by Alama Yusuf Binari in Binari town (near Karachi), educating 8,000 students (with its 12 affiliated *madrasas*). The Dar ul-Ulum Haqqaniyah Madrasa in Akora Khattak (Peshawar district), established in 1947, has educated one-third of the Deobandi ulema in Pakistan, even if today its influence is declining. The leader of this school is the secretary general of the Jamiyat ul-Ulema, Maulana Sami ul-Haq. Other *madrasas*, either belonging to the Ahl e-Hadith faction or linked to the Jamaat i-Islami, are more open to modernity, at least to technology (the English language and computers are taught for instance). The Jamaat i-Islami has opened 41 *deeni madrasas* in the NWFP, one-third of the new ones in the province, and 19 after the Soviet invasion, even though the Deobandis are still in a majority in the province. On the other hand, Saudi Arabia has financed the new Jamiyat Imam Bukhari Madrasa in Peshawar, officially opened in June 1999 in the presence of Mohammad Abdul Rahman, from the Saudi Ministry of Religious Affairs.[27] The director of this *madrasa* belongs to the Jamaat al-Dawa al-Coran wa-Sunna, a movement active in the Kunar province of Afghanistan (till the Taliban took over the place) and is close to the Ahl e-Hadith movement.

Since the war, the proportion of Afghan students in these *deeni madrasas* has increased noticeably. In 1982, approximatively 9 per cent of those belonging to the Taliban in the NWFP were Afghans, and this proportion has rapidly increased.[28] For example, the majority of the

750 students of the Jamiyat Imam Bukhari Madrasa that we mentioned earlier are Afghans. Likewise, 15 per cent of the students of the Dar ul-Ulum Haqqaniyah Madrasa were Afghans in 1960; a figure which rose to 60 per cent in 1985.[29] Afghan students generally join Deobandi *madrasas* because of the historical links between the Afghan ulema and the Dar ul-Ulum Deoband Madrasa (in India), even if, today, the relationship between this Madrasa and the Pakistani Deobandi movement is limited. Under the generic term 'Deobandi', one finds, in fact, different kinds of discourses and one cannot overestimate the education of their ulema and the coherence of their ideology.

Most of the Taliban ulema have been educated in the NWFP during the war. In particular, the Dar ul-Ulum Haqqaniyah in Akora Khattak (NWFP) has trained some of the most important cadres of the movement.[30] There are strong links of solidarity between the ulema trained in this *madrasa* and its Taliban students. The ulema who are in control of the Taliban movement have a strong sense of group identity even if, as in any other organization, they also have conflicts.

Besides the presence of the Afghan Taliban, Pakistani *madrasas* are directly linked to the Afghan war because participation in *jihad* is seen as a natural next step for its students. Most of the volunteers are Afghans, but some Pakistani citizens also participate in the *jihad*. They generally come from the NWFP and Baluchistan, and occasionally from Sindh or Punjab. When Kandahar was taken by the Taliban in September 1994, the first generation came from the *madrasas* in Baluchistan (Chaman, Gulistan, Jangal Pir Alizay, Pishin, Qila Abdullah). In December 1994, the 4,000 Taliban who took part in the war operations in Afghanistan came from different parts of the NWFP and Baluchistan.[31] The Deputy Chief of the Citizens–Police Liaison Committee of Karachi stated that 600 or 700 members of the Taliban were sent to Afghanistan in May 1997.[32] In August 1999, thousands of Afghan and Pakistani Taliban came to Afghanistan to reinforce Mullah Omar's troops.

Connection with Pakistani Fundamentalist Parties

Most of the Islamist and fundamentalist parties in Pakistan have the Afghan *jihad* on the top of their agenda. It is well known that most of these parties do not have any significant support during elections and they try to mobilize people with highly emotional issues, specially in relation to the *jihad* in Kashmir and Afghanistan. The bin Laden episode is a good example of such mobilization since the fundamentalist parties in Pakistan have successfully exploited the American strikes in Afghanistan.[33]

Yet, the Taliban do not have general support among these parties: the Deobandi movements are close to them, but the Islamists are clearly reluctant or opposed to them. The Taliban has well-known connections with the Jamiyat i-Ulama e-Islam which managed to gain support among the Durrani tribes in NWFP and Baluchistan during the 1990s. Maulana Fazlur Rahman, the leader of this party and himself a Pakhtun, was formerly Chairman of the Foreign Affairs Commission of the Parliament and was close to Benazir Bhutto. In addition, we have seen that the Dar ul-Ulum Haqqaniyah Madrasa led by Maulana Sami ul-Haq (leader of a splinter group of the Jamiyat i-Ulama e-Islam since 1986) has provided hundreds of recruits for the Afghan *jihad*. On the contrary, the Jamaat i-Islami supported the Hizb-i-Islami throughout the war and did not transfer its support to the Taliban.[34] Yet, there have been contacts between Taliban leaders and the Amir of the Jamaat-i-Islami, ʻQazi Husein Ahmed, who proposed a peace mission between Iran and Afghanistan. The Jamaat i-Islami, which was close to the Hizb-i-Islami, now seems to be seeking a rapprochement with the Taliban. The Ahl e-Hadith also have a rather distant relationship with the Taliban and they refuse to consider their fight as *jihad*. The Jamiat i-Ahl e-Hadith (Pakistani and Afghan wings) have made occassional official statements regretting the presence of the Taliban on the frontline.[35]

Fundamentalist groups have also established training camps for the Kashmiri Mujahideen in Afghanistan. The military wing of the Jamaat-i-Islami, the Hizbul Mujahideen, the Harkat ul-Ansar (also known as Harkat ul-Mujahideen), and other transnational groups such as bin Laden's Al-Qaida, are cases in point. For example, the Salman Farsi camp in Jawad (near the Pakistani border) was initially a Hizbul Mujahideen camp; then the militants of this organization were expelled by the Taliban and some were arrested by the Pakistani authorities. Later, the camp was used by the Harkat ul-Ansar, under the leadership of Mawlawi Jabbar in Afghanistan and Qari Fazlur Rahman Khalil in Pakistan. The militants were mostly from Punjab, who had received military training from one to six months.[36] Another camp in Darwanta, near Jalalabad, initially opened by Hekmatyar for Arab militants and which closed down after the fall of Jalalabad in September 1996, was also used by the Harkat ul-Ansar.

But the origin and the evolution of fundamentalist movements in Pakistan is clearly independent of the Afghan crisis, even if the policy of developing the network of *madrasas* is an offshoot of the Afghan war. The sectarian violence is not the result of the Afghan war nor a by-product of the emergence of the Taliban. For example, the Sipah e-Sahaba (Anjuman Sipah e-Sahaba Party), which was created in 1989 under the leadership of Maulana Azam Tariq Shias is most probably a result of the instrumentalization of Islam by the Pakistani government under Zia ul-Haq, even if the militants fought in Afghanistan, especially in the battle at Mazar-i Sharif where they massacred hundreds of Shi'ite Hazara people.

The Taliban and the Pakistani State

The long-term goals of Pakistan have remained more or less unchanged since the beginning of the war: to establish a protectorate state in Kabul to prevent the return of the traditional alliance between Afghanistan and India, and then to open Central Asia to Pakistani influence. The political dimension of the Afghan affairs was supervised by the military and the ISI, the diplomatic level by the Ministry of Foreign Affairs and the refugees by the Commissioner for Afghan Refugees.

The Pakistani strategy vis-à-vis Afghanistan, therefore, does not depend upon the political colour of the government. The initial support for the Taliban was provided by the government of Benazir Bhutto. The replacement of Benazir Bhutto by Nawaz Sharif did not signal any noticeable change in the Afghan policy. In fact, the Taliban was the cornerstone of Nawaz Sharif's policy in Afghanistan. Yet, all political bodies and institutions in Pakistan have not uniformly endorsed the Taliban. The Foreign Ministry and the ISI (which is Pakhtun-dominated) played a key role in developing support for the Taliban, in spite of the more balanced view of Nawaz Sharif and Army Chief of Staff Gen. Jahangir Karamat (both Punjabis).

Pakistani help to the Taliban is well documented, and the creation of the Taliban military force has obviously been made possible by the massive support of the ISI.[37] The point here is not to single out Pakistan for helping an Afghan faction, but to note that Pakistan's support was much broader and more effective than that of India or Russia for Massud or that of Iran for the Hizb-i Wahdat. Pakistani officers have fought alongside the Taliban on different occasions and Pakistani logistical support has been essential at crucial moments. For example, during the advance of Ismael Khan towards Kandahar in the spring of 1995, the logistical support of Pakistan was decisive, allowing the Taliban to resist and counter-attack successfully. Besides, since the fall of Kabul in 1996, the opponents of the Taliban living in the NWFP are under constant threat of assassination.[38] In 1999, the murder of Karzay in Quetta coincided with a new thrust by the royalists to push for a diplomatic solution. But the Taliban is by no means a puppet of the ISI. For instance, the premature move to take Herat in the spring of 1995 was made against the will of ISI officers.

The emergence of the Taliban is, in itself, a by-product of the Pakistani policy towards Afghanistan. In 1992, the Director of the ISI, Lt. Gen. Naved Nasir (appointed by Nawaz Sharif) supported Hekmatyar. The failure of the Hizb-e-Islami to take Kabul was also the failure of the ISI. After Nawaz Sharif's dismissal by President Ghulam Ishaq Khan in 1993, Gen. Nasir was also eased out in July as were dozens of Pakistani officers of the ISI. The new Director of the ISI, Lt. Gen. Javed Ashraf Ghani, was then under the authority of Gen. Naseerullah Babar, the Minister of Interior in Benazir Bhutto's Government and the special adviser to her father on Afghan affairs in the 1970s. Babar's policy towards Afghanistan was not very clear in the beginning. On 30 April 1994, he gave an interview to the *Frontier Post* in which he spoke in favour of the return of King Zahir Shah. But his main objective was the opening of a road towards Turkmenistan and Central Asia. In September 1994, Naseerullah Babar and Ismael Khan jointly inaugurated a new consulate in Herat. The Taliban militia was originally organized to ensure the security of the road and the free movement of the convoys between Quetta and Ashkabad. The Taliban launched its first military operation inside Afghanistan when it helped release a Pakistani convoy captured by the local commanders in November 1994. The convoy had been organized by the Pakistani National Logistic Cell. The surprising success of the Taliban provided a new opportunity to the Pakistani Government to prop up a pro-Pakistan government in Kabul.

PAKISTAN'S AFGHAN POLICY IN THE REGIONAL CONTEXT

The Taliban has its own agenda in foreign policy. Initially, it had revolutionary overtones and therefore resembled, in some respects, the agenda of the Iranian regime immediately after 1979. In particular, the Taliban was engaged in a confrontation with the Central Asian States and Iran. It still is. The Taliban has political ambitions directed against the post-Communist regimes that were established after the collapse of the USSR. Therefore, the Tajik civil war also has an Afghan dimension. About 40,000 Tajik refugees who entered Afghanistan were in part, under the control of different Afghan political parties (in Kunduz). The help that these parties provided to the Tajik refugees was not on an ethnic basis, as we see from the fact that Pakhtun-dominated parties like Ettehad or Hizb-i-Islami were the most important donors. Since the Taliban has been in control of the Kunduz province, it has helped Tajik refugees by providing arms and volunteers to fight in the name of *jihad*.[39] It is, of course, difficult to assess the number of Afghan Mujahideen in Tajikistan, but they probably number around a few hundred. In Central Asia, the Taliban is commonly seen as a major factor of destabilization.

Difficulties have also arisen in the relationship of the Taliban with Iran. It is important to note here that the two regimes are fundamentally different and have no ideological affinities whatever.[40] The killing of Iranian diplomats during the fall of Mazar-i Sharif was the most direct cause of tension. The build-up of a military force on the Afghan border led some observers to believe that Iran was on the verge of launching an attack on Afghanistan.

But the Taliban is also seeking the recognition of the international community for political and economic reasons. This trend seems more pronounced since at least the fall of Mazar-i Sharif in 1998, but the bin Laden affair has prevented it from making any progress in that direction. The missile attack of 20 August 1998 on alleged terrorist bases in Zhawar (Paktia) may have marked a turning point in the US policy towards Afghanistan. The US has ruled out any kind of dialogue with the Taliban since they have refused to act against Osama bin Laden. On 22 September the Taliban officially announced that it was closing the Osama bin Laden case because the US administration had failed to provide any evidence showing his involvement in terrorist activities. The Taliban has paid a high diplomatic price (in so far as it has been unable to get the US to grant it recognotion) and an economic one as well (no oil and gas pipeline from Central Asia) because of this affair. On the other hand, Saudi Arabia (one of the three States, with Pakistan and the United Arabs Emirates, which have recognized the Taliban Government) expelled the Taliban diplomatic representative on 22 September in reprisal for the Taliban's continued harbouring of Osama bin Laden. Saudi Arabia is also said to have reduced its aid to the Taliban and has initiated a rapprochement with Iran. In September

1998, Teheran asked for help from Riyadh to obtain the liberation of its diplomats in Afghanistan, and during this period Saudi newspapers were frequently critical of the Taliban. They remained neutral in the last crisis between Afghanistan and Iran.

The attitude of the Taliban towards human rights has also led to a series of confrontations with NGOs and UN agencies till, in July 1998, after unacceptable conditions had been imposed by the Taliban, most of the NGOs left Kabul. (They gradually began to return in 1999.) Afghanistan, under the Taliban is now a 'rogue State', defined as outside the set of the norms of behaviour acceptable by the international community (mostly the Western States). The relationship with Pakistan is, therefore, of great importance for the Taliban to avoid complete isolation on the regional scene.

The consequences of Pakistan's Afghan policy are such that we can wonder if they are really consistent with the official goals of Pakistan's foreign policy. More specifically, there are some contradictions in Pakistan's Central Asia policy. While Afghanistan is seen as a gateway to Central Asia, the support for the Taliban is inhibiting all forms of cooperation with the former Communist regimes, which are dominated by governments all extremely worried about destabilization by the fundamentalists. In others words, the new regime in Kabul is an obstacle to Pakistani projects in Central Asia. On the whole, the relationship between Central Asian countries and Pakistan has deteriorated because of Pakistani support to the Taliban.

Following the inroads of the Taliban in the north, Ministers of Defence from Central Asia met in Tashkent and Moscow to strengthen the security system on the Amu Darya. After the fall of Kabul in September 1996, Central Asian countries and Russia had already organized a meeting on security issues. During the ECO meeting in May 1997, Pakistan was accused of destabilizing Central Asia through the Taliban. The 1999 offensive provoked a new surge of protestations from regional powers and the UNO, against Pakistan as well as the Taliban. The presence of Afghans in Tajikistan fighting alongside local Islamists has been a source of constant worry in Central Asia.

On the commercial level, Iran is offering a way to bypass Afghanistan. The construction of a railway line from Turkmenistan to Iran is a case in point. Besides, Pakistan does not have the means to rebuild the Afghan infrastructure. For the almost six years that the Taliban has been in control of Kandahar, Pakistan has not been able to fund the building of a new road to Quetta.

Pakistan's relationship with the United States has been affected by its support to the Taliban and the bombing of Afghanistan was also, to a certain extent, a signal to the Pakistani Government. The diplomatic cost of its Afghan policy is, therefore, very high for Pakistan.

CONCLUSION

It is clear that the 1999 military coup has not changed the Afghan policy of Pakistan. The fact is that Pakistan has no alternative policy now. The defeat of the Taliban in the north would begin a new phase of disorder since Massud does not really offer a political alternative in Afghanistan, and his alliance with the former Communist militia and Shias would be short-lived even if it materialized. More disorder on its Afghan border is in no way a desirable state of affairs for any Pakistani Government.

There is no likelihood of the 'Talibanization' of Pakistan since the success of the Taliban movement has been the result of many different factors, notably the predominance of rural masses and poor social differentiation. The situation in Pakistan is quite different and the Taliban's impact on Pakistani politics will probably be limited. The Taliban runs training camps for fundamentalist organizations fighting in Kashmir or against the United States. To change this complex relationship with Afghanistan would need a profound modification in the foreign and domestic policies of Pakistan.

NOTES

1. For a general presentation of the war, see Gilles Dorronsoro, *La Rèvolution Afghane*, Paris: Karthala, 2000.
2. Charles Lindholm, *Frontier Perspectives: Essays in Comparative Anthropology*, Oxford: Oxford University Press, 1996.
3. Olivier Roy, 'Has Islamism a Future in Afghanistan?', in William Maley, ed., *Fundamentalism Reborn? Afghanistan and the Taliban*, London: C. Hurst, 1998.
4. David B. Edwards, 'Charismatic Leadership and Political Process in Afghanistan', *Central Asian Survey*, vol. 5, 1986, pp. 3-4.
5. Pierre Centlivres, 'Le Mouvement Taliban et la Condition Feminine', *Afghanistan Info*, March 1999.
6. Asta Olesen, *Islam and Politics in Afghanistan*, London: Curzon Press, 1995.
7. Despite the efforts of the State to develop a network of governmental *madrasas*, the State-educated ulema were a minority before the war, and part of them became Islamists.
8. M.N. Shahrani, 'Causes and Context of Differential Reactions in Badakhshan to the Saur Revolution', in M.N. Sharani and R.L. Canfield, eds., *Revolutions*

and *Rebellions in Afghanistan*, Berkeley: Institute of International Studies, 1984, p. 152.

9. Louis Duprèe, 'Comparative Profiles of Recent Parliaments in Afghanistan', *American Universities Field Staff Report*, vol. XV, no. 4, 1971.

10. See Leon Poullada, *Reform and Rebellion in Afghanistan, 1919-1929: King Amanullah's Failure to Transform a Tribal Society*, Ithaca: Cornell University Press, 1973.

11. A family of Naqshbandi pirs established in Afghanistan at the beginning of the nineteenth century, descendant of the Shaikh Ahmad Sirhindi [Kabul (1564) to Shihind (1624)].

12. A family of *pirs* from the Qaderi Sufi order which settled in Afghanistan in 1905.

13. See Mariam Abou Zahab, 'Les Liens des Taliban avec l'Histoire Afghane', *Les Nouvelles d'Afghanistan*, 85, 2nd trimester, 1999.

14. Ahmad Qeyamuddin, *The Wahhabi Movement in India*, Delhi, 1994. The Afghans were the most numerous group of foreign students in Deoband at the end of the nineteenth century: see Barbara Metcalf, *Islamic Revival in British India: Deoband, 1860-1900*, Princeton: Princeton University Press, 1982, p. 111.

15. Frederik de Jong and Bernd Radtke, eds., *Islamic Mysticism Contested: Thirteen Centuries of Controversies and Polemics*, Leiden: Brill, 1999.

16. Mawlawi B. Rabbâni was also elected Amir al-mominin, but his main source of legitimation was his appointment by a political *shura*.

17. Peter Marsden, *The Taliban: War, Religion and the New Order in Afghanistan*, London: Zed Books, 1998.

18. Hasan Kakar, 'The Fall of the Afghan Monarchy in 1973', *International Journal of the Middle East Studies*, vol. 9, no. 2, pp. 195-214.

19. The Loya Jirga is the Great or National Council, the highest organ of State power. The Loya Jirga was composed of tribal chiefs, members of the royal family and religious elders (plus elected members of the Senate and National Assembly after the Constitution of 1964). See Ludwig W. Adamec, *Historical Dictionary of Afghanistan*, London: The Scarecrow Press, 1991, p. 150.

20. Personal communication from Pierre Centlivres, March 1999.

21. The Taliban like to point out the non-Pakhtun members of their movement, for example, Gaysuddin Agha, member of the *shura* in Kabul and native from Badakhshan.

22. David B. Edwards, 'The Evolution of Shi'i Political Dissent in Afghanistan', in J.R.I. Cole and N.R. Keddie, eds., *Shi'ism and Social Protest*, New Haven: Yale University Press, 1986.

23. Jamal Malik, op. cit., p. 178.

24. *News International*, 28 May 1997.

25. *Herald*, December 1997.

26. Certain *madrasas* however refuse *zakat* to safeguard their independence.

27. *News International*, 25 June 1999.

28. Jamal Malik, op. cit., p. 206.
29. Jamal Malik, op. cit., p. 207.
30. Kamal Matinuddin, *The Afghan Phenomenon: Afghanistan 1994-1997*, Karachi, Oxford: Oxford University Press, 1999, p. 17.
31. The Maulana Nur Mohammad Saqib Madrasa in Kacha Garhi Camp, Zia-ul-Madrasa in Peshawar, Hashmia Madrasa in Bara, Dar-ul-Ulum Haqqaniyah in Akora Khattak, etc.; see *News International*, 11 December 1994.
32. Owais Tohid, *Herald*, December 1997.
33. Recently, 'Osama' has become a very popular name in the NWFP for the new-born *Khaleej Times Friday* (9 July 1999).
34. Qazi Husain Ahmad, the current leader of the Jamaat-i-Islami, was the middleman between the Mujahideen and the Pakistani Government. He once said, 'The Afghan case stands as the only tangible victory for Islam' (Seyyed Vali Reza Nasr, *Mawdudi and the Making of Islamic Revivalism*, Curzon Press, 1996, p. 75).
35. *Dawn*, 9 July 1997.
36. *News International*, 23 August 1998.
37. Ahmed Rashid, 'Pakistan and Taliban', in William Maley, ed., *Fundamentalism Reborn? Afghanistan and the Taliban*, London: C. Hurst, 1998.
38. *State and Human Rights in 1988*, p. 293.
39. The author interviewed Taliban Mujahideen who came from Tajikistan in January 1997. Interview in Ghazni province, January 1997.
40. Besides the fact that the two countries are respectively Sunni and Shia, the Iranian revolution was not essentially the product of the mobilization of the ulema: see Farhad Khosrokhavar, *L'Utopie Sacrifiée: Sociologie de la Révolution Iranienne*, Paris: Presses de la Fondation Nationale des Sciences Politiques, 1993.

REFERENCES

Adamec, Ludwig W., *Historical Dictionary of Afghanistan*, London: The Scarecrow Press, 1991.
Ahmad, Qeyamuddin, *The Wahhabi Movement in India*, Delhi: Manohar, 1994.
Ahmad, Qazi Hussein, *Pakistan and the Afghan Crisis*, Islamabad: Institute of Policy Studies, 1986.
Akram, Assem, *Histoire de la Guerre d'Afghanistan*, Balland, 1996.
Amin, A. Rasul, *Afghanistan Through a Critical Phase of History*, WUFA, 1996.
————, *Afghanistan: Grave Abuses in the Name of Religion*, AI Index: ASA, 11 December 1996.
Amnesty International, *Afghanistan: Report of Mass Graves of Taliban Militia*, AI Index: ASA, 11 November 1997.
Arif, General K.M., *Working with Zia*, Oxford: Oxford University Press, 1995.
Burdelein, Claude et al., *Report of the DHA Mission to Afghanistan*, UN, unpublished, 1997.

Centlivres, Piérre, 'Le Mouvement Taliban et la Condition Féminine', *Afghanistan Info*, March 1999.

Dorronsoro, Gilles, 'L'Économie de Guerre en Afghanistan', in *Les économies de Guerre*, ed. Jean-Christophe Rufin and François Jean, Hachette, 1996.

——, 'Désordre et Crise du Politique: Le Cas des Taliban en Afghanistan', *Cultures et Conflits*, April 1997.

——, 'Les Oulémas en Politique: Le Cas Afghan', *Revue des Sciences Sociales des Religions*, 1999.

Dorronsoro, Gilles, *La révolution afghane*, Paris, Karthala, 2000.

Duprée, Louis, 'Comparative Profiles of Recent Parliaments in Afghanistan', *American Universities Field Staff Report*, vol. XV, no. 4, 1971.

Edwards, David B., 'Charismatic Leadership and Political Process in Afghanistan', *Central Asian Survey*, vol. 5, nos. 3-4, 1986.

——, 'The Evolution of Shia Political Dissent in Afghanistan', in J.R.I. Cole and N.R. Keddie, eds., *Shi'ism and Social Protest*, New Haven: Yale University Press, 1986.

English, Richard, 'The Economic Impact of Afghan Refugee Settlement on the Tribal Areas of Northwest Pakistan', UNHCR, unpublished, 1989.

Foley, Paul, 'Hejrat: The Migration of Afghan Refugees to Pakistan, 1978-1991', unpublished Ph.D. thesis, University of Hawai, 1991.

Ghaus, Aisha, et al., *Provincial Governments and the Social Sectors in Pakistan*, Lahore: Vanguard Books, 1997.

Gilani, Ijaz S., *The Four 'R' of Afghanistan: A Study of Pak-Afghan Relations and their Impact on Foreign Policy Attitudes in Pakistan*, Islamabad: Institude of Strategic Studies, 1984.

Grare, Frédéric, *Le Pakistan Face au Cenflit Afghan (1979-1985): Au Tournant de la Guerre Froide*, Paris: L'Harmattan, 1997.

Human Rights Commission of Pakistan, *State of Human Rights in 1998*, Lahore, 1999.

Hussain, Fakir, 'Status of Women in NWFP', USAID, unpublished report, 1992.

Jalazai, Musa Khan, *The Sunni-Shia Conflict in Pakistan*, Lahore: Book Traders, 1998.

de Jong, Frederik and Radtke Bernd, eds., *Islamic Mysticism Contested: Thirteen Centuries of Controversies and Polemics*, Leiden: Brill, 1999.

Kakar, Hasan, 'The Fall of the Afghan Monarchy in 1973', *International Journal of the Middle East Studies*, vol. 9, no. 2, pp. 195-214.

Keiser, Lincoln, *Organized Vengeance in a Kohistani Community*, Holt, Rinehart and Winston.

Khosrokhavar, Farhad, *L'Utopie Sacrifiée: Sociologie de la Révolution Iraniènne*, Paris: Presses de la Fondation Nationale des Sciences Politiques, 1993.

Lindholm, Charles, *Frontier Perspectives: Essays in Comparative Anthropology*, Oxford: Oxford University Press, 1996.

Mahmood, Sohail, *Islamic Fundamentalism in Pakistan, Egypt and Iran*, Lahore: Vanguard Books, 1995.

Maley, William, ed., *Fundamentalism Reborn? Afghanistan and the Taliban*, London: C. Hurst, 1998.

Malik, Jamal, *Colonization of Islam: Dissolution of Traditional Institutions in Pakistan*, Delhi and Lahore: Manohar and Vanguard Books, 1996.

Marsden, Peter, *The Taliban: War, Religion and the New Order in Afghanistan*, London: Zed Books, 1998.

Matinuddin, Kamal, *The Afghan Phenomenon: Afghanistan 1994-97*, Karachi, Oxford: Oxford University Press, 1999.

Metcalf, Barbara, *Islamic Revival in British India: Deoband, 1860-1900*, Princeton: Princeton University Press, 1982.

Moshref, Rameen, *The Taliban*, The Afghan Forum, Occasional Paper no. 35, 1997.

Nasr, Seyyed Vali Reza, *Mawdudi and the Making of Islamic Revivalism*, Oxford: Oxford University Press, 1996.

Olesen, Asta, *Islam and Politics in Afghanistan*, London: Curzon Press, 1995.

Physicians for Human Rights, 'The Taliban's War on Women: A Health and Human Crisis in Afghanistan', Boston, unpublished, 1998.

Poullada, Leon, *Reform and Rebellion in Afghanistan, 1919-1929: King Amanullah's Failure to Transform a Tribal Society*, Ithaca: Cornell University Press, 1973.

Rittenberg, S.A., *Ethnicity, Nationalism and the Pakhtuns: The Independence Movement in India's North-West Frontier Province*, Durham, NC: Carolina Academic Press, 1998.

Robert, R. Nathan Associates, 'Profile of Private Cross-Border Trade Between Afghanistan and Pakistan', unpublished, 1989.

Rubin, Barnett R., *From Buffer State to Failed State*, New Haven and London: Yale University Press, 1995.

———, *Testimony on the Situation in Afghanistan*, United States Senate Committee on Foreign Relations, 8 October 1998.

———, 'Women and Pipelines: Afghanistan's Proxy War', *International Affairs*, vol. 73, no. 2, pp. 283-96.

Schetter, Conrad von, 'Pashtunischer Ethnozentrismus oder einigender Islam?', *Blatter fur Deutsche un Internationale Politik*, October 1997.

Shahrani, M.N., 'Causes and Context of Differential Reactions in Badakhshan to the Saur Revolution', in M.N. Sharani and R.L. Canfield, eds., *Revolutions and Rebellions in Afghanistan*, Berkeley: Institute of International Studies, 1984, p. 152.

Scofield, Victoria, ed., *Old Roads, New Highways: Fifty Years of Pakistan*, Karachi: Oxford University Press, 1997.

Shah, Syed Waqsar Ali, *Muslim League in NWFP*, Karachi: Royal Book Company, 1992.

The Economist Intelligence Unit, *Pakistan, Afghanistan*, 2nd quarter 1999, Country Report, 1999.

Tirmazi, Syed A.I., *Profiles of Intelligence*, Lahore: Intikhab-e-Jadeed Press, 1995.

8

The Islamic Dimensions of the Kashmir Insurgency

SUMIT GANGULY

$\mathcal{S}$ INCE 1989, THE Indian-controlled portion of Kashmir has been caught in the throes of an ethno-religious, secessionist insurgency. The origins of this insurgency are indigenous. However, Pakistan's involvement in the insurgency has expanded its scope, increased its intensity and prolonged its duration. In this uprising, more than 25,000 individuals have lost their lives since its outbreak. It has also dramatically strained Indo–Pakistani relations. Most recently, in May-June 1999, the two often antagonistic States again teetered on the brink of a full-scale war in Kashmir. This conflict, coming in the aftermath of the Indian and Pakistani nuclear tests of May 1998, also set off alarms about the dangers of escalation to the nuclear level.

A set of precipitate Pakistani actions coupled with India's initial failure to anticipate and promptly react to them contributed to the crisis. Specifically, Pakistan embarked upon a full-scale infiltration of insurgents across the Line of Control (LoC) at Dras, Kargil and Batalik in an effort to jump-start the flagging insurgency in Kashmir. Once the Indian military forces belatedly stumbled upon the Pakistan-backed infiltrators, they reacted with extraordinary vigour and even resorted to the use of air power.[1] By July 1999, the vast majority of the intruders had been evicted and the Indian forces had recaptured the lost territory and the strategic salients. Since the incursion of May-June 1999, the insurgency in Kashmir, which had ebbed significantly, has again shown signs of recrudescence.[2]

The insurgency has a distinctively Islamic component. At one level, Islam has been used instrumentally to advance State interests. To this end, Pakistani decision-makers, sensing an Indian window of vulnerability in Kashmir, have sought to exploit a notion of Muslim confraternity to support the insurgents.[3] On the other hand, Islam has also been used as a vehicle to mobilize a disaffected population and challenge the writ of the Indian State in Kashmir. This component of the insurgency is largely indigenous. However, over the last five years, outsiders, known as 'Mehmaan Mujahideen' ('guest militants') have entered the fray. Most of them are little more than mere condotierri. Their antecedents can be traced to States where political order has mostly collapsed, such as Sudan and Afghanistan. The Afghan Mujahideen, in particular, are battle-hardened zealots having previously fought the Soviets for the better part of a decade.[4] This paper will trace the origins of the two strands of Islamic assertion and discuss their role in fomenting and sustaining the Kashmir insurgency.

The (not only) Islamic Origins of the Insurgency

The incident that is widely seen as signalling the onset of the insurgency was the kidnapping of Rubaiya Sayeed, the daughter of then India's Union Home Minister, Mufti Mohammed Sayeed, in December 1989. Her kidnappers were not Islamic zealots but members of one wing of the Jammu and Kashmir Liberation Front (JKLF), the oldest, notionally secular, anti-Indian organization in the state of Jammu & Kashmir. Within weeks of the kidnapping, a variety of insurgent groups proceeded to wreak havoc throughout the Valley. Interestingly enough, divisions also quickly surfaced amongst the various insurgent groups. Few of these divisions, however, were as vicious as the one between the pro-Independence JKLF and the Pakistan-backed Hizbul Mujahideen (HUM). The HUM, which seeks merger with Pakistan, had little use for the JKLF's anti Indian but pro-independence stance. Furthermore, the HUM, unlike the JKLF, made no pretensions of having any concern for the nested Hindu minority in the Valley. Their interest in merging Kashmir with Pakistan stemmed from the latter's Islamic credentials. While the JKLF–HUM feud ensued, a number of other groups entered the fray, many also professing solid Islamic antecedents. The vast majority of these groups found both moral and material support from Pakistan.

To understand the Islamic dimensions of the insurgency, it is important to trace its origins. The insurgency, polemical accounts notwithstanding, does not amount to the sudden emergence of radical Islamic fervour in Kashmir.[5] Nor is it entirely the product of Pakistani machinations against India.

Its origins must be traced to the process of dramatic political mobilization and simultaneous institutional decay in Kashmir.[6] In attempts·to win the 'hearts and minds' of Kashmir's Muslim-majority population, various regimes in New Delhi lavished government resources upon the state. In the process they not only promoted a degree of economic development but also transformed the educational and communications infrastructure of the state.[7] These transformations contributed to the genesis of a new generation of Kashmiris who were far more politically conscious, sophisticated and knowledgeable than their forebears. Simultaneously, New Delhi pursued a strategy which tolerated deceitful and duplicitous electoral practices on the part of the principal political party, the National Conference. As long as the National Conference and its leaders did not raise the secessionist bogey, New Delhi ignored its malfeasant behaviour in the state. The immediate post-Independence generation of Kashmiris who lacked political awareness grudgingly tolerated the chicanery of the National Conference. Subsequent generations, specially that of the 1980s, proved to be quite different. Once they had the experience of two largely free and fair elections, in 1977 and 1983, they proved unwilling to countenance any efforts on the part of a regime in New Delhi to turn back the electoral clock. With few avenues available for expressing dissent, they resorted to violence.[8] However, Pakistan's systematic support to selected insurgent groups expanded and prolonged the scope, duration and intensity of the insurgency.

To understand these two closely interlinked processes, it may be useful to clarify Kashmir's special status and position within the Indian Union. Kashmir was, and remains, the only Muslim-majority state in India. In the years immediately after India's independence from the collapse of the British Indian empire, India sought to hold on to Kashmir to demonstrate its secular credentials. Since the founding of the Indian State was based upon civic nationalism, it was important for India to publicly demonstrate that a Muslim-majority region could live without fear under the aegis of her secular constitutional dispensation. For Pakistan, it was equally important to control Kashmir to bolster its self-image as a homeland for the Muslims of South Asia. Over the last several decades, India and Pakistan have both fallen short of the original, pristine principles that guided their founding.

Pakistan's failure to act as a guarantor of Muslim rights in the sub-continent came as early as 1971 when the Bengali population of East Pakistan rebelled. With Indian assistance, they successfully defeated the Pakistan Army and formed the new State of Bangladesh.[9] Two important consequences ensued from the break-up of Pakistan. At one level, its collapse demonstrated the falsity of the proposition that the Muslims of South Asia ever constituted a single, monolithic, primordial nation.[10] Logically, it also followed that the Pakistani irredentist claim to Kashmir was chimerical. If Islam alone could not be the basis of national cohesion, what claim did Pakistan have on its coreligionists in Kashmir?[11]

India's claim to Kashmir on the basis of its secular foundations also started to weaken in the 1980s. The rise of communal discord within India, the failure of various regimes to neutrally suppress such disturbances, and the resort to sectarian appeals in electoral contexts corroded India's commitment to and practice of secularism. By the late 1980s, it was hard to sustain the argument that Kashmir remained emblematic of India's secular status and credentials. Consequently, in the context of the 1990s, both India and Pakistan seek to hold on to Kashmir from the imperatives of statecraft and little else.[12] Simply put, States do not willingly and easily part with territory that they deem to be their own. More to the point, India (which has had to deal with its share of secessionist movements in the post-Independence era) also fears an internal 'domino effect'. If Kashmir is allowed to secede from the Indian Union, other disaffected states may be encouraged to follow suit. Pakistan, on the other hand, seeks to dislodge India from Kashmir to avenge the latter's role in the creation of Bangladesh and the break-up of Pakistan in 1971.

Despite the professed ideological commitments of both sides, from the outset neither State was able to live up to its lofty ideals. In Pakistan, sectarian and ethnic conflicts arose over the status of refugees from India, questions of federal power sharing and the adoption of a national language.[13] In India, the Hindu right-wing exemplified by the Bharatiya Jana Sangh remained unreconciled to the concept of a Secular State.[14] Its principal leaders saw little reason to grant Kashmir any special dispensation within the context of the Indian Constitution despite its predominantly Muslim population and the unique circumstances of its accession to India.

HISTORICAL BACKGROUND

Unlike other regions of South Asia, for the most part, Islam had come to Kashmir not as a conquering force. Instead, members of the mystic Sufi sect had first introduced Islam into Kashmir in the fourteenth century AD.[15] Subsequently, Kashmir had been under the control of various Muslim regimes centred in Delhi. In the waning days of the Mughal empire, the region passed into the hands of Maharaja Gulab

Singh, a Rajput Dogra, thanks to the assistance that he had rendered the British in one of their battles with Afghanistan.

The last ruler of Kashmir, a Dogra, was Maharaja Hari Singh, a rather ineffectual and authoritarian ruler. In the 1930s as the Indian and Pakistani nationalist movements gathered force, opposition to the Maharaja's rule started to emerge in Kashmir. Initially, the opposition was strictly along sectarian lines. The principal challenger were Sheikh Mohammed Abdullah, a former school teacher, Mirwaiz Yusuf Shah, a major religious figure of Kashmir, and Ghulam Abbas, prominent Muslim Kashmiri political activist.

Initially, Abdullah helped create a political party which reflected its Muslim antecedents. It was known as the All Jammu and Kashmir Muslim Conference. In the late 1930s, Abdullah, unlike his two other colleagues, came under the influence of the Indian nationalist leader of Kashmiri lineage, Pandit Jawaharlal Nehru. Nehru's socialist and secular views impressed Abdullah. As a consequence of this intellectual interaction, Abdullah embraced secular politics and also adopted a socialist-leaning economic platform. His association with the Indian secular Indian nationalists contributed to a rift with his more sectarian colleagues leading to a schism in the ranks of the National Conference. In June 1939, Abdullah, with the support of his Lieutenants Mirza Afzal Beg, Mohammad Syed Masoodi, Bakshi Ghulam Mohammed, G.M. Sadiq and others, changed the name and the underlying ideology of the party. From now on the party adopted an explicitly secular outlook and became known as the Jammu and Kashmir National Conference.[16] The Mirwaiz, at this juncture, became openly hostile to Abdullah and sought to boost the narrow interests of religious Muslims in the state. After Partition and the accession of Kashmir to India, he went over to Pakistan.

Shortly after the accession of Jammu & Kashmir to India, Sheikh Abdullah and the National Conference emerged as the two most powerful political forces in the state. Even before a constitution was written for Jammu and Kashmir and an assembly convened, Abdullah moved with speed and dexterity to pass two critical reforms. Specifically, he had passed the Abolition of Big Landed Estates Act and the Distressed Debtors Relief Act. Both of these Acts were designed to consolidate his position with the impoverished, predominantly Muslim peasantry of Jammu & Kashmir. These two pieces of legislation had the effect of ending landlordism in the state and provided considerable relief to the predominantly Muslim peasantry.[17]

The first stirrings of discontent with a distinct Islamic overlay emerged during the Hazratbal incident in December 1963. Owing to the peculiar features of Kashmiri Islam, the vast majority of Kashmiri Muslims revere the *moe-e-moeqaddas*, believed to be a hair of the Prophet Muhammad, which is kept in a sanctuary in the Hazratbal mosque in Srinagar. In December, some miscreants broke into the mosque and stole the relic. As word of this incident spread, widespread public protests and some rioting broke out throughout Kashmir Valley. Many of these protests had an anti-Indian component to them. Some of them, no doubt, were spontaneous. Others, however, had been carefully orchestrated. The person most responsible for the organized demonstrations was Maulana Masood Syed Masoodi, a former General Secretary of the National Conference. He organized an Action Committee which was devoted to the recovery of the holy relic. In this endeavour, he was supported by Mirwaiz Mohammed Farooq, whose grandfather Yusuf Shah had clashed with Sheikh Abdullah in the 1930s. After the relic was found, and duly authenticated, the members of the Action Committee turned to another cause, that of the unrealized plebiscite. Their renewed demand for a plebiscite, however, did not find widespread support amongst the populace. In fact, when the Pakistani politico-military leadership, on the basis of a series of dubious inferences, launched a war against India in September 1965 a second time over Kashmir, the vast majority of Kashmiris, their grievances against the Indian state notwithstanding, did not throw in their lot with their Pakistani co-religionists. Instead, they remained loyal to India and did nothing to undermine Indian military operations.[18]

THE RISE OF ISLAMIC SEPARATIST SENTIMENT

Between 1965 and the early 1980s, the Valley remained largely dormant. In fact, the pro-Pakistani forces in the state found themselves increasingly maginalized in the 1970s and the early 1980s. The principal reason for their peripheral position was the return of Sheikh Mohammed Abdullah to the helm in 1975 under the terms of the Baig–Parthasarathy Accord of 1975. Under the terms of the accord, among various other matters, the Sheikh was allowed to return to the state and resume political activity as long as he dispensed with any secessionist agenda.[19] Accordingly, in the 1977 election, Abdullah and the National Conference won an overwhelming and convincing victory. Even after Abdullah's death in 1982, when his son Farooq

Abdullah adopted his father's mantle, the 1983 elections were held without any significant allegations of electoral malfeasances. What then explains the seemingly sudden rise of violent, ethno-religious, secessionist sentiment in the late 1980s? The rise of separatist sentiment in Kashmir is inseparable from the process of political mobilization in the state. In the 1980s, the mobilization took place on religious lines because of three important factors. First, various national governments, most notably the Congress regimes of Indira and subsequently Rajiv Gandhi, showed a contemptuous disregard for electoral probity in Kashmir. They forged dubious electoral alliances and resorted to gross electoral malpractices reducing governments in Jammu & Kashmir to mere puppets of New Delhi. In 1984, for example, Prime Minister Indira Gandhi dismissed Farooq's regime on the most tenuous grounds. Subsequently, in 1986, her son and successor, Rajiv Gandhi, fashioned an ill-conceived electoral alliance with Farooq in an attempt to promote the Congress party in the state. This electoral combine resorted to the most blatant form of electoral fraud in the 1987 assembly elections in an attempt to counter the threat posed by the Muslim United Front, a loose collection of small political parties, opposed to the rule of the National Conference.

A new, politically astute generation of Kashmiris found these practices to be not only abhorrent but intolerable. As a consequence of their disenchantment, they turned their anger against a putative 'Hindu' regime in New Delhi. Their resentment took on this communal dimension because it was apparent that these large-scale electoral malpractices were mostly confined to the state of Jammu & Kashmir, India's only Muslim-majority state. In the minds of the young Kashmiris, they were being discriminated against because of the unique demographic features of their state.

At another level, their grievances took on a sectarian tenor because of the rising graph of communal sentiment, incidents and actions in the Indian polity. During the 1980s, as a consequence of a variety of factors, the belief in and support for secularism in India started to decline precipitously.[20]

Among other matters, politicians started to make blatant communal and sectarian appeals in efforts to bolster electoral fortunes. They resorted to these tactics as they faced a more sophisticated electorate throughout India which no longer appeared willing to vote in purely predictable patterns. As politicians stoked the anxieties of the majority community, Muslims across the country watched with growing misgivings. Some Muslim leaders, in turn, reinforced these fears through demagogic appeals of their own.[21] In effect, Muslim communalism in India and in Kashmir fed on the rise of Hindu fanaticism.

Last, as suggested earlier, a strain of Muslim separatist sentiment had always existed within Kashmir. These individuals and groups who constituted this body of separatist sentiment were now in a position of capitalizing on the first two factors to pursue their goals with renewed vigour. Pakistani decision-makers, aware of their existence, moved with considerable speed to organize, train and arm them, specially as political order started to collapse in the late 1980s.[22]

Who exactly were the participants in the uprising and which groups were most susceptible to influence from Pakistan? The vast majority of the insurgents were young men with a modicum of education. Many of them had found employment scarce and constituted a frustrated class of politically disaffected individuals.[23] Some, in fact, most notably Yasin Malik and Shabir Shah, were polling agents in the disastrously compromised election of 1987. The flawed election proved to be catalytic in precipitating the insurgency two years later.

What were and remain the principal insurgent groups and where did they spring from? The oldest insurgent group, of course, is the notionally secular Jammu and Kashmir Liberation Front. It was founded in the United Kingdom in June 1976 by Amanullah Khan and Maqbool Butt. The lineage of the organization can be traced to the Kashmir National Liberation Front, which was founded by Amanullah, Butt and Hashim Qureshi in the late 1960s. Amanullah continues to operate from Muzaffarabad, Pakistan in 'Azad Kashmir' ('free' or 'liberated' Kashmir). The JKLF (Valley) is an appendage of the parent organization and shares the former's ideological organization. In 1995, the JKLF (Valley) gave up its underground status and joined the All Party Hurriyat Conference, a disparate collection of political parties and groups opposed to the Government of India. Some of its members have a pro-Pakistani orientation while others, like the JKLF, seek an independent and united Kashmir. The release of Yasin Malik from Indian police custody enabled the JKLF to make this transition. Since then, Malik, though still subjected to periodic harassment from Indian authorities, has abjured violence and has focused on civil disobedience. Though the JKLF has no Hindus in its ranks, Malik continues to assert that a secular, independent Kashmir remains the eventual goal of the JKLF.

The JKLF, thanks to its pro-independence and professedly secular stance, has long been at odds with other more explicitly Islamic groups in Kashmir. One of the oldest of such groups is the Jamaat-i-Islami, an organization with a particularly austere vision of Islam.[24] The goal of the Jamaat as outlined by its founder, Maulana Abul Ala Mawdudi, is to create a *nizam-e-mustafa* or a political system guided by the precepts of the Prophet Muhammad. The extraordinary popularity of Sheikh Abdullah had kept the Jamaat at bay in Jammu & Kashmir.[25] After his demise, the Jamaat started to become more vocal and powerful. During this period, a Kashmiri politician, Ali Shah Geelani, emerged as the principal Jamaat leader. The armed wing of the Jamaat is the Jamiat-i-Tulba.[26]

Though the Jamiat-i-Tulba has been at odds with the JKLF, the principal threat to its operatives and activities has been the radical, pro-Pakistani, Hizbul Mujahideen (HUM). The HUM, one of the best funded and organized entities, has not only wreaked havoc within the Valley but has also been suspected of killing JKLF operatives. It is estimated to have 4,000 to 5,000 active members.

The Harkat-ul-Ansar, another pro-Pakistani group, was formed in 1993 through a merger of the Harkat-ul-Jihadi Islami (HUJI) and the Harkat-ul-Mujahideen. This group exceeded the viciousness of the HUM when it precipitated the destruction of Sheikh Nooruddin Noorani's (Nand Rishi) shrine in May 1995 in the town of Charar-e-Sharief. Its principal leader, the self-styled, 'Major' Mast Gul, is believed to have escaped to Pakistan after the confrontation with the Indian security forces at Charar-e-Sharief. In late 1997, probably as a consequence of being listed on the US State Department's annual report as a terrorist organization, the Harkat-ul-Ansar broke up into its original constituent parts. Since their break-up, the Harkat-ul-Mujahideen has been most active in Kashmir.

Another insurgent group, of primarily Afghan composition, is the Al-Faran. The Al-Faran, like the Harkat, has little or no grass-roots support thanks to its foreign composition and its ruthless methods. The Al-Faran was implicated in the brutal slaying of a Norwegian tourist in 1996, Hans Christian Ostro.

Quite apart from these groups which remain solely focused on keeping the Kashmir insurgency alive, another actor has recently entered the fray. This is the Taliban, a militant Islamic organization, based primarily in Afghanistan and in the Western reaches of Pakistan. It was spawned during the Afghan crisis years in the *madrasas* of the North West Frontier Province (NWFP) of Pakistan. Composed of young men, imbued with a form of radical Islamic fervour, they received considerable support from elements within the Pakistani State and from their extra-regional backers, most notably, the conservative Saudi, Wahhabi monarchy. The fond hope of Pakistani decision-makers, specially those in the upper echelons of the military, was that the Taliban could be used as a means for extending Pakistan's reach and influence into Afghanistan in the post-Soviet era. This goal proved to be quite illusory. The Taliban not only refused to serve as a conduit for the pursuit of Pakistani goals in Afghanistan, but became deeply implicated in fomenting sectarian conflicts within Pakistan. In early October of 1999, Prime Minister Nawaz Sharif publicly declared that the Taliban were involved in supporting sectarian violence within Pakistan and called on the Taliban regime to immediately desist from such activities.[27]

The Taliban, of course, have not just extended their activities into Pakistan. In the last few years, they have surfaced in Kashmir and constitute a new and more deadly force within the already-troubled state. In late 1998, they were implicated in a series of attacks on police and paramilitary personnel in Kashmir. They have demonstrated an extraordinary capacity to inflict pain upon the Indian security forces. However, they have failed to win much local sympathy because of their ideological beliefs and practices which are at odds with local religious customs and practices. Despite the communalization of the Kashmir conflict, their intractably austere and reactionary conception of Islam still does not have much resonance in the Valley despite Pakistan's ardent efforts.[28]

The Islamic dimensions of the insurgency were again underscored in late December 1999 with the successful hijacking of an Indian Airlines plane to Kandahar in Afghanistan in December 1999. In order to secure the release of the hostages, India agreed to meet several of the demands of the hijackers. Among these was the release of an incarcerated Pakistani cleric, Masood Azhar.[29] Shortly after his release, Azhar took refuge in Pakistan. Once ensconced in Pakistan, Azhar founded a new organization, the Jaish-e-Muhammad.[30] This group has vowed to wreak havoc throughout Indian-controlled Kashmir.

CONCLUSION

Today, the insurgency in Kashmir has lost much of its initial popular appeal. Several factors account for this sea change in the Valley. At one level, the entry of battle-hardened Islamic zealots, who lack any organic relationship with the Kashmiri Muslim populace has led to a decline in popular support. More to the point, the egregious behaviour of many of these 'Mehmaan Mujahideen', which includes rapine and pillage, also contributed to the loss of local support. At another level, India's well-established counter-insurgency strategy wore down much of the initial resistance. This strategy had three distinct components. It involved using overwhelming force against the militant groups to destroy much of their infrastructure, organization and firepower. Having severely degraded the capabilities of the insurgents, New Delhi successfully turned around some insurgents with the promise of money, employment and social status. These 'counter-insurgents', mostly of Kashmiri Muslim origin, worked in concert with the security forces to hunt down their former comrades-in-arms. The most prominent of these organizations was the Ikhwan-e-Muslimeen headed by Kukka Parray, a former insurgent leader. The third and final component of this strategy was the holding of elections both at national and state levels to improve political legitimacy in the state. The first election since 1989, held in May 1996, as part of the Indian Eleventh National Elections, was marred by allegations of voter coercion. Furthermore, the All Party Hurriyat Conference (APHC), a loose agglomeration of Islamic political parties which are bound by their common dislike of Indian rule, boycotted the election. However, the state assembly elections that were held in September 1996 proved to be of a markedly different order. Dispassionate observers commented that this election demonstrated a willingness of the vast majority of the Kashmiris to return to the ballot box.[31] (The APHC, however, again boycotted these elections.) Farooq Abdullah's National Conference won a substantial victory, gaining 57 out of a possible 87 seats in the State Assembly. It needs to be underscored that in the Valley, the principal locus of the insurgency, the National Conference won 40 out of a possible 44 seats.

Will Islam continue to play a mobilizational role in Kashmir and remain integral to the insurgency? The original, pristine quality of the insurgency has been all but lost. The 'mehmaan Mujahideen' supported by Pakistan and other outside powers have little standing amongst the Kashmiri populace. The most striking demonstration thereof was the ability of the Indian military to act with a free hand along the LOC in the summer of 2000 against the Pakistan-backed infiltrators. Had the local populace been well disposed toward the infiltrators, the Indian military would have encountered much greater difficulty in dislodging the well-armed and well-trained insurgents. Instead, they made quick work of the raiders despite considerable strategic and tactical disadvantages.

As support for their presence and activities have undergone a steady decline, the insurgents have now shifted the locus of their terror to other parts of the state, most notably the regions of Doda, Poonch and Rajouri. Today, more than ever before, they are willing to target fellow Muslims whom they do not deem to be adequately sympathetic to their cause or as loyal to any other entity. Simultaneously, they are targeting Hindu families with the hope of fuelling a possible anti-Muslim backlash in India.[32] The fecklessness of this new tactic underscores Pakistan's renewed failure to exploit the Islamic connection with Kashmir.

That said, much of the Kashmiri Muslim population remains understandably sullen, alienated and distrustful of the national government in New Delhi. Closer to home, the hopes that they had reposed in Farooq Abdullah's regime yet remain to be fulfilled. During the past three years, Farooq's Government has not moved efficaciously to address a range of extant grievances.[33] Simply because the insurgents are at bay does not mean that genuine peace has returned to the Valley.[34]

In late April 2000, the Central Government in New Delhi attempted to start a dialogue with the APHC. Very quickly, the prospects of a dialogue became mired in the divergent rhetorical positions the two sides adopted. The government in New Delhi, quite predictably, insisted that the APHC agree to uphold the territorial integrity of India as a prerequisite for any discussions. The APHC, in turn, issued its own preconditions. They included a categorical refusal to accept India's territorial integrity as a prerequisite for discussions and also an insistence that simultaneous negotiations be conducted with Pakistan.[35] The markedly divergent initial positions of the two sides led to a stalling of the talks. The future of the negotiations remains in abeyance.

NOTES

1. For a scathing indictment of the Indian intelligence failure see Praveen Swami, 'India and Pakistan: An Army Caught Napping', *Frontline*, vol. 16, issue 18, 28 August–10 September 1999 from http://www.the-hindu.com and also see Ishan Joshi, 'Loose Cannons', *Outlook*, 14 June 1999, p. 21.
2. See for example, Kashmir Times News Service, 'Chain of Explosions Rock Rajouri', *Kashmir Times*, 23 September 1999 from http://www.kashmirtimes.com.

3. The Pakistani official position holds that it does not provide the insurgents any material assistance. For evidence of Pakistan's complicity in the insurgency, see Edward Desmond, 'The Insurgency in Kashmir', *Contemporary South Asia*, vol. 4, no. 1, 1995, pp. 5-16.

4. For a discussion of the role of the '*Mehmaan* Mujahideen', see Manoj Joshi, *The Lost Rebellion: Kashmir in the Nineties*, New Delhi: Penguin Books, 1999.

5. For a particularly polemical formulation, see Samuel Huntington, *The Clash of Civilizations and the Remaking of World Order*, New York: Simon and Schuster, 1996.

6. For a statement of this argument see Sumit Ganguly, *The Crisis in Kashmir: Portents of War, Hopes of Peace*, New York: Cambridge University Press and Washington, DC: Woodrow Wilson Center Press, 1999.

7. For evidence to this end, see ibid.

8. It is worth pondering why the Kashmiris did not resort to mass civil disobedience. The answer probably lies in that they lacked a useful model for mass, non-violent civil disobedience. In this context, it needs to be underscored that political mobilization came slowly to Kashmir as in most princely states. The Indian nationalist movement's strategy of mass civil disobedience had been confined to the states of British India. On the role of the princely states during the last days of the British empire, see Ian Copland, *The Princes of India in the Endgame of Empire, 1917-47*, Cambridge: Cambridge University Press, 1997.

9. On the origins of the East Pakistan crisis and the emergence of Bangladesh, see Robert Jackson, *South Asian Crisis*, New York: Praeger, 1975.

10. For a particularly thoughtful critique of this concept, see Mushirul Hasan, 'The Myth of Muslim Unity: Colonial and National Narratives', in Mushirul Hasan, ed., *Legacy of a Divided Nation: India's Muslims since Independence*, Delhi: Oxford University Press, 1997.

11. Sumit Ganguly, *The Origins of War in South Asia: The Indo-Pakistani Conflicts Since 1947*, Boulder: Westview Press, 2nd edn., 1994.

12. Despite the infusion of Sufi beliefs and practices into Kashmir, some Kashmiri Muslim rulers proved to be violently intolerant of their Hindu and even Buddhist subjects. Consequently, some degree of tension did exist amongst the various communities at the onset of the nineteenth century when Kashmir came under Sikh and then Dogra rule. For a discussion of these matters, see the succinct account in Vernon Hewitt, *Reclaiming The Past? The Search for Political and Cultural Unity in Contemporary Kashmir*, London: Portland Books, 1995; for a more detailed and nuanced discussion, see R.K. Parmu, *A History of Muslim Rule in Kashmir*, Delhi: People's Publishing House, 1969.

13. Prem Nath Bazaz, *Kashmir in Crucible*, Delhi: Pamposh Publications, 1967.

14. For a sense of the debate, see Alastair Lamb, *Kashmir: A Disputed Legacy, 1946-1990*, Hertingfordbury: Roxford Books, 1991; *The Birth of A Tragedy: Kashmir*

1947, Hertingfordbury: Roxford Books, 1994 and Prem Shankar Jha, *Kashmir 1947: Rival Versions of History*, Delhi: Oxford University Press, 1996.

15. Lord Mountbatten also ruled that contiguous and predominantly Muslim areas would go to Pakistan. Kashmir posed a special problem because the ruler, Maharaja Hari Singh, was a Hindu, his subjects predominantly Muslim, and the state shared borders with both the nascent states of India and Pakistan. For a first-hand, if Indocentric account, see V.P. Menon, *The Story of the Integration of the Indian States*, Madras: Orient Longman, 1961; for a Pakistani perspective, see Chaudhuri Mohammed Ali, *The Emergence of Pakistan*, New York: Columbia University Press, 1967.

16. For evidence of Pakistan's complicity in the tribal rebellion, see H.V. Hodson, *The Great Divide: Britain-India-Pakistan*, Karachi: Oxford University Press, 1997.

17. For a discussion of Indian military operations in Kashmir, see Maurice Cohen, *Thunder Over Kashmir*, Hyderabad: Orient Longman, 1994.

18. Lars Blinkenberg, *India-Pakistan: The History of Unsolved Conflicts, Volume 1: The Historical Part*, Odense: Odense University Press, 1998.

19. The best discussion of the causes and consequences of the 1965 war remains Russell Brines, *The Indo-Pakistani Conflict*, New York: Pall Mall, 1968.

20. On this point, see the discussion in Ajit Bhattacharjea, *The Wounded Valley*, Delhi: USPBD, 1994.

21. For a discussion of these desecularizing propensities, see Subrata Kumar Mitra, 'Desecularizing the State', in Subrata K. Mitra, ed., *Culture and Rationality: The Politics of Social Change in Post-Colonial India*, Delhi: Sage, 1999.

22. For an analysis of this form of demagogic behaviour and its pernicious consequences in a polyethnic society, see Jack Snyder and Karen Ballentine, 'Nationalism in the Marketplace of Ideas', *International Security*, Fall 1996, vol. 21, no. 2, pp. 5–40.

23. For evidence of Pakistani complicity, see Desmond, op. cit.

24. For a discussion of this issue, see Prem Shankar Jha, 'Frustrated Middle Class: Roots of Kashmir's Alienation', in Asghar Ali Engineer, ed., *Secular Crown on Fire: The Kashmir Problem*, Delhi: Ajanta Publications, 1991.

25. For a particularly thorough treatment of the origins, ideology and organization of the Jamaat, see Syyed Vali Reza Nasr, *The Vanguard of the Islamic Revolution: The Jama'at-i Islami of Pakistan*, Berkeley: University of California Press, 1994.

26. The Sheikh had evolved a dexterous strategy to deal with the Jamaat. He would periodically remind them that if they become too obstreperous, New Delhi would respond with a mailed fist. On the other hand, he would let his interlocutors in New Delhi know that if they failed to back him, the Jamaat would come to the fore. His son and successor, Farooq Abdullah, lacked his father's political acumen and dexterity. It was during his years in office that the Jamaat, with Pakistani and possibly Saudi assistance, gained considerable

ground in Kashmir. Based upon personal communication with senior IAS officers with extensive professional experience in Kashmir, September 1997.

27. Joshi, 1999, pp. 8-12.

28. Sikander Hayat, 'Pakistan asks Taliban to Shut Terrorist Camps', *Frontier Post*, http://frontierpost.com.pk/top1.html

29. On the growth of the Taliban's activities in Kashmir, see Ahmed Rashid, 'The Taliban: Exporting Extremism', *Foreign Affairs*, vol. 78, no. 6, November/December 1999, specially pp. 27-8. For more specific evidence, see Praveen Swami, 'The Tales of a Bloody November', *Frontline*, vol. 15, no. 25, 5-18 December 1998, http://www.the-hindu.com/fline/fl1525/15250360.htm

30. For a critical discussion of the hijacking, see Ranjit Bhushan, 'Heads Don't Roll Here', *Outlook*, 17 January 2000, p. 35.

31. Praveen Swami, 'Of Theology and Terrorism', *Frontline*, 21 January 2000, pp. 14-17.

32. 'Pro-India Party in Kashmir Wins a Landslide Victory in Elections', *New York Times*, 3 October 1996, p. A6.

33. Jonah Blank, 'Kashmir's Crisis Goes Nuclear', *Foreign Affairs*, vol. 78, no. 6, 1999, pp. 1-17.

34. Mukhtar Ahmad, 'Death and Darkness Stalk Valley', *Telegraph*, 19 January 2000. For an excellent account of the sense of alienation that pervades the Valley, see Blank, 1999, op. cit., note 33.

35. Ajit Bhattacharjea, 'Restoring Letter and Spirit', *Outlook*, 1 May 2000 from http://www.outlookindia.com/20000501/affairs4.htm

9

Pakistan and the 'India Syndrome': Between Kashmir and the Nuclear Predicament

JEAN-LUC RACINE

I N MAY 1998, the open nuclearization of South Asia sharpened the wedge in the relations between India and Pakistan. While a number of Anglo–American observers considered the risk of the Kashmir conflict giving rise to a nuclear confrontation as very real, most Indian analysts asked why the principle of deterrence which worked between the USA and the USSR for decades would become less relevant in the South Asian context. Many Pakistani commentators endorsed that view, but Islamabad policy makers were not so unhappy with the dramatization effect: presenting Kashmir as the most sensitive potential nuclear flashpoint was supposed to help them in internationalizing this issue, a major objective of Pakistani foreign policy. While decade of insurgency had not drawn much attention from the global media or from the chancelleries, Kashmir was suddenly loaded with a new significance, and vindicated the arguments of analysts that after the end of the Cold War, regional conflicts would become the most serious factor of geopolitical destabilization, particularly where new nuclear powers were in confrontation. The rapprochement between Pakistan and India, nine months after the tests, illustrated by the joint Lahore Declaration of their Prime Ministers, made people believe that, after all, wisdom would perhaps prevail under the threat of Armageddon. Alas, the military adventure launched by the Pakistan Army at Kargil destroyed this hope in May 1999, and stalled the dialogue being engaged in. In October, the coup bringing Gen. Musharraf to power brought bilateral relations to a new low.

While it is best to refrain from any suggestion of impending catastrophe, the intensity of the Indo–Pakistani feud is obvious to all. The three open wars of 1947-8, 1965 and 1971, and the Kargil episode of 1999, are just its most acute phases. Beyond these, it is to the armed peace that attention needs to be drawn. The two States maintain diplomatic relations. They are members of a joint regional body, the South Asian Association for Regional Cooperation (SAARC). In the 1990s, their Prime Ministers used to meet fairly frequently, more often, it is true, on foreign soil than in their respective countries.[1] However, there is still no direct air link between Islamabad and Delhi, nor any direct shipping service between Karachi and Mumbai (Bombay). Each accuses the other of aggravating local tensions and stirring dissension in its country through its intelligence agencies. India denounces the 'proxy war' conducted by Pakistan in Kashmir, through Islamist militant groups instrumentalized by the Inter-Services Intelligence, the army-controlled ISI. Faced by a spread of murders in Karachi and sectarian killings in Punjab, Pakistan, on a subdued note, points to 'the foreign hand'—the Indian one.

The genesis of this uneasy peace, the lineages of this Cold War in South Asia, go back to an ideological discord prior to the Partition of 1947 which was meant precisely to resolve it. In his historic speech at Lahore on 23 March 1940, Mohammad Ali Jinnah, the Father of the Pakistani nation and its supreme leader (Quaid-i-Azam), who refused the arithmetics advantaging the Hindu majority community within the future independent India, had called for the recognition of a specifically Muslim nation. Once India would be divided into national States, he argued, there would be 'no reason why these States should be antagonistic to each other'. The States spawned by Partition would be able to 'live in complete harmony with their neighbours'.[2] The essence of the paradox of Pakistan lies in this very basic fact: born out of a partition chosen by itself, it appears to have found in independence neither the peace, nor the security, nor the freedom of spirit that would enable it either to live in harmony with India, or to ignore it. It seems impossible for Pakistan to forget India and to get along with it.

This chapter will consider, first, the India syndrome—born out of a fundamental dissymmetry—which afflicts Pakistan, and the major strategy elaborated for getting over the dissymmetry challenge, i.e. the nuclear deterrence policy, which came out in the open in 1998, following the Indian nuclear tests. Turning back to the structural dimension of the Pakistani–Indian feud, section two will analyse how the 'two-nation theory', which gave birth to Pakistan, found, after Independence, enough subjects of controversy for sustaining a culture of mistrust which sets the tune of the mainstream perceptions about

India. Section three will focus attention on the main dispute opposing India and Pakistan: what is called by Islamabad 'the core issue of Kashmir', which has been become more complicated than ever in the 1990s. Section four will present the practice of dialogue which has marked, intermittently, the official and non-official relations between Pakistan and India. The conclusion will suggest that Pakistan needs today to strike a delicate balance between its traditional perceptions, some of them wrong, some others legitimate, and the new realities which call for a positive adjustment to the growing role that India is bound to play in the new world order. In the present context, this challenge raises so many dilemmas in Pakistan itself that it is difficult to imagine a prompt improvement in bilateral relations, despite the culture of peace that people of goodwill from both countries are trying to develop.

The 'India Syndrome': From Asymmetry to Nuclear Deterrence

One tends too much to forget that Pakistan, with 135 million in-habitants, has the sixth largest population in the world, coming just after Russia. Although its GDP and its Human Development Index make it trail behind, such a size, and the memory of the sultanates, kingdoms and empires the Muslims built up in South Asia for centuries, give legitimacy to Pakistan's expectations to stand well in the comity of nations. However, the 50th anniversary of the country in 1997 generated more disturbing introspection than happy celebrations. In many quarters, a feeling of unaccomplishment prevailed. The Islamist forces were unhappy, for the Republic of Pakistan was not Islamic enough according to them. Liberals and most citizens were dissatisfied because the experiment in parliamentary democracy, launched in 1998 after the death of Gen. Zia-ul-Haq, has been disappointing: neither the Pakistan People's Party of Benazir Bhutto nor the Pakistan Muslim League of Nawaz Sharif offered good governance. In a leading publishing house, books written by academics or by members of the establishment offered depressing titles: *A Shattered Dream*; *A Dream Gone Sour*; *A Journey to Disillusionment*, to quote a few.[3] In October 1999, significantly, Chief Executive Gen. Musharraf sought to legitimize his military coup by advancing a similar rationale: 'Fifty-two years ago, we started with a beacon of hope and today that beacon is no more and we stand in darkness.' The General then listed the internal parameters of the structural crisis afflicting Pakistan: 'Our economy has crumbled, our credibility is lost, state institutions lie demolished, provincial disharmony has caused cracks in the federation, and people who were once brothers are now at each others' throat.'[4]

The 'India Syndrome' and the Asymmetry Challenge

An additional point might perhaps have been advanced here, a point that no Pakistani leader has ever recognized while being in power: after more than 50 years of existence, Pakistan has not overcome what I would call the 'India Syndrome'. Born of Partition, Pakistan has been self-defined at its birth as a Promised Land for the Muslims willing to escape from what the Muslim League defined as the 'Hindu rule' in India. However, its successive leaders have not been able to free the national mind from its Indian obsession—rather, they used it deliberately for their own purposes. A feeling of insecurity has been nurtured constantly since 1947, partly by India's realpolitik, but perhaps mostly by Pakistan's eagerness to take to task a much larger neighbour.

The asymmetry between the two countries, which became even more pronounced with the secession of Bangladesh in 1971, is striking. In terms of area, population, GDP and conventional forces, India has the advantage of magnitude. Admittedly, India fares less well than Pakistan in term of GDP per head, but during the 1990s, its new economic policies pushed up the country amongst the 10 largest national GDPs in terms of purchasing power. India is now recognized by Washington as a 'large emerging market', and voices ambitious designs to become a big power in the twenty-first century. Although in the midst of a multifaceted crisis, Pakistan still tends to define itself as a challenger to India, just as the Muslim League has been, in the 1930s and the 1940s a challenger to the Indian National Congress, as if India were not today, along with China, in a class apart.

Pakistan has tried for long—and still attempts today—to counter this asymmetry by apportioning an overwhelming share of its resources to defence expenditure,[5] and by seeking friends or allies, varying from Washington to Beijing, who were expected to provide military aid, openly or otherwise. India is seen by most decision makers and in many media as a 'born enemy'. On the one hand, it is considered as being hegemonic, unfair, obnoxious and resolute to weaken or even destroy Pakistan. On the other hand, it is perceived as undermined by its own weaknesses, be it the divisive caste factor for instance, or the Baniya culture as opposed to the virility of the 'martial races' of Pakistan. To quote an influential Pakistani Senator, India could be defined by a contradiction: 'large country, small people'.

In spite of the heavy military burden Pakistan imposes upon itself, the lack of symmetry has persisted. Hence, the nuclear logic that prevailed in Asia. After China's nuclear test in 1964, India intensified its nuclear research programme. India's test in 1974 heightened Pakistan's resolve to do the same (even were the Pakistanis to be reduced, as Z.A. Bhutto proclaimed, to 'eat grass' in order to finance their programme). Under Zia-ul-Haq, Pakistan's capability was confirmed but not official. India asserted that it was a widely imported capability and accused the supply of decisive technology and components on China most of all, even if some Western companies were also mentioned, and if some Arab countries helped with finances.[6] This capability enabled Pakistan to retaliate on 28 and 30 May 1998, with six tests, to the five Indian explosions of 11 and 13 May.

For those who accept the policy of deterrence, Pakistan has thus restored a balance of terror in the stand-off with its neighbour, for nuclear deterrence alone, working from the weak to the strong, offers decisive power without requesting symmetry. In the meantime, Pakistan has become the first Muslim State to be nuclearized. What has been labelled sometimes (including in Pakistan itself) as the 'Islamic Bomb' is, however, much more an answer to the asymmetry challenge and to the Indian syndrome, than a tool for ascertaining Pakistan's supremacy or leadership over the Middle East or Central Asia. To say the least, Islamabad's support to the Taliban and the financial crisis that it is experiencing have not been very flattering to its image in the 'brotherly Muslim countries'. The matters it has to deal with urgently are, therefore, on another plane: How to sustain the quest for a nuclear balance with India? And how to counter pressure from the US administration which aims at making it fall into line?

War and Peace Scenarios

Three hypotheses of a warlike situation and one peaceful hypothesis need to be examined. The first, Mutual Assured Destruction (MAD), is the most distressing, even if not—hopefully—the most probable one. Islamabad and New Delhi are at a distance of 600 km from each other. Lahore and Amritsar, the major cities of the two Punjabs, are virtually adjacent to each other. The time needed to react after a strike would be terribly short. This hypothesis assumes obviously that the two countries, after their tests, will have armed and deployed their missiles, which is apparently not the case. The prime requisite remains, on both sides, that of setting up procedures for the safe management of the nuclear arsenal, in order to avoid uncontrolled or accidental launching: all the sophisticated techniques of command, control and dependable information in real time, which cost much more than bombs or missiles. Where will Pakistan find the money for them, and at the cost of which investment for basic development, such as health and education? Whatever India and Pakistan might say, an arms race is not only inevitable, it is already on: Hatf 2 Pakistani missiles (280 km range), and M 11 (300 km range) received from China are to match India's Prithvi. The test of Ghauri (1,500 km range) in April 1998 was seen by New Delhi strategic circles as a threat, but was itself an answer to India's Agni. After the nuclear tests, Ghauri II quickly followed the missile test of Agni II. Officially, Islamabad's goal is not to match India, but to preserve enough poise for sustaining deterrence. But where to stop, as India plans to later induct nuclear missiles into its upgraded Navy? A future Indian intercontinental ballistic missile is obviously not needed for deterrence against Pakistan, but what will Pakistan do if India builds a neutron bomb?

A second hypothesis advances that deterrence works. As no one would want MAD, an intentional nuclear war has no chance to break out. This does not exclude the possibility of an accident, nor that of proliferation by an eventual extremist regime (the Jamaat-i-Islami pleads officially for sharing nuclear technology with Muslim 'brotherly countries'), nor that of a 'pocket edition' of a nuclear weapon of sorts falling into the hands of terrorists: shades of Osama bin Laden or of one of his clones are invoked now and then.

There remain two paradigms. One, the third hypothesis of a warlike situation (advanced by Indian analysts), submits that under cover of an 'impossible' nuclear conflict, hawks would take full advantage of deterrence. Pakistan may then pursue the strategy of low-intensity conflict aiming at 'bleeding India'. Hence, the proxy war in Kashmir or elsewhere, a war of infiltration and of sedition under the guidance of intelligence agencies. For the Government of India and for most observers, the Kargil adventure launched by the Pakistan Army in 1999 went even a step further, for it relied upon much more than infiltration of Islamist groups. This reading of Kargil suggests that the

Pakistan Army opted for direct (if limited) military intervention across the Line of Control (LoC), assuming that their level of pressure, supposed to be strong enough for facilitating the internationalization of the Kashmir issue by foreign powers afraid of a possible nuclear drift, would in fact be controlled enough for not pushing New Delhi to retaliate fully.[7] The miscalculation was patent. If New Delhi did react in taking great care to avoid a full-fledged war by deciding not to cross the LoC or/and the international border, this restraint turned to the disadvantage of Pakistan, which was clearly blamed by the international community for violating the LoC. The Kargil misadventure also offered the Indian Government a golden opportunity for strengthening consistently its long-term defence policy.

The last hypothesis is an optimistic one. For some analysts, to move from tacit to open nuclearization does not change the effective strategic balance, but may help to clear the way for negotiations in a global context favouring limited disarmament, calling for restraint, and giving emphasis to the command and control imperatives. Peace would then be the only way out. The Lahore agreement signed between Prime Minister Nawaz Sharif and Prime Minister A.B. Vajpayee in February 1999, along with additional documents calling for military restraint, would have validated this hypothesis, if Kargil had not followed, destroying whatever trust and hope emerged at that time. The military takeover which brought Gen. Pervez Musharraf to power in October 1999 (seen in India as 'the man responsible for Kargil') and the sustained activity of the jihadi groups in Kashmir which followed, further worsened the bilateral relationship, and stalled the dialogue.

Pakistan and the Strategic Triangle: India, America and China

Still shocked by the military and diplomatic defeat at Kargil, Pakistan learned about the 'Draft Nuclear Doctrine' released in August 1999 'for public debate' by the National Security Advisory Board set up by the Indian Government. Once again, Islamabad saw the proposed Indian posture as a threat, whatever be New Delhi's statements about 'minimal nuclear deterrence'. In fact, New Delhi's nuclear ambitions in the air, on land and at sea, address a much wider scope than bilateral relations, but obviously this offers no solace to Islamabad. In any case, there has never been much progress in any strategic Pakistan–India dialogue. After the Benazir Bhutto–Rajiv Gandhi agreement of 1986, the two countries exchanged (in 1992) the lists of their nuclear installations in order to rule out any strike against them. The same year, they signed a mutual information agreement concerning movements of troops and aerial reconnaissance flights on the borders and issued a joint declaration against chemical weapons. But the Pakistani proposal for the non-nuclearization of South Asia, formulated for the first time in the 1970s, and regularly reiterated afterwards, has been consistently rejected by New Delhi which does not want to de-link South Asia from the overall Asian scenario, knowing very well that China would not denuclearize itself even if South Asia were to do so. Furthermore, India is averse to any international conference in which nuclear powers from outside the region, viz., Russia, China and the United States, even to define what India should do in South Asia. Conversely, Pakistan has not responded to the proposal formulated by India after the tests of 1998, suggesting that both countries would take a pledge to not be the first to use nuclear weapons: this would mean, for Pakistan, an end to any efficient deterrence and would further widen the gulf in the field of conventional arms. At a more decisive level, Pakistan, being less in control of its strategic destiny than its neighbour, is driven to adopt a nuclear policy basically reactive to the initiatives taken by India. Despite strong and repeated American pressures, Pakistan decided, as India did: (1) to reject, in 1995, the indefinite extension of the Non-Proliferation Treaty (NPT); (2) not to sign the Comprehensive Test Ban Treaty (CTBT) negotiated by the international community in 1996; and (3) to conduct nuclear tests in 1998. In addition, a reactive policy cannot forget the risks of asymmetry. Thus, if the two countries were to end up by simultaneously becoming parties to the CTBT, Pakistan would consider itself in a safe position only on condition of possessing a nuclear arsenal able to deter, even if not equal, that of India. Similarly, Pakistan has accepted to take part in the negotiations on the future Fissile Material Cut-off Treaty (FMCT), but may hesitate to sign in due time, for its stocks of uranium and plutonium will remain far shorter than those of India.

This asymmetry favouring India plays a contradictory role in Pakistan's relations with the USA. On the one hand, it increases its vulnerability to American pressure, which exercises itself not just in defence matters, but also in the economic field. But on the other hand, Islamabad's policy on nuclear issues being largely reactive to New Delhi's initiatives, Washington's pressure is not always satisfied, when it comes to issues seen as vital by Pakistan. Islamabad knew that economic sanctions would be automatically imposed by Washington after the nuclear tests, and that these sanctions would harm more the crisis-ridden Pakistani economy than Indian interests. It conducted tests nevertheless. The US is not insensitive to this concern for balance, but what trump card does Pakistan hold to get itself heard for its own value, and not just as a follow-up of New Delhi's choices? It does not seem able to ease significantly the turn of events in Afghanistan, and underplays the influence it may have on the Taliban regime. As has been bandied about even in Islamabad, Pakistan could also gamble on its own crisis, as Nawaz Sharif seemed to have done for getting help. It did not prevent him being ousted in a coup, despite a US warning. More generally, and whatever be the reservations of the international community about the military regime, Gen. Musharraf's failure would be seen as a grave peril, as would open the way to radical political Islam. No one (India least of all) wants a Talibanization of Pakistan. Washington clearly expects the military regime to control the extremist groups, and has sent strong signals to Islamabad by engaging in an enduring dialogue with India of the problems raised by international terrorism, and on publishing a strongly-worded assessment of Pakistan in its *Report on Terrorism: 2000.* The different treatment meted out to India and Pakistan during President Clinton's visit to South Asia in March 2000 has highlighted the shift in US policy, which recognized India's position and rationale much better than before. In contrast, the US President linked up US willingness to help Pakistan with a return to democracy and clear dedication in the struggle against terrorist groups. In such a context, the 'eternal friendship' between Pakistan and Beijing is as precious as ever, but also subject to China's long-term interests. Beijing will certainly pursue its traditional policy of using (and arming) Pakistan in order to counter India's regional power, but Islamabad knows that nothing can be taken for granted in this regard. Beijing has not supported Pakistan on Kargil, and, more generally, avoids taking sides on the Kashmir problem.

The quest for understanding (if not alliances) for matching India's challenge is today more difficult than before. The global and regional geopolitical parameters have changed with the end of the Cold War, and have altered as well the significance of militant Islam projected during the war in Afghanistan. On the one hand, the old Western anti-Communist alliance set up in the 1950s, and even the Washington–Islamabad–Beijing axis have now lost their traditional rationale. On the other hand, jihad (not Islam per se, as too often argued in Pakistan) is anathema to Washington, Beijing and Moscow, and the correlation between jihadi forces active on the borders of Pakistan and national stability has evolved negatively. The need for adjustment is obvious. The policy of adjustment is, however, not easy to define and still more difficult to implement, because of the India syndrome. By simultaneously focusing their propaganda on internal reform and on Kashmir, Islamist forces, in a way, hijack (or outbid) the military regime's agenda.

In the new context where radical Islam is considered by many powers as being the latest peril, successive Pakistani authorities have tried to appear as vectors of moderate Islam. The exercise has not convinced many abroad. Observers have taken note of the overtures made from time to time by leading political parties to the proponents of political Islam. They are aware of the manipulation of armed extremist groups created or sustained by the army and the ISI, starting in 1994 with the Taliban in Afghanistan, followed by Kashmir with the Lashkar-e-Taiba and the Harkat-ul-Ansar (renamed Harkat-ul-Mujahideen after being classified as a terrorist outfit by Washington). The present situation in Pakistan seems uncertain if not confusing precisely because no one knows how the regime may be able to control the dangerous groups at home, if it believes that it needs them in Kashmir. To disband them without the approval of their parent bodies would draw the regime into a frontal showdown with the parties of political Islam. It would also imply either putting the Kashmir issue on the backburner, or entering into a genuine political dialogue with India, which has precisely that precondition: to stop the infiltration in Kashmir. Considering the legacy of half a century of bilateral relations developed on distrust and frustration, only a statesman with vision and strength would be ready for such a change.

BEYOND THE TWO-NATION THEORY: A CULTURE OF MISTRUST

The Partition of India in 1947 was seen by the founders of Pakistan as a victory gained with unexpected speed, but not without reservations. Jinnah had to reluctantly accept the division of Punjab and Bengal provinces, hence the frustrated reference to a 'moth-eaten Pakistan'. He had to adjust to the strategic loss of the Punjabi districts of Gurdaspur and Ferozepur. After his death, the ceasefire implemented in Kashmir on 1 January 1949 froze till date the divide of a highly symbolic Muslim majority land, and stalled Pakistan's hope of 'completing Partition'. In 1971, the loss of East Pakistan, which became Bangladesh, was traumatic. To Islamabad, India had taken advantage of the victory of the Awami League under the leadership of Sheikh Mujibur Rahman in the 1970 elections. By openly lending decisive military support to the secessionist forces, it had taken revenge on the Partition of 1947 by, in turn, breaking up Pakistan. Seen from India's viewpoint, the formation of Bangladesh was proof of the failure of the two-nation theory: Islam had not sufficed to cement together a disparate Pakistan.

The Legacy of Partition on Mainstream Perceptions

At the core of the dominant Pakistani perceptions stands the belief that India has never accepted the *rationale* of Partition, which is correct. The India of Nehru, such as defined in the Constitution of 1950, is pluralistic. Its philosophy of secularism does not place the foundation of the State and the nation on any privileged religious identity. The Muslims are not this other nation defined by Jinnah in 1940. They occupy a recognized place in a Republic of India which has already given itself two Muslim Presidents and whose Central and State Governments generally comprise Muslim Ministers too. Many in Pakistan, on the other hand, have considered the Indian National Congress as being an essentially Hindu body and recall that this party, under the leadership of Nehru, rejected coalition ministries with the Muslim League in 1937, has not implemented the Desai–Liaquat Ali Pact calling to form a temporary League–Congress coalition government in 1945, and finally refused the proposal put forward by the Cripps Cabinet Mission of 1946, which had suggested a federation in which the regions having a Muslim majority would have enjoyed wide-based autonomy. As independence was approaching, no consonance of views could be achieved through any formula for sharing of power between the Congress and the Muslim League. It was only after the Direct Action Day organized by the Muslim League on 16 August 1946, and the massacres which plunged Calcutta into mourning, that the top-rung leaders of the Congress (with the exception of Gandhi) became convinced that Partition was the inevitable price to be paid for obtaining the independence being conceded by the British. But many leaders in the Congress party were of the view that the two-nation theory was an artificial one and that it had no future. Vallabhbhai Patel, Nehru's Home Minister and Deputy Prime Minister, 'was convinced that the new State of Pakistan was not viable and that it would not last'[8] and the All India Congress Committee declared, in the document accepting Partition, that it 'believed firmly that when the present passions will have abated, the problems of India will be seen in their proper perspective, the false two-nation doctrine being then discredited and rejected by all'.[9] Immediately after Partition, the reluctance of Indian authorities to hand over to Pakistan its due share of financial assets and military equipment, and the controversy about the Indus waters added to existing frustrations.

This Indian feeling that Partition could have been avoided and that the tensions between Hindus and Muslims could not obliterate a shared heritage is alien to Pakistan where the Indian questioning of the *logic* of Partition is often perceived as a challenge to Partition itself. India is constantly suspected, even openly accused, of wanting to put an end to it, either by taking over Pakistan, or by destroying it as a State and a national entity. To those who argue that India has for long reconciled to the existence of Pakistan, the secession of Bangladesh, which occurred 30 years ago, is still advanced as testimony of its destructive intentions. This negative perception of India does not go as far as distinguishing between the Indian National Congress and its old rival, the communal *Sangh Parivar*, although, ironically, the Congress enjoyed for decades, after Partition, the electoral support of most of the Indian Muslims. Before and after Independence, the main opponent to Pakistan has been defined as being the Congress, not the Hindu nationalists now in power in New Delhi, for the Congress has been at the helm of affairs for more than 40 years, before and after Partition. While Hindu nationalists of the Hindu Mahasabha and the Rashtriya Swayamsevak Sangh have labelled the Congress as being pro-Muslim, the Pakistani leadership characterizes it as pro-Hindu. In other words, both Pakistani and Hindu nationalists would agree on defining the Congress practice as being, in fact, pseudo-secular.

Consider now the growing assertiveness of Hindu communalism during the 1980s, the violence against minority communities instigated by the *Sangh Parivar*, the destruction of the Babri Masjid in Ayodhya in 1992 and the killings which followed; the Bharatiya Janata Party coming to power in 1998 with an RSS agenda and quickly exercising the nuclear option. All these developments comfort the Pakistani mainstream rhetoric which equates India with militant and hegemonic Hinduism, and which recalls that the ideologues who theoreticized Hindu nationalism have put forward the concept of *Akhand Bharat*, the Greater India extending from the periphery of Afghanistan to the fringes of Burma. The fact that a number of Pakistani policy makers or intellectuals would make no difference between the Congress and its age-old opponent, the *Sangh Parivar*, goes beyond recalling the pro-

Hindu leanings of some prominent historical Congress leaders, such as Tilak or Patel, or quoting the intimidating remarks made by Indira Gandhi during the war of secession of Bangladesh. To the dominant Pakistani perspective, the Congress and the *Sangh Parivar* are only two sides of the same coin, and in a way, the BJP is, paradoxically, safer, for its philosophy is clear, while the Congress' leadership is always suspected of deceit.

This mainstream perception does not generate more trust in Indian liberals or in the Indian left. Every Indian, however conciliatory he may be, who invokes with nostalgia the pre-Partition days or conceives, in an undetermined future, of a more politically united South Asia, is seen by many commentators as desiring the annihilation of Pakistan. The doubts expressed now and then in India (outside official circles) on the viability of Pakistan and the hypotheses foretelling its breaking up into independent provinces give rise to added rancour, even though some Pakistanis themselves also conjure up the danger of implosion of their country.

A feeling of insecurity prevails at the core of the common Pakistani vision, and is fuelled by every event that takes place, and which projects India's leadership (whichever it is) either as bullying or tricky, stubborn or foul. This distrust, this lending of the darkest of intentions to its neighbour, this inability to come to terms with the past, this decisive weight of contradictory perceptions between the two countries, constitute the greatest obstacle to any lasting normalization of bilateral relations. True, there are also the burden of political strategies, the tactics of politicians and the interests of various groups, starting with the armed forces, in the chalking out of Pakistan's foreign policy, and the concern of the major parties which from time to time have tried to placate Islamist movements. The persisting tension with India is not without its advantages: in the context of the multiplicity of dissensions which plague Pakistan, India and the question of Kashmir offer an invaluable subject on which a near consensus prevails. But the reason for the persistence of this charged atmosphere has yet to be explained. Has Partition, sought after by the Muslim League, not brought the confidence and security that it was primarily meant to give?

Pakistan's Self and the Anti-Indian Rhetoric

The troubled political life of Pakistan gives us the first rudiments of an answer. As against the long stability of India, governed continuously by the Congress party from 1947 till 1977, Pakistan presents the image of turbulence and unsteadiness. The ailing Jinnah died in 1948 without having been able to firmly shore up the State or to work out for it a paradigmatic course of policy and practice. Liaquat Ali Khan, a key figure in continuity with his heritage, and Prime Minister since 1947, was assassinated in 1951. Six Prime Ministers followed in just five years. Three military regimes (Ayub Khan, 1958-69; Yahya Khan, 1969-71; Zia-ul-Haq, 1977-88), marked the first four decades after Independence, with Zia, moreover, getting his civilian predecessor, Zulfikar Ali Bhutto, hung. On the institutional plane, the first, long-delayed Constitution (1956) was never implemented, the second one (1962) was replaced in 1973 by a third text which was extensively amended in 1981.

A second series of queries arises over the nature of Pakistan. Is it a State of the Muslims? A nation state seeking to bring its ethnic diversity under the umbrella of a religious unity? An Islamic State? All these hypotheses involve, either directly or by way of comparison, a reference to India. Self-defined as a State of the Muslims of the former India, Pakistan has had to make do with half measures: right from 1947, a large part of the Indian Muslims did not join it; in 1971, the secession of Bangladesh deprived Pakistan of the majority of its population. However one may interpret it, the fact remains that Pakistan contains not much more than one-third of the Muslims of the subcontinent.

This being so, what should be its approach towards the Muslims in India, 'a minority in the land of the Hindus'? Attention could be drawn to the harsh treatment meted out to them. Indeed, the Pakistani Government did not fail to protest against the destruction of the Babri Masjid and the anti-Muslim riots that followed. This is one way of echoing the Pakistani reasoning behind Partition, by contending that the Muslims would inevitably be oppressed in a Hindu-majority India. There are also the more subtle overtones of the interpretation of the Hegira as a prophetic justification of the distinction between lands where Islam dominates (*dar-ul-Islam*) and lands where it is dominated (*dar-ul-harb*). The refusal by India to give the right of self-determination to the Kashmiris through a plebiscite promised long ago, and the harsh military repression it conducts against them, proffer also a manner of reasoning constantly advanced by Pakistan in favour of the equation that India is synonymous with Hindus, and all that supposedly follows as a natural corollary. A temptation might also exist: to help the few Indian Muslim fundamentalists engaged in subversion, and the most resolute militants of all shades disillusioned with the Indian system, as it did during the 1980s when it provided support for the Sikh secessionists struggling for an independent Khalistan. The Government of India (not only when led by the BJP) points at the ISI, accused of fishing in troubled waters, from Assam to Tamil Nadu, and alleges Pakistani connections for the Muslim team behind the Mumbai terrorist bombings after Ayodhya, or the Indian Airlines hijacking in December 1999.

The reasoning behind Partition originated in the refusal to see the Muslims of a united independent India subjected to the 'rule of the Hindu majority'. Does this imply that the Pakistani nation is bound to exist as a permanent adversary of India? The psychological dimension of the divide between the two neighbours cannot be ignored in Pakistan. However, how strong could be the impact of such collective perceptions, as they do not exist in a vacuum? They result partly from India's policies, but they also serve specific Pakistani purposes. While the exposure of India's damaging deeds—real or misconstrued—can be ignored in day-to-day life, it raises its head every now and then in the conscience of the nation, or at least in the discourse of its leaders, for at least four reasons.

In the first place, anti-Indian rhetoric always serves as an effective rallying point to consolidate national unity in times of crisis or of political difficulty. Gambling on Islamic identity, as Nawaz Sharif did with his failed Shariat Bill introduced after the nuclear tests, aimed at the same objective without necessarily achieving it better. In the second place, in the parliamentary set-up which existed from 1988 to 1999, the charged political rivalry between the two major forces, Nawaz Sharif's Pakistan Muslim League and Benazir Bhutto's Pakistan People's Party, has tended to paralyse whichever of the two was in power, which, whenever there was a slight improvement in bilateral relations, was quickly accused of weakness, if not of sacrificing the national interest. Hence, the hopes raised by the Benazir Bhutto–Rajiv Gandhi talks of 1985-6, and by the Nawaz Sharif–I.K. Gujral exchange of views in 1996-7, were quickly dissipated by the blows dealt by the political adversary of the moment, forcing the successive Prime Ministers to harden the stand taken in the face-off with New Delhi.

Third, the influence of the armed forces over the political power has been decisive since 1958 (even upon civilian governments), particularly in matters of international relations, beginning with urgent bilateral issues: Indo–Pakistan relations, Kashmir, Afghanistan. A military-bureaucratic complex has evolved, most of whose members have everything to gain by conserving a state of tension with India, as much to justify considerably large defence budgets as to shrink the diplomatic space of political parties in power. The controversial statement of Niaz Naik, former Pakistan Foreign Secretary, that the army launched the Kargil operation in 1999 for sabotaging the secret talks conducted with New Delhi on Kashmir, is only the latest occurrence of a structural parameter whose importance cannot be overemphasized. The fourth factor is no less important. It is epitomized in an unsolvable dispute, the crux of the matter being, precisely, the issue of Kashmir.

The Indo-Pakistan Dispute on 'The Core Issue of Kashmir'

Right from the first months after Independence, mistrust of India was fuelled by a multiplicity of tensions. Added to the massacres which accompanied Partition and claimed hundreds of thousands of lives, there were many issues of contention: landed properties of refugees, the use of Indus waters, the share of money in the coffers of the treasury devolving on Pakistan, the distribution of military forces and equipment. . . . At present, the Siachen Glacier, the Sir Creek Border, the Tulbul Waters are among the subjects of friction. Of all contentious issues, the dispute over Kashmir was, and still remains, by far the most crucial one, constantly defined by Pakistani authorities as 'the core issue of Kashmir', said to prevent the normalization of bilateral relations.

Kashmir as a Bilateral Bone of Contention

At the time of Partition, Jammu & Kashmir was one of India's largest princely states. Its ruler, the Hindu Maharaja Hari Singh, was tempted to remain independent, while the vocal Muslims were affiliated to one or the other of the two main political parties: the Muslim Conference, which advocated accession to Pakistan, and the National Conference, under the leadership of Sheikh Abdullah, which empathized more with India, subject to the latter granting a very substantial degree of autonomy to Jammu & Kashmir. The Poonch uprising against the Maharaja made him vulnerable, all the more so as the Pathan tribals coming from the north were advancing towards Srinagar. Hari Singh finally appealed to India for help. Before sending Indian troops to his rescue, Nehru called upon the Maharaja to sign a Treaty of Accession to India—Hari Singh did it on 26 September 1947—and undertake to form a government under the leadership of Sheikh Abdullah. The insurgency turned into outright war with the arrival of regular Pakistani troops in 1948. The cessation of hostilities on 1 January 1949 under the auspices of the United Nations delineated a ceasefire line which, with slight alterations, became the 'Line of Control' (LoC) after the 1971 war. Since 1949, the former kingdom of Kashmir has thus been divided into two main parts, China being in control of a third part.[10] The portion of Kashmir to the west and to the north of the LoC is under Pakistan's control (what India calls Pakistan-occupied Kashmir). In Poonch, in the west, the Muslim Conference had proclaimed as far back as in 1947 an 'Independent State of Jammu & Kashmir' ('Azad Jammu & Kashmir'). This so-called independent State (with a President and a Prime Minister) is in fact controlled by Islamabad, and provided with a Council presided over by the Prime Minister of Pakistan. To the north of the LoC, the Northern Territories group together with the tribal principalities which had formerly pledged their allegiance to the Maharaja of Kashmir. The Pakistani troops are stationed all along the LoC, which stops at point NJ 9842, at the foot of the Siachen Glacier without going right up to the Chinese border. India and Pakistan both claim this glacier (which is an enormous reservoir of sweet water), where the two armies have taken positions at very high altitudes, and have been exchanging artillery fire since 1984.

To the south of the LoC stretches the land under India's control (Pakistan calls it Indian-occupied Kashmir) which constitutes Jammu & Kashmir, one of the 25 states of the Indian Union. Its jewel is the Valley of Kashmir. To the south-west, the Jammu region has a Hindu majority, but some districts have a large Muslim population. To the east, Ladakh has a Buddhist majority in the district of Leh while that of Kargil now has a Muslim majority. The population of the Srinagar Valley is more than 90 per cent Muslim, but is home since centuries to a Brahmin community, the Pandits, who traditionally occupy a place in the Kashmiri identity, known as *Kashmiriyat*. Most of these Pandits have fled out of the Valley when the insurrection gained momentum in 1990. Their fate and the conditions of their resettlement add to the complexity of the Kashmir problem.

Having been the cause of the first Indo–Pakistan war in the days just following Independence, Kashmir remains today the most dramatic point of discord between the two countries. What is at stake here? Over and above its strategic importance, located as it is between China, the Central Asian Republics, India, and the Middle Eastern Muslim continuum ending in Afghanistan, Kashmir represents, for Pakistan and for India, more than a territory. It stands as a symbol of the idea of nationhood on which each of the two States has been founded. For Islamabad, Kashmir should have belonged to it by right, in line with the very reasoning behind Partition: it had, after all, a Muslim majority and was contiguous to Pakistan. New Delhi vindicates its stand by referring to the Treaty of Accession to India signed by the Maharaja. Among Pakistan's arguments, some are procedural, but there are two which are more valid. The first is the condition laid down by Lord Mountbatten, the first Governor-General of Independent India, on the acceptance of the choice of the Maharaja, which was given 'subject to the condition that the people would be consulted'. Nehru was in agreement with this at that time. The second takes note of the case of the principalities of Junagadh (adjacent to Pakistan) and of Hyderabad (in the heart of India). The two instances, antithetic to that of Kashmir (both had a Muslim ruler with a Hindu–majority population) were settled to India's advantage, even though the princes had chosen either to accede to Pakistan or to remain independent.

India's way of reasoning is different. Its Constitution is based on the principle that religion is not a factor to be taken into account in national identity. A secular State, India is the home of about as many Muslims as Pakistan itself. A Muslim-majority State can very well exist within its frame, and, in fact, vindicates the concept of a pluralistic India. India adds to this another historical argument: the Pathan hordes which sought to overthrow Hari Singh in 1948 were simply instruments of the Pakistani authorities (Islamabad denies this, but the role of Pakistani officers is attested to) who thus committed a masked aggression against the princely state, before intervening openly through their army. On the legal plane, India maintains that the Security Council distorted the meaning of the appeal that it made to the UN against Pakistani aggression. Even though India at the time accepted in principle a plebiscite, as suggested by the United Nations Commission for India and Pakistan (resolution of 5 January 1949), this involved the withdrawal of Pakistan's armed forces—one of the necessary preconditions to any consultation for determining the people's wishes (resolution of 13 August 1948), and this withdrawal never took place.

While Pakistan insists on the implementation of the UN resolutions favouring a plebiscite, India considers these as having become obsolete, for the above reason and for two additional ones. The first is that in the Indian part of Jammu & Kashmir, a Constituent Assembly was set up, followed by a parliamentary regime. New Delhi considers that the repeated exercise of the electoral process by the Kashmiris is a substitute for the plebiscite, and recalls that the Jammu & Kashmir Assembly has renounced, in 1957 and in 1965, to the original special autonomous status. Pakistan challenges, as does also the Security Council (resolution of 24 January 1957), the fact that successive elections could be a substitute for the plebiscite, and, in fact, denies the fairness of the electoral process, which has certainly been too often manipulated. In the second place, India interprets the Simla Agreement, signed between Indira Gandhi and Zulfikar Ali Bhutto in 1972, as a commitment to solve disputes within a bilateral framework, and no longer under the supervision of the United Nations or through third party intervention. Islamabad challenges this interpretation, as well as India's assertion that Bhutto had made a verbal commitment in Simla to work towards the acceptance of the status quo in Kashmir, giving de jure sanction to the division of the former kingdom, permitting the transformation of the LoC into an international border.

To sum up, India's official maximalist position holds that the entire Jammu & Kashmir (occupied or not by Pakistan or by China) is its by rule of Hari Singh's accession. Pakistan's official position is more nuanced. It defines Kashmir as 'a disputed territory' (a qualification rejected by New Delhi), and does not define its status before a plebiscite could decide about it. Beyond official statements, India would, in fact, be satisfied with a settlement confirming the status quo, with minor adjustments, while Pakistan would be ready to abandon to India the districts of Jammu and Ladakh having a non-Muslim majority. As such, the two unofficial 'solutions' are irreconcilable, for no party is ready to leave to the other one the cultural and economic heart of Kashmir, the Vale of Srinagar and its surroundings districts.

The Third Party: The Kashmiris' Experience

And now, the Kashmiris themselves—more precisely, the Kashmiris from the state of Jammu & Kashmir effectively under Indian law (for Pakistan has cleverly succeeded in controlling its own side of Kashmir, despite local movements for more rights). The Constituent Assembly of Indian Jammu & Kashmir, which met in 1951, gave to this state a special status, formalized five years later and recognized through Article 370 of the Indian Constitution. This wide autonomy was very quickly suppressed. New Delhi's relations with Sheikh Abdullah turned to the worse, and the charismatic leader of the National Conference party, suspected to favour independence, spent long years in detention after 1953. Most Indian observers acknowledge that the Government of India, since the Nehru era, is largely responsible for the deterioration of relations with Kashmiris, which were aggravated after 1982, the year of the death of the Sheikh. The strong sense of identity of the Kashmiris, the errors committed by New Delhi which disrupted the interplay of local politics and offered the Kashmiris neither the plebiscite nor the promised autonomy, and the very progress of education amongst unemployed and frustrated Kashmiri youth explain, essentially the feeling of alienation which has grown and led to insurgency.[11]

This insurgency has changed the face of things on at least two counts. Launched in 1989 by the secular and pro-independence Jammu and Kashmir Liberation Front (JKLF), it gave a new tone to the expression of Kashmiri feelings. To be against Indian rule was no more necessarily connotative of pro-Pakistan leanings. The Kashmir problem, seen for long as a matter of confrontation between two powers, has become tripartite with the 'independentist current' entering the fray. Pakistan did welcome Amanullah Khan, founder of the JKLF, but quickly preferred to support pro-Pakistan and Islamist Kashmiri militant groups, such as the Hizbul Mujahideen, much more than the JKLF. In 1992, it restrained the JKLF from marching from Azad Kashmir and openly crossing the LoC. The UN resolutions being fairly vague in nature, would not be absolutely antagonistic to the 'third option', the independence of Kashmir, becoming the subject of a plebiscite along with the two others, accession to India or to Pakistan. But Islamabad does not have a clear-cut attitude on this point, while India rejects any prospect of independence.

Has the containment of the armed groups by the Indian paramilitary and military forces, accompanied by the human rights violations denounced both by Indian and international human rights groups, finally led to normalization? Is the slow and constrained resumption of the electoral process in Jammu & Kashmir, from 1996 onwards, fully convincing in this regard? Hardly so, but once again, the analysis offered is different in India and in Pakistan.

For Islamabad and for the leaders of 'Azad Kashmir', the Kashmiris on the Indian side are freedom fighters carrying on a 'heroic fight' for national liberation and the right of self-determination. They will content themselves with nothing less than the holding of the plebiscite promised in 1947. For New Delhi, the armed revolt by 'misguided youths' is in the process of dying out, as can be testified by the peace that has been more or less regained (under the deep shadow of the army) in the Srinagar Valley. The conflict which continues outside the valley is just the last manifestation of the proxy war that Pakistan is conducting against India. Local militants are said to have surrendered in numbers, the fighting continuing mostly through Pakistani agents or volunteers, veterans of the Afghanistan war, militants fighting a jihad, mercenaries fighting for a wage. What Delhi is said to suppress is no more a local insurgency, but foreign-sponsored terrorism. Beyond the propaganda of both sides, Pakistan's involvement, officially denied by Islamabad, is evident. The most active groups, such as the Lashkar-e-Taiba and the Harkat-ul-Mujahideen are the armed wings of Pakistan-based recognized organizations which recruit and train the Mujahideen, and openly celebrate the *shahid*, the 'martyrs' who died in their struggle. In 2000, the appearence of suicide commandos bombing army camps, both in Kashmir and Chechnya, was not missed by observers of transnational radical Islamist movements. On the other side, it is as well established that the repression launched by the Indian forces has targeted not just insurgents for years, but the local population at large. The figure of 20,000 dead since 1989 is not official. Pakistan puts it at much higher. The 'tragedy of errors', to quote Indian journalist Tavleen Singh,[12] is apparently not coming to a close.

In the early 1990s, the Russian withdrawal from Afghanistan and the independence acquired by the republics of Central Asia gave rise to hope in Srinagar and in Islamabad that the moment had arrived for big changes to take place in Kashmir. But many have misread New Delhi's rationale and India's resilience. Kashmir is certainly important to India, but not a subject of narrow focus as it is in Pakistan. Kashmiri insurgency, stirred by Islamabad, is a sore, and costs the Indian Army a lot, but India may afford to stick for long to its policy, however inefficient it be. To put it briefly, the Pakistani strategy of 'bleeding India', as defined by New Delhi strategists, is not operative, for India may afford to wait, or might even boost its national morale when Islamabad engages itself in a Kargil-like adventure which backfires. Whatever be the cost of the Kashmir tangle, New Delhi prefers to support it, and to suffer from a negative image on this account

(Pakistan's image not being better, at any rate) rather than to open the Pandoras box of rethinking afresh the status of Kashmir. The Indian political philosophy accepted by all the mainstream parties advances (in unison with the leadership of many multicultural countries, including Russia and China) that the right to self-determination was valid only against colonial states. Kashmir is thus treated in India as a purely internal matter, and New Delhi, whichever be the party in power, will hardly contemplate a plebiscite which would not turn in its favour. Besides the image of a pluralistic nation which is at stake, a victorious secession might stimulate other militant groups in north-east India or elsewhere. With the independence movements apparently wearing thin, we seem to be back to the original binary scenario, with a difference, however: the drift of the 1990s has not changed the status of Kashmir, but has certainly brought in a militant radical Islam, alien to the Kashmiriyat tradition, and connected with international networks.

The International Dimension of Kashmir

Between 1994 (when the local insurgency gave signs of weakening) and 1998 (when the nuclear tests projected Kashmir as a potential flashpoint), New Delhi might have believed that time was in its favour. The greater involvement of radical Islamist groups armed and trained in Pakistan was a challenge, but it did not affect the great transformations India was engaged in on the socio-economic front. Furthermore, the setting up of the All Parties Hurriyat Conference sent mixed signals. The Conference does voice the anti-status quo perspective in Jammu & Kashmir, but what freedom (hurriyat) it struggles for is not defined the same way by its various components. To bring together so many different groups, from the Jamaat-i-Islami to the JKLF, does not help to define a clear political perspective, nor to identify any charismatic Kashmiri leader enjoying wide acceptance.

Pakistan has not succeeded in internationalizing the Kashmir issue the way it hoped to. However, the nuclear tests on the one hand, and the willingness of India to project itself as a country with growing ambitions, has drawn external powers to pay more focused attention to the Kashmir problem. In the new, openly nuclearized context calling for upgrading missile potential, the issue of security in South Asia has acquired increased relevance. On the other front, the promise of economic development and the realization that India is a big emerging market calls for peace and negotiation rather than confrontation.

The external powers, however, are not much interested in Kashmir per se, and in the fate of the Kashmiris. What they hope for is *any* durable settlement of the Kashmir tangle, not necessarily a plebiscite. This adds to the frustration of many Pakistanis, who denounce the supposed anti-Muslim bias of the international community, and compare its restrained comments on the fate of the Muslims in Bosnia, Kashmir and Chechnya, with its prompt intervention in Timor, for supporting Christian Timorese against Indonesian rule. (The Western support to Muslim Kosovars is strangely not recognized as a counterclaim.) The Kashmir issue is not just a bone of contention between India and Pakistan. It feeds on Pakistani anti-Western feelings, the West, and other powers as well, being seen as unprincipled, treacherous, and deeply opposed to Islam. This is obviously something of a paradox, as Pakistan, in the meantime, is constantly asking for international mediation for solving the Kashmir problem. Added to the legitimacy of the Kashmiris' expectations, the feeling of being unheard or misunderstood generates self-righteous justification which helps also to underestimate (or be deliberately silent about) the extent of Pakistani responsibilities in the military and ideological radicalization of the Kashmir problem. This, in turn, does not facilitate a fruitful dialogue with India.

In March 2000, the visit of Bill Clinton to South Asia has satisfied New Delhi much more than Islamabad. In a rare speech 'to the People of Pakistan' broadcast on Pakistan TV, the US President asked Pakistan 'to reduce tensions with India' and to 'intensify its efforts to defeat those who inflict terror'. Two messages were given to the public, not much in tune, to say the least, with the predilections of the country's leadership: (1) 'There is no military solution to Kashmir. International sympathy, support and intervention cannot be won by provoking a bigger, bloodier conflict'; (2) 'We cannot and will not mediate or resolve the dispute in Kashmir. Only you and India can do that, through dialogue.' While Pakistan opposes India's expectations to become, in due time, a permanent member of the Security Council on the ground that a country not respecting UN resolutions cannot reasonably receive support for such upgrading, the US President chose to say not a word about the plebiscite Islamabad harps upon as the only solution to the Kashmir tangle.[13]

The US might not mediate officially in Kashmir, but it certainly puts pressure on both Pakistan and India. No public statement indicates what could be the best hypothesis for progressing to an agreement. Various compromises are imagined, some of them abroad. None seems easy to implement. In any case, the history of negotiation between Pakistan and India is not encouraging, and it must also be acknowledged, as Pakistan avers, that no policy either imposed by India, or agreed to by Pakistan and India, could be viable if the Kashmiris do not truly accept it.

INTERMITTENT DIALOGUE: STRAINS AND PROSPECTS

Going around in circles: that is the protracted story of the Pakistan–India dialogue. Furthermore, agreements arrived at often leave a bitter taste. New Delhi contests the turn given by the UN to its 1948 complaint and considers, not without reason, that the Tashkent Agreement signed through Russian mediation after the 1965 war has brought nothing concrete. Many believed in Pakistan that the Simla Agreement was signed 'under duress'. Notwithstanding the worsening of the Kashmir crisis in the 1990s, the dialogue, with some interruptions, continued till the Kargil crisis and the military takeover of 1999. A dialogue mostly of the deaf, in which each party followed the tactics of blow hot, blow cold: the artillery shelling along the LoC often intensified whenever diplomats met. Today, the shelling continues, but the official dialogue is at a standstill. Gen. Musharraf's proposal to renew it 'anywhere, anytime, at any level' leads nowhere, as long as Pakistan does not satisfy the precondition set by India: the end—or at least a significant slackening—of infiltration of jihadi commandos in Kashmir. The stalemate does not preclude discreet contacts, nor 'individual' initiatives (involving, recently, noted Kashmiris settled in the USA). Whatever the future holds in store, it could be instructive to draw some lessons from past dialogues, and to identify what seem to be the present positions of the different parties involved.

The Practice of Dialogue: The Stop-and-Go Strategy

The last two recent steps of bilateral relations have offered very quick volte-faces. The first phase started with the nuclear tests of May 1998 and went up to April 1999, when the 'Lahore process' was still promising. The second phase started in May 1999 with the Kargil exposure and still runs (at the time of writing, in July 2000).

In the context of the deep-rooted reciprocated mistrust which has crystallized decade upon decade, there are, first, some questions of method which get formulated. As mentioned earlier, the heads of the Pakistani and Indian Governments generally used to meet each other (usually in third countries) during annual international conferences. After the acid comments generated by the nuclear tests of May 1998, the Indo–Pakistani dialogue was not really stopped. The tones alternated rapidly from being frigid (at Colombo, on the sidelines of the SAARC summit in July 1998) to being a little more urbane (at New York, at the time of the General Assembly of the United Nations in September 1998) with the dialogue often being suspended. While Prime Ministers and Ministers for External Affairs set the tone, it is generally the Foreign Secretaries who negotiate. This procedure restricts the room for manoeuvre and political initiatives.

Even as regards the proposed conduct of the dialogue, the attitudes are divergent. Islamabad insists that progress on the 'core issue' of Kashmir is a necessary precondition for moving towards a normalized relationship. Contrarily, New Delhi feels that giving priority to Kashmir, which is a matter of major friction, is counterproductive. It argues that it would be better to achieve some progress on the side issues and thus create a better climate for bilateral discussions. Talks are, therefore, held mostly on what the subject of the talks should be. In June 1997, eight points were retained, the first two within the competence of the Foreign Secretaries, the others pertaining to other officials: Kashmir; peace and security; Siachen; navigation on the Tulbul; the Sir Creek Border; terrorism and drug traffic; economic and commercial cooperation; cultural cooperation and reciprocal visits.

Whatever be the government in power, Pakistan argues that foreign mediators are indeed needed for progressing on Kashmir, as bilateral discussions have failed for years. It recalls that the Indus Treaty, in the 1950s, was successfully negotiated thanks to the mediation of the World Bank chief. Islamabad also asks for Kashmiris being associated with the discussions. It has proposed that India should come forward on the Kashmir issue by making some distinct gestures: withdrawal of a part of the armed forces (6,00,000 men according to Islamabad, probably less but India does not give figures), recognition of the Hurriyat Conference as the interlocutor representing the Kashmiris, free elections under the supervision of foreign observers. Pakistan insists that a plebiscite is the only way out, and that the 50 years old UN resolutions in this regard are still valid. The unofficial suggestion to hold plebiscites at district level is seen in Islamabad as a concession permitting the non-Muslim district of Jammu & Kashmir to remain within India. It does not really open new vistas, for New Delhi objects to any plebiscite on principle, Kashmir being not considered as 'a disputed territory', but just an internal problem.[14]

India officially rejects any type of mediation, and, whatever be happening behind the scenes, would oppose any mediated build-up of the Camp David style, which would be found offending its status (an Oslo-type procedure would certainly be more acceptable). As far as Kashmiris are concerned, New Delhi maintains contacts with the Hurriyat leaders (whether in jail or free) and certainly tries to divide them, as some might be tempted by compromise after a decade of unsuccessful armed struggle. But which type of compromise? Even the loyal Assembly of Jammu & Kashmir met with a strong rebuttal from the BJP-led Government in July 2000, when it passed a resolution favouring the restoration of the pre-1953 full-fledged autonomy. While Pakistan's policy on Kashmir is very vocal, India keeps silent on its options: no official statement on the change of status of the LoC, no proposition for granting significant autonomy to Jammu & Kashmir, which seems, however, the only way offered for eventually changing the mood of the Kashmiris.

In contrast, India is vocal on Pakistan's intrusion in Kashmir, and on opposing 'international terrorism'. In this regard, New Delhi has scored some points in its own way, with the American attack on Osama bin Laden's camp in 1998 (which is actually in Afghanistan, but just two steps away from the border with Pakistan, having some Pakistani Mujahideen preparing themselves for operations in Kashmir. It provided a perfect opportunity for calling on the international community to organize a large conference against terrorism which India complains of enduring since a long time, in Kashmir and elsewhere, at the instigation 'of one of its neighbours'. The new regular dialogue engaged between India and the US on terrorism is another victory of sorts, even if Washington, eager to keep contacts with Islamabad, stops short of defining Pakistan as a terrorist state. The course of events, at any rate, has added pressure on Pakistan.

Track II and Track III Diplomacy

Other channels and other dialogues attempt to go beyond the often sterile formalism, however indispensable, of official meetings. Many well-meaning persons, whether retired army officers, former high-ranking diplomats and bureaucrats, or academics with political contacts, meet influential colleagues from the other side and test new ideas, with the knowledge of the two governments, without committing them officially. The Neemrana Initiative has been the most well-known among the instruments of what is known as 'Track II diplomacy'. Less close to those in power and much more critical of the authorities in both camps, 'Track III diplomacy', conducted by NGOs, aims at promoting a people-to-people dialogue: it organizes public meetings and annual conferences, alternately in India and in Pakistan, with participants from both countries, if visas are granted. The Pakistan and Indian People's Forum for Peace and Democracy is one of the most active of these. It is encouraging to note that although the official dialogue and the Track II channel have been paralysed since Gen. Musharraf's takeover, Track III has been left open.

Some people express doubts on the effectiveness of such movements which are said to catch the attention of only those who are already convinced. This is a short-sighted assessment. In the context of the general suspicion continuously kept alive since half a century, everything that promotes respect for the other side, every initiative favouring publicized dialogues between concerned citizens from both countries, prepares the ground for possible steps forward, while not necessarily yielding on basic issues. If confidence building measures have to be decided mostly by authorities in power, the culture of peace is a common good. It would be wrong to underestimate the relevance of Pakistanis who voice appeals for 'burying the hatchet', or for 'getting back to the right side of history'.[15]

Geo-Economics versus Geopolitics?

There remains the economic channel. Is the geopolitical heritage, replete with strife, sustained by deep-seated ideological differences and by sentiments of identity, instrumentalized by political circles for half a century, ready to yield ground in the face of the geo-economic imperative, in an era of globalization which necessitates strong regional structures, woven into forceful internal exchanges? The first economic effect of bilateral tensions, and not the least for Pakistan, is its cost in terms of defence budgets. But these tensions have also prevented intercourse which could have contributed to the prosperity of the two neighbours. A number of studies, as well as chambers of commerce from both countries (before the nuclear tests), have stressed on their potential complementarities and have denounced the absurdity of a situation in which indisputable possibilities of exchange are never the less ignored, or are conducted through indirect or clandestine channels, enriching competitors, intermediaries or smugglers. This is an area holding vast potential for dialogue, sustained by shared interests, which would in all likelihood strengthen the prospects of regional security. A better relationship between the two stronger pillars of SAARC, India and Pakistan would help the association to progress, instead of paying the price of their dispute. As no one knows when the South Asian Preferential Tariff Agreement (SAPTA) will actually give place to a South Asian Free Trade Area (SAFTA), a number of States— India included—devise alternatives, either on bilateral lines or focused on a different core area, such as the Bay of Bengal rim States. For the time being, the Economic Cooperation Organisation, whose members include Turkey, Iran, Azerbaijan and the Central Asian Republics, does not seem to offer Pakistan much prospect in the short run. It would be a victory of geo-economics over geopolitics if Pakistan could one day benefit from the links to be established between India, Iran and Turkmenistan for a regular supply of gas and oil. In between, Islama-bad still refuses to grant to India Most Favoured Nation status, but will have to yield on this point, since the two countries are members of the World Trade Organisation.

PAKISTAN'S DILEMMA

Nothing illustrates better the dilemma Pakistan is facing than the quick succession of the events of 1999. In February, a new symbolic gesture revived hope of an improvement in bilateral links and was accompanied by cordial words on both sides: riding in the first bus linking New Delhi to Lahore, the Indian Prime Minister, Atal Behari Vajpayee, was received at the border post by his Pakistani counterpart, Nawaz Sharif. The two heads of government made an appeal to 'remove the bitter-ness of the past' and to work 'towards peace and harmony'. Once again, the press, thwarting pessimists on all sides, hailed 'this moment of history' and laid stress on what the two countries and their neighbours would gain from a normalization of relations. Kargil followed three months later, killing in the bud any prospect of improvement in bilateral relations, and eventually thwarting the dis-creet dialogue open on Kashmir. As Kargil was prepared for with at least the basic knowledge of Nawaz Sharif before the Lahore meeting,

Indian hawks had all good reason to repeat that decidedly, no Pakistani leadership could be trusted.

However, the parameters defining Pakistan's policy cannot be simply confined to any collective psychological dimension. The duplicity theory does not bring us very far. True, the traditional perceptions we have defined as 'the India syndrome' affecting mainstream Pakistani ideology do hold sway over the shaping of the bilateral relationship. But even those who think afresh for charting a path out of the present difficulties have no readymade answer to offer. But they may at least raise good questions, and identify stumbling blocks, some of them being structural (the power structure and the deficit of representative democracy, for instance), while others result from risky strategies implemented since the 1980s and 1990s (particularly as far as the Islamicization of the Kashmir policy is concerned). Ayesha Jalal offers interesting reflections in this regard. She recognizes, first, that the 'policy of sustaining low intensity warfare against India' cannot succeed in Kashmir, then goes further, echoing a question heard more often privately than publicly: 'Should the Kashmir cause take precedence over Pakistan's own internal and external security?' Perhaps 'Pakistan can court peace and economic prosperity' if it were to give up Kashmir, but would it be realistic, asks Jalal. She answers 'no' for three reasons. First, because of the domestic scenario and 'the deeply entrenched interests of the army' and various intelligence agencies. Second, because the organizations which train and arm militants for Kashmir would certainly not reduce the internal security risk they represent for Pakistan, if they were to face such a drastic shift in Pakistan's Kashmir policy. Third, on a less practical and more principled stand, because 'Pakistan has a moral responsibility in supporting the freedom struggle of a people so long denied the elementary right of choice in shaping their own destiny.' In other words, the officialization of the LoC is unacceptable, for it would amount to 'sanctifying territorial borders at the cost of human beings'.

Retract from any territorial claim; be ready for all options (including Kashmir's independence) other than the status quo; stop the jihad rhetorics and focus on the human rights issue: some of Jalal's proposals go far from the established paradigm, although calling the international community to 'enforce restraint on India's military war machine'[16] is much more consistent with the standard Pakistani expectations. Whatever be the degree of representativeness of Ayesha's Jalal analyses, they illustrate do how uncertain the road to a settlement of the Indo–

Pakistani dispute will be, as goodwill alone does not permit defining wa compromise between Indians who reject a plebiscite and Pakistanis who reject the status quo.

On the whole, Pakistan finds itself confronted with many dilemmas. The new configurations of the world order favour India for the time being, but they could favour as well a reformed Pakistan charting a new path towards democracy, peace on its borders, and economic recovery. The core of the problem lies inside Pakistan itself. It has a right to external security, but has also to define, or redefine, a national ideology which serves its internal security as well. It may certainly keep the Kashmir issue alive as a matter of principle, and make proposals for solving it, as long as it does not exacerbate the issue, and does not sabotage the compromise that India might eventually forge with the Kashmiris, if New Delhi were to choose at last to listen to them. But to define Kashmir as 'the core issue' would probably bring to Pakistan no more significant result in the future than it did in the past. More generally, Pakistan has to free itself from the India syndrome. It has to recognize the fact that India is a regional power, which is only bound to grow. On the other hand, India has to be, vis-à-vis its western neighbour, the 'benevolent power' that it argues it is (in the BJP electoral manifesto). Benevolence must start in Kashmir, provided that it is more than a mere paternalistic slogan. It must expand to Pakistan, which waits for a sign from New Delhi. The 'Gujral doctrine' suggesting to offer to neighbouring South Asian countries facilities without immediate reciprocity must be extended to Pakistan. But how to enlarge it after the Kargil trauma, whose impact on the Indian mind, coming so soon after the Lahore Agreement, is apparently not rightly evaluated in Islamabad?

The time is not ripe for optimism, nor for despair. Incertitude will prevail till men or women of vision take charge, and would work patiently and dedicatedly to 'remove the bitterness of the past'. This will be a time-consuming process. In between, armed peace has somehow to be preserved, although threatened by possible relapses. More than a billion human beings live under its wing.

NOTES

1. The diplomatic regional and international calendar offers annual conferences which provide (on their sidelines) opportunities for 'informal' Indo–Pakistani contacts at the highest level, particularly the meetings of SAARC, of the

Commonwealth, of the Non-Aligned Movement and the UN General Assembly.

2. Presidential Address delivered by Quaid-i-Azam Mohammad Ali Jinnah at the 27th Session of the All-India Muslim League, Lahore, 22-4 March 1940.

3. Ghulam Kibria's *A Shattered Dream*; Roedad Khan's *A Dream Gone Sour*, and Sherbaz Khan Mazari's *A Journey to Disillusionment* have all been published by Oxford University Press, Karachi.

4. Gen. Musharraf's Address to the Nation, 17 October 1999.

5. Defence expenditure and debt repayment account for more than 60 per cent of the State expenditure. In the mid-1990s, the defence expenditure ratio has been declining from 6 per cent to 5 per cent of the GDP in 1996, not counting a part of its military nuclear programme, as against 2.5 per cent for India, with the same reservations. After the nuclear tests of 1998, the Indian Government, led by the nationalist Bharatiya Janata Party, has substantially raised its defence budget. Pakistan could follow suit only at the cost of its basic economic equilibrium and sustainability.

6. For Pakistani analyses of Pakistan's nuclear programme and nuclear policy, see Munir Ahmed (1998), and Munir Ahmad Khan (1998). For Indian perspectives, see Sumita Kumar, 'Pakistan's Nuclear Weapon Programme' and Ruchita Beri, 'Pakistan's Missile Programme', in Jasjit Singh, ed., 1998, pp. 156-208.

7. This is what Indian defence expert Jasjit Singh hints at when he notes that the nuclear weapons tests gave the Pakistani leadership 'a false sense of security that the nuclear umbrella would allow its military strategy to succeed' Singh (1999), p. vii.

8. Maulana Abul Kalam Azad (the main Muslim leader of the Congress), in the unexpurged version of his Memoirs (1988), p. 242.

9. V.P. Menon (1957), p. 384.

10. In the 1950s, China occupied Aksai Chin, expanded it a bit at the cost of Indian Ladakh during the Sino-Indian war of 1962, and exchanged territories with Pakistan, east of the Karakoram, in 1963.

11. See Ganguly (1997).

12. Tavleen Singh, *Kashmir: A Tragedy of Errors*, New Delhi: Viking, 1996.

13. The White House, Office of the Press Secretary: *Remarks by the President to the People of Pakistan*, 25 March 2000.

14. The proposed redefinition of the administrative boundaries inside the Indian state of Jammu & Kashmir can hardly appear as a step in direction of the Pakistani proposal of holding a plebiscite at district level, although it appears to emphasize the local dimension of religious identities in Jammu, Ladakh and Kashmir.

15. To quote here, amongst many other writings, the titles of two opinion pieces published by *Dawn* one year after the Kargil episode unravelled. Sher Khan's 'Time to Bury the Hatchet' (*Dawn*, 5 May 2000), contrasts the enduring Indo-Pakistani stalemate with the evolution of bilateral relations between the

USA and Vietnam, North and South Korea, Egypt and Israel, etc. Ayesha
Jalal's 'Getting Back to the Right Side of History' (*Dawn*, 4 May 2000) will
be referred to in more detail later.
16. All these quotes are from Ayesha Jalal: 'Getting Back on the Right Side of
History', *Dawn*, 4 May 2000.

REFERENCES

Ahmad, Rafique, ed., *Pakistan India Relations: Prospects for a Durable Peace*, Lahore:
Pakistan Institute of National Affairs, 1989.
Ahmed, Akbar S., *Jinnah, Pakistan and Islamic Identity: The Quest for Saladin*, Karachi:
Oxford University Press, 1997.
Ahmed, Munir, *How We Got It: A True Story of Pakistani Nuclear Programme*, Lahore:
Sham-Kay-Baad Publications, 1998.
Azad, Maulana Abul Kalam, *India Wins Freedom*, Delhi: Orient Longman, 1988.
Behera, N.C., P.M. Evans and Gowher Rizvi, *Beyond Boundaries: A Report on the State
of Non-Official Dialogues on Peace, Security and Cooperation in South Asia*,
North York: University of Toronto–York University, 1997.
Blinkenberg, Lars, *India–Pakistan: The History of Unresolved Conflicts*, Odense: Odense
University Press, 1998.
Bose, Sumantra, *The Challenge in Kashmir: Democracy, Self-Determination and a Just Peace*,
Delhi: Sage, 1997.
Burke, S.M., and Lawrence Ziring, *Pakistan's Foreign Policy: An Historical Analysis*,
Karachi: Oxford University Press, 1990.
Dixit, J.N., 'Indo-Pak Relations: Reasons for Adversarial Drift, Future Prospects', in
Foreign Service Institute, *Indian Foreign Policy: Agenda for the 21st Century*,
Delhi: Konark, 1998, vol. 2, pp. 216-27.
Ganguly, Sumit, *The Crisis in Kashmir: Portents of War, Hopes for Peace*, Cambridge
University Press, 1997.
Harrison, Selig, Paul Kreisberg and Dennis Kux, eds., *India and Pakistan: The First Fifty
Years*, Cambridge: Cambridge University Press, 1998.
Hussain, Ijaz, *Kashmir Dispute: An International Law Perspective*, Islamabad: Quaid-i-
Azam University, 1998.
Jalal, Ayesha, 'Getting Back on the Right Side of History', *Dawn*, May 2000.
Jha, Prem Shankar, *Kashmir 1947: Rival Versions of History*, Delhi: Oxford University
Press, 1996.
Kashmir Study Group, *1947–1997: The Kashmir Dispute at Fifty, Charting Paths to Peace*,
New York: Kashmir Study Group, 1997.
Khan, Munir Ahmad, 'Nuclearisation of South Asia & its Regional Implications',
Regional Studies, vol. XVI, no. 4, 1998, pp. 3-59.
Khan, Sher, 'Time to Bury the Hatchet', *Dawn*, 5 May 2000.
Krepon, Michael and Amit Sevak, eds., *Crisis Prevention, Confidence Building and
Reconciliation in South Asia*, Washington: Henry L. Stimson Center, 1996.
Lamb, Alastair, *Kashmir: A Disputed Legacy, 1846–1990*, Hertingfordbury: Roxford
Books, 1991.
———, *Birth of a Tragedy: Kashmir 1947*, Hertingfordbury: Roxford Books, 1994.
Menon, V.P., *The Transfer of Power in India*, Princeton: Princeton University Press, 1957.

Samad,Yunas, 'Kashmir and the Imagining of Pakistan', *Contemporary South Asia*, 1995, vol. 4, no. 1, pp. 65-77.

Shafquat, Saeed, *Civil-Military Relations in Pakistan, From Zulfikar Ali Bhutto to Benazir Bhutto*, 1997.

Singh, Jasjit, ed., *Nuclear India*, New Delhi: World Knowledge Publications, 1998.

————, ed., *Kargil 1999*, Delhi: World Knowledge Publications, 1999.

Thomas, Raju, ed., *Perspective on Kashmir: The Roots of Conflict in South Asia*, Boulder, Colorado: Westview Press, 1992.

Wirsing, Robert, *India, Pakistan and the Kashmir Dispute: On Regional Conflict and its Resolution*, New York: Saint Martin's Press, 1994.

10

The Geopolitics of Pakistan's Energy Supply

FRÉDÉRIC GRARE

T HE SUPPLY OF energy has for long been one of the crucial
problems for the economic development of the Indian subcontinent. Despite a specific slowing down of economic growth, due
partly to the consequences of the nuclear tests conducted by India and
Pakistan, it will undoubtedly constitute one of the major challenges
that the region will have to confront at the turn of the millennium.

Pakistan, whose nuclear tests have served as a reminder of the importance of this country for the security of South Asia, is no exception
to the rule. Though endowed with considerable potential, it is, to a
large extent, not able to meet its energy needs. Its population,[1] its
economy and its rate of urbanization are growing at a pace that is faster
than the development of its energy resources. The chronic shortage of
electricity, for instance, is likely to increase further during the coming
years and will force the country to continue its arduous efforts at
structural adjustment. Hence, the urgent need to evolve development
strategies that will make it possible to meet the growing demand for
energy in keeping with the objectives of development.

While substantial efforts are being undertaken to exploit the existing resources and to develop a solid, indigenous base in the matter of
exploration and exploitation, Pakistan will nevertheless be obliged, in
the near future, to meet a growing part of its demands for energy
through increased imports; this will not fail to aggravate its already
burdensome balance of payments deficit. Pakistan, with some 37 billion dollars of external debt, equivalent to more than half its gross
national product, a trade deficit of 150 million dollars a month, foreign
exchange reserves amounting to 1.3 billion dollars,[2] and the servicing
of the interest on its debt oscillating between 200 and 500 million
dollars per month,[3] is totally dependent on foreign aid. The American
sanctions that followed its nuclear tests have increased the social

tensions undermining the already fragile cohesiveness of the country, and are intensifying its chronic instability.

This issue on both the economic and the social plane is compounded by yet another, of a geopolitical nature. It concerns not only the relations between Pakistan and its traditional sources of supply in the Middle East, but also those of this 'Land of the Pure' with the new producers of energy in the Caspian Sea basin, the Himalayas or the Pamirs. These relationships, which Pakistan appears to have counted upon for supplying a not negligible part of its future energy needs, are giving rise to misgivings on two counts.

1. First of all, they involve countries at war or operating in a climate of conflict and/or political uncertainty. The persistence of the Afghan conflict, for instance, rules out for the present any hope of the import of natural gas from Turkmenistan. Similarly, the Tajik civil war precludes for the time being any possibility of materialization of the contracts signed with Tajikistan for the supply of electricity. Last, the difficult political relations prevailing between Iran and Pakistan are causing substantial complication in the development of trade exchanges between the latter and the countries of Central Asia.

2. They give rise, next, to the question of the possibilities of a bilateral and multilateral cooperation between the states of South Asia on the one hand and the member states of the Organisation for Economic Cooperation on the other hand, as well as the question of the possibility of cooperation between these two entities. What is at stake here is the eventuality of an integrated approach to the question of energy, and the pivotal role that Pakistan might subsequently be led to play in this perspective. It, is indeed, the issue of how Indo–Pakistan relations evolve that is thrown up here, as well as that of the still incomplete geopolitical realignments subsequent to the end of the Cold War.

The present study aims at examining, basically the topic of oil and gas. Starting off with the present projections concerning the growth of demand, and an analysis of the structural constraints that Pakistan is faced with, it aims at concentrating on Pakistan's energy situation, keeping in view the geopolitical dimension of the problem. To do this, it will examine the political risks entailed by the dependence of the 'Land of the Pure' on the Middle East exclusively, as well as those involved in an eventual diversification of its sources of supply. In this perspective, special attention will be paid to Pakistan's relations with Central Asia and Iran.

Its canvas is, however, wider, and states are not the only players that figure in it. Over and above Pakistan, it is in fact India, seen as the largest emerging market in the world, which is the object of the envy of oil companies. The problematic of this study revolves entirely around the present and the potential link between South Asia, West Asia and Central Asia, or, to use an Anglo-Saxon term that is in vogue, between South Asia and the 'greater Middle East' in which Pakistan plays a pivotal role. It brings out a contradiction between the political difficulties in the short run, the crisis created by the Pakistani and Indian nuclear tests being just one more among such episodes, and the long-term necessities which point towards a reconciliation between the two regions, implying a normalization of Indo–Pakistan relations. It, therefore, proposes to examine the possibilities and conditions associated with increased regional cooperation in the matter of energy. On the one hand SAARC, and the OEC on the other hand, might constitute, if necessary, the institutional frameworks for such cooperation. This study proposes also to examine the consequences of these factors on the geopolitical situation of Pakistan and of the region as a whole.

The present work does not claim, obviously, to be exhaustive, on a subject whose scope extends far beyond the aspects examined here, that too only partially and in an incomplete manner. It expects more modestly to contribute towards focusing attention on a problematic whose importance has still remained ill perceived. For beyond the purely economic dimension of a still very hypothetical potential link, what is at stake is also the political stability of one of the most populated regions of the globe, skirting, what is more, the borders of the strategic waterways of communication between the Persian Gulf and the rest of the world.

DEPENDENCE AND SECURITY IN THE FIELD OF ENERGY

Although frequently utilized, the term 'energy security' is relatively ambiguous. With the passage of time, its distinctly military connotation—it meant initially the safeguarding of supplies during wartime—has taken on the significance more associated with economics, denoting the long-term protection against effects of oil crises. It is, however, in both cases, connected as much with the situation of dependence of the consumer country/countries on the producer country/countries, as with the political stability of the latter.

In the case of Pakistan, this dependence has been established at around 38 per cent of the available energy.[4] Out of the 39.25 million tonnes of oil equivalent, 15.08 are imported.[5] Out of this 5,52,636 tonnes represent coal equivalent[6] oil and 14 million 4,96,637 tonnes oil.[7] The magnitude of this dependence is not enough by itself to define the level of security or lack of security of the country on the energy front.[8] The real problem lies much more, in the present case, in the specific context of dependence on three countries alone, Iran, Saudi Arabia and the United Arab Emirates, whose stability is uncertain.[9]

Political Dimension of Energy Security

Rather than recapitulate the events which had led to the oil crises of the past two decades,[10] it is undoubtedly preferable here to lay stress on two recent events likely to affect the security of oil supplies and for which Pakistan, among others, would inevitably have to pay the price.

1. *The renewed growth in the demand for oil*: While the demand for oil stagnated during the 1980s, it is, on the other hand, likely to increase significantly once again during the coming years. According to the International Agency for Energy, this demand is likely to grow by 2 per cent per annum (as against 0.3 per cent per annum during the decade 1980–90), the growth of Asia's economies being largely responsible for this situation.[11]

2. *The growing concentration of production in the Middle East alone*: A renewed growth is taking place in the context of an ever-increasing concentration of the production in the Middle East alone, where the political conflicts and tension that have been responsible for the oil crises in the past are still very prevalent. The stagnating 'peace process', the growing disenchantment with the Middle East policy of the United States, the political and economic difficulties[12] facing the States of the region, are the many factors liable to singularly complicate the geopolitics of the region.[13]

In a context of increased demand of oil and of the concentration of its production in a geopolitically unstable arena, it would be no exaggeration to consider the possibility of a stoppage of supply as a potential danger.

TABLE 10.1: A COMPARISON OF ALTERNATIVE OIL PRICE PROJECTIONS

Source	1995	2000	2005	2010	2015	2020
OWEM Reference Case (1996$/b)	17.2	17.6	19.4	21.4	23.6	26.1
IIASA/IEW Poll Response (medians), January 1996	20.5 (1990)	19.0	—	26.0	—	33.3
P.R. Odell, 'Is Middle Eastern Domination of the International Oil Market Inevitable?' IIASA International Energy Workshop, Laxenburg, Austria, 1995	15.8 (1993)	16.5	—	18.3	—	21.0
International Energy Outlook, 1996, EIA/DOE	16.8	19.3	21.9	23.7	25.4	—
World Energy Outlook/IEA, 1996	16.3	17.0	17.0	25.0	17.0	25.0
Petroleum Economics Ltd., Oil and Energy Outlook to 2010, December 1995	16.4	14.7	14.6	12.3	—	—
Data Resources Incorporated, Oil Market Outlook, October 1995	16.5	16.8	20.8	23.2	24.8	—
Petroleum Industry Research Associates Inc., 'World and US Oil', October 1995	17.7	14.7	15.4	—	—	—
The WEFA Group, 'US long-term economic outlook', 4th Quarter 1995	17.2	19.6	21.3	22.1	—	—
Gas Research Institute, 'Baseline Projection of the US Energy Supply and Demand', October 1995	—	16.2	16.2	16.2	16.2	—
National Economic Rsearch Associates Inc., 'NERA Energy Outlook', February 1996	16.9	21.6	27.1	21.5	—	—
EC 'European Energy to 2020', Spring 1996	17.6	21.10	—	29.0	—	31.0
Bonner & Moore Associates, in Arab Oil and Gas, 1 February 1996 (1995$/b)	17.1	17.2	18.5	—	—	—
Median Growth in forecasts other than OWEM	1995-2010: 0.9% pa			2010-20: 1.4% pa		

Source: Oil & Energy Outlook to 2020, January 1997, OPEC Secretariat, Vienna.

Note: The forecasts made in Table 10.1 are to be taken as indicators of trends. The author has neither the desire, nor the ability to discuss the hypotheses on which each of the models whose results appear here is based.

The Economic Dimension

More disquieting perhaps, being relatively more probable (keeping in mind, moreover, the above-mentioned elements), are the projections concerning the trend of prices of oil. Given in Table 10.1 is a convincing comparison of the projections made in the matter by various specialized agencies.

THE NATURAL GAS OPTION

Of the commercial energy consumed by the 'Land of the Pure', 37 per cent being made up of imported oil, Pakistan has to disburse a sum of some 2.5 billion dollars, amounting to one-fifth of its export earnings. About one-third of this oil is used for generating the electricity consumed. Now, both from the economic as well as the ecological point of view, it could be replaced to advantage by natural gas, which would also enable better control over the increase in the dependence on oil.

A projection (Table 10.2) for the horizon 2002/3 (end of the 9th Five-Year Plan) based on the increase observed during the last five years would indicate the near doubling of imports of oil.[14]

TABLE 10.2: PRIMARY ENERGY DEMAND PROJECTIONS BASED ON
HISTORICAL GROWTH DURING LAST 5 YEARS

			(in barrels of oil equivalent per day)
	1995-6 *Actual*	*2002/3* *Projections*	*Annual Compound* *Growth Rate*
Indigenous			
Oil	57,549 (7.3%)	71,000 (5.4%)	*
Gas	2,90,735 (36.8%)	4,09,000 (31.2%)	5.0%
Coal	33,147 (4.2%)	42,000 (3.2%)	3.6%
Hydro	1,12,809 (14.3%)	1,58,000 (12.1%)	4.9%
Nuclear	2,347 (0.3%)	12,000 (0.9%)	†
Imported			
Oil	2,78,139 (35.2%)	6,00,000 (45.8%)	11.6%
Coal	14,471 (1.8%)	17,000 (1.3%)	2.15%
Total	7,89,197 (100%)	13,09,000 (100%)	7.5%

Source: Ministry of Petroleum and Natural Resources, Islamabad.
Notes: * Assumed a 3 per cent overall growth rate as a sum total of declining production from existing fields and addition from new discoveries as a result of ongoing exploration programmes.
† Assuming commissioning of 300 mw Chashma Nuclear Power Project in 2001.

TABLE 10.3: PRIMARY ENERGY SUPPLIES DIVERSIFICATION
FROM OIL TO GAS

('000s barrels of oil equivalent)   *(Desired 2002/3)*

	Present (1995-6)	After Substitution	Growth Rates
Indigenous			
Oil	57 (7.3%)	71 (5.5%)	3.0%
Gas	291 (36.8%)	485 (37.5%)	7.6%
Coal	48 (6.0%)	90 (7.0%)	9.5%
Hydro	113 (14.3%)	144 (11.1%)	3.6%
Nuclear	2 (0.3%)	33 (2.6%)	45.9%
Imported			
Oil	278 (35.3%)	264 (20.4%)	-0.7%
Gas	163 (12.6%)		
Coal	44 (3.4%)		
Total	789	1,294	7.4%

Source: Ministry of Petroleum and Natural Resources, Islamabad.
Assumptions: 1. Energy consumption to increase at 7.4 per cent p.a.; 2. All new thermal power to be fuelled by gas/coal.

Keeping in mind the fluctuations in the prices per barrel, it is not certain that such a trend would lead systematically to a similar doubling of the oil bill. It would, nevertheless, worsen the balance of trade deficit and would necessitate massive investments in the field of infrastructure for the storage and the transportation of the oil. Hence, the objective of increasing the share of natural gas in the overall consumption of energy by 50 per cent and decreasing that of oil by 30 per cent.

Pakistan is itself a producer of natural gas and is reported to possess considerable resources of the same. Some 7,250 km of pipelines and a

TABLE 10.4: POTENTIAL RESOURCES

	Potential Resource	Proven so far
Oil (billion barrels)	40	0.5
Gas (trillion cft)	200	31
Coal (billion tonnes)	185	2.9
Hydro (mw) (Economically viable)	30,000	4,826

Source: Ministry of Petroleum and Natural Resources, Islamabad.

distribution network stretching over 46,500 km ensures the distribution of an indigenous production which has increased at the rate of 5 per cent per annum during the course of these last few years.[15] But despite recent and promising discoveries in Baluchistan, the demand for natural gas is increasing faster than its supply.

Pakistan's proximity to the producer countries of West and Central Asia, notably Qatar, Iran and Turkmenistan, is the cause of this country becoming both a market as well as a natural middleman for the transport of, and the regional trade in, natural gas.

Pakistan and the Regional Development Projects

It was only logical that Pakistan would play a role in the regional projects for development of the trade in natural gas which made an appearance in the early 1990s when it became obvious to all that this source of clean energy, less expensive than oil and likely, moreover, to generate considerable foreign exchange earnings, was an important one. However, Pakistan initially figured in these projects only as a medium, the necessary location for the gas to cross through from the Persian Gulf on its way to India.

1. In 1990, the construction of a pipeline of 3,300 km and a capacity of almost 36 billion cubic metres per year was proposed, which was to connect Bandar Abbas with Calcutta. The western provinces of Iran would have received 10 per cent of the exported gas and Pakistan 20 per cent, the balance going to India. Its cost was estimated at about 12 billion dollars. The project however did not materialize.[16]

2. The Australian company Broken Hill Petroleum Corporation proposed the construction of a pipeline meant also for the export of Iranian gas intended for the west coast of India. From its starting point on the island of Qeshm, this gas pipeline would have been constructed along the Iranian and Pakistani coasts up to India. It would have been possible to also connect the gas from the South Pars offshore field and even from Qatar, to this line. This project also was abandoned following a change of management at the head of the company.[17]

3. In early 1992, Chiyoda Corporation made a proposal for an even more ambitious project, contemplating the linking together of several producers and consumers extending from the Mediterranean to India. The cost of this project, meant to link together Europe,

North Africa, the Middle East and India, was estimated at 38 billion dollars. In September 1993, the size of the project was reduced to a considerable extent and its South Asian dimension was abandoned.[18]

4. On the other hand, the gas pipeline project between Qatar and Pakistan, proposed in 1991 by the Crescent Petroleum Company of Pakistan, still remains a possibility. The project, extending over a length of 1,600 km at an estimated cost of 3 billion dollars, initially encountered some feasibility problems; the necessity of crossing through water at a great depth (nearly 3,000 m) in the Arabian Gulf would have considerably increased the price of the gas and reduced thereby the economic benefit to be derived from this project. It was recast in 1992, and Crescent Petroleum announced that the gas pipeline would be routed from Qatar to Dubai and would then cross through the Strait of Hormuz to subsequently border the Iranian coast up to Pakistan. It was on the basis of this plan that the Pakistani company joined the TransCanada Pipelines Ltd and Brown & Route Inc. in 1994 to develop a transmission system thereafter named 'Gulf-South Asia Gas Project' (GUSA).[19] This project has, however, yet to come into being.

One major event was to take place in the early 1990s, which, without changing the basic nature of the problem that Pakistani decision-makers had to face (and still continue to face), brought a distinct element of complexity into the matter. The emergence of the Central Asian republics as independent producers of energy, joined to the obsession with security of the 'Land of the Pure' and to the chronic instability of the region, introduced into Islamabad's calculations considerations of a geostrategic nature which vied in importance with its purely economic motivations. Indeed, few pipelines will have been the subject of as much controversy as the one meant to bring Turkmeni oil and gas to Pakistan through warring Afghanistan.

Afghanistan and the Energy Projects of Pakistan

The Story of an Incomplete Project

Before becoming a point of focus of regional relations and an object of international disgrace on account of the alleged links of one of the promoters with the Taliban, the aforementioned project was at first the subject of bitter rivalry between two competitor oil companies, Bridas and UNOCAL.

The Argentinean company Bridas was the first Western company to show an interest, in 1991, in the hydrocarbon products of a newly independent Turkmenistan. The Yashlar fields to the east of the country, near the Afghan border, were allotted to it. Two years later, the Keimir oil field near the Caspian Sea was also assigned to it.[20] Right from 1994, Bridas began to export oil from the Keimir field and in 1995 it discovered a new gas deposit estimated at 27 billion cubic feet[21] in the Yashlar zone. Considering the magnitude of the discoveries, the Turkmeni Government, which had initially granted very advantageous terms to the Argentinean company, demanded a periodical renegotiation of the current contracts, with the result that Bridas began to fear soon thereafter that it would not be able to make a profit on its investments.

It was at this time that, looking for a market for the gas from the Yashlar deposit, it tried to arouse the interest of Pakistan in the construction of a pipeline joining Yashlar (in Turkmenistan) to Sui (in Pakistan), crossing through Afghanistan. Islamabad had already started negotiations with Teheran for the delivery of Iranian gas, but on 15 March 1995, Benazir Bhutto and the Turkmeni President Nyazov signed an agreement for the preparation of a feasibility study.[22]

At the same time, desirous of reducing the risks arising out of the Afghan civil war, Bridas tried to bring some other companies into the picture, among these being the American oil company UNOCAL, which had established itself in Pakistan since 1976. It would seem that at the instigation of Bridas, some Turkmeni officials met representatives of UNOCAL in Houston in April 1995.[23]

The negotiations which then began, however, moved away quite rapidly from the initial plan, and on 25 October 1995, President Niyazov signed an agreement with UNOCAL and its Saudi partner Delta Oil for the construction of a gas pipeline crossing Afghanistan, joining the Daulatabad field, with reserves estimated at 708 billion cubic metres, to Multan in Pakistan.[24] The project was to be operated by a consortium in which UNOCAL had 70 per cent of the shares, Delta Oil 15 per cent, the Russian company Gazprom 10 per cent and the Turkmeni State company Turkmenrosgas 5 per cent.[25]

UNOCAL signed a second agreement with the Turkmeni Government, the Central Asian Pipeline Project, with the intention of exporting oil from the Turkmeni field of Chardzou towards a new terminal (Gwadar) situated on the Pakistan coast, from where it was then to be transported to India and South-East Asia. This project itself formed part of a more ambitious pattern in the framework of which (from the starting point of this initial pipeline) the oil from Turkmenistan, Uzbekistan, Kazakhstan and western Siberia would be linked to the Indian Ocean.[26]

At the same time, as Bridas still refused to renegotiate its contracts with the Turkmeni Government, the latter stopped all exports of the company and put an end to all the operations of the company on its territory. The Argentinean company then took UNOCAL to court in the county of Fort Bend, Texas, alleging interference in its pipeline project and claiming several billion dollars in damages and interest. It demanded the arbitration of the International Chamber of Commerce (ICC) against the Turkmenistan Government for breach of contract.[27] At the same time, it kept up its presence among the Taliban, which by then had taken control of Kabul, and signed an agreement with the latter as also with Rashid Dostum for the construction of a gas pipeline.

In May 1997, during a summit meeting of the Organisation for Economic Cooperation (OEC) held at Ashkabad in Pakistan, Turkmenistan and the two companies UNOCAL and Delta Oil signed a new agreement for the construction of a dual pipeline (one gas and one oil), as well as for the finalization of the consortium entrusted with the financing and implementation of the project before the end of 1997. On 4 and 5 June 1997, the inaugural meeting of the joint Turkmenistan–Afghanistan–Pakistan working group brought to light a difference of interpretation between the partners. What the Pakistani and Turkmeni authorities considered as the deadline for the start of the work was considered by UNOCAL and Delta only as a desirable objective.[28] The setting up of the new consortium, CENTGAS, was nevertheless, finalized at the end of the month of October 1997. UNOCAL now owned 46.5 per cent of the capital, Delta Oil 15 per cent, Tukmenrosgas 7 per cent, the Pakistani company Crescent Group 3.5 per cent, the Japanese companies Inpex and Hitochu 6.5 per cent each, and the South Korean Hyundai 5 per cent. Gazprom showed some interest by reserving 10 per cent of the shares.[29]

Till the American bombardment of the Mujahideen camps in Afghanistan and the announcement on 21 August 1998,[30] of the suspension of its activities in the country, UNOCAL enjoyed the staunch support of Pakistan and Turkmenistan. Its position with regard to the Taliban, however, remained ambivalent, the latter having declared that they would give their support to whichever company was the first to start work on construction of the pipeline. With the suspension of the project, however, the uncertainty on this matter became, for the time being, inconsequential.

The Stakes of Rivalry

To understand the overall stakes at peril, it is undoubtedly desirable to examine the energy problem in the wider context of Pakistan's general policy with regard to Central Asia. The objectives of this policy are indeed not limited to the economic field alone. The competition between Bridas and UNOCAL, then with BHP Petroleum, would well have been just anecdotal, a simple rivalry between commercial enterprises, had it not been for the crucial role of Afghanistan as the place where these regional rivalries were being played out.

INDO–PAKISTANI ANTAGONISM: PAKISTAN'S EFFORT
TO REVITALIZE ITS RELATIONS WITH THE US

Indo–Pakistani antagonism played a crucial role in this tussle. This was not only because it was a factor to contend with in the wider context of the Cold War, but also because, in the struggle for influence between the US and the USSR in the region, it was used to advantage as an instrument.

While the Central Asia policy of Pakistan did indeed take note of the continued war in Afghanistan, neither the fear of the Soviet Union, nor the threat presented by the Afghan claim to 'Pakhtunistan'[31] were ever the only, or even the main, Pakistani priorities in this conflict. Islamabad continued to consider India as its foremost threat. However, the presence of the Red Army in Afghanistan enabled Zia-ul-Haq to acquire state of the art American armament systems and to thus partially compensate for its quantitative inferiority with regard to India, and above all, to develop its nuclear programme for military purposes, relatively freely. This situation could last, however, only as long as the Soviet presence itself lasted, and, in fact, the US progressively lost all interest in Afghanistan, and subsequently in Pakistan, once the Red Army had completed its withdrawal. In accordance with the agreement concluded in 1987 between Islamabad and Washington, American money and arms continued to flow into Pakistan till 1992, but non-proliferation and armaments control once again became matters of priority for the State Department at this time, and American aid was stopped. What was more serious in Pakistan's view, the economic liberalization that the Rao Government was initiating in India at this time made it clear to Pakistani decision-makers that the new formulations of American policy then taking place in the subcontinent could well, and in all likelihood would indeed, be to the advantage of India.

Under such conditions, the collapse of USSR and the emergence of newly independent energy-producing countries were seen by Pakistan as an unexpected opportunity to breathe new life into the privileged relationship that had united these two countries throughout the Afghan war. Islamabad tried from then onwards to become the preferred route for export of Central Asian hydrocarbon products to the markets of the world, thus hoping to develop its influence in Central Asia, and at the same time to prevent India from becoming Washington's chosen ally in the region. To do this, it had to ensure the stability of Afghanistan, and in some form or the other, keep it under its control in order to ensure access to the hydrocarbons.

Till 1994, however, Islamabad proved to be incapable of putting an end to the civil war which had followed the Soviet withdrawal from Afghanistan. The policy of splitting up of factions, which had basically constituted its Afghan policy throughout the Soviet presence, now proved to be counterproductive. Its attempts at imposing the setting up of a government of national union, then the Islamabad, Peshawar and Jalalabad agreements, all ended in failure. The antagonism persisting between the main factions, notably the Hizb-e-Islami of Gulbuddin Hekmatyar and the Jamaat-i-Islami of Burhanuddin Rabbani and Ahmad Shah Massud not only prevented the development of any economic and political link with Central Asia, but, what is more, drew Afghanistan itself into a growing state of anarchy.

It was in this situation that the Taliban movement emerged in the autumn of 1994. A popular movement (at least initially), born out of the discontent aroused by the anarchy which then prevailed in the southern part of the country, it rapidly obtained the support of Pakistan, and then began its advance towards Kabul which fell to it on 27 September 1996. The effect of the movement for the reunification of the country, which then began, was to alienate Pakistan from the near totality of the regional powers.

Reactions of Regional Powers

The emergence of new, independent, regional players was not looked upon in as favourable a manner by all the regional powers. India, notably, initially saw in the independence of the former Soviet republics of Central Asia a strengthening of the position of Pakistan in the region. In the view of Indian decision-makers, as in that of their Pakistani counterparts, their common adherence to Islam did indeed make the five Central Asian republics potential allies of Islamabad. New Delhi hence tried to prevent its turbulent neighbour from achieving its ends by strengthening its own relations with each one of the Central Asian capitals, and did this by playing on their fear of Islamic fundamentalism.[32] Seeking to isolate Pakistan, India, at the same time, strengthened its links with Iran. In exchange for Iranian neutrality in the Kashmir conflict,[33] India systematically adopted attitudes contrary to those of Islamabad and vigorously opposed the American embargo against Teheran,[34] obtaining, in addition, facilities for passage towards Central Asia.

Fearing that the penetration of Western capital into Central Asia would be accompanied by a possible loss of influence in its 'close foreign neighbour', Russia let it be known soon enough that it would not allow the power vacuum prevailing in the post-Soviet arena to be occupied by external interest groups, this warning being aimed naturally at the Pakistani or Afghan Islamic groups, and the Western interests which, rightly or wrongly, were associated with them.

Iran, which, on its part, entertained ambitions in Central Asia similar to those of Pakistan could not but experience anxiety over the advance of the Taliban. For ideological reasons first of all, since the Islamic Republic could obviously not but condemn the violently anti-Shia nature of the movement. This anti-Shiaism was a threat, moreover, to the Hazara minority, and more specifically the Hizb-e-Wahadat, on which Iran had built the (very limited) influence it wielded in Afghanistan.[35] More important, however, Teheran interpreted the prominence given to the 'students of theology' as a veritable Saudi–Pakistani–American conspiracy aimed at isolating it even further. The pipeline project of the two companies, Delta and UNOCAL, seemed to give to this (theory of conspiracy) a semblance of reality.[36] It was, therefore, appropriate that its implementation be prevented, contributing to maintaining the country in a state of civil war.

Even before the Taliban could advance in a decisive manner by occupying the cities of Mazar-e-Sharif and Bamyan in the summer of 1998, Pakistan already found itself isolated. With the exception of Turkmenistan, it had alienated the entire sum total of the regional powers. Iran, Uzbekistan, Russia and India supported (to different degrees, it is true), the Northern Alliance made up of the Hizb-i-Wahadat, the Jumbesh of Dostum and the Jamaat-i-Islami of Massud and Rabbani, while Pakistan, for its part, constituted the most solid supporter of the Taliban.

The 'Iran Pakistan Pipeline Project': A New Factor of Discord

The energy question complicated the situation even further in early 1998. On 24 January 1998, a press release of the Australian company, BHP Petroleum and of the National Iranian Gas Company announced in fact that 15 billion cubic feet of gas from the vast deposits of South Pars had been allocated for consumption in Pakistan, and that the two companies proposed to construct a gas pipeline of some 2,500 km from Assaluyeh, in the south of Iran, to Multan in Pakistan (this pipeline might subsequently be connected to India) at an estimated cost of 2.7 billion dollars.[37]

This new project gave rise to competition between two routes; the Iranian route and the Afghan route, and above all between two countries, Iran and Turkmenistan, on account of the varied advantages and disadvantages of each of the two routes. The Iranian route had the advantage of being clearly less risky from the political angle, but involved, on the other hand, a higher cost than for the Turkmeni gas on account of the construction of the infrastructure required for its exploitation. In Turkmenistan, the latter was already in place.

This competition, in fact, existed only on account of the con-

TABLE 10.5: GAS IMPORT PROPOSALS

From Qatar	
Total pipeline length	1,620 km
Proposed route	Qatar–UAE–Iran–Pakistan
Capacity (flow rate)	Committed: 1,500 MMCFD
	Design: Over 2,000 MMCFD
From Iran	
Total pipeline length	1,740 km
Proposed route	Iran–Pakistan
Capacity (flow rate)	Committed: 1,500 MMCFD
	Design: Over 2,000 MMCFD
From Turkmenistan	
Total pipeline length	1,540 km
Proposed route	Turkmenistan–Afghanistan–Pakistan
Capacity (flow rate)	Committed: 1,500 MMCFD
	Design: Over 2,000 MMCFD

Source: Ministry of Petroleum and Natural Resources, Islamabad.

tradictions between the long-term perspectives and the short-term realities that the oil companies were faced with. It is the Indian market, considered as the largest emerging market in the world, that all the companies involved in the region are eyeing. With the exception of liquefied petroleum gas, which is more expensive, all the means of export of Iranian or Central Asian gas going to India have necessarily to cross either the continental plateau or Pakistani territory.

In the absence of a significant improvement in the political relations between the two countries leading to the possibility of real co-operation between India and Pakistan, they have to be content with the Pakistani market to make their investments worthwhile and profitable. Now, while the magnitude of the energy shortage in Pakistan opened the door to the simultaneous development of several projects, the discoveries of gas made in Baluchistan during the course of 1997 changed the situation to a remarkable degree. While it is still impossible to determine the extent of the deposits, they do seem to be large enough to warrant the immediate execution by the Ministry of Petroleum and Natural Resources of Pakistan of one project, the necessity of a second one being considered only by the year 2007.

Considering what has been said till now, it would obviously be absurd to view the Iranian support to the Northern Alliance through the single prism of the energy wager. In their dual aspects, the defensive one (preventing the circumvention of Iran by adopting an Afghan route) and the offensive one (promoting the construction of a pipeline connecting the Iranian gas reserves to the Pakistani consumer centres), these have, none the less, constituted an important determining factor in the formulation of Iran's recent Afghan policy.

The US–Pakistan Relationship:
Story of a Misunderstanding

Paradoxically however, while the national interests of the regional powers in the neighbourhood of Pakistan reveal the game of alliances being played in the Afghan conflict and the subsequent halt to all development in the sphere of energy, it was America's policy in the region which put an end (provisionally?) to Pakistani hopes in this field. It was subsequent to the American bombings of the Mujahideen camps based in Afghanistan that UNOCAL announced, on 21 August 1998, the suspension by the consortium CENTGAS, of all its activities concerning the pipelines crossing Afghanistan.[38] Indeed, the history of American–Pakistani relations with regard to Afghanistan since the fall of Najibullah appear to resemble a misunderstanding for which each of the protagonists must share a part of the responsibility.

THE DISPARITY BETWEEN PAKISTANI AND AMERICAN INTERESTS IN CENTRAL ASIA

Their lack of interest in the projects in question or at least their view of them as not enjoying a high priority, did not date back to the summer of 1998. Totally immersed in their desire to revitalize the privileged relationship that had existed between the two countries throughout the course of the Soviet presence in Afghanistan, Pakistani decision-makers visibly overestimated the importance of their own patterns of development for the Americans.

The latter probably helped them in holding this view. Shortly after the capture of Kabul in September 1996, Robin Raphel, Assistant Secretary of State for South Asia, during a speech in the United Nations had, stressed on the necessity for recognizing the Taliban as an indigenous movement and a lasting power.[39] A little later, on 28 October 1996, the American Consul in Karachi declared that his country was in favour of increased economic links between Pakistan and the CIS crossing Afghanistan, and he recalled the interest shown by American businessmen in a development of this kind.[40] He was probably just making a statement of fact. His declaration, which indicated that such objectives could only be met when peace would have been restored in Afghanistan, hardly involved the US.[41] It was, none the less, interpreted at the time as an encouragement to the Pakistani projects.

It was too quickly forgotten that the implicit acceptance of the Taliban by the US was due essentially to the hope it gave rise to of an end to the anarchy that prevailed in a not negligible part of the country, and notably of the closing down of the training camps of the Mujahideen and an end to the peddling of drugs. But while order was restored, a certain number of camps (those of the Harkat-ul-Ansar which was active basically in Kashmir) were reopened under Pakistani pressure and the drug peddling continued.

It was being forgotten also that American concerns were not confined to the interests of their oil companies alone and that in the US, more probably than anywhere else, foreign-policy decisions were the outcome of the interplay of a multiplicity of influences and contradictions. Seen from this standpoint, the CENTGAS consortium project constituted just one possibility among others of the opening up of Central Asian hydrocarbons. And, in the view of the American administration, the pipeline projects crossing the Caucasus were more important than the project opening up from the south. The American bombings in Afghanistan only made apparent, in a spectacular fashion, an option that had already been selected much earlier.

THE OBSTACLES OF FINANCING:
THE SHORT-TERM AND LONG-TERM DILEMMA

The Afghan situation alone does not explain the dead-end at which the energy development projects of Pakistan find themselves today. It undoubtedly constitutes the most immediate and the most evident hurdle, but it conceals at the same time other difficulties, not the least of these being that of financing.

The consequences of the American economic sanctions which followed the nuclear tests are not the only ones involved. Pakistan has, for many years, imported more than it could export, using international aid, loans from abroad, foreign exchange earnings repatriated by its expatriate workers, and foreign investments to partially make good the deficit. This deficit has incessantly continued to increase, and the country has several times been on the verge of declaring suspension of payments. In October 1997, the debts of the main public enterprises in the energy sector rose towards each other and towards their external creditors, to more than one and a half billion dollars. The largest among them, the Water and Power Development Authority (WAPDA), was close to bankruptcy. It alone owed more than 400 million dollars to its creditors, and its debt kept increasing by around 50 million dollars every month.[42]

The suspension of direct American aid and of loans from the International Monetary Fund only further aggravated the situation. Fearing a flight of foreign exchange, the government immediately froze, after the nuclear tests, some 11 million dollars lying in local accounts, which did not prevent the rate of the rupee from immediately plunging downwards. Foreign investments came to a halt almost as rapidly,[43] and Pakistani expatriates stopped sending their capital home through official channels on account of the difference of the extent of 25 per cent between the official and the market rates of exchange of the rupee.[44] At one stroke, the government lost almost all its foreign exchange sources (which brought in almost 3 billion dollars a year), while inflation set in once again, sustained partly by the rise in the price of petroleum products.

The fact that one of the first agreements concluded by Pakistan in an attempt to redress the situation was an oil loan granted by Saudi Arabia, is something that should not be ignored. But over and above the matter of Pakistan's ability to surmount the present crisis (and in addition even the question of regaining the goodwill of the international community towards it), there is indeed the problem of its capacity to honour its long-term commitments with regard to its options in the matter of energy. As a matter of fact, as against oil, whose modality of purchase is very often negotiated in international markets on the basis of short-term payments, the trade in gas involves long-term contracts (twenty to thirty years). Now, not only does Pakistan's internal debt, which today has reached more than 20 billion dollars,[45] portend in the short, middle and long term, a worsening of the difficulties in the matter of payments, which is hardly likely to reassure investors, but the recent affair already mentioned concerning the Independent Power Plant (no. 45), has made an even further dent in the credibility of the government.

The latter is hence confronted with a dilemma difficult to resolve. It has the choice of either continuing to pay, with ever-increasing difficulty, for energy that is expensive and thereby increasing its deficit, or to opt for less expensive energy, which is likely to relatively alleviate the burden of the energy bill on its balance of payments, but for which it is more and more incapable of offering the financial guarantees likely to inspire necessary confidence in investors, required for its development.

INDO–PAKISTAN RELATIONS IN THE FIELD OF ENERGY

It may seem incongruous, to say the least, to attempt here to examine the subject of cooperation between India and Pakistan in the matter of energy. For not only have most of the projects likely to have led to such cooperation been suspended,[46] but the crisis set in motion by the nuclear tests of both countries seems to have taken the relations between them back to where they were several years earlier. However, it would probably not be an exaggeration to consider the present tension as yet one more brief but tumultuous episode in the history of the relations between these two rivals in the subcontinent.

More important is the fact that the problematic of energy has figured till recently on the agenda of the bilateral negotiations between the two countries. India and Pakistan were even on the point of signing a memorandum of understanding when the first series of India's nuclear tests temporarily put an end to what might have been the start

TABLE 10.6: PROJECTION FOR THE DEMAND FOR
HYDROCARBONS IN INDIA

	Unit	2001	2006	2011
Oil products	mt (million tonnes)	87	115.8	149
Gas	bcm (billion cubic metres)	36.6	43.8	61.3

Source: Tata Energy Research Institute, New Delhi.

of some kind of cooperation.[47] It is probably better not to read too much into the import of such a step. Never the less, it does bring out the awareness, at least in this specific field, of the need for a real commonality of interests. In fact, energy does constitute a recurrent subject matter for discussions between the two countries (even though their commitment never really goes beyond simple declarations of intention).[48] Like Pakistan, India also faces a chronic and growing shortage of energy. Like Pakistan, it considers the recourse to natural gas (a less expensive and cleaner alternative)[49] as being one of the possible options if it wants to reduce its dependence on oil. Last, its potential suppliers also are the same as those of Pakistan, namely, Iran and Central Asia.

All studies, moreover, concur in the view that, from the strictly economic standpoint, cooperation between the two countries, more specifically for the utilization of joint pipelines for the import of natural gas, would enable vast economies of scale resulting for each of them out of a substantial decrease in the unit cost of gas.[50]

The construction of the already mentioned pipelines poses no technical problem: the obstacles in the way of the implementation of bilateral cooperation between the two countries in this sector are manifestly of a political and psychological nature. The Kashmir conflict—needless to recall here that it has been the reason for three wars in 1948, 1965 and 1999—which came in the aftermath of an incomplete partition, has envenomed the relations between the two countries ever since independence. Their antagonism also has its roots in certain psychological factors. 'A nation of refusals', Pakistan has always opposed what it perceives as India's aspirations to leadership in the region on account of its size, its population, its technological and industrial progress and its military superiority.

Apart from the two wars already mentioned (to which should be added the 1971 conflict over the secession of East Pakistan), these different factors had consequences in the military sphere—among these being an armaments race which culminated in the acquisition of nuclear weapons by the two protagonists—as also political and diplomatic ones. It has already been mentioned during the course of this study that India and Pakistan have been adopting reciprocally opposite policies in Central Asia, where India today has an edge over Pakistan. Similarly, their respective support has gone systematically to opposite factions or alliances throughout the Afghan conflict, during and after the Soviet invasion. In other words, their respective attitudes, in the field of energy, which is the subject of this study, run systematically counter to their common interests.

Perspectives Concerning Supplies to Pakistan

This being so, what are the likely perspectives regarding Pakistan's future supply of energy? They do not appear too bright at present. Over and above the State of permanent tension vis-à-vis India, which deprives the 'Land of the Pure' of large economies of scale (but which, on the strictly economic plane it can manage to do without), three points still cast a shadow, in the short term, over the picture rapidly sketched in the preceding pages.

LIKELY DETERIORATION OF THE AFGHAN SITUATION

The feeling of rejection aroused in the near totality of the Central Asian States by the advance of the Taliban during the summer of 1998 is not the only obstacle that Pakistan has, in all likelihood, to surmount during the coming months, in Afghanistan. It is not unreasonable, if the Afghan fundamentalists were to remain in power and consolidate their hold over the country, to consider a very progressive process of normalization of relations, or at least of the appearance of some compromise between Afghanistan and its neighbours, which would be accompanied by a similar easing of tensions between Islamabad and the Central Asian capitals. In this perspective, Pakistan could, under certain conditions, revive its projects and would thus demonstrate the soundness of its Afghan policy.

However, the hypothesis of a lasting consolidation of power by the Taliban, while not being totally impossible, does appear at this juncture to be improbable. The question here is not of the capture of Kabul by Massud—quite possible but which is not likely to change much on the national plane—nor is it a question even of the future of the peace process launched in March 1999 at Ashkabad, but that of the movement running out of steam and even of its veritable collapse. There are signs which indicate that it has already lost a part of its dynamism. Contrary to the policy adopted till then, and which consisted in not allowing any person to govern a region for more than a few months, the Taliban have now carved out some veritable strongholds for themselves. Similarly, the threat of a conflict with Iran has led them to rearm populations in a zone they cannot totally count upon. None of these is manifestly a crucial element, but they do lead to the fear (or hope, depending on one's point of view) of an eventual implosion of the movement, the tribal, clannish or very simply the local logic then coming into their own. The absence of an alternative centre of power leads one in this event to foresee the risk of generalized chaos in the whole of the country, preventing any kind of development in the region for a long time.

Last, it is obvious that while Pakistan and the Taliban do partially share some common interests, the latter will in no way be docile executors of the dictates of Islamabad, and that, even in the hypothesis of an evolution of the situation in favour of the 'student militia' (with which Bridas has forged closer ties than its competitor, UNOCAL), the Pakistani Government will have to come to terms with them on the question of energy, as in other matters.

DETERIORATION OF IRAN–PAKISTANI RELATIONS

Although the relations between the two countries markedly improved since the Turkmen gas pipeline project was postponed, the second crucial point with regard to Pakistani ambitions is the difficult relations between Islamabad and Teheran. While this has crystallized around the Afghan situation, the latter is not the only element it is made up of. The wave of sectarian violence which has once again swept over the Pakistani scene since two years had already strained the relations between the two capitals, Teheran not ceasing to blame Pakistan for its lack of eagerness to protect the Pakistani Shias who constitute between 15 and 20 per cent of the total population of the country. The assassination on 17 September 1997 of five Iranian trainee officers near Islamabad had aroused the ire of Iran, and the assassination by the

Taliban of nine Iranian diplomats during the capture of Mazar-e-Sharif only strengthened an animosity that the repeated visits of Pakistani officials to Teheran could not camouflage.

For the time being, however, Teheran is certainly the best lobbyist and it now seems to be taken seriously by the Indian authorities as well as the Pakistani ones.

GROWING RISK OF POLITICAL INSTABILITY IN CENTRAL ASIA

It needs finally to be noted that the further the possibility of the gas projects coming into being recedes, the more the conditions for their implementation are likely to deteriorate. The risk of political instability is constantly on the increase in some of the Central Asian republics. This is particularly true of Turkmenistan, whose real gross domestic product has not ceased to decline since independence. Having fallen by around 30 per cent between 1993 and 1995 and an additional 3 per cent in 1996, it is reported to have declined by another 15 to 25 per cent in 1997, on account of the drop in its exports of gas.[51] The monthly salaries, for their part, have declined by 80 per cent since 1993. This situation will continue to deteriorate if Turkmenistan does not find any markets for its gas. Endowed with an essentially rural population occupied in subsistence agriculture, and in the absence of an alternative to the present President, the economic crisis has not yet degenerated into a political crisis, but President Nyazov's 'dream of a Central Asian Kuwait' could well find itself transformed, at the time of his succession, into a political nightmare, curbing still further the development of the exploitation of hydrocarbons.

Is There Reason for Hope?

THE PERSISTENCE OF THE DEMAND

It would be a mistake to give a hasty burial to Pakistan's energy projects in Central Asia on account particularly of the persistence of a certain number of structural constraints. Indeed, however serious the present difficulties of Islamabad, they do not but point for the time being, in the medium and the long run, to a slowing down of the growth in demand rather than a reversal of this trend. At the same time, these same financial difficulties make the search for less expensive (and incidentally less polluting) types of energy ever more necessary. Last, these energy projects linked with Central Asia enter a much more vast plan of action, already examined in these pages, which Islamabad is unlikely to abandon in the short term.

EXTERNAL INTERESTS

The projects for construction of infrastructure enabling the export of Central Asian hydrocarbons to the markets of South Asia bring into play an array of interests which are outside the canvas of Pakistan alone.

There is little possibility for the export of gas to the markets of the West as they are already saturated, while these very States have an ever-increasing need of foreign exchange which the Central Asian markets will eventually be in a position to supply to them.

The oil and gas companies which are all eyeing the Indian market are fully conscious of the stakes, and have built up their regional strategy keeping this perspective in mind.[52]

The international community, on its part, should take into consideration the fact that growing regional cooperation in this field would help to bring stability to those States that are fragile, both because of the indispensable financial inputs that it would not fail to create, as well as the interdependence that it would bring about.

Finally, the Indian and Pakistani nuclear tests will—paradoxically have—contributed towards promoting a dialogue between Islamabad and New Delhi. By creating a sort of psychological parity between the two countries, likely to reassure Pakistani public opinion, they have indeed given back to Pakistan's decision-makers a part of their lost legitimacy, thus conferring on them, in their negotiations with their powerful Indian neighbour, a limited but real margin for manoeuvre.

Bringing Reassurance into the Regional Environment

Pakistan has some reason for hope, but if it wants to see its aspirations take shape, it must attempt to smoothen matters in its regional environment. It must, among other things, try to improve further its present relations with Iran. Islamabad must, to this end, cease to appear, in the view of the Iranian decision-makers, as the instrument of American policy in the region. Normalization of Iran–American relations, very unlikely in the near future, and for which it has no means of action, would help it by putting an end to the Iranian paranoia, sustained by a difficult environment. It will also have to find an alternative to its Afghan policy, although it is difficult at present to make out what shape this would take.

INDIA: KEY TO THE FUTURE OF PAKISTAN IN THE MATTER OF CENTRAL ASIAN ENERGY?

Paradoxically, Pakistan's salvation in Central Asia lies perhaps in the at least partial normalization of its relations with India. India too, like Pakistan, must find new sources of energy if it wants to maintain its rate of economic growth, and it must necessarily diversify its sources of supply. Central Asia constitutes, at this stage, just one of the medium or long-term options, but it remains a real option. Its negotiations with Iran are, from the point of view of the problematic of energy, at a much more advanced stage than those with the Central Asian republics. Any significant progress achieved with regard to the former, however, prepares the ground for establishment of links with the latter. In both cases, the necessity for having the eventual gas pipelines cross Pakistan's territory or continental plateau constitutes a stumbling block in the negotiations. New Delhi fears that its vulnerability would increase as Islamabad could cut off its supply.

Apart from the already mentioned economic argument, several factors speak in favour of the construction of joint pipelines, these being the following:

1. There are precedents for the construction of gas pipelines between countries or regions in a state of conflict. The gas pipeline linking Russia to Europe, constructed during the Cold War period, is an example.
2. There are also means for reducing the risks of stoppage of supply or their consequences: (a) On the technological plane, it is possible to make a choice of installations utilizing multiple types of energy and/or to build up underground reserves, or to set up links with networks utilizing liquified gas; (b) There is also a whole arsenal of legal techniques and political means, such as the 'Take or pay clause', for the intermediary consumer. Pakistan would have to purchase the entire gas consumed by itself as well as its neighbour, and would thus be obliged to resell the remaining quantity to the Indian consumers. Agreements involving the cessation of all supply

by the producer country to Pakistan if the latter were to stop supplies to India, can also be considered.

3. India's presence in the paradigms for the opening up of Central Asia's energy from the south are such finally as to facilitate their implementation. Not only has India been a steadfast ally of the USSR, but even today it shares some common interests with Russia. Both consider that eventual instability in Central Asia would be harmful for their own security and would, among other things, have a snowballing effect on their Muslim minorities.

Contrary to Pakistan, India enjoys an excellent reputation in Central Asia, and its participation in the eventual operation of the pipelines would reassure the local authorities against the possible utilization of the latter by Pakistan for the spread of its Islamic polity. It would also bring to Russia and to Iran some guarantees that Central Asia would not be left at the mercy of Pakistani and Saudi influences alone. This could in the end make each one of these regional players modify its attitude on the Afghan conflict.

It is also in the interest of New Delhi to develop closer links with the OEC to counterbalance Pakistan's influence in it.

Conclusion

It would be manifestly premature to draw any conclusion about the outlook for Pakistan's energy supply, even if the future perspectives are perhaps not as grim as the present situation would lead us to suppose. It seems possible at this stage to assert that this development will only take place if it is in line with the wider perspective of development of South Asia as a whole. Both for the political reasons already mentioned as for economic ones, the emergence of India as a future economic giant is a matter of good fortune for Pakistan as it opens up a series of opportunities without posing any threat to it. Contrary to numerous plans for trade agreements in which Pakistan's hesitations are explained primarily by Islamabad's fear of Indian hegemony, be it economic, Pakistan finds itself, in the energy sector, in a position to negotiate with India on an equal footing as it is geographically impossible to bypass it.

Numerous obstacles and uncertainties, however, persist. The normalization of Iran–American relations, possible in the medium term, but still problematic, delays to that extent investments which are indispensable, and indirectly affects the totality of the relations between South Asia and Central Asia. The demand for energy continues to grow in the subcontinent, and must, in one way or another, be met, but the establishment of solid links with Central Asia will obviously be, in the best of events, a long and difficult process.

NOTES

1. The 1998 census brings out a total population of 130.57 million as against 84.25 million in 1981, namely, an increase of 46.32 million during the last 17 years: *Pakistan Political Perspective*, vol. VII-8, August 1998, p. 65
2. Before the coming into force of American sanctions.
3. 'Pakistan Country Analysis Brief', United States Energy Information Administration.
4. This was the total of the energy imported and the energy produced in Pakistan.
5. *Pakistan Energy Yearbook 1997*, Islamabad: Hydrocarbon Development Institute of Pakistan, Ministry of Petroleum and Natural Resources, January 1998.
6. Ibid., p. 48.
7. Ibid., p. 25.
8. This relationship between dependence and security in the matter of energy is itself a subject of debate. Some assert that there is no direct link between these two realities. On the other side, the argument according to which dependence on imports is a security threat has represented in the past the main rationalization for numerous energy policies. See, notably, Ken Koyama, 'Growing Energy Demands in Asian Countries: Opportunities and Constraints for Gulf Energy Exporters', in *Gulf Energy and the World: Challenges and Threats*, Abu Dhabi: Emirates Center for Strategic Studies and Research, 1997, p. 59.
9. This relates to import of oil. Coal has been deliberately left aside here.
10. The Yom Kippur war, the Iran revolution of 1978, the Iran-Iraq war and the invasion of Kuwait. Even if the resultant price increase was on each occasion a temporary one, it none the less underlined the vulnerability of the more fragile economies, Pakistan being one of these.
11. It is still difficult to determine to what extent the financial crises that these same economies are experiencing will affect, in the long run, this growth.
12. These issues are relatively new but are nevertheless very real risks for the Arab monarchies of the Gulf. As Gregory Gause writes, 'The welfare states built in the 1970s, with seemingly limitless resources for very small populations, are now strained by high population growth rates and flat oil prices. Indigenous middle classes, created by state education and employment policies, expect remunerative employment and increasingly seek an outlet for their hope of political participation' (Gregory F. Gause, 'The Gulf Conundrum: Economic

Change, Population Growth, and Political Stability in the GCC States', the *Washington Quarterly*, vol. 20, no. 1, pp. 145-65, specially p. 146). In fact, each one of them finds itself faced with the same problem: how to do more politically with distinctly decreasing economic resources. Each government thus finds itself confronted with the need to decrease its expenses, while the population continues to grow at a high rate. These economic difficulties are, however, less important by themselves than because of the fact that they are occurring during a period when the regimes in position are experiencing a crisis of legitimacy, a crisis which they contribute singularly towards strengthening. Although in a different context, Iran is faced with a relatively similar situation.

13. Ken Koyama, 'Oil Supply Security in Asian Economies: Growing Oil Imports and their Response Measures', *Energy in Japan*, no. 149, January 1998, pp. 31-46, specially p. 34.

14. Gulfaraz Ahmad, 'Pakistan Energy Demand and Supply Outlook and Prospects for Oil and Gas Imports from Central and West Asian Countries', speech delivered at the First Ever Conference in Asia Pacific on Central Asia Oil & Gas Market & Pipelines, Singapore, 23 February 1998.

15. Gulfaraz Ahmad, op. cit.

16. Narsi Ghorban, 'The Evaluation of Recent Gas Export Pipeline Proposals in the Middle East', the *Iranian Journal of Iranian Affairs*, vol. VII, no. 2, Summer 1995, pp. 449-65, specially p. 450.

17. Ibid., p. 451.

18. Ibid., p. 453.

19. Ibid., p. 451. Much of the credit for what is found in this chapter must go to an article by Ahmed Rashid, entitled 'The Turkmenistan-Afghanistan-Pakistan Pipeline', published in *Petro Finance Focus on Current Issues*, of October 1997.

20. Ahmed Rashid, 'The Turkmenistan-Afghanistan-Pakistan Pipeline', *Petro Finance Focus on Current Issues*, The Market Intelligence Service, October 1997, pp. 1-16, specially p. 2.

21. Ibid., p. 2.

22. Carlos Bulgheroni, President of Bridas, reportedly spent nine months in trying to convince the Pakistan Prime Minister and the Turkmen President about the viability of the project. He then spent almost as much time in convincing the chiefs of the Afghan factions. In February 1996, Bridas signed a 30-year agreement with Burhanuddin Rabbani, then officially President of the Afghan State, for the construction and exploitation of a gas pipeline. Agreements were also entered into with Rashid Dostom, head of the Uzbeki militia, Jumbesh, which controlled the north of the country and the Taliban. Ahmed, op. cit., p. 2.

23. Ibid., p. 2.

24. UNOCAL, Delta Oil Company, Turkmenistan–Afghanistan–Pakistan Gas Pipeline Project.

25. Turkmenrosgas itself is controlled to the extent of 45 per cent by Gazprom while Itera, a company registered in the United States but controlled by Russian and Turkmeni interests, owns 4 per cent. Ibid., p. 3.

26. UNOCAL, Delta Oil Company, Central Asian Pipeline Project.

27. On 28 January 1997, the International Chamber of Commerce ruled partially in its favour, ordering the Turkmeni Government to authorize the resumption of exports of oil from the Keimir field. Ahmed, op. cit., p. 3.

28. Inaugural Meeting of the 'Turkmenistan–Afghanistan–Pakistan' Gas Pipeline Joint Working Group, Islamabad, Pakistan, 4–5 June 1997.

29. http//www.pakistanlink.comheadlines/Oct/29/09.html

30. Position Statement, Proposed Central Asia Gas (CENTGAS) Pipeline Project, 21 August 1998.

31. Pakhtun irredentism, which made an appearance at the time of the partition of India in 1947, related to the territory situated between the Afghan–Pakistan border, the 'Mortimer–Durand Line' and the Indus, the majority of whose inhabitants are Pakhtuns. The geographic expanse encompassed by this claim varies, however, according to its authors. For the Pakhtuns living in Pakistan, it encompasses just the present North West Frontier Province. For the Afghan Government of 1947 on the other hand, it covers this province as well as Baluchistan. Last, in its most extreme interpretation, Pakhtunistan extends from the Indian Ocean till Gilgit and the 'Mortimer–Durand' line at the Kashmir border.

32. Between 1992 and 1997, there was not a single official visit between Indians and Central Asians which did not end with at least one declaration against Islamic fundamentalism. The headlines in the Pakistani press testify eloquently to this. To quote some among these, 'Nazarbayev Allays Fears on Islamic Bloc', *News*, 23 December 1992; 'India Seen as Bulwark Against Fundamentalism', *Herald*, 25 May 1993; 'Indo-Uzbek Vow to Counter Fundamentalism', *Pioneer*, 6 January 1994; 'India, Kyrgyzstan Oppose Terrorism', *News*, 22 September 1995.

33. 'Teheran Not to Interfere in Kashmir Affairs', *Herald*, 21 September 1993.

34. 'India Opposes Embargo on Iran', *Pioneer*, 9 May 1995.

35. The degree of control that Iran exercises over the Hezb-i-Wahadat is, however, relatively limited. Teheran did indeed help the Hazara Party in 1990 to put an end to the veritable civil war which then reigned in Hazarajat, but the party was able to absorb the other Shia movements only marginally, abandoning its revolutionary and religious ideology close to the Iranian model for a 'Hazara nationalism' more capable of bringing together in a federation the different politico-military groups of the region.

36. It is also necessary to point out that this project was being planned within a regional environment that already posed a threat to the Islamic Republic. Apart from the American embargo, the presence of the US fleet in the Gulf, the never-ending Iraqi crisis and the Nagorno-Karabakh crisis were factors which added to Teheran's insecurity.

37. NIGC, BHP Press Release. Iran–Pakistan Pipeline Project, 24 January 1998.

38. Position Statement, Proposed Central Asia Gas (CentGas) Pipeline Project, http://www.unocal.com/globalops/asiapipe.htm, 21 August 1998.

39. Richard Mackenzie, 'The United States and the Taliban', in William Maley, ed., *Fundamentalism Reborn? Afghanistan and the Taliban*, London: C. Hurst, 1998, pp. 90–103, specially p. 91.

40. 'US Wants Trade Links Between Pakistan, CIS', *Dawn*, 29 October 1996.

41. It was not appreciably different from the one made by Secretary of State Madeleine Albright, who asserted in November 1997 in Peshawar that the US would only recognize a broad national union government: *International Herald Tribune*, 19 November 1997.

42. Ahmed, op. cit., p. 13.

43. On account also of the unilateral denunciation by the Pakistan Government of a contract binding it to an electric power station sponsored by Canada as well as eight other projects involving American and Japanese capital, and this in spite of the guarantees initially provided by the State. The concerned companies were accused by the latter of corruption and of overbilling of the electricity supplied: Rashid Ahmed, 'Its no Party', *Far Eastern Economic Review*, 16 July, p. 70.

44. *The Economist*, 22 August 1998.

45. Ibid.

46. There is, however, talk of UNOCAL returning to the Pakistan scene.

47. Conversation with Hilal A. Raza, Director General, Hydrocarbon Institute of Pakistan, Islamabad, 20 May 1998.

48. After the partition of 1947, modest cooperation did, however, exist between the two countries for a very brief period. Pakistan imported a small quantity of electricity (which is outside the scope of this study) from the Indian power station at Jogendar Nagar on account of the difficulties it encountered in the maintenance of its own stations as the majority of their staff and technicians being Hindus, had migrated to India: Aurangzeb Z. Khan, 'India and Pakistan Bilateral Cooperation in the Energy Sector', in Sony Devabartuni, *Regional Cooperation in South Asia: Prospects and Problems*, Washington DC: The Henry Stimson Center, 1997, p. 75.

49. The continuation of the present energy policy would lead to a multiplication by 3.5 times of the emissions of carbon during the course of the next forty years. P.R. Shukla, 'Final Demand Energy Scenarios for India', International Seminar on India and the World: Stakes and Prospect for a Sustainable Energy System, Geneva, 8–9 June 1998.

50. See tables in annex. Source: Hilal A. Raza, 'Natural Gas Import Options for South Asia', Fourth meeting, India and Pakistan Opportunities in Economic Growth, Technology and Security, Muscat, Oman, 21–3 March 1998. See also Rahul Tongia, TransAsia Pipeline System: A Pre-Feasibility Study on the Delivery of Natural Gas to Pakistan and India from West/Central Asia',

Department of Engineering & Public Policy, Carnegie Mellon University.

51. Thiery Kellner and Mohammed Reza Djalili, 'Oil and Gas in the Caspian: Between Myth and Reality', *Transitions*, November 1998.

52. The objection can justifiably be raised that this latter assertion is in contradiction to the objections formulated earlier as regards the ability to pay and the credibility of States such as Pakistan, but this problem has partly been envisioned. The UNOCAL project, for instance, consists of a dual pipeline, one of which is an oil pipeline meant to bring Turkmeni oil into Pakistan where it would be refined before being exported to the South-East Asian markets, thus partially financing the imports of gas. Similarly, BHP Petroleum intends to develop, parallel to its gas pipeline, some projects for the extraction of copper ores meant for export.

PART III

How to Project Nationalism?
The Foreign Policy of Pakistan in its Region

11

The Dialectic between Domestic Politics and Foreign Policy

MOHAMMAD WASEEM

LL FOREIGN POLICY is ultimately the expression of a world-view reared by the ruling elite of a country. It is based on specific considerations relating to the general objective of projection and security of the national interest. However, the direction and scope of implementation of foreign policy as well as the level of diplomatic effort in pursuit of policy goals at any given time depend on a complex interplay of forces working on complementary, parallel or even contradictory lines. As conventional wisdom has it, the more democratic a political system is, the more its ruling elite is influenced by public opinion, and, therefore, the more representative of national aspirations is public policy.[1] The typical examples of this model are drawn from Western democracies. Conversely, the more authoritarian a State is, the greater is the concentration of decision-making power in the hands of the ruling elite which is typically shielded from the deterministic influence of the public opinion. Due to Pakistan's chequered constitutional history punctuated by three military governments, the country is typically put in the category of those States where policy input into the business of State from the public at large is somewhat limited.

However, in reality things can be far more complex. Governments generally exercise a great influence over the communications network, and tend to manipulate public opinion in favour of their own policies. During election campaigns, the process of issue-formation itself is controlled by the ruling elite which operate in various fields of public activity. This allows only a limited number of policy choices.[2] Second, as compared to policy in various other fields, foreign policy generally carries a low priority because it impinges on public life relatively indirectly and causes a somewhat delayed response as compared to economic, political and administrative policy measures which can elicit a direct and immediate response. This factor is responsible for providing a certain level of immunity for the way external relations are handled from pressures of the wider public even in the most developed democratic systems such as the US and UK. Last, in the case of States locked up in endemic and existential conflicts with other States for a long time, policies involving large financial and human input can be pursued with relative impunity. The Cold War between the US and USSR, the Arab-Israel conflict and the Indo–Pakistan conflict are typical examples of overarching dichotomous models of hostile relations between nations. In this context, certain policies are considered as 'givens', because these enjoy a high level of legitimacy in the public eye. Policies relating to these fundamental conflicts are pursued without any risk of close scrutiny or accountability. In other words, certain policies are pursued irrespective of the changing regional climate of international relations or the shifting social base and the rationale for them at home.

In the case of post-colonial States such as Pakistan, the dialectics between domestic politics and foreign policy can be even more complicated. Here, certain policy choices are simply inherited from the erstwhile colonial set-up, often under some kind of continuing tutelage of the latter in the form of the personnel policy, or more directly through organizations such as the British Commonwealth. The institutional ethos and geostrategic perspective of the colonial government is often carried over to the successor State after Independence. For example, the way the British Government at Delhi perceived the role of Russia in terms of its southward expansion in the context of the Asian geopolitical system during the late nineteenth century substantively influenced the world-view of the Government of Pakistan after 1947.[3] The educational background and professional training of Pakistani diplomats kept them firmly committed to operate through the established communication channels within the British Commonwealth. It is true that the Foreign Office in London showed gross scepticism about continuing to share the confidential information with the new dominions of India and Pakistan, and became very selective in this regard.[4] However, the practice of sharing information of a less confidential nature with other capitals of the old and new Commonwealth countries continued, along with the high drama of annual conferences of Commonwealth Prime Ministers involving discussion on serious and contentious matters. On the eve of their departure, the British had argued that future Pakistan was ideally situated as a bulwark against Soviet Communism.[5] This argument strongly influenced the strategic thinking of the emergent State. All this pointed to continuity of the old institutional ways of handling diplomatic issues without recourse to eliciting public opinion. Often, entry into international agreements was disclosed to the Constituent Assembly of Pakistan as a fait accompli. Not surprisingly, there was hardly any serious scheduled debate on foreign-policy issues on the floor of the parliament, not the least because it was considered dangerous due to the confidential nature of the country's international commitments.

Second, in post-colonial States such as Pakistan, representative institutions and public organizations have been kept out of operation for long periods of time whenever the army took over. This further reduced the level of input into policy making from informed public opinion. Under Ayub's Martial Law Government (1958-62) which dissolved the national and provincial assemblies and banned political parties, foreign policy (like other fields of public policy) became an exclusive preserve of the State apparatus.[6] Under the new dispensation, the army leadership was able to influence diplomatic activity more directly and decisively than before. This situation left a deep imprint on all decision-making in this field for the following four decades under both civilian and military governments. Politicians continued to be subjected to gross mistrust by the military establishment. Some of them, such as Benazir Bhutto, were considered a security risk in matters of foreign and defence policies.[7]

Last, one can mention the way the unstable regional setting around Pakistan has contributed to the perceived legitimacy of exclusive control over foreign policy exercised by the State machinery. Pakistan was born out of a conflict over the issue of Partition in the teeth of opposition by the All India Congress. It has fought three wars with India, two of them over Kashmir in 1947-9 and 1965. It lost half of the country in the 1971 war. Other conflicts with India include Siachen Glacier, Wular Barrage and Sir Creek. The tension over these conflicts has been compounded by the nuclear rivalry between the two hostile neighbours. Pakistan vehemently embarked on its nuclear programme following India's explosion of a nuclear device in 1974. The May 1998 nuclear explosions have now pushed the two countries into a nuclear arms race in South Asia. In view of the armed conflict in Kargil in the north of Kashmir Valley in mid-1999, the tendency of monopolizing the diplomatic initiative got further entrenched in the two countries. Along the northern border, the resistance movement against the Soviet forces in Afghanistan and their puppet regime in Kabul from 1979 to 1992, followed by several years of internecine war between various Mujahideen groups, kept the Pakistan Army and Inter-Services Intelligence (ISI) deeply involved in the war. This took the initiative for strategic decision-making away from the hands of the Foreign Office in Islamabad. Under the post-Zia elected governments, the ISI seems to have exercised a veto power in certain matters of strategic importance in the region. It has been widely held responsible for involvement in the Kashmir insurgency and insurrection in east Punjab in India as well as in the rise of Taliban in Afghanistan.[8] Similarly, nuclear diplomacy has been dominated by the military's strategic preferences. Political governments along with the Foreign Office bureaucracy have generally played a conformist role in this regard. Relations between Iran and Pakistan reached an impasse in the context of the Taliban's onward march to conquer the whole of Afghanistan, and in the process alienate and emasculate Iran-backed Hizb-i-Wahadat. While the ISI seemed to be supportive of the Taliban's push forward at any cost, the Foreign Office was more sensitive to the grievances of Iran and other countries further West. However, matters less directly related to strategic operations in the region, for example the US aid and relations with the Middle Eastern countries, are typically handled by the Foreign Office. The continuously unstable regional environment along the eastern, northern and now even western borders with India, Afghanistan and Iran respectively has brought about a pattern of decision-making in the realm of foreign policy which allows wide margin to the country's bureaucracy for bypassing any substantive input from the public. Not surprisingly, a direct fallout of regional instability is reflected by a high level of general conformity to the official version of events in the backdrop of public commitment to national security.

Our observation that the location of real decision-making power in the realm of foreign policy in Pakistan lying in the State rather than the society does not imply that the two operate on parallel or contradictory lines in terms of their preferences and commitments. For several decades, there has been an underlying consensus on national issues such as the Kashmir dispute, the nuclear programme, Middle Eastern orientation, and support for Islamic causes in Palestine, Afghanistan, Bosnia and Chechnya. The more an issue is understood to be national or civilizational rather than partisan and parochial, the more the government has control over it as a symbol of the State. The underlying consensus on foreign-policy issues helped the decision-makers at the top to pursue diplomacy with relative immunity. However, we must qualify this argument about consensus by bringing in the factor of ethno-spatial dimensions on the one hand, and temporal dimensions on the other. In spatial terms, those regions which were not fully represented in the mainstream politics of the Pakistan movement, or failed to move to centre stage in the emerging State system, did not necessarily share what is otherwise billed as national consensus. Indeed, the more the State apparatus of Pakistan—which is identified with Punjab and increasingly NWFP—centralized all meaningful authority in its own hands, the more such federating units as East Bengal, Sindh and Baluchistan opposed the Centre's policies in both domestic and foreign contexts. The official sponsorship of the Kashmir cause was not welcomed by many Bengalis. For them, Kashmir was remote, both geographically and historically, while proximity with India, represented by West Bengal, was too real to be ignored in geographical, historical, cultural, linguistic and economic terms. The situation in Sindh and Baluchistan has not been very different inasmuch as the two provinces produced a world-view which was parallel and often contrary to the dominant world-view of Punjab. Therefore, when we discuss domestic politics as a factor in foreign policy, we should also take into account the smaller currents of public opinion in terms of their limited input or none at all.[9]

Last, in Pakistan (as elsewhere), priorities and preferences of policy have changed over time, perhaps not so much in the way the world-view of the ruling elite is shaped anew as in the means adopted and resources committed to pursuit of policy goals. For example, on several occasions in the short history of Pakistan, the State was ready to commit its vital political, diplomatic and military resources to the maximum limit, short of endangering its own security to pursue its goal in Kashmir. This happened during the 1947-9 and 1965 wars, and at various points during the insurgency in Kashmir Valley during the 1990s. Some even point to the 1999 flare-up in Kargil as an extension of this commitment to take grave risks. On the other hand, the same Kashmir dispute had been put on the backburner for nearly two decades after Pakistan lost the 1971 war. A parallel example of change in public mood and policy over time is the Afghan policy. Islamabad's commitment to support the Afghan resistance movement in 1979-80 initially enjoyed a national consensus. However, by the mid-1980s, the consensus had given way to controversy in the wake of hot pursuit of Afghan Mujahideen into Pakistani territory by the Soviet forces, bomb explosions in NWFP and further south, as well as the emerging pattern of conflicts between Afghan refugees and the local population in the two northern provinces. Similarly, there was a continuous, though passive, consensus about pro-US policies of the government among various sections of the ruling elite who enjoyed some input in policy making at some levels. However, at other times, this latent consensus was shattered, for example when Washington's military might moved against Muslims either indirectly (such as in the Arab–Israel wars of 1967 and 1973) or directly such as in the bombing of Iraq during the 1991 Gulf war and missile attacks against Sudan and the training camps of Osama bin Laden in Afghanistan in 1998.

How far can we locate the origin of decision-making about foreign policy in Pakistan in the dynamics of political change? Did a change in the constellation of powers ruling Pakistan at any given time lead to a corresponding change in the procedural aspects of decision-making only, or did it go beyond that stage to redirect the substantive aspects of foreign policy? In other words, what explanatory potential does regime change in general, and shift of power from one political party to another in particular, have for understanding foreign policy in Pakistan? How far did the changing regional scenario around Pakistan, characterized by revolutions in Iran and Afghanistan in the late 1970s, the proxy war along Pakistan's western borders between the two superpowers during the 1980s, and the perceived Indian bellicosity in the context of Delhi's commitment to a nuclear weapons programme influence the dynamics of policy making in Islamabad? We can attempt to answer these questions by arguing in favour of a fourfold model: (1) the constitutional factor, i.e. whether political or martial law governments ruled Pakistan, and what difference the changing balance of civil–military relations made for the purposes of designing foreign policy; (2) the level of direct input from the public into policy making through the media, professional associations and political parties; (3) the institutional factor, i.e. inputs of the Foreign Office which is formally responsible for developing policy options and implementing any policy agreed upon by the powers that be; and (4) the personality factor, insofar as some leaders left a strong imprint of their thought or action either on the government or on relations with the outside world. Four distinct phases of Pakistan's history can be outlined in terms of the constitutional (or extra-constitutional) set-up, level of public input into foreign policy, institutional framework of decision-making and personality input. These phases comprise the following historical periods: 1947-71; 1971-7; 1977-88; and from 1988 to date.

The first phase (1947-71) is characterized by domestic 'non-politics' rather than politics. No general election based on adult franchise was held at the national level for 23 years. From 1947 to 1958, political leaders sitting in the parliament increasingly lost touch with the public in the absence of elections. In this set-up, the hastily organized and skilfully centralized bureaucracy kept the initiative in its own hands. It enjoyed clear backing of the two charismatic leaders, Jinnah and Liaquat Ali Khan.[10] Successive governments were installed in office on the basis of coalitions of factional groupings operating on the floor of the parliament, which was itself elected by Provincial Assemblies before Independence. In 1955, i.e. eight years after the previous indirect election and one year after the dissolution of the first Constituent Assembly, the second Constituent Assembly was elected, again by Provincial Assemblies without any recourse to mass voting. In this set-up, foreign policy largely remained a preserve of the Foreign Office bureaucracy. Pakistan's Foreign Minister, Sir Zafrullah (1947-54), who later rose to become Chief Justice of the International Court of Justice and President of the UN General Assembly, steered the country's foreign policy firmly along pro-Western and pan-Islamic lines. Sir Zafrullah left a deep imprint on the way Pakistan perceived its role in the global and regional frameworks. Under his long tenure, the Foreign Office enjoyed a situation of splendid isolation from the wider political scene, which was understood to be given to factional intrigues, ideological battles and ethnic strife among politicians. It emerged as a pool of conventional wisdom about the geostrategic environment of Pakistan. It operated relatively autonomously in processing information and implementing cabinet decisions. Sir Zafrullah soon became the target of mass agitation during the anti-Ahmadiya movement in 1953 which led to the overthrow first of the Punjab Government, and then the Federal Government at Karachi.

The autonomy of the Foreign Office from the routine operations of political governments remained intact even after Sir Zafrullah left the scene soon after. From 1954 when Pakistan developed a strategic relationship with the US to 1958 when the military under Ayub took over power, close cooperation between the Foreign Office and the Defence Establishment became a routine matter. Pakistan's entry into

CENTO and SEATO confirmed its pro-Western policies, which did not necessarily reflect public opinion, and at times even went against it. For example, the 1956 attack on the Suez Canal by France, Britain and Israel led to intense mobilization of the nation against the West, even as Suhrawardy's Government in Karachi defended its pro-Western policies. Ayub's coup in 1958 symbolized the fact that the civil–military establishment had finally managed to control the levers of power without sharing them with political elements in a substantive sense. During the martial law (1958-62) and post-martial law (1962-9) periods of Ayub's rule, the country's march forward along the lines set out in various areas of public policy during the early and mid-1950s gained momentum. Foremost among them was the security orientation, with its centre of gravity lying in threat perceptions surrounding India's military occupation of the Muslim-majority state of Jammu & Kashmir. Gen. Ayub took the initiative to send Pakistani commandos into Indian-held Kashmir in August 1965. This led to the September war, and finally to the controversial Tashkent Declaration of January 1966. A decade of close security relations between Pakistan and the US involving meaningful military aid thus came to an end as the latter put an arms embargo on the former and turned to appease India and bolster Iran's role in the region.[11] The Kashmir dispute, which was the most sensitive foreign-policy issue during this phase of Pakistan's history, started to slip from the top position for the next quarter of a century. However, the 1965 war represents a watershed in the growth of the decision-making mechanism in the realm of foreign policy. It pushed the Foreign Office bureaucracy to a secondary role in the context of shaping the post-war diplomatic position in the South Asian region. The 1971 war with India further weakened the hold of the diplomatic service over foreign policy, as military considerations overtook diplomacy in shaping the world-view of the ruling elite. The influence of the army's high command over foreign-policy objectives and deliberations reached a critical point under Yahya in an operational sense.

Indo–Pakistan relations remained the focal point of regional politics in this period. While a pervasive Indocentric security orientation characterized Pakistan's foreign policy during the two decades after Independence, the ideological orientation couched in the Islamic idiom remained a constant—though somewhat static—feature of foreign policy in this period. Immediately after Independence, Governor-General Jinnah sent Feroz Khan Noon as his emissary to

Muslim countries to apprise them of the emergence of a new entity on the world map and to extend moral support to Arab countries on the issue of Palestine.[12] Later, various proposals for economic and political cooperation between Islamic countries emerged from official quarters from time to time. Within Pakistan, the political influence of the ulema in general, and Islamic parties in particular, was limited to constitutional demands at home and projection of a pro-Islamic profile of the country abroad. The 1953 anti-Ahmadiya movement was brutally suppressed. However, its fallout on the incumbent governments in Karachi and Lahore turned out to be negative inasmuch as they succumbed to mutual lack of trust. Successive governments freely used Islamic rhetoric without compromising their pro-Western policy commitments. The only major policy initiative was the opening up with China in 1963. This was due to the changing regional scenario after the 1962 Sino–Indian conflict which activated Western support in favour of India. Pakistan felt that it was abandoned by its traditional allies. For the ruling elite of Pakistan, it was very difficult to overcome its anti-Communist line of thought and commitment in the field of diplomacy. But the generational transition represented by the young firebrand Foreign Minister Z.A. Bhutto made it possible to look for new patterns of alliance in the region.

Last, it was the development orientation aspect of foreign policy that made Karachi most anxious to go West. The Ayub period was especially characterized by resource inputs from abroad which ushered the country into the industrial age.[13] The foreign missions of Pakistan took on the additional functions of gathering economic information, establishing communication with multinational companies as well as financial apparatuses of the donor countries and creating a profile of political stability in the country. Under Ayub, the Foreign Office bureaucracy generally flourished. It enjoyed a considerable level of autonomy in decision-making from public inputs as well as from public accountability. The role of the military establishment in directing specific aspects of foreign policy enormously expanded after 1965.

The Yahya Government (1969-70) initially committed itself to more of the same, with only a change of guard at the top. However, after the December 1970 elections, things started to go wrong as the government searched for ways and means of extricating itself from the responsibility of transferring power to the majority-party Awami League. From March 1971, when military operations started in East Pakistan, to

December 1971 when the armed forces surrendered in Dhaka, the Yahya Government was engaged in a major damage control operation as one foreign policy disaster followed another. Diplomatic activity was reduced to a unidimensional approach to the world at large, inasmuch as the government was put on the defensive for explaining its actions in East Pakistan.[14] No new initiatives were possible in this atmosphere. The movement in foreign policy came to a halt, except for meeting the challenge of hostile world opinion.

Indeed, the 1970 election results had presented a devastating critique of the existing power structure which had its epicentre in the military-bureaucratic establishment. While the Awami League represented an anti-establishment mood in the eastern wing in pursuit of the demand for provincial autonomy couched in Bengali nationalism, the Pakistan People's Party (PPP) rode the groundswell of protest against the ruling elite—the military and bureaucracy as well as industrial and landed elite—in the western wing from a populist perspective.[15] Z.A. Bhutto's Government (1971-7) brought into play new ideological and diplomatic positions such as socialism, Third-Worldism and anti-Westernism. It is interesting to compare the new shift in foreign policy with the two previous grand policy initiatives, i.e. the pro-Western policy symbolized by Pakistan's entry into CENTO and SEATO in the 1950s, and a policy of friendship with China in the early 1960s. The previous policies were largely based on a calculated response of the Foreign Office to changes in the strategic environment of Pakistan—characterized by India's preponderant military position in Kashmir combined with its non-alignment policy—and the 1962 Sino–Indian war leading to Delhi's Westward orientation respectively. Foreign policy remained a closed diplomatic affair in both cases.

However, the new policy initiatives in Islamabad in the wake of Z.A. Bhutto's ascendancy to power were part of the populist upsurge in domestic politics. The socialist idiom reflected opposition to concentration of wealth in the hands of capitalists—the so-called 22 families—as projected by organized labour and the leftist intelligentsia. These capitalists along with their perceived support base in the military-bureaucratic establishment were condemned as agents of Western imperialism. Bhutto represented the 'second-wave revolution' against the traditional power structure and its alleged Western patrons.[16] He found himself in the company of such leaders as Col. Gaddafi of Libya, Allende of Chile and to some extent Indira Gandhi of India. An undercurrent of solidarity with other Third World countries which were similarly caught in a complex network of asymmetrical relations with the West defined Bhutto's world-view. He publicly identified himself with Palestinian leader Yasser Arafat, Kim Il Sung of North Korea and Hafeez Assad of Syria. However, populist anti-Westernism remained limited in scope because the new idiom fell far short of radically changing the goals of Pakistan's foreign policy. Islamabad's threat perceptions vis-à-vis India continued to be at the centre of its security considerations, along with its need to seek Western support. For example, the Bhutto Government vehemently pursued the goal of getting the US arms embargo lifted. On the other hand, Pakistan–China friendship continued to be firmly based on the perceived need for strategic partnership involving the two military establishments. The socialist rhetoric was largely superfluous to the ongoing friendly relations between the two countries. In other words, the populist idiom of Bhutto did not necessarily make the foreign policy of Pakistan change its course. This was not so in other fields of public policy, such as education, industrial relations, land reform, administrative reforms and nationalization of the banking and insurance sectors. A major reason of this state of affairs was that the PPP's populist movement during the late 1960s and early 1970s put up somewhat clearer demands in these fields, such as redistribution of land, decentralization and nationalization. On the other hand, foreign-policy demands were relatively vague, general and ideological. Second, changes at home were obviously easier to pursue than changes abroad, where strategic and economic interests of other States were clearly involved and where the writ of the government in Islamabad had a limited impact, if at all. Last, the mechanism of collecting, pruning and evaluating information and suggesting the broad outline of policy continued to be in the hands of the Foreign Office bureaucracy.

The two substantive policy initiatives taken by the Bhutto Government which continued to be operative during the following decades were rooted in regional dynamics far more than domestic politics. The Indian nuclear programme had triggered an acute sense of insecurity in Pakistan from the late 1960s onwards. The debacle at Dhaka in 1971 followed by India's nuclear explosion in 1974 pushed the country to a quest for national security by developing a nuclear device of its own. Islamabad was able to resist US pressure against the development of its nuclear programme, even though its attempt to buy a nuclear reprocessing plant from France was finally aborted by Washington.

Public opinion had rapidly moved to endorse the official nuclear programme in reaction to the Indian nuclear explosion. It grew increasingly critical of the US pressure against Pakistan's acquisition of nuclear technology. It was wary of Washington's perceived inability to help Pakistan in the 1971 war, beyond what was considered to be an empty gesture of sending the Enterprise into the Bay of Bengal. It perceived the US role in the 1973 Arab–Israel war as anti-Arab and anti-Muslim. Last, the continuing US embargo against Pakistan grossly alienated the articulate sections of the public. Given this framework of diffuse and latent anti-Westernism, Islamabad was able to pursue its nuclear programme without seriously compromising its general pro-Western policy orientation. This dual policy later survived even close US–Pakistan security relations during the next decade.[17] However, it was followed by another decade of Washington's cooling off towards Pakistan under the Pressler Amendment.

While the nuclear initiative developed into a constant feature of Pakistan's foreign and defence policies for the following three decades, the second substantive initiative in the realm of external relations in the 1970s related to policy orientation towards the Middle East. Traditionally, the State and society in Pakistan looked at the region from an ideological perspective as the classical homeland of Islam, and, therefore, the right place to pursue pan-Islamist policies. However, in the aftermath of the 1973 Arab–Israel war which was followed by a fourfold increase in the oil price and accumulation of huge oil revenues by the Gulf States, which in turn led to a demand for migrant workers from abroad, Islamabad opted for entry into the region in a big way.[18] The general public was awakened to the new reality of the Arabian peninsula as the home of petro-dollars. Unlike Pakistan's old Middle Eastern orientation for classical religious ties, the new orientation was predominantly market-based. Islamabad's view of Arabs as remote co-religionists changed to a perception of their role as economic, diplomatic and even strategic partners. Already, Pakistan had effectively turned its back on South Asia after the emergence of Bangladesh. The new Middle East orientation further consolidated this trend. During a decade and a half following the oil price hike in 1973, the flow of remittances from the Gulf to Pakistan amounted to $22 billion.[19] This underlined Pakistan's relatively independent pursuit of a strategic role in the region, specially in the field of nuclear policy. One can observe that both the nuclear and Middle East policies were largely reactive in nature. In the former case, it was the Indian nuclear programme which involved Pakistan in a spiral of reactive strategy for decades. An unstable situation on the border immediately after the 1971 war followed by the 1974 Indian nuclear test degenerated into a race for nuclear weapons. In the latter case, the opening up of Pakistan to South-West Asia was indeed a result of a chain of events unfolding in that region after the 1973 Arab–Israel war. Thus, regional inputs in foreign policy were decisive in both cases. Of course, hostility against India and feelings of brotherhood for Muslim countries of the Middle East operated as given in this framework, and provided legitimacy to the State for pursuing these policies.

It is true that the PPP Government in the 1970s was relatively less beholden to the administrative hierarchy than its predecessors. Under Bhutto, the bureaucracy in general lost its pre-eminent role in decision-making at the top. The new populist trend was relatively open-ended, without any well-defined direction for public policy.[20] However, the Foreign Office was relatively less influenced by direct political interference. Still, two aspects of the regime change left an imprint on the functioning of Pakistani diplomats. First, as compared to previous chief executives, Z.A. Bhutto put the seal of his own thoughts on Foreign Office deliberations more forcefully. In this, he drew upon his experience as Foreign Minister a decade earlier and by his position as Bonaparte in the new constellation of powers ruling Pakistan.[21] Apart from Bhutto's personality factor, which operated as long as he was in power, there was the indirect and long-term impact of those who joined the Foreign Service as well as the secretariat group through lateral entry.[22] These people brought a new outlook to the service which was not necessarily in tune with the old institutional ethos of the Foreign Service. In this way, the dialectics between domestic politics and foreign policy which had remained limited in operational terms, acquired a new level of dynamism during the 1970s which had not been known for a quarter of a century. Therefore, one can argue that political change in the country at large is reflected in foreign policy only indirectly through change in the internal dynamics of the institutional apparatus of the State and the changing idiom of mass politics. Bhutto's efforts to prop up Pakistan's profile of independence from the West, and to neutralize Soviet hostility to some extent relied heavily on populist rhetoric accompanied by some half-measures such as cultivating relations with North Korea and be-friending Gaddafi and Yasser Arafat.

The third phase (1977-88) of foreign policy in Pakistan can be described in terms of rediscovering the Soviet Union and reinventing the West. From the mid-1950s to the mid-1960s, Indo–Pakistan diplomacy surrounding the Kashmir dispute in and around the UN reflected deep hostility towards Moscow and total reliance on Washington on the part of Islamabad. These attitudes relaxed after Soviet diplomatic efforts brought the two South Asian adversaries to the conference table which led to the Tashkent Declaration in February 1966. Ayub, Yahya and Bhutto successively visited Moscow. On the other hand, Washington had steadily cooled off towards Islamabad after the 1965 war. Especially, it did not look favourably on Bhutto's relentless use of a 'socialist' and anti-Western idiom of politics, and opposed his pursuit of a nuclear programme practically. The Soviet incursion into Afghanistan changed all that. The Red Army on the borders of Pakistan presented a challenge hitherto unknown to the State as well as society. It was as if the old fears of British India about the southward expansion of the Soviet Union had suddenly come true. The situation neatly fitted in the Cold War scenario where the US felt obliged to roll back the Soviet presence in Afghanistan. For both the US and Pakistan, the situation looked more grim than in the 1950s when the Soviet forces were not actually deployed anywhere in the Middle East. The new strategic environment got the two countries deeply embroiled in the war effort of the Afghan resistance movement. Moving forward from India-centred security arrangements, Pakistan adopted a two-front approach to national strategy in the 1980s.

As mentioned earlier, the informed public in Pakistan was generally shocked by the Soviet military incursion into the neighbouring Muslim country. There was a general consensus about the need to resist the Soviet move in official circles, Islamic parties and groups, the industrial and landed elite as well as Afghan refugees.[23] Only pockets of leftist groups as well as Pakhtun and Baluch nationalist elements saw it as a positive move in the context of their own fight against Zia's military dictatorship. However, as the war in Afghanistan spilled over into northern Pakistan and the 1983 MRD (Movement for Restoration of Democracy) agitation shook Zia's military rule—which was closely identified with the war effort—the consensus gradually broke down. In the mid-1980s, an intense debate started in the media about the efficacy of Islamabad's policy commitment to the Afghan resistance movement. Prime Minister Junejo held an all-party conference in Islamabad before going to Geneva for negotiations with Moscow and Kabul in 1987 to apprise himself of public opinion. He was alerted to public fatigue with the Afghan war. He took it into consideration when he signed the Geneva accord which set a timetable for with-drawal of Soviet forces from Afghanistan. It involved a marginal loss of initiative by the military. Similarly, it was a major development in the context of dialectics between domestic politics and foreign policy. It can be argued that the lifting of martial law and installation of an elected government in office in 1985 created some strategic space for dialogue in public. Junejo was able to respond to the public mood. He chose to wriggle out of the Afghan imbroglio and got a reasonable deal from the war-weary Soviet Union.

Foreign policy under Zia (1977-88) reflected not only the regional scenario but also the preferences and predilections of persons in charge. Sahibzada Yaqub Ali Khan, who survived in office longer than any other Foreign Minister under the successive Governments of Zia, Benazir Bhutto and Nawaz Sharif, put Pakistan firmly back on the track of pro-US foreign policy. Under Zia, several army officers joined the diplomatic corps. This generally helped the incumbent government in terms of both the input function of diplomacy by way of churning out relevant information and policy recommendations, and the output function inasmuch as implementation of policy was carried out as an in-house matter. As the war in Afghanistan progressed, the diplomatic initiative slipped into the hands of the military high command. The army's intelligence outfit, the ISI, especially managed to move to centre stage in the Afghan war. And yet, when expression of public opinion in a relatively free political atmosphere under the elected government of Junejo was allowed, public discontent with the Afghan policy helped Islamabad to chalk out its negotiating position in Geneva. It can be argued that in a situation of war, including the civil war in East Pakistan in 1971 and the guerrilla war in Afghanistan during the 1980s under Generals Yahya and Zia respectively, foreign-policy initiatives slipped to the army as well as the military intelligence. This severely undermined the autonomy of the Foreign Office. Also, it typically barred the way to societal input into policy considerations about external relations. We can argue that Pakistan operated in a regional setting which was characterized by far too many wars and warlike situations along its borders, along with the continuing hostile relations with its eastern neighbour to make its foreign policy open-ended and amenable to influences from the wider society. Centralization of the State's authority further discouraged input from outside official circles. In other words, a relatively peaceful and stable situation on the borders and a regional scenario not characterized by endemic and existential conflict as well as a democratic political system are necessary conditions for an enhanced societal input into foreign policy.

In the fourth phase of foreign policy (1988-99), characterized by successive party-based civilian governments in a post-Zia scenario, two issue areas from the previous phase revolving around the Kashmir dispute and war in Afghanistan have continued to determine the direction of foreign policy. There is a consensus among people on the official policy on Kashmir, specially in north Pakistan. A policy of support for the struggle of Kashmiris for independence from India throughout the 1990s has enjoyed considerable backing from the public. Indeed, the Kashmir policy always got full support from the articulate sections of the society for the past half century. In public view, Kashmir is a part of the incomplete agenda of Partition based on Muslim nationalism in British India. In the 1980s and 1990s, it was additionally couched in nuclear nationalism. The sensitivity of the Pakistani public on Kashmir was amply demonstrated when the two countries started exchanging gunfire as well as hot words over the battle for Kargil in north Kashmir in May 1999. The initiative for pursuit of policy on Kargil remained with the two establishments on both sides of the border.

On a parallel line, Afghanistan is projected in the Pakistani media in the context of an internecine war, in which one faction, the Taliban have now taken control of 90 per cent of the territory. The world media have often pointed to Pakistan's role in determining the fate of the war in that country. During the last five years, more than a million Afghan refugees went back. The spillover effect of the Afghan war in terms of militant Islamization in Pakistan has been somewhat contained. The informed public seems to be cognizant of the underlying logic of the official Afghan policy in terms of the ultimate goal of opening up to Central Asia once political stability in Afghanistan is achieved. There is obvious discrepancy between the viewpoints of Pakistanis and the West in general on the role of the Taliban in Afghanistan. Pakistan looks at it in terms of Pakhtun nationalism which underlined state-hood in that country for two centuries. Also, it has a strategic importance for its southern neighbour which has its own Pakhtun population on its side of the border along with the latter's ethnic aspirations. From Islamabad's perspective, the Taliban delivered on two key issues: the pro-Pakistan stance of Kabul, and political stability in the country which is the key to future cultural and commercial links with Central Asia. On the other hand, the world media and Western diplomacy have generally looked at the Taliban in terms of their perceived fundamentalist policies and alleged violation of human rights at home, and alienation of neighbouring countries such as Iran and Tajikistan abroad. As far as the mobilized mass public in Pakistan is concerned, Islamabad's Afghan policy remains a favourite, because it first led to Soviet withdrawal from Afghanistan, and second, it was perceived as helping a pro-Pakistan militia—the Taliban to establish stability in that country.

An important development in the field of strategic policy was the detonation of nuclear devices by Pakistan as a follow-up of the Indian nuclear tests in May 1998. The nuclear programme of Pakistan has attracted maximum attention abroad in the context of the changing geostrategic environment in recent years. By the mid-1980s, Pakistan had developed the capacity of putting together a rudimentary form of nuclear bomb. Islamabad's nuclear diplomacy has revolved around three aspects: alarming the world about India's nuclear weapons programme and pressing for establishing a Nuclear Weapons Free Zone in South Asia; approaching India directly with a series of suggestions for Confidence Building Measures (CBMs) starting from the proposal for renunciation of acquisition and manufacture of nuclear weapons in 1978 to the offer of a bilateral CTBT arrangement in 1987 and a meeting of five nuclear States comprising the US, Russia, China, India and Pakistan in 1991; and pursuing a nuclear deterrence doctrine in South Asia which perceived the bomb as insurance against India's superior conventional and nuclear weapons.[24] There was a nuclear stand-off with India in 1990 when it was widely feared that the latter would attack Pakistan's nuclear installations. The period of nuclear opacity is over after the nuclear tests detonated by India and Pakistan in May 1998. As the two countries have moved from recessed deterrence to weaponized deterrence, the security situation in South Asia is more unstable than before.

The official nuclear policy has all along enjoyed public support. In 1996, the Joan B. Kroc Institute for International Peace Studies at the University of Notre Dame in the US sponsored a survey of public opinion in Pakistan on the nuclear issue.[25] While the Kashmir dispute topped the list of issues of public interest, the nuclear issue stood at the sixth position. However, 85 per cent of the respondents favoured the policy of going nuclear if India opted for a nuclear test. Generally, people were not sensitive about the cost in human life in the case of a nuclear war or the devastating effect of economic sanctions. The role of India in the region remained the highest determining factor in foreign policy in the public eye. The tiny anti-nuclear lobby in Pakistan has ascribed the relative insensitivity of the public to the horrors of a nuclear arms race in South Asia to domestication of the nuclear language by official circles which reduced the whole issue to a matter of selecting between 'options'.[26] One can argue that there is a passive consensus on the issue of Kashmir, Afghanistan and the nuclear programme which is activated whenever there is a crisis situation. This fact is responsible for making these issues least debatable in public. Indeed, the relative absence of these issues from successive election campaigns can sometimes be mistaken as their irrelevance for the public, or even its opposition to the official policy in these matters. Pakistan has been in the midst of a controversy about signing the CTBT after it detonated nuclear tests in May 1998. The opinion on the right, represented by Islamic parties and conservative sections of the middle class as well as elements of the top military hierarchy opposed any move towards signing the CTBT. From the left, Sindhi and Baluch nationalisms and the liberal English press were in favour of such a move. The imposition of US economic sanctions on Pakistan in the aftermath of the May tests created a financial crisis in the country which marginally tilted public opinion in favour of the latter position.

It is generally known that the defence policy in general, and India as well as Afghan policies in particular, are under the deterministic influence of the army and ISI. Such foreign-policy orientations as nuclear nationalism, anti-India stance and overtures to the Middle East and Central Asia remain socially embedded in the regions and communities operating within mainstream politics such as Punjab and NWFP. Those operating outside the mainstream such as in Sindh and Baluchistan, remain sceptical about some of these goals. On the other hand, those issues which were close to their heart, such as repatriation of Biharis from Bangladesh pursued by Mohajirs and repatriation of Afghan refugees from Baluchistan demanded by the Baluch remain low-priority areas of foreign policy.[27] They have a limited potential for input into the policy-making at the federal level.

We can conclude by observing that the dialectics between domestic politics and foreign policy in Pakistan at best operate indirectly. The institutional ethos inherited from the pre-Independence period continues to exert pressure in favour of exclusive foreign policy deliberations. The peculiar pattern of civil-military relations in the country undermined the growth of political institutions, which further limited public input into foreign policy. On the other hand, regional instability all around Pakistan has grossly influenced both public opinion and official policy. Within the country, those regions and communities which are not fully represented in the State feel alienated from the established foreign-policy orientations. Even mainstream public opinion drifted away from the official line over some issues for some time in the past. However, the underlying consensus in the society continues to provide legitimacy to the decision-makers at the top in pursuit of their policies on Kashmir, Afghanistan, India and the Middle East. The broad foreign-policy outline characterized by pro-Western, pro-Chinese and pro-nuclear policies has generally survived the regime change.

NOTES

1. Benjamin Ginsberg, 'Elections and Public Policy', *The American Political Science Review*, March 1976, p. 41.
2. Charles E. Lindblom, 'Another State of Mind', *The American Political Science Review*, March 1982, p. 11.
3. Alastair Lamb, *Asian Frontiers*, London: Pall Mall, 1968, pp. 12-13.
4. Foreign Office Minute: Ashton Gwatkin, 12 August 1947, W/6142, FO371/ 65574; also addendum dated 15 August 1947.
5. See Mohammad Waseem, 'Pakistan's Perceptions of the Impact of US Politics on its Policies Towards Pakistan', in Noor Husain and Leo Rose, eds., *Pakistan-US Relations: Social, Political and Economic Factors*, Berkeley: University of California, 1988, p. 306.
6. See Herbert Feldman, 'The Experiment in a Presidential System', in S.H. Hashmi, ed., *The Governing Process in Pakistan: 1958-69*, Lahore: Aziz Publishers, 1987, pp. 30-5.
7. Mushahid Hussain and Akmal Hussain, *Pakistan: Problems of Governance*, Lahore: Vanguard Books, 1993, p. 96.
8. Ibid., pp. 73-80; also Diego Cordovez and Selig Harrison, *Out of Afghanistan: The Inside Story of the Soviet Withdrawal*, New York: Oxford University Press, 1995, p. 62.
9. For a discussion of parallel ethnic world views in Pakistan, see Mehtab Ali Shah, *The Foreign Policy of Pakistan: Ethnic Impacts on Diplomacy, 1971-1994*, London: I.B. Taurus, 1997, pp. 66-79 and 105-13.
10. See Mohammad Waseem, *Politics and the State in Pakistan,* Islamabad: National Institute of Historical and Cultural Research, 1994, pp. 137-8.
11. Hasan Askari Rizvi, *Pakistan and the Geostrategic Environment*, Basingstoke: Macmillan, 1993, pp. 88-9.

12. Sir D.D. Kelly (Angora, Turkey) to Foreign Office London, F 15381/8800/85, no. 298, dated 13 November 1947.

13. Gustav Papanek, *Pakistan's Development: Social Goals and Private Incentives*, Cambridge, Mass: MIT Press, 1967, p. 9; and Rashid Amjad, *Industrial Concentration and Economic Power in Pakistan*, Lahore: Vanguard, n.d., p. 60.

14. A good example of this approach is Qutubuddin Aziz, *Mission to Washington*, Karachi: United Press of Pakistan, 1973.

15. Waseem, op. cit., pp. 250-4.

16. John Kautsky, *Political Consequences of Modernization*, New York: Wiley, 1972, p. 197.

17. Rizvi, op. cit., pp. 92-101.

18. See Mervin Weinbaum and Gautam Sen, 'Pakistan Enters the Middle East', *Orbis*, Fall 1978.

19. See Akmal Hussain, *Strategic Issues in Pakistan's Economic Policy*, Lahore: Progressive Publishers, 1988.

20. Waseem, op. cit., pp. 304-6.

21. See Khalid B. Sayeed, *Politics in Pakistan: The Nature and Direction of Change*, New York: Praeger, 1980, pp. 89, 94.

22. Charles H. Kennedy, 'Analysis of the Lateral Recruitment Programme to the Federal Bureaucracy of Pakistan 1973-78', *Journal of South Asian and Middle Eastern Studies*, vol. 3 (4), Summer 1980, pp. 46-7.

23. See Rasul Baksh Rais, *War Without Winners: Afghanistan's Uncertain Transition After the Cold War*, Karachi: Oxford University Press, 1994.

24. Stephen P. Cohen, 'Policy Implications', in Stephen Cohen, ed., *Nuclear Proliferation in South Asia*, Boulder: Westview Press, 1991, p. 359; and William Walker, 'International Nuclear Relations after the Indian and Pakistani Test Explosions', *International Affairs*, vol. 74, no. 3, 1998, pp. 516-18.

25. Samina Ahmed and David Cortright, 'Pakistani Public Opinion and Nuclear Weapons Policy', in Samina Ahmed and David Cortright, eds., *Pakistan and the Bomb: Public Opinion and Nuclear Options*, Indiana: Notre Dame University Press, 1998, pp. 17-22.

26. Zia Mian, 'Renouncing the Nuclear Option', in Samina Ahmed and David Cortright (eds.), ibid., p. 47.

27. Shah, op. cit., pp. 59, 111.

12

The 'Multi-Vocal State':
The Policy of Pakistan on Kashmir

AMÉLIE BLOM

I N MAY 1947, Mohammad Ali Jinnah was strongly against the idea of using force to incorporate Kashmir into Pakistan. But at the same time, he declared that the new State would be incomplete without the Himalayan kingdom being part of it. Even before Partition, when the idea or 'imagining of Pakistan' was still being discussed, it was already taken for granted that Kashmir was an integral part of Pakistan[1] as the letter 'K' in 'Pakistan' suggests. The dispute with India over Kashmir is therefore a highly emotional and ideological issue in contemporary Pakistan. How can this be explained? One simple answer would be that it is Pakistan's duty to keep the issue alive. Official statements repeatedly refer not only to India's failure to implement the United Nations' resolutions calling for a plebiscite since 1948, or to organize free and fair elections and respect Article 370 of its Constitution protecting the autonomy of the State, but also to the UN Security Council's remarkable indifference—only 44 UN military observers monitor ceasefire violations along the entire Line of Control (LoC).

Such feelings and explanations may be prevalent in Pakistan,[2] but they do not account for the decades following the 1965 war and the 1972 Simla Agreement during which Kashmir became almost a dead issue. The picture radically changed in the late 1980s for two reasons. First, following the 1987 elections which were rigged a grassroots armed insurgency arose in the Kashmir Valley in the form of the 'azadi or freedom movement'[3] which initially had very little to do with Pakistan. And as Gen. Zia as well as Pakistani leaders of Islamist movements were at that time much more preoccupied with the Afghan war, conditions inside Pakistan and Azad Jammu & Kashmir (AJ&K)[4] were not conducive to establishing training camps there before the mid-1980s, as recalled by a Kashmiri militant leader.[5] Pakistani authorities as well, were not comfortable with a rebellion spearheaded by the Jammu & Kashmir Liberation Front (JKLF), an outfit which proved too difficult to control.[6] Second, with the Soviet threat vanishing after 1989, for several Pakistani Islamist groups, who had support from sections of the Pakistani military, Kashmir became the new '*jihad*' and the Hindus the new 'infidels'.

The level of importance given to the Kashmir issue in Pakistani politics is dictated by external circumstances. Domestic factors too play a decisive role. Historical sociology has shown how important territorial conflicts are for nascent States—legitimizing their coercive apparatus (police and army), nurturing their national feelings, accelerating the process of centralization and modernization of their administrative structures, and reinforcing their call for sovereignty at the international level.[7] Indeed, the Pakistani State and its army came into existence with a war on Kashmir and developed in the framework of a quasi-permanent confrontation with India. The 1949 ceasefire line (transformed into the LoC in 1972) which divides Kashmir between Pakistan and India remains a temporary demarcation and does not even appear in official Pakistani maps wherein the whole of Jammu & Kashmir with the boundaries of the former Princely State is depicted as a 'disputed territory'.[8] Kashmir has been at the heart of two wars (1947-8 and 1965), almost provoked two others (in 1987 and 1990), and finally caused one of the most serious military confrontations between nuclear India and Pakistan in May 1999. In between, the 'proxy war' in Kashmir has claimed more than 25,000 victims (since 1990).[9] Sporadic but intense firings between the two armies across the LoC have become a routine affair and have almost transformed both parts of Kashmir into garrison states.[10] Seen from this perspective, the official Pakistani viewpoint that 'Kashmir is the unachieved agenda of the 1947 Partition' goes further than it appears to: the possibility of a war with India over Kashmir, which hangs like Damocles' sword over Pakistanis' heads, is not only a constitutive part of Pakistan's official nationalism but also a structural element which helps the institutions of the State to 'achieve' a complete control over the society by keeping it in a constant state of mobilization.

Though it helps in understanding the importance of the Kashmir issue for the Pakistani State and its policy towards it, the link that one could establish in this macro-sociological perspective between war and State formation appears to be too tenuous. The relation between the conflicts with India and the process of centralization of the Pakistani

State is far more complex. With a mere 200 million rupees as its opening cash balance just after Partition, and its defence expenditure soon exceeding that of the undivided Government of India (with an estimated 35 to 50 million rupees a month to be spent in the upkeep of its defence forces alone), the centre could not sustain military hostilities with India without depriving the provinces of their right to a whole range of taxes.[11] Therefore, as Ayesha Jalal forcefully put it, 'if defence against India provided added impetus for the consolidation of state's authority in Pakistan, paradoxically enough, it also served to distort the balance of relations between the newly formed centre and the provinces',[12] a trend which will weaken the centre's authority in the long run. The macro-sociological approach is all too structuralist: it hardly incorporates the agents who influence, frame and implement the defence policy of a state. For whom is the Kashmir issue relevant and who actually elaborates the Kashmiri policy of Pakistan? The fact that Pakistan can send contradictory signals regarding Kashmir (the contrast between the February 1999 Lahore Declaration and the Kargil crisis three months later being the most amazing one) is precisely the reason why an analytical perspective centred on the actors (institutional and individual) of this policy is required. According to Ahmed Rashid, 'an attempt to understand' the decision-making process in foreign policy towards India (and towards Pakistan in India) 'is perhaps the first step in trying to formulate a more coherent debate on how the Kashmir dispute can be resolved'.[13] It also demonstrates, as former French Ambassador in Pakistan Pierre France points out, that 'We can not analyse Pakistani domestic policy, its economic, financial, and religious aspects included, without keeping in mind the Kashmir issue.'[14]

The agents of the Kashmir policy during the 1990s, their different voices and decisions, hence the expression 'multi-vocal state',[15] are the main foci of this article. The central hypothesis is that the specific civil-military balance of power during 1990s (and particularly before the October 1999 military coup) as well as the numerous, and sometimes very influential, social and political groups who have vested interest in the Kashmir dispute explain why this dispute is as much a domestic issue as a foreign policy one.

IS THERE A COHERENT KASHMIR POLICY?

There are certainly some recurring elements in the official position that Pakistan holds on Kashmir: (1) the former Princely State is a 'disputed territory' since 1948; (2) the right of self-determination has to be given to the Kashmiri people via a UN-supervised plebiscite; (3) such a plebiscite should offer accession either to India or to Pakistan; and (4) the Simla Agreement does not rule out international mediation.[16] Pakistan also frequently proclaims its commitment to help 'politically and morally' the 'azadi movement'. The regularity of bilateral talks with India from 1972 up to 1999, inspite of the tensions between the two States, is also an important, and often forgotten, characteristic of Indo-Pakistan relations: at the Foreign Secretary level almost every one or two years and at the President or Prime Minister level more than eight times.

Yet some analysts and officials, with very distinct ideological backgrounds, question the coherency of Pakistan's policy towards India. According to them, it has, in fact, no clear direction and remains purely a knee-jerk reaction. This is the claim of the Institute of Policy Studies (the research centre of the Jamaat-i-Islami in Islamabad): Kashmir is one such issue where Pakistan is 'like a blind man'[17] and acts only after India gives the impulse or the United States pressurizes it. Former Director General (DG) of the Inter-Services Intelligence (ISI), Hamid Gul, shares this opinion. For him, 'there is a great deal of ambivalence in Pakistan's policy on Kashmir'.[18] Commenting on the Kargil crisis, the former Chief of Army Staff (COAS) in 1996-8, Jehangir Karamat, credits more wisdom to the Cheshire cat of *Alice in Wonderland* than to Pakistani authorities: while the former's advise to the lost Alice is that the way she ought to go depends a good deal on where she wants to go, the latter had no clear-cut aims, no idea about the image Pakistan wished to project and no ability to coordinate.[19] The conclusion of the current Pakistani Ambassador to the United States, Maleeha Lodhi, is even more critical: the Kargil affair has exposed 'systemic flaws in a decision-making process that is impulsive, chaotic, erratic, and overly secretive'.[20]

Some concrete inconsistencies seem to confirm these severe judgements. The most recent being the striking contrast between the images of the Pakistani and Indian Prime Ministers shaking hands at the Wagah border (and signing the highly symbolic Lahore Declaration in which they promised to 'make all efforts' to resolve the Kashmir issue) in February 1999, and less than three months later, those of both armies getting into a clinch once again in one of the most serious military and diplomatic crisis of their post-nuclear era. This limited conventional war in Ladakh, during which India used the Air Force for the first time in Kashmir, started only after India discovered on 6 May that guerrilla fighters backed by Pakistan (presenting themselves as Mujahideen) had infiltrated into the Kargil and Drass hills more than 15 km away from the LoC. Interestingly, a similar paradoxical situation arose nine years earlier when, soon after the Pakistani and Indian Foreign Ministers met to discuss Kashmir (in January 1990, after three years of silence), a very serious crisis was shortly averted thanks to US intervention, as Gen. Aslam Beg (COAS of Pakistan at that time) and retired Gen. Sharma (ex-chief of the Indian army) have recently disclosed.[21] It is also well known that firings along the LoC (without, at times, being fully controlled by the respective army, as local Brigadiers may act independently) can intensify even as scheduled bilateral talks draw near, as was the case before the Summer 1998 Foreign Secretaries meet. It was also not rare during Nawaz Sharif's second government (February 1997-October 1999) to read contradictory statements from the Secretary General of the Ministry of Foreign Affairs rejecting mediation by a third country in the Kashmir dispute one day, and calling for it the next day. Finally, it will be recalled that in 1993, the Government of AJ&K sent its own delegation abroad without informing the Foreign Office, and that the same year, Pakistan Foreign Minister allowed a JKLF conference to be held while the Prime Minister of AJ&K had decided to ban it.

Graham Allison, in his comparative study of the decision-making process in the USA and USSR during the Cuban missile crisis, has shown that what we often take to be as incoherences in decision-making process reflects most of the time our own misinterpretation of foreign policy as simply being the 'nation-state's foreign policy'.[22] States rarely behave as monoliths which choose the more rational action given the national interest at stake and the constraints they face (as the 'realist' approach of foreign policy would have us believe). They are 'black boxes covering various gears . . . in a highly differentiated decision-making structure'. Foreign policy decisions are 'consequences of innumerable and often conflicting smaller actions by individuals at various levels of bureaucratic organizations' whose reactions depend on the positions they occupy and what they have previously learned to perform (according to the 'organizational process model'). They also result from 'compromise, coalition, competition, and confusion among officials'. It is the priority, ability, perception and hierarchical position of these officials which will determine the outcome of the bargaining process (according to the 'bureaucratic politics model').

Robert Putnam, on his part, has completed Allison's models by studying the wider domestic constraints imposed not just on executives and institutional arrangements but also on institutions such as parties, social classes, interest groups, legislators, and even public opinion and elections which help determine foreign policy. Foreign policy is thus conceived as a 'two-level game' whose 'paradoxical interactions' may create inconsistencies:

At the national level, domestic groups pursue their interest by pressuring the government to adopt favourable policies, and politicians seek power by constructing coalitions among those groups. At the international level, national government seek to maximize their own ability to satisfy domestic pressure, while minimizing the adverse consequences of foreign developments.... The unusual complexity of this two-level game is that moves that are rational for a player at one board ... may be impolitic for that same player at the other board.[23]

These two analytical frameworks help to understand Pakistan's policy on Kashmir. Indeed, the multiplicity of institutions and actors involved in framing this policy during the 1990s is one important factor which explains why it was such a 'multi-vocal' policy. There is, truly, a plethora of agencies in charge of Kashmir: the army and its several divisions, the ISI (which is sometimes credited as having its own policy), the Prime Minister's Secretariat, the Foreign Office (and its Kashmir Directorate), the Defence Secretary, the Ministry for Kashmir Affairs, Northern Areas and Frontier Regions (KANA and SAFRON), the Kashmir Council (acting as a link between the Federal Government and the AJ&K Government), the Kashmir Committee of the Parliament, etc. But then it is also true that these institutions frame their policies while taking into account wider political and social domestic forces: Kashmiri 'public opinion' (political groups and non-political associations settled in Pakistan as well as in AJ&K), political parties, Islamist movements active in Kashmir, as well as the Punjabi media and pacifist NGOs.

INSTITUTIONAL 'PLAYERS' IN PAKISTAN'S KASHMIR POLICY

The Army

The importance of the army in decision-making process regarding Kashmir is universally acknowledged. Even during the period of relative democratization during 1988-99, no defence policy could be framed without the blessing, and the active involvement of the army. The Defence Secretary was himself a high-ranking officer, as was the Minister for Kashmir Affairs. The GHQ (General Headquarters), the Corps Commanders' Conferences (CCC) and the Joint Chiefs of Staff Committee (JCSC) are said to have been the main bodies in the decision-making process during this period. During the CCC convened by the COAS, where, interestingly, the DG ISI was believed to have been absent, the nine Corps Commanders, the COAS and six members of the General Headquarter (all from the Army Staff) provided inputs to the JCSC and in return implemented the joint decisions taken at this level. Although the COAS is all-powerful, he needs the support of the CCC for any major change in foreign policy.[24] The JCSC, together with the COAS and the Chiefs of Naval and Air Force Staffs, directly makes recommendations to the Prime Minister and to the Defence Secretary. It appears that the inter army-civilian bodies, the Defence Committee of the Cabinet (DCC) for instance, frequently mentioned as being important did not have any role to play most of the time. Some specific military forces are central to Pakistan's Kashmir policy. The key role that CCC plays in the Kashmir policy comes, of course, from the presence of the 10 Corps Commander (headquartered in Rawalpindi).[25] This Corps gained greater importance during martial law periods when it became the military government's main power base.[26] It was, above all, the biggest operational corps of the Pakistan army defending the LoC. The Northern Light Infantry (NLI), in charge of the defence of the Northern Areas, is another crucial structure. This paramilitary force, supervised by army officers, has been fully integrated into the army after the Kargil crisis in 1999, where it lost more than 300 men. The ISI, one of the most renowned Pakistani intelligence's services, is, ofcourse, another one.

What is the influence of ISI and how autonomous is it in framing and implementing the Kashmir policy? For some, the ISI cannot be dissociated from the army as high-ranking Generals head it and as most of its civilian members are in fact retired officers. The new DG ISI appointed after the October 1999 coup (Lt. Gen. Mahmood Ahmed) is, for instance, the former head of the 10 Corps which is, as mentioned previously, central to the protection of the LoC. On the other hand, others insist on the ability of the ISI to have its own policy designed in its 'Kashmir cell'. Given the obvious absence of studies on the ISI, this is a mere conjecture. It is clear, however, that the ISI has two strong tools of influence: knowledge and manpower. It assesses intelligence from India and Kashmir, plans secret operations, executes them and undertakes counter-intelligence. It is the principal operational institution in the 'proxy-war' in Kashmir and years of experience in Afghanistan have given it an 'expertise' in the field of guerrilla warfare. As it is also the principal source of information, the ISI is frequently seen as a 'conceptualizer' and, therefore, as widely dominating the dialogue with the army and the government on Kashmir.

In addition to the spectre of another major war with India, the military has other specific strategic concerns that guide its policy towards India and Kashmir. First, the conflict has hydraulic implications (as the accession of Kashmir to India deprived Pakistan of the control over the important rivers which water the plains of the Indus valley). But the fear expressed by a Pakistani General that 'India might make a desert of Pakistan' (allegation based on the construction of the Wular Barrage) is not without a sense of dramatization. Indeed, the 1960 Treaty regulating the shared water resources has been neither contested nor violated by both countries. Second, it is important to understand that what Pakistan can do, in military terms, to further its claims on Kashmir is quite limited. Given Pakistan's conventional military inferiority compared to India, and the difficulty in targeting civilians in J&K without alienating its supporters, Pakistan has only three options as recalled by a former DG ISI: rely on nuclear deterrence, locally respond to Indian attacks, and help the insurgents in J&K. The first option was ofcourse at the heart of the nuclear tests of May 1998 (the third one will be developed in the third part of this article). The second option, less frequently analysed, is absolutely central to the day-to-day policy regarding Kashmir. It can be summarized by what is called the 'offensive defence doctrine' of the army.[27] This implies, as it was stated during one of the CCC in 1998,[28] that Pakistan should be able to give to India a 'befitting response' each time ceasefire violations occur along the LoC.

This aspect of the army's policy was one of the most important causes of the spring 1999 confrontation with India. Indeed, since the summer of 1998, India has dramatically intensified its firings on villages in the Neelum and Jhelum valleys in AJ&K arguing that it needed to prevent Pakistan-trained militants' infiltration into J&K. This situation confronted Pakistan with three major problems: the heavy losses suffered by its troops controlling the southern part of LoC; the blockade of the supply roads to these troops; and the very difficult handling of the dilemma the displaced people in AJ&K.[29] Therefore, the Kargil operation had a defensive side that went generally unnoticed by the Western media: to create a mutual vulnerability along the LoC. The plan was in response to the escalation of Indian artillery firings in the Kel-Kotli sector; Pakistan would retaliate in the north-western portion of the LoC[30] and make it difficult for India to maintain control of the positions it had snatched from Pakistan in the Siachen Glacier area since 1984.

But the Pakistan's army policy towards Kashmir is not only driven by strategic concerns, it is also a matter of perception. There is, first, a deeply rooted feeling that Indians cannot be trusted. According to Stephen Cohen, this line of thinking of Pakistani officers is now less a product of their experience before Partition than of crude images of India that have become part of their education—both formal and informal—and which are documented in numerous policy studies coming from the GHQ.[31] The recently developed 'new thinking' of the army has far from softened this sense of distrust: the Indian threat remains but in a changing fashion, not in conventional wars any more, but through sponsoring of internal warfare.[32] For one defence analyst, 'the Army is very clear that today if the enemy wants to attack, it will attack from within' and former COAS Gen. Karamat confirmed it by saying that '[India] wants to remove the irritant by weakening us, splintering us not through a direct approach but through low intensity conflicts within Pakistan'.[33] The fragile cohesion of Pakistan and the trauma of the 1971 independence of East Pakistan determine this 'cognitive fusion' of the external and domestic enemy. It can also be seen as a functional perception since it helps the army to project itself as the ultimate guarantor of law and order within, and thus, remain a major political force. Saeed Shafqat convincingly shows that there is, traditionally, a strong correlation between the political salience of the military in politics during civilian interludes, and what he calls the 'manipulation of geopolitical factors'. 'In the post-military hegemonic period' (1972-7), he writes, 'Pakistan was faced with both external threat and internal dissension. With the military defeated and its top brass in disarray, these threats seemed larger than they really were.'[34] The army's perception that India will continue to take any advantage to weaken Pakistan goes along with another notion which becomes crucial when it comes to holding official talks with the neighbouring state: Pakistani politicians are even more untrustworthy, as they are extensively corrupt, preoccupied only by the short-term agenda of re-election and unable to frame and defend the 'national interest' of the country.[35] The army assumes therefore that it has to maintain the upper hand in foreign policy towards India.

The position of the army regarding Kashmir is also determined by the strength of its emotional involvement. This emotional approach in its relations with India, and in the Kashmir dispute, has been underlined by several former high-ranking Pakistani officers, as well as by foreign diplomats during their talks with Pakistani army men.[36] This 'passionate' approach is, of course, nurtured by the sense of struggle for a 'just cause' (presently, roughly 80 per cent of the officers are convinced that J&K is an integral part of Pakistan and is not negotiable)[37] and by India's recurrent shelling across the LoC. But that is not the only reason. The army's ethnic composition is another important factor. Officers from the Punjab (more precisely, from Northern Punjab, and adjacent districts of the NWFP, Kohat and Mardan),[38] the province which suffered most from Partition, constituted more than 70 per cent of the officer corps in 1979. The traumatic memories of their families has made them more reluctant to compromise on Kashmir. The generation factor also plays a role. Officers who suffered the 1971 defeat are still at the top of the army's hierarchy. After the 12 October 1999 takeover the two most important military leaders of the country (and the principal decision-makers during the Kargil operation) have led a life and charted a career marked by tense relations with India. COAS Gen. Musharraf, whose family hails from Delhi, migrated to Pakistan after Partition when he was a child. He was active as a member of the Elite Special Services Group during the 1965 and 1971 wars. Lt.-Gen. Muhammad Mir Aziz Khan, former Chief of General Staff (CGS) and recently appointed by Gen. Musharraf as Commander 10 Corps, was born in the year of Partition in Rawalkot in AJ&K, and has occupied key posts related to Kashmir affairs: he has served in the Force Command Northern Areas, the NLI and the ISI.

The Government

It is common public perception in Pakistan that, even during the phases of democratization, the government had no autonomy in framing its policy towards India as that process was the monopoly of the army. Such a view has to be qualified, at least as far as the second government of Nawaz Sharif (1997-9) is concerned. This politically very interesting period gives a more complex picture of the main axes of Sharif's policy regarding the Kashmir dispute. As opposed to Benazir Bhutto (who was quite a hardliner vis-à-vis India), Nawaz Sharif took several steps to show his commitment towards normalizing his country's relations with India. Some observers even consider that such steps could be seen as signs that a real civil foreign policy, autonomous of the army's inputs, was firmly in the making. Nawaz Sharif truly played a significant role in the revival of the dialogue with India under Inder Kumar Gujral's government. He was the first Punjabi politician to have publicly declared, in 1997, that he was prepared to reconsider the position of Pakistan on Kashmir. The dispute also became part of a larger package of several disputed issues which Pakistan and India had agreed to discuss (peace and security, terrorism and drug trafficking, Siachen Glacier, Wular Barrage Project, Sir Creek delimitation, economic and commercial cooperation, and promotion of friendly exchanges in various fields). New rounds of bilateral talks were even undertaken with the NDA government in which the ultra-nationalist Bharatiya Janata Party (BJP) is a major partner. Even when the Pakistani government kept repeating that it would not start (and continue) the talks if the Kashmir dispute was not settled,[39] it nonetheless did begin a dialogue after India merely promised to 'talk on Kashmir'. Indian strategy to 'de-link' Kashmir from other issues had succeeded. And though this dialogue had yielded tenuous results (no agreement on Siachen and not even the beginning of a consensus on Kashmir) relations between India and Pakistan did improve during the months preceding the limited war in Kargil. A new visa regime for Pakistanis visiting India was established, a regular bus service between Lahore and Delhi was introduced, exchanges of civil prisoners allowed, and visits of commercial and cultural delegations to each other countries were organized. The perception that a 'personal' Indian policy framed by the prime minister was being implemented, without being fully approved of or controlled by the army, was further sustained by Indian Prime Minister Atal Behari Vajpayee's visit to Lahore in February 1999 at Nawaz Sharif's initiative. It was further strengthened after the Indo–Pakistani press revealed of secret negotiations being conducted between a former Pakistan Foreign Secretary and an Indian emissary, even while the Kargil war was on, and an informal sugar trade deal between the two countries was taking place.[40]

This process of normalizing relations with India was nevertheless replete with contradictions. More glaring of all was the entire management of the Kargil episode by Prime Minister Nawaz Sharif, who is believed to have first supported it,[41] before he was requested to present himself in Washington on 4 July 1999 to make a joint statement with

US President Bill Clinton. Pressured by Clinton, Pakistan had to unilaterally stop the confrontation and ask the 'mujahideen', who had been named earlier, in bilateral phone talks and in the US Congress, as 'Pakistani forces', to withdraw. This act by itself almost sanctified the LoC. If international pressure is seen as the main reason for this lack of coherency in Pakistan's foreign policy (the G-8, the American Congress and China openly targeted Pakistan as being responsible for the crisis, and the Americans even threatened to impose diplomatic sanctions), the schizophrenic policy of the government and the domestic political situation are other important factors to consider. Nawaz Sharif's policy towards Kashmir was indeed a Janus-faced one. Each time negotiations were on (openly or secretly), the Pakistan government insisted on their 'failure', while ironically the very subject of the rounds of talks was 'confidence-building measures'. And each time, the intense anti-Indian propaganda on PTV, i.e. the national TV channel—whose chairman in 1998 was a Senator from the Pakistan Muslim League, the party then in power—would be at its height.

All governments in Pakistan are careful of not being seen as 'soft on Kashmir'—this is as true of Sharif as it was of Benazir or even Gen. Zia—domestic pressures being very strong. As far as Nawaz Sharif was concerned, these pressures came first from his own family which belongs to the Punjabi 'Kashmir *mohalla*' ('community' or 'neighbourhood' of Kashmiri migrants), and especially from his powerful father (well-known for being reluctant to compromise with India). This abiding influence was frequently featured in the press as cartoons showing a baby Nawaz Sharif asking his father, 'And now, *abbaji*, what do we do?' These domestic pressures also came from his own party, the Muslim League, and through the National Assembly Special Committee on Kashmir. This committee, a creation of Benazir, which was given lots of funds to promote the Pakistani cause abroad, acts as a sounding board for the opinions of Muslim Leaguers on Kashmir. There were, finally, more politically threatening pressures from the opposition parties like the Pakistan People's Party (PPP) and the Islamist parties. Kashmir has traditionally been part of the politics of personal vendetta, rivalry and revenge between Bhutto and Sharif from 1988 to 1999. Islamist parties like the Jamaat-i-Islami did not hesitate to brand Sharif as a traitor in the face of a huge 'Hindu conspiracy'[42] and it, therefore, decided to use its well-organized politics of the street (as during Vajpayee's visit to Lahore in February 1999).

The personal policy on India which Nawaz Sharif tried to implement was bound to fail because it had been developed in an atmosphere of mutual tension with the army, a fact which explains the many contradictions in the way the Kargil crisis was managed. These tensions became apparent during the crisis since the Defence Committee of the Cabinet (DCC, constituting of the President, the Prime Minister, the Foreign Minister, the Defence Secretary and the three Army Chiefs), the unique civil-military body where a concerted Indian policy is supposed to be framed, and officially the sole arbiter in matters of strategic affairs, met only in the final phase and after two years of inactivity.[43] These tensions were also highlighted by Pakistani journalists who tried to identify the men responsible for this crisis: Zaffar Abbas, for instance, asked, 'Whodunnit?'[44] This cryptic query best encapsulates the depth of crisis in governance of the Pakistani state. During the two years relations between the Prime Minister and the army had deteriorated to an unprecedented level. Indeed, since the 1997 elections, Pakistan had witnessed a growing centralization of power in the hands of the Prime Minister who could not only appoint the COAS but also keep the portfolio of Defence and appoint Lt. Gen. Khawaja Ziauddin (a close family friend) as the new DG ISI. More decisively, during the year preceding Kargil, he managed to amend the Constitution doing away with the President's power to dismiss the government and sacked not only the President but also the Chief Justice. Above all, in October 1998, the COAS Gen. Jehangir Karamat, who discussed on public forums governmental performances, along with the Naval Chief were forced to resign. Finally, members of Sharif's cabinet started to criticize the military institution in the press. The Kashmir policy could not remain immune to this continuous arm-wrestling between the Prime Minister and the army: it prevented Pakistan from speaking with 'one voice' on the domestic and on the international front.

In this struggle, and because of his specific style of governance, the Prime Minister lacked the support of the third institutional player of the Kashmir policy, the Foreign Office. He deliberately kept it at bay, as is evident from the Kargil crisis. A Pakistani diplomat in Washington disclosed effectively that, 'They [the Government of Pakistan] have not even asked for a summary from us since the crisis began. They have not discussed any strategy or given any line of action. We are working in a vacuum.'[45] This astonishing situation of a crisis dealt without any diplomatic preparation, explains why Pakistan so hastily succumbed to international pressures. It definitely weakens the realist theory hypothesis mentioned earlier: 'the State' is not a monolithic actor in foreign policy. Though the influence of the Foreign Office in the framing of the Kashmir policy is seen as traditionally weak, it still plays a significant role by advising the political leadership, and most importantly, by being at the forefront of the talks with India. What then is the vision of this bureaucracy on the Kashmir dispute? Some Pakistani analysts consider that hardliners dominate the civil administration but this opinion clearly underestimates the plurality of opinions which prevails in the Foreign Office, in the Foreign Service Academy (FSA) as well as in the Civil Service Academy (CSA). A former director of the FSA, interviewed in 1998, is of the opinion that negotiations are useless given the duplicity of India as according to him, 'Mohajirs are being blackmailed when they ask for visas for India, and compelled to destabilize Pakistan'. But another Foreign Office official does not hesitate to offer imaginative solutions for the Kashmir dispute: he suggests that during an interim period Pakistan and India could first demilitarize the area, then put it under UN administration and discuss the modality of a plebiscite which would only concern AJ&K (excluding then the Northern Areas) and the Kashmir Valley (excluding then Jammu and Ladakh), and which would also include the third option (independence), so as not to alienate the JKLF.

NON-STATE ACTORS AFFECTING THE KASHMIR POLICY

Kashmiris

Can the state of Azad Jammu & Kashmir be another centrifugal force in Pakistan? One reason cited by some Pakistani officials to explain why neither the army nor the government can compromise on Kashmir is that, if it were so, AJ&K will rebel. Is this opinion based on any empirical evidence? Theoretically, the 2.5 million Azad Kashmiris[46] are politically autonomous (while the one million living in the Northern Area are under the direct administration of the Centre). AJ&K has its own Constitution (since 1974), its own Legislative Assembly and Supreme Court. It is fully autonomous in local affairs (education, forestry, local administration, etc.) but its foreign policy, defence and currency are directly under the control of the Federal Government. Islamabad supervises the state through the intermediary of the Ministry for Kashmir Affairs and Northern Areas (considered to be so useless, given the prominent role of the Kashmir Council, by some civil servants of AJ&K that they call it only by its acronym 'KANA', which means 'one-eyed' or 'foolish' in Urdu), and more decisively through the Kashmir Council. This Council, headed by the Chief Executive of Pakistan (the President of AJ&K being its vice-chairman) is, for instance, in charge of collecting income tax in AJ&K (20 per cent of the total amount collected is used for the administration of the Kashmir Council and 80 per cent is returned to the AJ&K government) and is the main source of the total development budget of the state. Despite its weak position, the AJ&K Government is clearly conscious that it has some room of manoeuvre in the implementation of the Kashmir policy. The Federal Government has to be very careful in not destabilizing the state because it will be seen as doing to its Kashmiri population exactly the thing it accuses India of perpetrating in J&K. The authorities of AJ&K count also in the vigorous international lobbying that the Pakistani government is promoting abroad and they frequently meet foreign officials for this purpose. They also play a part in the decision of relocating local population when firing from across the LoC intensifies. They also deal with the problem of Indian refugees.[47] There are, therefore, more important issues to deal with than merely playing the card of independence. The AJ&K entry checkpoint proclaims in big white letters in Urdu: 'Kashmir belongs to Pakistan'. Indeed, AJ&K cannot really afford to promote a separatist agenda. It is a poor area, living marginally from forest income, informal trade of wood, small industries, but mainly from Kashmiri migrants' remittances, federal subsidies (almost 50 per cent of its budget come from Pakistan), and the very presence of the army. Nowadays its priority is to attract tourists.

There are, nevertheless, some issues at the grassroots level which demonstrate an uneasy relation with the Centre: the growing resentment against the incapacity of the State to protect villagers from indiscriminate Indian firings, and against the international community to take care of the refugee camps. The burgeoning sense of insecurity related to the internal feuds between Mujahideen groups in the mid-1990s, the atmosphere of intimidation those groups can impose on the population,[48] and a general unstable situation (the Muzaffarabad-Kohala road is frequently subjected to gangs' attacks), may as well alienate the population. But, this feeling of insecurity will not be easily transformed into an appeal for independence because of the ambiguities of the 'Kashmiri identity' of today's AJ&K. What does it actually mean to be a Kashmiri in Pakistan? It is mainly a territorial identity. It means being born in the territory belonging to the former Princely State or to be sons and daughters of migrants. For one JKLF leader based in Pakistan, any 'Kashmiri *mohalla*' abroad is part of the *Kashmiriyat* which is, first, 'a meeting of minds'. But, even if some people still have members of their families, or some properties, on the other side of the LoC, there is almost no linguistic and communicational link between Azad Kashmiris and their Indian counterparts. In the Indian Valley, people speak Kashmiri, but in AJ&K the majority speak Punjabi or Pahari (a Punjabi dialect spoken in mountainous areas), others Potohari (mainly from Mirpur) or Pashto; only a small minority speaks Kashmiri: the refugees from India, significantly referred to by the name of 'true Kashmiris'.[49] The main road from Muzaffarabad to Srinagar is closed and even communication through the phone is not easy. The LoC has, therefore, been able to create two distinctive political, as well as cultural, communities. This does not mean that a sense of a shared Kashmiri identity—in its territorial understanding—does not exist in AJ&K. But it takes, as in the Valley, the form of a strong political attachment to the principle of a plebiscite if ever it occurs in the territorial limits of pre-1947 Kashmir. Even if people largely anticipate that the choice to belong to Pakistan will prevail, being consulted is as important for them as it is for Indian Kashmiris. This desire of being politically heard is indeed the principal aspect of the socially constructed 'Kashmiriyat' identity, as John Cockell believes.[50]

Kashmiri migrants in Pakistan—the 'Kashmiri *mohalla*'—are also an important constituent of the 'public opinion'. There are, roughly, two million people who migrated from J&K before, or just after 1947, mainly to the big and medium cities of Punjab: Lahore, Gujranwala, Sialkot, satellite town of Rawalpindi; and more marginally in Abbotabad, Peshawar and Karachi.[51] They matter as voters not only in the National Assembly, but also for the twelve specific seats reserved for them in the AJ&K Legislative Assembly. They are also very active in the handicraft and shawl business and are well represented in the judiciary, the Urdu press, and at the governmental level. The sense of a Kashmiri identity is strong for those who have experienced Partition, and among those of the next generation who still speak Kashmiri. It is politically translated into several Kashmiri think-tanks. Nevertheless, for the new generation born in Pakistan, this sense of 'belonging' is more emotional. This is quite different from the diaspora, and especially the Kashmiri migrants in UK (they constitute almost 90 per cent of the Pakistani community in a city like Bradford), among whom most of the Kashmiri political groups are represented. A scandal (revealed in 1998) about funds allocated to a British MP to defend Pakistani cause on Kashmir, showed, for instance, how much Kashmiri constituencies count for in British local politics (fifty seats in the House of Commons depend partly on Kashmiri constituencies, according to an official of AJ&K).

Kashmiri political movements fostered by Pakistan concentrate their activities on the civil war in Indian Kashmir. The All Parties Hurriyat Conference (APHC), formed in 1993 in J&K as a broad-based and multi-party coalition of almost thirty Kashmiri political, religious and social organizations, is well represented in Pakistan, with offices in Islamabad and Muzaffarabad. The APHC is an active member of the Kashmiri policy. Its intense lobbying abroad—in UK, the US or at the Organization of Islamic Conference, for instance—makes it a necessary partner of the government in its Kashmiri policy which reiterates that it is the true representative of Indian Kashmiris. If it resented not being consulted during the Kargil crisis, and having been betrayed by withdrawal of the guerrilla fighters, it was earlier party to trilateral secret negotiations organized for the first time in UK in 1996, where the Deputy High Commissioner of Pakistan and an advisor of ex-Indian Prime Minister Narasimha Rao were believed to be present. The APHC's official position as the representative of Kashmiris, and its links with Indian Kashmiri militants, assures it a real level of influence in Pakistan, as is evident from its briefings to Pakistani newspapers. Despite the tensions from within, the APHC has remained united since 1993, thanks to an overall consensus that exists on three basic issues: (1) the entire former Princely State is a disputed territory (from Ladakh to Gilgit Agency), (2) its fate can only be determined by a plebiscite according to the UN resolutions, (3) any bilateral negotiation has to integrate them. However, strong differences remain. For the Jamaat-i-Islami only two choices have to be given to the Kashmiris: India or Pakistan. For the JKLF,[52] on the other hand, a third option has to be taken into consideration: total independence, the 'best reward expected from the very high price people have paid in the *azadi* struggle' and 'the only language foreigners understand'.[53] Pakistan's claim of speaking for the Kashmiris is not fully accepted either: if the Jamaat-i-Islami Kashmir remains silent on this issue, the JKLF regularly reiterates that Pakistan does not represent the Kashmiris and is even an 'occupation power' ('the struggle against India is military, the struggle against Pakistan is political').[54] No wonder then that the JKLF is in an uneasy position in Pakistan.

Jihadist Organizations

Several Pakistani Islamic groups which are active in Indian Kashmir can be called 'jihadist' as their *raison d'être* is to fight, wherever Muslims are perceived as being oppressed, which they proclaim to be a *jihad* (or holy war). Even if they have close links with them, they are distinct from the main religio-political parties in Pakistan (they have their own leadership and headquarters). Labelling the outfits as '*jihadist* organizations' helps us to distinguish them from other guerrilla fighters in Kashmir, like the JKLF's armed branch, who are inspired, not by Islam, but by secular ideologies (mainly nationalism). The more important *jihadist* organizations active in Kashmir at the end of the 1990s, and which have claimed their participation in the Kargil operation, are: the Hizbul Mujahideen, Al-Badr Mujahideen, Harkat-ul Mujahideen (another name for Harkat-ul Ansar) and the Lashkar-i-Taiba. Though their social and political profile as well as their influence on Pakistani politics has seldom been analysed, and is difficult to document, some facts and hypotheses can nevertheless be advanced.

The total number of fighters from these four groups is allegedly 3,00,000 men.[55] But this may well be an exaggerated figure as the infrastructure to train such a number would be equivalent almost to that of half the regular army. Even if they belong to different Islamic ideologies or traditions, they can organize joint military actions just as the Al-Badr and Harkat-ul Mujahideen ones did in Kundi on 28 October 1999. There are established links between the groups: a deputy *amir* of the Jamaat-i-Islami lost two of his nephews in a Lashkar operation in J&K, for instance. They mobilize young people mainly through the students' unions of the Islamic political parties or through their own universities (the Lashkar has such institutions), also during the funerals of their 'martyrs' to which a lot of care and publicity is given, and through the medium of their open offices. Mujahideen are often young (between 15 and 25 years old) and single men. They come mainly from poor sections of the society educated in *madaris* (religious schools) though this is not always the case: they can be scions of Islamic party leaders. One of the Harkat-ul Mujahideen leaders active in

Kashmir was the son of a rich businessman settled in UK who came to Pakistan at the age of 16 to join the movement. The reasons why they join these organizations are many: from firm ideological commitment to a search for material welfare. Also for a reassuring human environment (young recruits are educated, housed, fed and strictly trained), or for giving a firm direction to their lives. Concerning the leadership, it is interesting to note that the original founders of the four groups, were all veterans of the 1979-88 Afghan war. And, except for Al-Badr, founded during the 1971 war to fight secessionist forces in East Pakistan, the three others have been structured during the 1980s Afghan *jihad*.

Their influence on Pakistan's policy towards Kashmir stems from several factors. First, if these groups are generally considered as receiving ISI's support to operate in Kashmir (this is difficult to prove with data),[56] they are neither the products of the army's intelligence nor a simple puppet in a proxy war.[57] These religiously inspired fighters are not merely mercenaries whose indoctrination can be easily changed, but often 'genuine Mujahideen' who are deeply committed to the 'cause'. Second, the *jihadist* groups have strong ties with Islamic Sunni political parties in the opposition: Hizbul Mujahideen and Al-Badr with the Jamaat-i-Islami; Harkat-ul Mujahideen as well as the newly created Jaish-i-Muhammad with the Jamiat Ulema-i-Islam (JUI); and the Lashkar with the Jamiat Ulema Ahl-e-Hadith (JUAH).[58] The government, as well as the army, cannot ignore the opinion of these parties which have proved capable of destabilizing it, because of their capacity to organize massive street demonstrations, their wide networks of *madaris* and mosques all over the country, and their almost daily declarations in the Urdu press reminding national leaders not to 'betray Kashmir'. Therefore, the visibility and strength of these *jihadist* groups is dependent on their growing political ambition domestically: the Hizbul Mujahideen has been since 1993, interestingly as in Afghanistan, superseded by the Deobandi Harkat-ul Mujahideen, which itself is now in competition with the more and more influential Ahl-e-Hadith Lashkar-i-Taiba. Third, the growing influence of these *jihadist* movements, which is evident from the new training camps they have opened in the Northern Areas and the waiting list of Mujahideen they announced after the Kargil crisis,[59] can have negative effects on the army itself. Some Pakistanis are inclined to comment that while the army has lost three wars, the Mujahideen fight Indians effectively without costing much to the national exchequer. For some young men, it becomes therefore more self-enhancing to join their ranks where justice and egalitarian spirit seem to be respected. This can be a worrying factor for the army in the long run as autonomous political ambitions of these groups cannot be ruled out: after the 12 October coup when the Constitution was suspended, the Lashkar-i-Taiba leader, for instance, did not hesitate to declare 'I present to General Musharraf the constitution of Allah' (i.e. the Koran).[60]

Let us look at the relations between the *jihadist* movements and Kashmiri political organizations. Even if the religiously inspired fighters are represented in a United Jihad Council (founded in 1991 or 1992), itself linked to the APHC, this latter organization has to take into account, the opinion of the people in the Valley who view the *jihadists* as 'foreigners'. Neither the lack of support for the *jihadist* organizations in J&K (which would make any guerrilla operations against Indian forces very difficult), nor the number of militants trained in Afghanistan in the Kashmiri '*jihad*' (the only evidence being the death of Harkat-ul Mujahideen militants during the US bombing on Osama bin Laden's camps during the Summer of 1998) should be overestimated. But it remains true that the 'martyrs' of these groups come mostly from outside both parts of Kashmir: they are from Punjab (Kahota, Toba Tek Singh, Bahawalpur) and NWFP.[61] This may, therefore, lead to a widening rift with the Kashmiri population which, if we rely on the works of three Western researchers who have been able to visit the Valley recently, favours secularist groups having affinities with the majoritarian Sufi and syncretic Kashmiri-Islamic tradition.[62]

The 'Public Opinion'

Because Kashmir is often regarded as a highly emotional issue, it is common to consider that Pakistani public opinion largely supports a non-compromising line. In fact, this perception needs to be strongly qualified. First, people of different regions hold different opinions regarding the Kashmir dispute: while it is an extremely sensitive issue in Punjab (mainly in central and upper Punjab as well as in cities where there is a strong presence of Kashmiri minorities), and in parts of NWFP (bordering the AJ&K and the Northern Areas), it is barely acknowledged in Sindh and even less in Baluchistan. And surprisingly, the option of J&K joining Pakistan is not so readily favoured: recently, an opinion poll showed that even among the Lahoris, one-third of the interviewees preferred an independent state for Kashmir than it to be a part of Pakistan (a majority of the interviewees from Karachi and Quetta supported this opinion).[63] Second, who makes Pakistani public opinion anyway? For French sociologist Pierre Bourdieu, the 'public opinion' doesn't exist and is just a misnomer for groups and agencies in competition for imposing their pretension to speak on behalf of the 'public opinion'.[64] This is a convincing argument. Such Pakistani groups and agencies in Pakistan will now be discussed.

The Urdu press is most of the time virulently anti-Indian. This concerns mainly the heart of the Urdu media circle: Lahore. *Nawaz-e-Waqt*, the second most important Urdu daily after *Jang*, is a case in point. Run on by M. Nizami, a Pakistani of Kashmiri origin, this newspaper, while being very supportive of the PML and the Sharif family, launched a campaign against any normalization with India during the October–November 1998 talks. The English-speaking press too, surprisingly, is not clearly in favour of such normalization. The State-owned television channel, PTV, is very active in the propaganda against human rights violations committed by Indian forces in Kashmir. In 1998, for instance, in a quiz programme the host repeatedly asked during the day: 'In 1989, how many people died in Indian Occupied Kashmir?' The right answer according to him was '60,000' (which actually is the figure that even Kashmiri associations give for the entire decade of 1990s). PTV was also broadcasting, during the same year, a popular drama about a young, happy boy in the Valley whose fight for revenge started after his house was set on fire by Indian security forces. This kind of propaganda indoctrinates the younger generation to distrust India. A seven year-old girl, for instance, told me that after watching the programme she had horrific nightmares in which she saw Indians invading her house and setting her parents on fire. In such an atmosphere chances of any rapprochement are very remote.

Some groups, however, advocate that Pakistan must have better relations with India. This is line of thought of pacifist movements and several NGOs. The Human Right Commission of Pakistan, based in Lahore, plays an active role in promoting contacts and intellectual exchanges between Indian and Pakistani human rights activists. Other organizations are more directly involved in the promotion of friendly relations between India and Pakistan, like the Pak–India People's Forum for Peace and Democracy, the recently created Indo–Pak Friendship Association, or the very active South Asia Citizens Web on the Internet. Their main task is to promote debates, to convince people of the necessity of a peaceful settlement of the Kashmir conflict, and to struggle against stereotypes in both countries. They organize, as they have been doing since February 1995, peace conferences where both Pakistani and Indian delegates participate. They have managed to attract some high profile officials from both countries to these debates. They have also been able to promote a dialogue between social workers, trade unionists, retired defence personnel and intellectuals from both countries. Even if the means and the audience of these pacifist movements remain very limited, their initiatives have to be taken note of, as they are a new phenomenon in the history of Indo-Pakistan relations.

CONCLUSION

The predominant preoccupation of Pakistani politics is not simply the Kashmir dispute with its neighbour. It is, indeed, the outcome of a complex interplay of actions and perceptions, driven by a set of institutions, groups and individuals who, during the Kargil crisis, can be engaged in strong rivalries. The 'multi-vocal state' syndrome of Pakistani politics on Kashmir during this period is one important reason for the diplomatic and military impasse in which the two countries are locked. But, as Jonah Blank writes:

Kargil may also, paradoxically, have laid the groundwork for a stable peace. Demonstrating the dangers of the status quo may jolt New Delhi and Islamabad out of their complacency. Politicians in both capitals see only the Kashmir they wish to see: for Pakistanis, a Muslim land pining to join its Islamic neighbour and welcoming the intervention of mujahideen; for Indians, a state ravaged by terrorism and sedition but now largely brought under control. Both visions are clouded by self-delusion.

Though Blank presents the politicians as a monolith, which is not the case, his views are by and large convincing. The mere fact that a wide consensus on what has to be done in Kashmir does not exist anymore in Pakistan is itself significant and lays the groundwork for a significant debate on the issue.

NOTES

1. Yunas Samad, 'Kashmir and the Imagining of Pakistan', *Contemporary South Asia*, vol. 4, no.1, 1995, pp. 65-77, especially p. 67. The word 'Pakistan',

etymologically 'the land of the pure', is an acronym invented in 1933 by a student in Cambridge, Choudhry Rahmat Ali, who composed it by taking certain letters from the names of Muslim homelands in India and Asia: Punjab, Afghania (or the North-West Frontier Province), Kashmir, Iran, Sindh, Tukharistan, Afghanistan and Baluchistan. See Khalid Bin Sayeed, *The Political System of Pakistan*, Boston: Houghton Mifflin Company, 1967, p. 39.

2. See, for instance, Ijaz Hussain, *Kashmir Dispute: An International Law Perspective*, Islamabad: Qaid-i-Azam University, 1998.

3. For a detailed account of the origins and evolution of this movement, based on fieldwork in Indian Kashmir, see Victoria Schofield, *Kashmir in the Crossfire*, London: I.B. Tauris, 1996, pp. 221-96, and John Cockell, 'Ethnic Nationalism and Subaltern Political Process: Exploring Autonomous Democratic Action in Kashmir', Paper presented at the ECPR Third Pan European IR Conference, Vienna, September 1998. The principal factors of this insurgency are either the growing gap between a politicized (and educated) Kashmiri youth and the closing of institutional channels for voicing discontents, acording to the 'institutionalist approach'. See Sumit Ganguly, *The Crisis in Kashmir: Portents of War, Hopes of Peace*, Cambridge: Cambridge University Press, 1997, or Balraj Puri, *Kashmir: Towards Insurgency*, London: Sangam Book, 1993. The exasperated expression of a desire for political autonomy progressively ridiculed by New Delhi but well entrenched in a 'Kashmiriyat' identity (and a long tradition of social movements in J&K since the 1930s) is the analysis favoured by the 'ethnicity approach'. See Cockell, op. cit.; Scholfield, op. cit.; Reeta Chodhari Tremblay, 'Nation, Identity and the Intervening Role of the State: a Study of the Secessionist Movement in Kashmir', *Pacific Affairs*, vol. 69, no. 4, Winter 1996-7.

4. The names by which the two governments call the part of Kashmir they control will be used here (and not the one they use to label each other): 'Azad Jammu & Kashmir' (AJ&K) and 'Northern Areas' for Pakistan; 'Jammu & Kashmir' (J&K) for India (which includes the Kashmir Valley, Jammu and Ladakh).

5. Firdous Ahmad Baba, chief commander of the Muslim Janbaaz Force, quoted in Cockell, op. cit., p. 24.

6. They also remembered their inability to foment, a rebellion in Kashmir just before the 1965 war: Sumit Ganguly, *The Origins of War in South Asia: Indo-Pakistan Conflicts Since 1947*, Lahore: Vanguard Books, 1988, pp. 85-90.

7. See Charles Tilly's study of the 'war making/state making process', in *Coercion, Capital, and European States: AD 990–1990*, Cambridge: Blackwell, 1990; and Michel Foucault, *Il Faut Défendre la Société*, Paris: Gallimard, 1997 (1976).

8. Strangely enough, portions of the Pakistani Northern Areas to the west of a line running down from the Nanga Parbat mountain to the Panma glacier are excluded from it.

9. Figure given by Jonah Blank, 'Kashmir: Fundamentalism Takes Root', *Foreign Affairs*, vol. 78, no. 6, November-December 1999, p. 38. But, the APHC talks

of 60,000 lives lost since 1989, and the UNMOGIP (United Nations Military Observer Group in India and Pakistan) estimates that 10 to 20 people are wounded or killed every day, both parts of Kashmir included (interview with an UNMOGIP officer, Islamabad, November 1998).

10. Some 6,00,000 Indian army, police and paramilitary troops are stationed in J&K and some 80,000 Pakistani troops are deployed along the LoC. See Ahmed Rashid, 'The Decision-Making Process in Pakistan: Implications for India-Pakistan Relations', in Saeed Shafqat, ed., *Contemporary Issues in Pakistan Studies*, Lahore: Azad, 1998, pp. 151-68, especially p. 151.

11. Ayesha Jalal, *Democracy and Authoritarianism in South Asia: A Comparative and Historical Perspective*, Cambridge: Cambridge University Press, 1995, pp. 22-3.

12. Ayesha Jalal, *The State of Martial Rule: The Origins of Paksitan's Political Economy of Defence*, Lahore: Sang-e-Meel Publications, 1999, p. 49.

13. Ahmed Rashid, op. cit., p. 152. The work of this senior Pakistani journalist is, perhaps the only one dedicated to the decision-making process in Pakistan's foreign policy.

14. Pierre Lafrance, 'Et Pourtant le Pakistan Existe', in Christophe Jaffrelot, ed., *Le Pakistan, Carrefour de Tensions Régionales*, Bruxelles: Complexe, 1999, p. 127.

15. It is borrowed from Ivo Duchacek's analysis of subnational governments' foreign policies that lead nation states to act nowadays as 'multivocal actors' on the international scene: Ivo Duchacek et al., *Perforated Sovereignties and International Relations: Trans-Sovereign Contacts of Subnational Governments*, New York: Greenwood Press, 1988, p. 4.

16. Kashmir Study Group, *1947-1997: The Kashmir Dispute at Fifty: Charting Paths to Peace*, USA: Kashmir Study Group, 1997, p. 32.

17. Tariq Jan, ed., *Pakistan Foreign Policy Debate*, Islamabad: IPS, 1993, p. 9.

18. Ibid., p. 175.

19. Jehangir Karamat, 'Learning from Kargil', *The News*, 5 August 1999.

20. Maleeha Lodhi, 'The Kargil Crisis: Anatomy of a Debacle', *Newsline*, July 1999. M. Lodhi held this position in 1994-7 and again since November 1999.

21. *The News*, 2 November 1998. The spirals of growing help from Pakistan to Kashmiri militants (Pakistani troops probably entered Kashmir in the Poonch and Kupwar sectors) and massive Indian deployment of troops in Punjab, led the two countries almost to a direct confrontation between March and May 1990. See the detailed account of this crisis, based on interviews with retired US, Pakistani and Indian officials, by Seymour M. Hersh, 'On the Nuclear Edge', *The New Yorker*, 29 March 1993, pp. 56-73.

22. Graham T. Allison, *Essence of Decision: Explaining the Cuban Missile Crisis*, Boston: Little Brown, 1971.

23. Robert D. Putnam, 'Diplomacy and Domestic Politics: The Logic of Two-Level Games', in Peter B. Evans et al., eds., *Double-Edged Diplomacy: International Bargaining and Domestic Politics*, Berkeley: University of California Press, 1993, pp. 434-5.

24. Rashid, op. cit., p. 153.

25. He was an ex-DG of Military Intelligence in October 1998. *Friday Times,* 23-9 October 1998.

26. See the memoirs of its head in 1980, Lt. Gen. Jahan Dad Khan, *Pakistan: Leadership Challenges,* Oxford: Oxford University Press, 1999, pp. 209-35.

27. Stephen Cohen, *The Pakistani Army,* Oxford: Oxford University Press, 1998 (1st edn. 1994), p. 145.

28. *The Muslim,* 29 September 1998.

29. The Indian mortar firings in summer 1998 created the third-most important displacement of Pakistani Kashmiris after 1965 and 1971: 105 people were killed, 334 injured and 75,000 have been driven from their homes (*The News,* 15 October 1998). The growing number of displaced people from villages bordering the LoC in AJ&K (1,00,500 in 1998 according to AJ&K official sources) is a major concern for the authorities of the State. They are reluctant to go back to their villages (500 people from Chakothi have been waiting in a temporary camp in Hatian which we visited in October 1998), but giving them fixed settlement will endorse India's policy of terrorization.

30. Karamat, op. cit.

31. See Cohen, op. cit., pp. 79 and 167; and Kotera M. Bhimaya, *Civil-Military Relations: A Comparative Study of India and Pakistan,* Dissertation, Rand Graduate School, n.d.

32. This new doctrine is detailed in Azhar Abbas, 'The Creeping Group', *The Herald,* May 1999, pp. 28-41.

33. Ibid., p. 29.

34. Saeed Shafqat, *Civil-Military Relations in Pakistan,* Boulder: Westview Press, 1997, p. 169.

35. See interviews in Cohen, op. cit., pp. 59-63.

36. See, for instance, Dad Khan, op. cit., p. 222 and the comments of an anonymous US official accompanying President Clinton during his March 2000 visit to Pakistan who described the attitude of COAS Gen. Pervez Musharraf as 'strong and passionate' when the US President started to talk about the Kashmir dispute: *The News,* 27 March 2000 (Internet edition).

37. Bhimaya, op. cit., p. 141.

38. Shafqat, op. cit., p. 173. See also Ian Talbot, 'The Punjabisation of Pakistan: Myth or Reality?', in this volume.

39. In October 1998, the Foreign Minister declared in the press that 'without some progress on Kashmir' there would be 'no point in continuing talks in New Delhi'.

40. For the first point, see *The Nation,* 1 October 1999. For the first time, the two parties would have envisaged all options concerning Kashmir (even the transformation of the LoC into an international border) and engaged themselves to lower their propaganda, to discuss openly the question of transborder infiltrations and to keep secret the negotiations which were to start in October 1999. For the second point, see *Newsline,* October 1999. Sonia Gandhi, Congress candidate in the autumn 1999 general elections,

accused Vajpayee's government of what was then called 'Sugargate': a deal between the Army Welfare Trust of Pakistan and the Kundan Rice Mills of India to export 225 million dollars of Pakistani sugar with a benefit of 40 million dollars for eight companies owned by close acquaintances of Nawaz Sharif or his own family (the Ittefaq group).

41. Nawaz Sharif then declared that he was not aware of the operation. But it is difficult to understand why the army would have imposed on him on this occasion, whereas it held back when Benazir Bhutto refused to endorse it twice during her second Government. See Abdul Hayee, 'Ms Bhutto's interview', *The Nation*, 14 August 1999.

42. *The Nation*, 14 October 1998.

43. See Lodhi, op. cit.

44. See Zaffar Abbas, 'Whodunnit?', *The Herald*, August 1999.

45. Quoted in Hassan Ali Shahzeb, 'Clueless in Washington', *Newsline*, July 1999.

46. Numbers in *Spotlight on Regional Affairs: Uprising in Indian-held Jammu & Kashmir*, Islamabad: Institute of Regional Studies, March–April 1991.

47. There are presently 16,982 registered, and 35,000 non-registered refugees from India in AJ&K. Majority of them are from the cities of Kupwar and Baramula in India, who moved across the LoC in early 1990s. This information was given to the author by the assistant to the Relief and Rehabilitation Commissioner for Refugees (Muzaffarabad).

48. A resident of Muzaffarabad said that, although he found that the Jihadi movements' militants kept a low profile, as they lived away from the local population, he was recently shocked to see them forcing drivers to stop listening to the radio in buses.

49. Tariq Rehman, *Language and Politics in Pakistan*, Karachi: Oxford University Press, 1998, pp. 226-7.

50. For this understanding of '*Kashmiryat*' in Indian Kashmir, see Cockell, op. cit.

51. Figures given by the Kashmir Action Committee, interview, Lahore, November 1999.

52. The JKLF was formed in the 1970s in UK and now has three branches (J&K, AJ&K and UK). It split into two sections in 1995: Yasin Malik's (part of the APHC representation in Pakistan) and Amanullah Khan's (well established in the Northern Areas).

53. Interview with a JKLF leader (Malik faction), Islamabad, November 1998. Therefore, 'independence' is not necessarily an accurate translation of the aspiration for political autonomy which has characterized the Kashmiri movement since 1930s.

54. Ibid.

55. This is a personal—and unverified—estimation which lowers figures advanced by Jamaat-i-Islami leaders (5,00,000) and takes into account the 2,00,000 participants of the Lashkar-i-Taiba's, convention in Muridke (Pakistan) in November 1999.

56. Nevertheless, they could not be trained in AJ&K, the Northern Areas and

NWFP, or even cross the LoC, without ISI's blessing. See Schofield, op. cit., p. 271.

57. To be sure, those who had this feeling, quickly changed their colour. See the testimony of a former rebel who, after being trained in Gilgit, came back to Srinagar and became the 'renegade leader' of a militia with the status of Special Police Officer (SPO). Blank, op. cit., p. 48.

58. For an analysis of Pakistani Islamic parties, see Amélie Blom, 'Les Partis Islamistes à la Recherche d'un Second Souffle', in Jaffrelot, op. cit., pp. 99-115.

59. See Arif Jamal, 'Camping for *Jihad*', *The News*, 14 August 1999.

60. *Jihad Times* (Urdu weekly of the Lashkar-i-Taiba), 13 November 1999.

61. See the list of martyrs (*shahid*) published by the Harkat-ul Mujahideen, *The Nation*, 2 November 1998.

62. Blank, op. cit.; Cockell, op. cit.; Schofield, op. cit.

63. *The Herald Annual*, January 1997, p. 166.

64. Pierre Bourdieu, 'L'Opinion Publique n'Existe Pas', in *Question de sociologie*, Paris: Minuit, 1984.

13

Does the Army Shape Pakistan's Foreign Policy?

IAN TALBOT

HE CONTROVERSY surrounding Prime Minister Nawaz Sharif's knowledge of the planning of the ill-fated Kargil adventure of early summer 1999 reopened questions concerning the influence of the Pakistan Army in the foreign policy field. Earlier, in February 1990 during Benazir Bhutto's first administration (November 1988–August 1990), a Pentagon official had hinted to Iqbal Akhund, her Adviser on National Security and Foreign Affairs, that the intelligence agencies or the army were conducting a covert operation in Kashmir behind the Prime Minister's back.[1] Benazir herself had initially raised concerns about the initiative allowed to the political leadership by claiming that her government's freedom of action was 'institutionally, economically, politically (and) structurally' constrained.[2] Not only was the defence budget sacrosanct at this time, but the military retained a veto on vital foreign policy and security matters including policies relating to Kashmir, Afghanistan and the nuclear issue.

Nawaz Sharif, who succeeded Bhutto following her dismissal in 1990, was widely regarded as Zia's protégé and as such was considered to enjoy the wholehearted backing of the military establishment. This was to be increasingly withdrawn, however, as he strayed off message with respect to the Gulf war and challenged the army's ally, President Ghulam Ishaq Khan over his power to appoint the Chief of General Staff. Following a hint from the army, Ghulam Ishaq Khan used his power under the Constitution to dismiss the Government of Nawaz Sharif on 18 April 1993. Another palace revolution which cut short Benazir Bhutto's second administration, saw Sharif returned to power in 1997 with a massive parliamentary majority. His clipping of the powers of the President[3] and his triumph over both the Supreme Court Chief Justice, Sajjad Ali Shah and the President Farooq Leghari in tests of his authority presaged what some commentators saw as a new era of elective dictatorship. The Prime Minister also got Gen.

Jahangir Karamat to submit his resignation on 7 October 1998, three months ahead of his official retirement, and appointed his own choice, Gen. Pervez Musharraf as Chief of Army Staff, despite the fact that he was junior to the Chief of General Staff, Lt. Gen. Ali Kuli Khan. Musharraf was to prove Sharif's nemesis, just as Zia had been for Zulfikar Ali Bhutto, who had similarly fast-tracked his promotion.

Nawaz Sharif undoubtedly brought a populist approach to both domestic and foreign policy. The latter was exemplified in the 'bus diplomacy' with the Indian Prime Minister Atal Behari Vajpayee early in 1999 which led to the triumphant Lahore Declaration of 21 February. This was designed to symbolize the maturity in the relations of the two new nuclear powers in the subcontinent and to demonstrate that political will could break through the logjam of complex issues in bilateral relations. Doubts remained, however, whether the army had been sidelined completely by the powerful Prime Minister. His curbs on independent journalists in mid-1999, when Pakistan had not fully mended its bridges with the West after the nuclear explosions a year before, smacked of anxiety, rather than self-confidence. Each successive act of centralizing authority in the Prime Minister's hands had, ironically, undermined the legitimacy which had accompanied his return to power. The Sharif family was embroiled in corruption charges, and Pakistan's collapsing institutions saw the army inducted into such routine activities as running the Karachi Electricity Supply Corporation and the Water and Power Development Authority. Moreover, for all his authority, it was widely believed that the Pakistan Prime Minister still lacked control over nuclear weapons policy and that the final control of the nuclear button rested with the Army-dominated Central Command and Control System. Furthermore, the murky background of the fighting in the Kargil mountains in May 1999 again raised the spectre of an independent army foreign policy with respect to Kashmir. Indeed, Indian Defence Minister George Fernandes on 29 May pointedly blamed neither Nawaz Sharif nor the ISI for the 'infiltration', attaching this instead to the Pakistan Army. The Prime Minister's 'surrender' to Indian demands for withdrawal after a hasty trip to Washington, according to some commentators precipitated the October 1999 coup which brought down the curtain on the populist interlude. Its immediate catalyst was his dismissal of Gen. Musharraf and the refusal to allow the commercial aircraft on which he was returning from an official visit to Sri Lanka to land at Karachi although it was running out of fuel.

The above narrative hints both at the zero sum game of Pakistan politics and the constraints which hemmed in successive administrations in the post-Zia era. Their existence should not, however, encourage a simplistic view of the Prime Minister and foreign ministry acting as mere cyphers for the GHQ in Rawalpindi. The return of democracy ensured that the total subordination of the foreign ministry during the Zia era with respect, for example, to Afghan policy, could not be repeated.[4] The political leaders' similarities of outlook with the army on key issues was the result not only of deference,[5] but of a common stance based on realpolitik and response to popular opinion.[6] Last, it is important to see the army as part of a wider establishment with which the politicians had to contend. This included the civil bureaucracy, the President who wielded considerable autonomous power, and the intelligence agencies which were prone to act independently in pursuit of gains in their turf wars. Any assessment of the army's role must take into consideration the growth in importance over the last decade and a half of its intelligence wing, the Inter-Services Intelligence (ISI). This organization worked closely with the CIA during the Afghan war and channelled weapons to Pakistan's client faction of the Mujahideen under Gulbuddin Hekmatyar's leadership. Although headed by a senior army officer, the ISI has operated autonomously of the Pakistan Army and has kept as careful a watch on generals as on politicians to ensure their 'reliability'.[7] In the post-Zia era, it has seemed at times to be acting independently of any civilian and command structure, not only in its activities in Afghanistan and Kashmir, but in the ethnic conflict which has raged in the port city of Karachi. The lack of supervision became clear in 1993 when, under American pressure, there was an attempt to haul in its activities. Following the sacking of the ISI chief, Gen. Javid Nasir, Nawaz Sharif discovered that an unaccounted ISI budget of around $3.3 million a month had been spent on assisting Kashmiri militants.

Last, the question concerning the extent to which the Pakistan Army shapes the State's foreign policy requires a historical awareness of the pre-1988 period. Parallels need to be drawn, for example, between the 1990s and the 1950s when there was evidence of informal military pressure on the policies of elected governments. It is also useful to consider over a length of time whether civilians have acted differently than the generals when confronting Pakistan's security requirements. Moreover, a historical contextualization can shed light on the extent to which the contemporary Pakistan Army has shifted the sources of its influence (and possibly its priorities) from the first martial law period of the Ayub era. Before turning to this historical overview, it is necessary, however, to briefly reflect on an understanding of the motives for the Pakistan Army's much greater involvement with foreign policy than is usual in most States.

INTERPRETATIVE APPROACHES

There are two conflicting responses to the question as to why the Pakistan Army concerned itself so much with the State's foreign policy. The first sees this in terms of the geopolitics of the region and Pakistan's strategic insecurity regarding its mighty Indian neighbour. This is encapsulated in depictions of Pakistan as 'a garrison state surrounded by three of the world's top four military powers and haunted by a history of wars with India'.[8] The second understanding focuses on the emergence of the military as a powerful interest group unwilling to see any thaw in the subcontinental Cold War, as this would endanger the swollen defence budget.[9] Certainly as early as 1958, an American intelligence report assessed that the 'Pakistan Army had developed as a pressure group' and would 'continue to have priority over economic development for appropriations' irrespective of the Indian factor.[10]

Geopolitical explanations undoubtedly bring out the insecurity which has been the hallmark of both Pakistani domestic and foreign policy. The strategic balance tilted even further in India's favour with the secession of East Pakistan in 1971. Some commentators have claimed that this has resulted in a 'fragility syndrome' marked by repression of internal dissent and defensiveness in relations with India. Such circumstances perpetuate the Pakistan Army's influence in domestic and foreign affairs, as well as encourage the adoption of a nuclear weapons strategy to restore the strategic balance. The weakness in a purely geopolitical understanding lies in the failure to explain why alternative strategies of rapprochement with India have not been adopted to remove this fear.

The depiction of the military as a powerful pressure group usefully highlights the Pakistan State's overriding priority of building up the armed forces. The scene was set when the years 1947–50 saw up to 70 per cent of the national budget being allocated to defence.[11] But this argument assumes too readily that material self-interest rather than ideological motivations have influenced the army's thinking on foreign-policy matters. Patriotism and a commitment to Islam, in fact, dominate its ethos. The belief that a strong army equates with a strong nation may be misguided, but it is not merely self-serving.

Moreover, it is important not to see the army as just a powerful institution with its own agenda, but as a predominantly Punjabi-based force. The Punjabization of the colonial predecessor of the Pakistan Army helped pave the way for the Punjabization of Pakistan itself. It is impossible to appreciate the impact of the army on contemporary domestic and foreign affairs without acknowledging the congruence between its interests and those of significant sections of Punjabi society. This helps to explain, in part, the continuities in policy between periods of civilian rule and martial law. An interest group interpretation which sees the army as standing apart from society ignores this reality. It posits a dichotomy between development-minded politicians and security-driven generals, which has seldom existed. As we shall see in the ensuing section, politicians have been every bit as hawkish on the key issue of Kashmir, as have the military commanders. The reality of the army's involvement in the shaping of foreign policy is thus, in fact, considerably more complex than strategic or interest group interpretations allow. It requires the kind of historical grounding to which we will turn in the section below.

THE ARMY, THE STATE AND FOREIGN POLICY: A HISTORICAL OVERVIEW

The army's involvement in both domestic politics and the foreign-policy process is rooted in the turmoil which accompanied Pakistan's birth. The massacres and migrations of 1947, disputes over the division of assets,[12] and specially the armed conflict in the former Princely State of Jammu & Kashmir in 1947-8 provided a defining moment. Although the fighting in the first of Pakistan's two wars to date over Kashmir was confined to the disputed territory, it brought home the strategic dangers facing Pakistan, the weaker of the protagonists. The priority of building up the Armed Forces was spelled out by Liaquat Ali Khan in a broadcast to the nation on 8 October 1948. 'The defence of the State is our foremost consideration,' declared the Pakistan Prime Minister, 'and has dominated all other governmental activities. We will not grudge any amount on the defence of our country.'[13] Henceforth, in Ayesha Jalal's telling phrase, scarce resources were devoted to the establishment of 'a political economy of defence'. The army regarded itself (and was perceived by others) as the ultimate guarantor of national security. Recruitment continued, however, to be centred around the 'martial castes' region of north-west Punjab. The Pakistan Army was, consequently, a predominantly Punjabi-officered and manned force.

The decision to prioritize defence expenditure did not in itself create a determining role for the armed forces in the conduct of foreign policy. Under both the ailing Jinnah and Liaquat, priorities were set by the politicians. The longer term conditions for military involvement were established, however, as funds were pumped into the army at the same time as political institutionalization remained weak. Moreover, the lack of expenditure on what would today be termed 'human development' hampered the emergence of a civil society which might have questioned the growing influence of the army.

Despite Pakistan's skewing of its economy to meet its strategic defence requirements,[14] it could not—unaided—match the resources of its Indian neighbour. This fact was recognized from the outset. Indeed, as early as October 1947, Pakistan unsuccessfully requested a 2 billion dollar loan from the United States.[15] Britain lacked the financial resources to provide major assistance, and also needed to appear evenhanded in its dealings with the Indians and Pakistanis. The Americans thus appeared a better bet, specially in the light of their requirement for regional Cold War allies as part of their containment policy of the Soviet Union and China. When external US military and economic assistance eventually arrived in 1954, it inevitably came with the strings attached of membership of CENTO, SEATO and the Baghdad Pact. The US–Pakistan strategic relationship was to be filled with tensions because, in the words of an administration position paper on the eve of Gen. Ayub Khan's July 1961 visit to Washington, 'Pakistan's concern over Communist bloc threats is secondary to its preoccupation with India'.[16]

Despite such frustration, both sides saw sufficient gains in the relationship to persist with it. The Pakistan authorities thus eschewed ties with the Muslim world which would have commanded popular support[17] and became increasingly locked into a dependent relationship with the United States. It provided the bureaucrats and their military allies at the Centre with both the motives, i.e. the exclusion of political interference on foreign-policy issues, and, increasingly, the resources to tilt the balance of power away from representative parties and politicians. A full five years before Ayub's takeover of October 1958, the Governor-General, Ghulam Muhammad, had appointed a political non-entity, Mohammad Ali Bogra, as Prime Minister because of his pro-American stance.[18]

Bogra was a Bengali, but he did not share the outlook of the majority of his compatriots who were active in politics. They increasingly lined up against the Punjabi-dominated West Pakistan establishment not only on such issues as the need for greater provincial autonomy, but on the need for better foreign relations with India in order to free the budget from the grip of defence expenditure. The Kashmir issue in the mid-1950s (as it still does today) held the key to Indo–Pakistani relations. The Bengali political elite was able to adopt a less uncompromising stance, because the Kashmir dispute was much less portentous in East than West Pakistan not only because of geography, but because there was no refugee community to keep it alive. Kashmiri migrants in West Pakistan could not only count on the sympathies of the large East Punjabi refugee community, but on the Mohajirs from UP and Delhi. One important reading of Ayub's coup which ushered in Pakistan's first period of martial law is to see it as a pre-emptive strike against the possibility of Bengali interests running the show following the impending national elections.

THE AYUB ERA

The decade during which Ayub Khan dominated Pakistani politics sheds further light first on why the army has constantly taken upon itself the task of shaping foreign policy, and second on how it has attempted to implement this. Ayub expressed contempt for the professional politicians,[19] whom he depicted as bringing the country to its knees through their selfish bickering. Military involvement in foreign policy was premised on the general rationale for the coup, i.e. the feeling that the army was the only properly functioning institution, and that its responsibility was to protect the State from both external and internal dangers. While the coup marked a sharp discontinuity in such areas as social reform (the 1961 Muslim Family Laws Ordinance) and Land Reform (1959), foreign policy, however, appeared for a number of years to follow the same track as before.

The lack of a clear martial law stamp to foreign policy rested on two major factors. First, the army had, in any case, been pulling the strings of successive elected governments when it came to such matters as relations with the US and the Kashmir dispute. Ayub had himself—not least during his visit to America in 1953—played an important role in the establishment of close defence and diplomatic ties. Second, Ayub was as reliant on the bureaucracy as his civilian predecessors, when it came to the formulation as well as the implementation of policy. Significantly, the major deviations in policy, the swing towards China and the abortive military solution to the Kashmir dispute in 1965 had both been urged upon Ayub by his firebrand civilian Foreign Minister Zulfikar Ali Bhutto. They reflected not only Bhutto's emerging populist touch, but a realpolitik response to the changed military balance in the subcontinent following the West's arming of India in the wake of its humiliating defeat in the 1962 Sino–Indian war.

Ironically, Ayub was undone by his out-of-character military adventurism in the abortive Operation Gibraltar. The operation was promoted by Bhutto, but was the brainchild of the Pakistan Army's 12 Division Commander, Gen. Akhtar Husain Malik. This attempt to resolve the Kashmir dispute by infiltrating five thousand insurgents into the valley foundered on the twin misconceptions that the Kashmiri people were ready to rise against their 'Indian oppressors', and that India would seek to limit the conflict to Kashmir. Ayub's regime never regained the ground lost after the resultant 1965 war with India and the 'humiliation' of the Tashkent Treaty brokered by the Soviet Union. Ayub was hounded for his 'unpardonable weakness' in purchasing peace at the cost of 'national honour' and betraying the 'just cause' of Kashmir.[20] The army as an institution, however, survived with its reputation intact, and was still popularly regarded as the pillar of the State. This image was dealt a major blow with the bungling of Yahya Khan, Ayub's successor as Chief Martial Law Administrator.

Yahya oversaw the descent to civil war in East Pakistan following the failure of Bhutto and Mujibur Rahman to share power in the wake of Pakistan's first national elections held in December 1970. The break-up of Pakistan became inevitable when Yahya misguidedly sanctioned Operation Searchlight on 25 March 1971. The butchery which followed in Dhaka was at first hidden from the West Pakistani populace. It was impossible, however, to hide the defeat of the Pakistan Army at the hands of the Bangladeshi freedom fighters and the regular Indian forces. The surrender of 93,000 troops in Dhaka at the end of the war dealt a shattering blow to the myth of the Pakistan Army's invincibility.

BHUTTO AND THE POPULIST INTERLUDE

The Bangladesh debacle enabled Zulfikar Ali Bhutto to assume greater power than any civilian had wielded since the days of Jinnah. Hopes in some quarters that a powerful popularly elected Sindhi Prime

Minister might shape a new foreign policy towards India were soon dispelled. Bhutto showed no inclination to build a better relationship with India following the Simla Accord, but instead embarked on a nuclear capability programme which had earlier been disavowed by Ayub.

The 1972 Simla accord was touted as a triumph by Bhutto, and contrasted with Ayub's capitulation at Tashkent. Despite Pakistan's material weakness and the unresolved position of the prisoners of war, Bhutto was careful to make no territorial concessions on Kashmir, or to be drawn into a no-war pact, or to recognize Bangladesh. Indian hopes for a 'final' solution on Kashmir were dashed, although Indira Gandhi claimed that the agreement of both sides to settle their differences by peaceful means through 'bilateral negotiations' buried the dispute as an international issue which could be brought before the United Nations. This interpretation was immediately challenged by Bhutto. Neither the Pakistan leader, nor Mrs Gandhi were temperamentally inclined to use the Simla accord as a departure point for a wide-ranging transformation in Indo–Pakistan relations.

Bhutto injected a strong flavour of Islamic socialist and Third Worldist rhetoric into the conduct of foreign policy. New departures included the decision to leave the Commonwealth (30 January 1972) and the SEATO security pact (8 November 1972). Bhutto also intensified existing ties with China and the Middle East. The most spectacular example of Sino–Pakistan cooperation was, of course, the construction of the strategic Karokoram Highway which, on completion in 1978, connected Pakistan's Northern Areas with Xinjiang province through the Khunjerab Pass. Pakistan's emerging role in the Muslim world was symbolized by the February 1974 Islamic Summit in Lahore which brought together on the same platform Yasser Arafat, King Faisal of Saudi Arabia, Col. Gaddafi and Presidents Assad, Sadat and Boumedienne. A euphoric crowd packed the new Gaddafi stadium to hear the Libyan leader declaim that Pakistan was the 'citadel of Islam in Asia', and 'our resources are your resources'.[21]

Bhutto's policy was driven in part by the need to restore the national morale shattered by the 1971 war, and to secure his own power. It was shaped no less than Ayub's, however, by the desire to maintain Pakistan's security vis-à-vis India. Significantly, more resources were poured into the military by Bhutto than under any previous martial law regime. Defence expenditure rose by over 200 per cent, with $8 for every Pakistani citizen being spent on the armed forces throughout the Bhutto era.[22] The US once again became a major source of military hardware, following the lifting of its arms embargo in 1975. By then, China had become a major supplier of tanks, naval vessels and F-6 combat aircraft. The Chinese also constructed a tank rebuild factory at Taxila and an Air Force repair facility at nearby Kamra. Every dollar spent on weaponry, however, reduced Bhutto's ability to meet the demands of his poorer supporters for improved education, healthcare and housing. It also led to the unpopular step in April 1974 of cutting food subsidies in order to control the spiralling budget deficits. Bhutto's re-equipment of the army marked its post-Bangladesh re-habilitation, and its increasing use by Bhutto to maintain internal security helped create the conditions for the 1977 coup against his regime.

In one important respect, Bhutto went further than Ayub had ever done in the search for strategic balance. From the mid-1960s onwards, he had argued that Pakistan should acquire a nuclear capability. Ayub had opposed this argument, however, even in the wake of the 1965 war. In January 1972, two years before India's 'peaceful' nuclear explosion at Pokhran, Bhutto gave the go-ahead to produce a nuclear bomb. In addition to the motivation to restore a strategic balance in the face of India's vastly superior conventional weapons, there may have been a 'hidden' domestic agenda in that the bomb programme was to be independent of military control. Pakistan eventually acquired a nuclear capability by the uranium rather than plutonium enrichment route envisaged by Bhutto. Significantly, the clandestine efforts to obtain a 'bomb in the basement' reached fruition in the Zia rather than Bhutto era, when Pakistan had emerged as a 'frontline' State in the struggle against Communism following the 1979 Soviet occupation of Afghanistan. Prior to this, the Americans had looked askance at Pakistan's public attempts to acquire a power programme generated by nuclear fuel. France suspended a deal in 1978 under pressure from the Carter administration for the supply of a nuclear power station and reprocessing plant.

According to one version of events, including that propounded by Bhutto in his death-cell memoirs, *If I am Assassinated*, his decision to obtain a nuclear military capability[23] despite the existence of the Nuclear Non-Proliferation Treaty may have led to his ouster from power.[24] Bhutto claimed that he was warned by his Minister of Production, Rafi Raza[25] in January 1977 not to proceed with the nuclear reprocessing plans, and that external funding for the opposition's March election campaign and the motive for the subsequent military coup was the desire to dislocate and destroy Pakistan's nuclear programme.[26]

ZIA AND PAKISTAN'S FOREIGN POLICY

The return of the Army to centre stage, following the Zia coup of 5 July 1977 code-named Operation Fairplay, ushered in a series of dramatic domestic developments. With respect to foreign policy, there was again the search for security, which we have noted has motivated all regimes. Zia adopted different methods to achieve this common goal, but these reflected as much the changed strategic environment following the Afghan war as any especial military slant on policy. It should be noted, however, that Zia (unlike Ayub) bent the bureaucracy much more to his will. The army retained a much closer influence on the running of the government, even after the civilianization of martial law in 1985. The greatest influence was exerted over Afghan policy. In the words of one diplomat, 'Ziaul Haq had run the Afghan war on his own with the help of the intelligence agencies . . . leaving to the foreign ministry the job of explaining the policy to the world.'[27]

Zia's Army was more middle class and Islamically oriented than the Sandhurst-trained force of Ayub's day. Zia was profoundly influenced by his family's uprooting from Jalandhar (Jullundur) to Peshawar at the time of the 1947 Partition. Years later, when he was Pakistan's President, he declared at an International Islamic Conference in Islamabad, 'I will tell you what Islam and Pakistan means to me. It is a vision of my mother struggling on, tired, with all her worldly possessions in her hands, when she crossed the border into Pakistan.'[28] Significantly, Zia picked Gen. Arif (who came from East Punjab) as his Vice-Chief of Army Staff, while Gen. Akhtar Abdur Rahman from Jalandhar commanded the powerful Inter-Services Intelligence (ISI) in 1984-8. Operation Fairplay, had been executed by Zia's fellow Arain from Jalandhar, Lt. Gen. Faiz Ali Chishti.

Zia's personal piety and patriotism chimed with the ethos of the East Punjabi refugee community. This explains his popularity to the end amongst certain classes of Pakistanis. From the perspective of the refugee trading classes of the Punjab, the army was not shaping foreign policy to its interests, but representing their heartfelt views of the need for a strong stance on Kashmir, and vigilance in the face of an Indian threat.

Pakistan's attempts to counterbalance India's strategic superiority were assisted by the Americans' willingness to once more distribute their largesse to the Pakistan 'front-line' State. Within weeks of the Soviet occupation of Afghanistan on 28 December 1979, President Carter had despatched his National Security Advisor Zbigniew Brzezinski to Pakistan. This was the prelude to an offer of a $400 million economic and military aid package. Zia disdainfully rejected this as 'peanuts', but eagerly accepted the incoming Reagan administration's offer of $3.2 billion spread over a six-year period. Reagan's preoccupation with the 'evil empire' also created a more favourable environment for the clandestine nuclear policy. While once again playing the role of America's 'most allied ally' in Asia, Zia cultivated ties with China and the Islamic world. Not surprisingly for an officer who had served in Jordan at the time of operations against the PLO, he reached out to the conservative monarchies rather than the radical Arab States.

Under Ayub, the army was seen as the ultimate guarantor of the country's internal stability and territorial integrity. Zia extended this, and saw the army as indispensable for the maintenance of Pakistan as an ideological State. In May 1982, for example, he declared that the 'preservation of that Ideology (Pakistan ideology) and the Islamic character of the country was . . . as important as the security of the country's geographical boundaries'.[29] This sentiment lay behind the attempt to rewrite the history of Jinnah's intentions in the creation of Pakistan. Newspaper articles on the occasion of Jinnah's birth anniversary in December 1981 omitted the words from his speech to the Constituent Assembly that 'Hindus would cease to be Hindus and Muslims would cease to be Muslims, not in the religious sense, because that is the personal faith of each individual, but in the political sense as citizens of the state.' When the veteran Muslim Leaguer Shaukat Hayat objected to such puerile attempts to show Jinnah favouring the establishment of an Islamic State (as did the former Chief Justice, Muhammad Munir in his book *From Jinnah to Zia*), a resolution was moved in the Majlis-i-Shura that sought to ban any verbal or written comment that 'would in any way, directly or indirectly, detract from, or derogate [Jinnah's] high status, position and achievements'.[30]

In another crucial respect, the Zia era also marked a discontinuity. This involved the growing influence of the army intelligence agency, the ISI, in the conduct of covert activities. The rise of the ISI resulted from its use by the Americans as an arms conduit to the Afghan Mujahideen. This established a field of operations for the organization in Afghanistan which continues to this day in its support for the Taliban. The ISI shared Zia's aim of establishing a client state in Afghanistan, which in the wake of the collapse of the Soviet empire would enable links to be forged with the newly emerging Muslim States of Central Asia. Pakistan would not only secure trading advantages and access to oil, but, it was anticipated, would have finally redressed the strategic balance with India.

More controversial than the ISI's involvement in Afghanistan was its role in the 'proxy' wars being fought in the Indian Punjab and Kashmir. The insurgencies in both regions were not created by Pakistan, but by the Indian State's mishandling of ethno-nationalist demands. The Zia regime was, none the less, well prepared to profit from this. There was an element here of revenge for the Bangladesh breakaway. Involvement in the Kashmir *intifada* was, however, rooted in the long-standing Kashmir dispute rather than merely being opportunistic. It was to become clear, however, that Pakistan stopped short of backing the JKLF's demand for the 'third option' of Kashmiri independence. As in Afghanistan, the ISI influenced the course of the struggle by favouring pro-Pakistan and Islamist militant groups with its weapons supplies at the expense of the JKLF.

Three points emerge from this brief overview of the military's involvement with Pakistan's foreign policy in 1947-88. First, it should be noted that civilian and martial law regimes possessed very similar conceptions of policy objectives. This reflects, first and foremost, the overriding security anxieties, although important additional factors include both the informal army influence on popularly elected governments and the congruence of military and East Punjabi refugee interests. Second, it is clear that Kashmir and a preoccupation with India dominated all other foreign policy concerns even during the populist interlude of Zulfikar Ali Bhutto. Third, it is important to note that direct army control through the curbing of the bureaucracy and the rise of the ISI was much greater in the Zia era than before. We shall turn now to examine how this legacy from Zia has impacted on the army's ability to influence foreign policy in contemporary Pakistan.

THE ARMY'S INFLUENCE ON FOREIGN POLICY IN POST-1988 PAKISTAN

The military considerably influenced those areas of foreign policy linked to its security concerns, i.e. Afghanistan and Kashmir during the 1988-99 period. The nuclear weapons programme also continued largely under military control. In addition, the ISI operated independently of civilian command. It continues to inhabit the murky world of the secret state which seems to be marked out by institutional factionalism and parallel lines of command. Significantly, the much trumpeted 'accountability drive' of the Musharraf regime has excluded the ISI from its reach.

Evidence of the army's influence can be pieced together from such developments as the retention of Zia's Foreign Minister Yakub Khan in Benazir Bhutto's cabinet. A further indication was provided by the extreme discomfort Nawaz Sharif displayed when the Chief of Army Staff Gen. Beg, smarting under the cessation of US economic and military aid, questioned the Western coalition policy adopted by the government during the Gulf war and hinted that Pakistan should adopt a posture of 'strategic defiance' like Iraq's.[31] The army's role became slightly more transparent with the creation (during Meraj Khalid's caretaker Government in 1996) of the Council of Defence and National Security (CDNS).[32] The notification order at the time of its establishment referred to the fixing of priorities in the coordination of defence policy with external and domestic policies, and of advising the Government on economic and fiscal policies affecting defence and national security.

It is even more difficult to assess the extent of the ISI's influence and the degree of its autonomy. Piecing together press reports, it can be seen that in the post-Zia era, it has continued to run its own foreign policy in Afghanistan and Kashmir. In 1993, for example, it established the Markas-Dawar as a front organization based in Peshawar to channel weapons to Islamist groups fighting in the Valley in a repeat of the earlier Afghan operation.[33] While the ISI's autonomy from civilian control enabled the Indian charge of Pakistan's fighting 'proxy wars' to be rebutted, the spasmodic attempts by both Benazir Bhutto and Nawaz Sharif to influence appointments to its leadership and to play off the civilian Intelligence Bureau against it revealed their unease at its lack of supervision.

This was hardly surprising, as the ISI did not just fight proxy wars on the soil of Afghanistan and Kashmir, but involved itself in the ethnic turmoil in Karachi. Some of its members went even further than this, and attempted to subvert the elected government of Benazir Bhutto. The most notorious of these covert actions which has come to light involved a clandestine 'night jackals' meeting of 6 October 1989 in Rawalpindi between two leading ISI officials, Maj. Aamer and Brig. Imtiaz, opposition MNAs and Sindhi PPP members.[34]

What was extraordinary about this particular meeting was not ISI involvement in 'horse-trading' to unseat the Bhutto Government (such actions dated back at least to the previous spring), but that the government had got wind of the activities and set a trap to record the conspirators in the hope that Punjab Chief Minister Nawaz Sharif might himself be implicated. In the event, Nawaz Sharif stayed away from the meeting, which marked a further escalation in the tussle between the government, its IB 'ally' and the ISI. Earlier that summer, Benazir Bhutto had taken advantage of the failed ISI backed Mujahideen assault on Jalalabad to replace Gen. Hamid Gul as ISI head.[35] His replacement, Gen. (retd.) Shamsur Rahman Kallue, was, however, virtually boycotted by the ISI. The Prime Minister also appointed a committee under the chairmanship of Air Marshal (retd.) Zulfikar Ali Khan to investigate the intelligence agencies. His report was considered, but then quietly shelved. These steps, however, created further enemies without securing civilian control of the secret state.

It is much easier to analyse the causes of the army's involvement in security-related foreign-policy issues than to assess the extent of its influence. The major factors include, first, the nature of Pakistan's transition to democratic rule and especially the power vested in the office of the President; second, the continued, weak institutionalization of Pakistan's political parties and the personalization of power within them. Before examining these features, the point requires reiteration that the military's desire and ability to shape foreign policy following the restoration of democracy should not evoke any surprise. This is precisely what happened from the early 1950s onwards until the formal coup of 1958.

Many commentators, buoyed up by the optimism surrounding the return of the PPP to power under Benazir Bhutto's youthful leadership, however, overlooked this historical perspective. Moreover, there was hope that the presence of two national leaders in Benazir Bhutto and Rajiv Gandhi, who were born post- and pre-Partition respectively, might herald a breakthrough in Indo–Pakistan relations. This was regarded as especially important in the light of the war scare arising from the Indian Army's Brasstacks manoeuvres in 1987.[36] Further euphoria was generated by the collapse of the Soviet empire and the emergence of a so-called 'third wave' of democratization.

The new departure in Indo–Pakistan relations with its hopes of a 'peace dividend' did not dawn. A breakthrough on the Siachen Glacier conflict stalled. Following the outbreak of the *intifada* in

Kashmir, Indo–Pakistan relations worsened to such an extent that the US claimed that it had prevented the two countries standing on the brink of nuclear war in 1990.[37] Although disaster was averted on this occasion, talks even at Foreign Secretary level were in abeyance from 1994 onwards. The thaw brought by the short-lived I.K. Gujral Ministry which came to office in April 1996 did not survive the election of a BJP-led Government the following spring. To add to democratic Pakistan's catalogue of foreign policy woe, the United States had suspended all economic and military aid from 1 October 1990 onwards because of the inability to certify under the terms of the Pressler Amendment that Pakistan did not possess a nuclear weapons programme. This meant not only the loss of $564 million of economic and military aid, but prevented the delivery of 71 F-16 fighters and spare parts to the Pakistan Air Force.

Political-science writing on the recent democratic transitions across the globe conceptualize these processes in terms of 'transformation', 'transplacement' and 'replacement'. Early studies did not always draw a definitional clarity between democratic transition and democratic consolidation. Subsequent works have linked the nature of the original transition with the prospects for democratic consolidation.

The democratic transition in Pakistan can be best conceptually understood as a 'transformation'. Despite the formation of the multi-party Movement for the Restoration of Democracy in 1981, democracy 'emerged' following the voluntary withdrawal of the military after Zia's sudden death in the plane crash of 17 August 1988. It owed more to the decision of the Chief of the Army Staff Beg to go down the democratic route than to the institutional strength of these groups which had opposed the Zia regime. Beg could also rely on the ISI's behind-the-scenes brokering of a deal which ensured the unity of anti-PPP political forces under the leadership of Nawaz Sharif. This ensured that the PPP would not sweep the polls. The strong showing of the Islamic Alliance in the key Punjab province increased the army's leverage over the PPP. Benazir Bhutto succeeded to office following a series of 'understandings' which revolved around the assurance that the defence budget was sacrosanct, and that the army retained a veto in vital foreign policy and security matters.

The army's informal influence was further strengthened through its allies in the bureaucracy. These were led by the President, Ghulam Ishaq Khan. Zia, as part of the transition to civilian 'rule' in the mid-1980s, had appreciably strengthened the office of President who, under the terms of the Eighth Amendment of the Constitution, could dismiss the Prime Minister and the National and Provincial Assemblies. The use of the Eighth Amendment hung like a Damocles sword over successive Prime Ministers until it was removed by Nawaz Sharif in the flush of his stunning 1997 election triumph. Some commentators were to presciently note at the time, however, that a 'safeguard' to an outright military coup had now been dismantled, and that Sharif's action increased rather than diminished the prospects of martial law.

Benazir Bhutto, and later Nawaz Sharif, in both their first ministries were the least powerful of a troika which included the President and the Chief of the Army Staff. It would be simplistic, however, to see the President as merely the army's catspaw. Both Ghulam Ishaq Khan and Farooq Leghari possessed their own institutional bases of support and political interests which were independent of the army. It is similarly simplistic to see Nawaz Sharif's removal (by means of the Thirteenth Amendment) of the Eighth Amendment ending military behind-the-scenes influence in both domestic and foreign affairs. The army continued to act as an arbiter, as can be seen during Nawaz Sharif's clash with Chief Justice of the Supreme Court Sajjad Ali Shah in the winter of 1997. The clash increasingly involved a tussle with President Farooq Leghari, who was smarting at the clipping of his wings by the Pakistan Prime Minister. The attitude of the army COAS, Gen. Jahangir Karamat, appeared to be decisive in the outcome. The military's stepping back ensured that, in contrast to 1993, Nawaz Sharif emerged triumphant from his conflict with the Presidency. Leghari following Justice Shah's removal from office, announced his resignation to a packed press conference at the Aiwan-e-Sadr in the afternoon of 2 December. The army had distanced itself from the President long before the clash, and knew that it could exercise its influence either informally or through the CDNS rather than the office of President. It could also rest content that no bold initiatives would be taken without its approval because of the twin threats of economic collapse and ethnic conflict in urban Sindh which hung over the heads of successive governments. Indeed, some commentators even alleged that the ISI deliberately kept the violence on the boil in Karachi to provide a reason for the dismissal of any government which failed to meet the army's approval.

The personalization of power and the bitter conflicts between the government and the opposition during the period 1988-96 further diminished the politicians' room for independent action. A kind of zero sum politics prevailed, in which opposition was not regarded as legitimate. Much energy was dissipated in street demonstrations, attempts to involve rivals in legal cases, and the bandying about of charges of corruption. The weakness of the government was laid bare by, for example, the inability of Benazir Bhutto's first ministry to bring forward any meaningful legislation during a two-year period. Indeed, Pakistan's experience throughout the period 1988-96 lends weight to those understandings which maintain that transitions unilaterally imposed by armed forces are likely, at best, to result in fragile democracies which eschew the improvement in economic equity, whilst maintaining guarantees for political freedom, but which are more likely to produce a hybrid mix of electoral forms and authoritarianism which has been dubbed 'electocratic rule'.

Ironically, given his questionable democratic credentials, Nawaz Sharif was in a stronger position than his PPP predecessor when he came to office in 1990 to tilt the balance of power in favour of the assertion of elected institutions over the state structure. This resulted both from his power base in the politically crucial Punjab region, and his greater acceptability to the Islamic parties. Nevertheless, although the civil-military bureaucracy had engineered Nawaz Sharif's rise to power in 1990, the relations between the new Premier and the establishment became increasingly uneasy as he sought to carve out an independent political agenda. His government was also undermined by the constant sniping of the opposition, along with his inability to meet the unrealistic demands of the Islamist groups. Attempts to exert his influence over the army and the ISI marked the final parting of ways. This state of affairs owed much to the ISI's covert activities untrammelled by civilian control. Ironically, however, Nawaz Sharif was to suffer from it. Although the charge list cited 'corruption' in the wake of the collapse of the cooperative societies in the Punjab and the spiralling disorder in Karachi as the motives for his dismissal, it is probable that the army-supported action was prompted in part by the consideration that Benazir Bhutto with her allies on Capitol Hill was more likely to get US sanctions against Pakistan lifted than Nawaz Sharif.

The dramatic events of April 1993 which surrounded Nawaz Sharif's dismissal, subsequent reinstatement by the Supreme Court and eventual simultaneous resignation with the President in an army-brokered deal need not concern us here. What is significant, however, is the fact that the men in khaki did not want to assume direct responsibility, but were content to continue the troika arrangement with a chastened Benazir Bhutto. They saw her more positive image in America and friends on Capitol Hill as holding out the possibility of improving relations with the Americans which had sunk to an all-time low by the end of Nawaz Sharif's tenure as a result of the over-zealous pursuit of the proxy war option by the ISI. Indeed, Pakistan was pla-ced on the watch list of potential terrorist states for six months. In all probability, the army also saw Benazir as a better bet for heading off the hostility which was continuing to accrue as Pakistan pursued its quest for a nuclear weapons capability.

Following the October 1993 polls, Benazir Bhutto returned to power in apparently a much stronger position than five years earlier, not just because of a better PPP showing in the key Punjab region, but because a PPP loyalist, Farooq Leghari, replaced her erstwhile nemesis Ghulam Ishaq Khan in the office of President. It was not so much Benazir's new strength which led to a lifting of the army straitjacket, but her successful carrying out of many of the military's aims in the foreign-policy field. A clear case of the military tail wagging the civilian dog.

Benazir Bhutto's 'charm offensive' ensured an improvement in relations with the United States, which had been further jeopardized by Nawaz Sharif's statement of 23 August 1994 that Pakistan possessed nuclear weapons. To many, this was the major achievement of her government. There was no breakthrough in Indo–Pakistan relations, however, although this held the key to a reduction in military expenditure and improved trade relations which would be of immense benefit to the majority of Pakistan's population.

Benazir Bhutto was at her most effective when addressing Western audiences. She projected an image of Pakistan as a moderate Islamic State, open for business and willing to assist the West in its international struggle against drugs and terrorism. Diplomacy was linked with the encouragement of foreign investment. Considerable progress was made in this respect with regard to the energy sector, particularly following the visit to Pakistan of US Secretary of Energy Hazel O'Leary in October 1994.[38]

By far the most important overseas trip made by Benazir Bhutto was the visit to Washington at cherry blossom time in April 1995.[39] This had been accompanied by a pre-visit publicity blitz. A favourable impression had also been created by Pakistani participation in UN peacekeeping activities in Somalia, Haiti and Bosnia, and in the extradition of terrorists[40] and drug traffickers. Whilst the nuclear issue and the continued sanctions under the terms of the Pressler Amendment remained high on the agenda, considerable attention was devoted to investment opportunities. Maleeha Lodhi, the extremely able Pakistan Ambassador[41] and assiduous lobbyist, built on the favourable impression created by the visit. Indeed, the former journalist was able to run rings around her Indian counterpart, Siddhartha Shankar Ray. This bore fruit on 21 September, when the Senate voted in favour of the Brown Amendment. This proposed a waiver of the August 1990 Pressler Amendment which had cut off aid to Pakistan and halted arms sales until Pakistan agreed to a verifiable capping of its nuclear programme. Under the terms of the Brown Amendment, over 350 million dollars worth of military equipment would be released which Pakistan had paid for but not received. Equally important, however, was the paving of the way for economic aid to Pakistan, as the Brown Amendment deleted the Pressler Amendment requirements for economic sanctions. President Clinton ratified the Brown Amendment on 27 January 1996.

While Pakistan's relations with the USA had thus improved from their 1993 low point, the Cold War continued with India. The two countries accused each other of fishing in the troubled waters of Sindh and Kashmir. The Indian consulate in Karachi was closed amidst claims that RAW (Indian secret service) agents were attempting to destabilize the country in retaliation for Pakistani involvement with Kashmiri separatists.[42] Earlier, the fire which severely damaged the parliament building in Islamabad in November 1993 was blamed on RAW agents. Kashmir continued to be the major hurdle to the normalization of economic and political relations. Following fruitless talks early in 1994 and continued clashes between the security forces and Kashmiri militants, the Pakistan Government unsuccessfully attempted to move resolutions on Kashmir in the UN Human Rights Commission (March 1994), and later in the General Assembly (November). The Casablanca meeting of the Organisation of Islamic Conference (OIC) did, however, pass a condemnatory resolution along with establishing an OIC contact group on Kashmir.

None of these endeavours compensated for the deteriorating domestic scene dominated by economic crisis, bitter political infighting and the ongoing violence in Karachi which had even claimed the life of her own brother, Mir Murtaza Bhutto. The Prime Minister's increasingly acrimonious relations with the judiciary and with the President further undermined her position. Nevertheless, Farooq Leghari would not have moved to dismiss her on the eve of the 1996

US Presidential elections without the backing of the military high command. Yet further evidence was provided of the army's pivotal role in Pakistan's politics.

It would be tendentious to blame the military's behind-the-scenes influence solely for the worsening Indo–Pakistan and US relations which dispelled the initial optimism surrounding the restoration of democracy. Extraneous developments, such as the ending of the Cold War and the Afghan conflict, the Kashmir uprising which New Delhi put down to Pakistani meddling and the election of a BJP Government in India would have in any case exerted a deleterious impact. Moreover, an electorate emotionally committed at least in Punjab to the Kashmiri cause would have boxed in any government wishing to make concessions in the search for better relations even without the prospect of the military breathing down its neck. Nevertheless, it cannot be denied that the continuing security-driven military approach to Indo-Pakistan relations stultified attempts to put these on a new footing. In different circumstances, Nawaz Sharif might have been more responsive to those commercial interests which wished to see Kashmir put on the back-burner in order to take advantage of the economic opportunities which would have flowed from a normalization of relations with India.

It, of course, takes two to tango or engage in a diplomatic minuet. With the exception of I.K. Gujral, and, more surprisingly, of Atal Behari Vajpayee, the head of the BJP coalition Government following the February 1998 elections, successive Indian Prime Ministers have not displayed any appreciation of the need to make the running in any improvement of relations with Pakistan, the psychologically and strategically less secure of the two subcontinental protagonists. It could be argued why they should show accommodation at the same time as they believed that the ISI encouraged the activities of Islamic militants in Kashmir. In sum, therefore, it would be fair to conclude that the Army/ISI influence on security and foreign-relations issues hindered new departures, although the ruling PPP and Muslim League Coalitions during 1988-99 for their own political reasons eschewed initiatives which might have eased the subcontinental Cold War.

CONCLUSION

It is undeniable that the military has exercised considerable influence over key areas of Pakistan's foreign policy. This reflects, in part, the entrenchment of the army in the political process following successive martial law regimes. Linked with this, of course, has been weak political institutionalization and an underdeveloped civil society. The major cause of the military role, however, has been Pakistan's 'strategic deficit' vis-à-vis India, and the consequent emphasis on security-driven rather than other aspects of foreign policy. This explains the continuities in attitude to the key Kashmir issue across both civilian and martial law regimes. The only serious challenge to the establishment/army supported view was provided by the Bengali elite in the former East Pakistan. Their marginalization ensured that the 'official' view would prevail. Since 1971, significant sections of Punjabi society have identified both their domestic and foreign-policy concerns with those of the army. The PML(N) inherited the congruence of interests forged during the Zia era.

Zia's martial law entrenched not just the army, but saw the rise to prominence of the ISI. This intelligence agency has followed its own institutional interests in both domestic and foreign affairs untrammelled by civilian control. The politicians' room for manoeuvre following Zia's demise was also limited by the powers which had been vested in the President. Although the civil bureaucracy, the President, the security agencies and the army did not possess identical foreign-policy interests, or invariably pull in the same direction, they represented a formidable establishment with which both the 'outsider' Prime Minister Benazir Bhutto and the 'insider' Nawaz Sharif had to contend. Both elected leaders expressed their opinions firmly and were not mere onlookers even with regard to the sensitive Afghan policy. But in 'post-martial law Pakistan, the civilian government had to take into account the army's concepts and feelings'.[43]

The October 1999 coup did not, however, necessarily signal a return to the complete military domination of the key Afghan and Kashmir foreign-policy areas of the Zia era. This reflected not only the personality differences between Musharraf, the self-styled Chief Executive, and his predecessor, but the changed international climate and regional ground realities. A post-Cold War scenario has encouraged not only US linking of economic aid with pressure for rapid democratization, but also for a resolution of regional conflicts. In such circumstances, despite the army's hawkish role at Kargil, in the straitened diplomatic and economic circumstances Pakistan finds itself in at the beginning of the new century, Musharraf's authoritarian regime may have to not only sign-post the return to democracy, but show 'flexibility' over Kashmir. The key to a breakthrough, however, lies with an enlightened Indian Government initiating renewed bilateral dialogue from a position of increasing moral, economic and political strength.

NOTES

1. Iqbal Akhund, *Trial & Error: The Advent and Eclipse of Benazir Bhutto*, Karachi: Oxford University Press, 2000, p. 222.
2. Hasan-Askari Rizvi, 'The Legacy of Military Rule in Pakistan', *Survival*, vol. 31, no. 3, May-June 1989, p. 266.
3. The Thirteenth Amendment of the Constitution repealed the Eighth Amendment under which the President had dismissed successive elected Prime Ministers.
4. By the time of the restoration of democracy in Pakistan, the Afghan crisis had moved from a military to a diplomatic stage with the emphasis on the post-Soviet power structure. This in itself encouraged a greater civilian output than during the Zia years, when the emphasis was on military advice and operational support for the Mujahideen.
5. Its extent may be seen in the fact that the PPP Minister of State for Defence in Benazir Bhutto's first administration advised journalists not to report on matters relating to the army or national security: Iqbal Akhund, *Trial & Error. The Advent and Eclipse of Benazir Bhutto*, Karachi: Oxford University Press, 2000, p. 121.
6. Benazir Bhutto lamented shortly before Zia's death that the PPP's foreign policy echoed the government's on all major issues, ibid., p. 20.
7. I. Malik, *State and Civil Society in Pakistan: Politics of Authority, Ideology and Ethnicity*, Basingstoke: Macmillan, 1997, p. 97.
8. Kamal Afzal, *Pakistan: Political and Constitutional Dilemmas*, Karachi: OUP 1987, p. 138.
9. In the 1996-7 budget, for example, Rs. 131 billion was earmarked for defence, a 14 per cent rise on the previous year, compared with a meagre Rs. 1,625 million for education and Rs. 3,219 million for health expenditure. The annual development programme expenditure was set at about 30 per cent less than this gargantuan military spending.
10. A. Jalal, *The State of Martial Law: The Origins of Pakistan's Political Economy of Defence*, Cambridge: Cambridge University Press, 1990, p. 238.
11. Y. Samad, *A Nation in Turmoil*, New Delhi: Sage Publications, p. 128.
12. In principle, Pakistan was entitled to 17.5 per cent of the assets of undivided India, but it was not until December 1947 that an agreement was reached on its share of the cash balances. The bulk of this (Rs. 550 million) was held back by the Government of India as a result of hostilities in Kashmir. It was only paid on 15 January 1948 following Gandhi's intervention and fast.
13. Muhammad Ali, *The Emergence of Pakistan*, New York: Columbia University Press, 1967, p. 376.

14. In 1953, the Economic Appraisal Committee conceded that Pakistan's annual expenditure on defence and civil administration was wholly out of line with available resources: Jalal, *The State of Martial Rule*, p. 237.

15. Ibid., p. 55.

16. M.R. Gannett, 'Position Paper on CENTO in advance of 11-13 July 1961'. Declassified Papers, LBJ Country Files Box 4, National Security Archive, George Washington University.

17. Liaquat Ali Khan was toying with alternatives to a pro-Western foreign policy shortly before his assassination on 16 October 1951. Popular opposition to the pro-Western stance of the establishment was especially evident during the July 1956 Suez crisis.

18. Bogra had previously been the Pakistani Ambassador in Washington.

19. In his first broadcast as Chief Martial Law Administrator on 8 October 1958, Ayub had declared that the politicians had 'waged a ceaseless and bitter war against each other regardless of the ill effects on the country, just to whet their appetites and satisfy their base demands'. Ayub Khan, *Speeches and Statements*, Karachi: Pakistan Publications, 1961, vol. 1, p. 2.

20. American Embassy, Karachi, to Secretary of State, 31 January 1966, Central Policy Files 1964-6, Political and Defence Files Pol. 27, Military Operations India–Pakistan National Archives at College Park.

21. S. Wolpert, *Zulfi Bhutto of Pakistan*, Oxford: Oxford University Press, 1993, p. 234.

22. S.J. Burki, *Pakistan Under Bhutto 1971-1977*, Basingstoke: Macmillan, 1980, Table 5.2, p. 105.

23. Official diplomacy throughout the post-1972 period stressed that Pakistan's nuclear programme was entirely peaceful in character.

24. Henry Kissinger is reported to have threatened to make a 'horrible example of him' if he did not abandon his plans to reprocess plutonium. A. Kapur, *Pakistan's Nuclear Development*, London: Croom Helm, 1987, p. 145.

25. During the course of an interview on 2 January 1997, Rafi Raza maintained to me that he had warned Bhutto about sabre rattling on the nuclear issue because of its impact on American opinion. While he believed that the USA was happy about Bhutto's fall, it had not engineered the PNA campaign which Bhutto had to a large extent brought upon himself.

26. Z.A. Bhutto, *If I am Assassinated*, New Delhi: Vikas, 1979, pp. 106-7, 135-8.

27. Akhund, op. cit., p. 191.

28. K.B. Sayeed 'Pakistan in 1983', *Asian Survey*, vol. 24, no. 2, February 1984, p. 1084.

29. Hasan-Askari Rizvi, *The Military and Politics in Pakistan 1947-86*, Lahore: Progressive Publishers, 1986, p. 242.

30. *Al-Mushir*, vol. 24, no. 2, 1982, p. 93.

31. *Dawn*, 7 December 1990.

32. The CDNS membership was to comprise the President, Prime Minister, Foreign Minister, Defence Minister, Interior Minister, Minister/Adviser for

Finance, Chairman of the Joint Chiefs of Staff Committee, Chief of the Army Staff, Chief of the Naval Staff and Chief of the Air Staff. Significantly, it was to be headed and convened by the President rather than the Prime Minister.

33. V. Hewitt, *Reclaiming the Past, the Search for Political and Cultural Unity in Contemporary Jammu and Kashmir*, London: Portland Books, 1995, p. 186.

34. See *Dawn Magazine*, 11 September 1992.

35. See Shaheen Sehbai, 'The Day of the Night Jackals', *Dawn Overseas Weekly*, week ending 14 June 1989.

36. K. Bajpai et al., *Brasstacks and Beyond: Perception and Management of Crisis in South Asia*, New Delhi: Manohar, 1995.

37. See D.T. Hagerty, 'The Theory and Practice of Nuclear Deterrence in South Asia', unpublished Ph.D. thesis, University of Pennsylvania, 1995.

38. A large number of memoranda of understanding amounting to 4 billion dollars were signed with foreign investors in the energy field.

39. See *Newsline*, April 1995, pp. 24-32.

40. Ramzi Yusaf, who was wanted in connection with the World Trade Center bombing in New York, was arrested in Islamabad and extradited to America shortly before Benazir's visit.

41. She relinquished her post on 31 January 1997 and was replaced by the Pakistan Ambassador to India, Riaz Khokhar. The Government of Meraj Khalid had, in fact, asked her to stay on another year.

42. For a comment on this development, see I.A. Rehman, 'Unholy Acrimony', *Newsline* (Annual), January 1995, pp. 125-6.

43. Akhund, op. cit., p. 191.

And Yet, Pakistan Exists

PIERRE LAFRANCE

AKISTAN IS TOO OFTEN and too conveniently viewed as a sort of deliberately created territory in the region, all the more artificial as its borders were defined in a hurry, without any of the explicit—if not unequivocal—historical or administrative references that have served as the foundation for establishing the borders of most of the States born of the decolonization process. In other words, Pakistan is viewed simply as a part of India, just as an iceberg is part of the icecap, as if it faces the same centrifugal forces and the same identity problems as India. However, India is able to establish its national unity on the basis of its 'Indianness', the common denominator of all its constituents, and its distinct stamp on the regional map. Hence, there would be some basis—identifiable by cultural anthropology—on which the Indian nation would have the right to claim its unity.

Why, then, doesn't one speak of 'Pakistanness'? Indeed, this term, bizarre as it may sound, is never used. Moreover, we know that ever since the birth of the state, Pakistan's unity has been seriously damaged by all the stresses and strains born of the struggle between the two notoriously heterogeneous elements of which it was composed at the time, and of which one was to break away to become Bangladesh in 1971, after a short but bloody war. The conclusion drawn was that the 'Islamness' that was mooted as a unifying force both in Karachi and Dhaka (then Dacca) factored only partially in the identity of the two countries concerned, since the aim of religion is not that of creating countries, which would amount to denying its own universality. 'Indo-Islamness' too would not be any basis for the existence of a nation state, since India harbours more than 100 million Muslims who, since Partition, accept or have adjusted to being a part of an Indian Union that claims to be secular although it is strongly marked by Hinduism (as recent developments have shown). Given this situation,

Pakistan and Bangladesh would have no *raison d'être* or justification for their existence other than a sort of heightened 'Islamness'; in other words, something that has more to do with passions than substance, and which can only get increasingly diluted over time, particularly as the hope for a Caliphal restoration embracing the entire ummah, with no distinctions, withers away, thereby dissuading the two countries with their heterogeneous components, to form subcontinental wholes after 1971 second Partition.

This kind of identity-related affliction could only worsen the effects of all the forces that play a hand in Pakistan's fragmentation—Pathan and Baluchi irredentism or autonomism, for example—which are the source of the problems at the Afghan and Iranian borders; Sindhi nationalism, at the moment neutralized by the Mohajir upsurge in Karachi and Hyderabad, but which could well call into question the role the Punjabi majority plays in cementing national unity, particularly if this community were to reach some kind of understanding with the Mohajirs (which is a possibility that cannot be ignored).

In the light of such a scenario, we would be inclined to draw the conclusion that Pakistan, in the way it perceives itself, is the victim of an illusion, that it wrongfully believes that it exists, and will sooner or later have to acknowledge its error.

There is a very glaring contradiction in this viewpoint: the fact that the elements believed to be centrifugal forces or claiming to be such are evidently peripheral, not so much vis-à-vis Islamabad, but definitely so in terms of the subcontinent. From this point of view, the Baluch would belong far more to the eastern fringes of the Iranian plateau, while the Pathans would belong to the southern Afghan mountains. As for the Sindhis, they traditionally look as much towards the Arabian peninsula as to the other peninsula whose boundaries start toward the east of their territory. Thus, Pakistan has at least as many grounds for distinguishing itself from India as it may have for differentiating itself from its other neighbours. In other words, the effects of the ethnic and religious forces at play in its territory are centrifugal with regard to Delhi, while at the same time laying the foundations for its specificity.

However, there are other reasons—even more convincing ones—that make Pakistan a very distinct entity within the surrounding territories, with the borders it has at present. These are reasons that are geographic and historic in nature.

GEOGRAPHIC COHESION AND HISTORIC CONTINUITY

As it stands today, and after Bangladesh asserted its Gangetic and Islamo–Bengali identity, Pakistan, at first glance, seems to comprise the enormous Indus Valley along with the mountains and plateaux that bear its tributaries while also forming natural borders. There is an obvious geographic cohesion that would establish Pakistan as a separate country, even if we were to ignore the history of the settlement of populations in this area.

In fact, we find here the natural framework for the constitution of a specific human culture, since culture can be likened to collective fertilization and fecundity. Indeed the most material, say agricultural element of fecundity is present here. In the same way, the other basic element of culture, the one that actually gives it all its dimensions as a ground for community life, i.e. communication, is also present, through all the waterways but also the surface roads that border these waterways, or connect them. Finally, the natural ports that can be seen along the approximately 800 km of its coastline and the famous mountain passes that enabled some to use them as 'invasion routes' and others as 'silk routes' provide an opening to the outside world, another important component of culture.

As it happens, history largely confirms what geography allows one to sense. What, indeed, does history tell us? It tells us about the birth of one of the most accomplished civilizations of its time, in the third millennium before our era and in the same area that is called 'Pakistan' today. It was a civilization comparable to its contemporaries in Sumer and Memphis. This civilization spread widely towards the west (today's Baluchistan) and the north, right up to the banks of the Amu Darya. However, it barely spread into the east and did not reach the Gangetic Valley, in spite of its proximity, which indicates that there were cultures in the peninsula proper (as, indeed, in the Iranian Plateau) that were cohesive and well-established enough to remain impervious to the diffusion of the Harappan and Mohenjo Daro civilization, a civilization that was so closely linked to its land of origin.

Another major event would later separate the Indus even more from what India is today, only to bring them closer together further on— the Aryan invasion. While we may know very little as yet about its rise and fall—an indication of the fact that this migratory movement, unlike others, did not lend itself to any epic recollections—it appears that since the end of the second millennium before our era and at the beginning of the first, it was in the Indus Valley that the religious Vedic culture and Sanskrit developed, to spread to almost the whole of the subcontinent later.

However, the merger of the Indus, the Ganges and the Deccan was not to last very long. In the sixth century, a large part of the Indus Valley came under the influence of Persia's Achaemenid empire. Fate willed that today's Pakistan be distinct from today's India, not only because of geographic constraints but also due to the effects of physical, cultural or spiritual conquests sweeping in from the west or the north, and fate was not to be denied.

While the echoes of Alexander's conquests in the area were to be heard far into the territory, although he was more or less confined within the boundaries of what is, today, Pakistan, they left their imprint on the valley not because of the endurance of a notoriously ephemeral conquest, but more so due to the effects they produced. Indeed, all through the Seleucid, Parthian and Greco-Bactrian interludes in the west and the great Mauryan adventure in the east, the valley re-established its originality and flourished, in the sense that it came under the influence of two spreading currents that were not so much antagonistic as inclined to commingle—the Hellenistic and Indian currents. After the humanistic contribution of Ashoka's policies and the contributions of Bactrian Greeks, particularly under Menander, these were to light the way to the blossoming of Buddhist philosophy and to the development of a very original civilization inspired by it in the Indus basin and its surrounding territory.

Present-day Pakistan found itself encompassed within a civilizational area that spread towards Trans-Oxiana, but one that was clearly demarcated both in the east and the west. The area took the name of its centre of development—Gandhara. While we must endeavour not to give in to the temptation of going into a lengthy treatise on the history of this civilization which reached its zenith in the first and second century AD under the Kushan empire, we must never the less highlight the craze of art lovers for original sculptures of this period, which reveal the confluence of Greek, Persian, Indian and even Roman influences. Any references to the long list of discoveries by the various British, Pakistani, French, Italian and Indian archaeologists who made this civilization known would, of course, be irrelevant. However, an observation by Mario Bussagli that reminds us of the extent to which Gandhara art is distinct from Indian art does deserve to be mentioned. The historian wrote, 'Basically, the region in which Gandhara art flourished remains culturally different, if not estranged from the very vibrant Indian traditions prevailing in other parts of this immense peninsula.'[1]

This regional individuality, which had already been asserted by history, was undoubtedly diminished during the short century (AD 350-450) of the primacy of the Gupta dynasty in this valley, competing with the influence of the Sassanids. However, this individuality was underlined by the persistence of Buddhism in what is present-day Pakistan. Hence, the latter is distinguished from the rest of the Peninsula by remaining one of the major centres for the conservation and spread of this religion, as testified by the accounts of Chinese and Korean pilgrims.

When Hinduism once again conquered the banks of the Indus, it was under the impelling force of non-native conquerors who swept in from the north, like others before them—Hephtalite Huns first, followed by the Turkishahis, who were to heighten the cultural distinctness of the Indus Valley basin while seeming to wipe out its religious specificity.

A Specific Islamic Stamp

At the end of the first millennium, present-day Pakistan gradually entered the sphere of influence of Islam, before the rest of the subcontinent. We know that conversions took place in three different ways. One through the Arab conquest, since AD 711, enabling Muslim principalities to settle in Sindh (Bambore) and southern Punjab (Multan). Conversions at that time followed paths very similar to those observed during the same period in the Middle East and Central Asia. Moreover, a balance of forces and peaceful coexistence soon developed between the Muslim and Hindu princes. The second way in which conversions were carried out was far more brutal, imposed by Turkish and Afghani conquerors who did not seem to hesitate in forcing conversions, massacring and destroying temples—painful episodes that essentially took place between the tenth and twelfth centuries. Finally, the most sustained conversions—sustained because they were based on conviction, or even a certain passion—took place through preaching and through the examples set by mystics, most of whom came from some of the major brotherhoods that were to flourish in the ancient land of Gandhara: the Qadiriyas, the Nakshbandiyas and the Shishtiyas. This is an important factor, since it appears to translate a certain continuity in the spiritual history of the region. Apparently, it was not merely by chance that most of the places in which these initiators, with their mystic wisdom, first taught and were then interred, are located in the same areas where, in more ancient days, Buddhist hermits once welcomed their followers, nor is it merely by chance that the objects used to keep holy texts open at the required pages in Islamic schools are shaped like stupas. Everything happened as if a tradition had been preserved—one whose origins were unknown even to those who were promulgating it.

Nevertheless, influxes of ever-new populations and influences from the west and north have always flooded the Indus Valley. The valley has proceeded to integrate them within its own persona, but during the reign of the various major dynasties that have left their stamp on this region in the course of the second millennium, these influences have enhanced the Muslim character of the valley as well as its content of elements foreign to the Indian world—Turkish or Turko-Mughal, Pakhtun, Baluch or Iranian elements. But it is important to note that most members of the Pakistani elite claim precisely the kind of ancestry that is linked to these migrations and conquests—Rajputs descending undoubtedly from the Hephtalites in the case of the Bhuttos, from the Pakhtuns for the Lodhis, Babars, Durranis or Khattaks, the Baluch for the Legharis or Jatois, the Persians for the Afshars or Shirazis. In a word, a population of more or less powerful country squires who came from elsewhere over the centuries to shape the lives of the natives, unaware that they were the heirs of one of the oldest civilizations in the world.

PAKISTAN AND THE 'TWO-NATION THEORY'

However, one fact that proved to be the determining factor in the genesis of Pakistan was the irreducibility of the two major religions in the subcontinent vis-à-vis each other, i.e. Islam and Hinduism. It is apparent, in particular, that the vitality of the latter religion, endowed with multiple facets and the ambition to determine laws capable of governing the cosmic and spiritual balance, made its followers little inclined to admit the validity of laws derived from other religions, if not totally insensitive to their 'message'. On the other hand, Muslims, loyal to the 'seal of the Prophecy', were at least equally intransigent.

Can dharma and shariah coexist? And if yes, how? This, in essence, is the crux of the issue underlying the subcontinent's history in the second half of this millennium, specially during the Mughal empire.

Attempts at creating harmony and understanding between the two religions sought by Akbar gave way to a cultural divorce. First Aurangzeb, then the Marathas put their seal on this separation, but a powerful reaction to it was syncretism based on a mystical and messianic approach. Consequently, Sikhism, by extending its ascendancy from Amritsar to Peshawar, with Lahore as its hub, appeared as a dominant force vis-à-vis the headway gained by British colonization. Even within Islam itself, efforts made to implement radical spiritual reforms under the dual influence of confraternal traditions, and, no doubt, Hindu asceticism, resulted in the elaboration of doctrines, such as those by Ahmadi and Zhikri, that were deemed heterodox by rigid Muslims.

Nonetheless, the incongruity between the rival ambitions of the two large religions ended up in making their followers distrustful of any fusionist or confusionist attempts, specially during the British era. Furthermore, we saw each community becoming more protective of its identity. Thus, whereas on the one hand, the Jamaat-i-Tabligh saw the light of day, on the other, Hindu nationalism emerged. Although Hindus and Muslims fought against British colonization together at the end of the nineteenth century, the differences between the two started becoming more pronounced. The fact that Mahatma Gandhi held a Koran in one hand and a Hindu book of wisdom in the other while on his famous peregrinations in itself showed that the British Raj's spiritual identity revolved around these two distinct poles. Indeed, this foreshadowed the two-nation theory that Mohammad Ali Jinnah put forward after lengthy vacillation.

Curiously enough, the abominable massacres that took place at the time of Partition were hardly a surprise for the region's experts. It is well known that both British as well as Hindu and Muslim political watchers had feared 'a blood bath'. In fact, a certain amount of hatred had been smouldering, explained by the existence of two very emotional issues: fury at seeing one's own universality being radically denied by the other group, and a panicky fear that the latter would constitute a mass and turn into a demographic force.

It was only normal—perhaps even too normal according to some— to direct the regrouping of religious communities seeking a physical divorce from the other towards areas where each predominated such as the Indus Valley, where eight centuries of successive demographic sedimentation had left an indisputable Muslim mark. It had long been the area least marked by Hinduism, and as the boundaries of India redefined themselves around the peninsula proper, it became the area marked by the least amount of Indianness. Thus, this very real Indus 'country' was to become the State that it was perhaps bound to be since the dawn of history.

THE ISLAMIST THREAT

The fact that religious criteria were at the root of Partition had created a certain Islamoduly in the mentality of Pakistan's citizens and in the ideology the State took inspiration from, which is still present to some extent. This trend turned at times into Islamolatry (which was, by definition, foreign to Islam as it substituted the 'we' cult for that of the Divinity). Already perceptible in the Tablighi movement or in the writings of Mawdudi, the founder of the Jamaat-i-Islami, although it was never clearly admitted, this trend is undoubtedly related to what we call 'Islamism'. Consequently, ever since that period, and specially over the last several years, it has become common to describe Pakistan as a country that is 'threatened by the Islamist peril'.

And yet, the reverse is not too far from one's mind, for if Pakistan (naturally inclined to see salvation only by and through Islam) has not resorted to an Islamic revolution or religious fundamentalism despite the social and political upheavals that have taken place since its birth, it is obviously because there have been obstacles on the way.

Perhaps in this instance, we must examine the difference in the manner in which Pakistan lives out Islam and the way it celebrates it. Pakistani piety is, in fact, just as serene and unobtrusive, as its attachment to Islam can sometimes be declamatory. There seem to be two explanations for this. First, the people, who were mostly converted to Islam by mystics in the first few centuries of the first millennium AD, have largely remained attached to Sufism. One of the most glaring signs of this is the role played by qawwali songs in the country's artistic expression. We also know that it is difficult for spiritual pursuits and rigid orthodoxy to live in harmony for long. On the other hand, the ruling elite in Pakistan follows the Aligarh school of thought which is open to contemporary intellectual and scientific developments, rather than the Deoband school which is resolutely impervious to discoveries and innovations—a school from which a sort of minority set of teachers and preachers claim to draw inspiration. The Constitutions of the country and its political life, in particular, have been fashioned by people who directly or indirectly stem from the Aligarh school. Thus, the entire population has since become accustomed to compatibility, indeed a harmonious coexistence between Islam and democracy. In fact—and this is quite rare—in Pakistan, democracy is designated by an Arab term, 'jumhuriya', analogous with religious concepts, while in the rest of the Muslim world, it is the Greek term that has been adopted. In short, while it is true that Islam imposes moral rules for the Pakistani people, politics is for the most part a matter of electoral choice and the balance of power. Thus, the Islamist discourse, which can hardly be termed scandalous given the fact that it glorifies Islam, only partially mobilizes the people and even less the voters when it comes to supporting a government project in this regard, except perhaps in the event of extreme disarray and the peremptory failure of both democracy and nationalism.

It is true that just as in the case of many other Muslim countries, Islamism still has, to a certain extent, the power to lead to a certain polarization of the discontent, of the frustration and disappointments stemming from the distorted or perverse practice of democracy, within the country itself or amongst Western partners. Nevertheless, it is not the only recourse available and the Pakistanis—in spite of low literacy rates, limited access to information and the means of influence that the imam of the mosque in each village or city district may have—are still able to make a distinction between present-day democracy and what it could really be. They, therefore, find recourse in the power play between political parties or changes in the Constitution rather than in an unlikely transformation of the political field into a purely moral and religious one. They are all the more wary of such a prospect because of the examples set by other regimes that have failed to convince them of their feasibility—even those supposed to be the most friendly ones like that of the Taliban—and in which there is so little difference between the holy and the profane.

However, religious intimidation retains some of its effects on their consciences. The various regimes that have come to power in Pakistan have often been tempted to exploit the leverage that fanatic militants could place at the service of national interests, particularly at the country's doorsteps (Afghanistan, Kashmir and tribal areas).

All this results in a situation where the various forums of power, believing that the people are immunized against Islamism, do not hesitate to promote it as a weapon of defence—or even of offence. That is a somewhat cynical policy, since an entire series of institutions of religious education and training in Pakistan, or in some parts of the Afghan territory subject to Pakistani influence, are being transformed into nurseries for indefatigable fighters. At the present time, these combatants, who constitute a strategic mass of a few hundreds of thousands of young people, seem to have the wind in their sails, since their participation in the restoration of peace in many parts of Afghanistan and in the establishment of a regime in this country that knows no other law than the shariah. Their rise is in sharp contrast to the slow sliding of the government into a morass of indebtedness, authoritarianism and unpopularity. However, the situation has not yet reached the stage of the colonization of Pakistan by the Deobandi Taliban. They have no means of training entire peoples. Their simp-listic discourse is far from attractive. What is more, elitist religious movements like the Jamaat-i-Islami are not really on their side.

In brief, it would be wrong to say that Pakistan is threatened by Islamism. It would be more correct to say that Pakistani Islamism is a threat to countries other than its land of birth.

THE REALITY OF PAKISTAN'S PROBLEMS

If we put aside the perspective of uncertainty about its identity or of the Islamist threat, we would inevitably wonder about the nature of the problems that Pakistan has to face. The reality of these problems cannot be denied because of the fact that, since Partition, this country has witnessed a series of upheavals, political adventures and crises.

There seem to be two kinds of explanations for this state of affairs. First of all, the heart of the country's cultural, political and administrative activities, i.e. the region of western Punjab, including Islamabad, Rawalpindi and Lahore, is too close to Kashmir and the tragic events taking place there, inevitably drawing Pakistan into spiralling interaction with its affairs.

Hence, instead of living up to its non-Indianness by engaging in the kind of normal relations with India that ordinarily exist between neighbouring countries, Pakistan finds itself trapped in anti-Indianness, with all the tragic consequences that an arms race can have on a country whose population is eight times less than that of its rival (the recent nuclear tests have only underlined a very old phenomenon). Such a situation of permanent alert obscures the economic and social stakes involved in the political debate and leads the Pakistani author-ities to various kinds of excesses of Islamolatry. (That is what hap-pened in Gen. Zia's time, for example, but the Communist attack in Afghanistan as well as a certain atmosphere prevailing in the Muslim world at that time also had a role to play.) Indeed, the 'endemic turbulence' drives the Pakistani State towards a tenacious indulgence in the most combative Islamist influences (which has led to the absurd acts of violence of 'sectarian' groupings in the recent past). In other words, Pakistan's internal politics, with all its economic, financial and religious aspects, cannot be analysed without bearing the Kashmir issue in mind.

The second element is social in nature. Since the death of Moham-mad Ali Jinnah in 1948, a certain prosperous oligarchy took up the major political posts in the country. As a result, all democratic and economic activities are two-faced. On the one hand, there is a very visible side consisting of the preparation, defence and implementation of programmes aimed at increasing prosperity and distributing wealth on the basis of an acceptable degree of equality—in fact, Pakistan has witnessed periods of rapid growth and the improvement of the living condition of the poorest sections of the population—and on the other, a more hidden side, devoted to the replication of existing structures and hierarchies by any means possible.

In the long-term, this has resulted in the development of networks of supporters that distort the very meaning of the electoral process, as also the way the administration functions. Indeed, this has led to the establishment of a parallel society and economy exposed to increasing criminalization and inclined to play with clan loyalties or ethnic rivalries. Along with this world of networks, Pakistan also has a very vigorous civil society, increasing its ties with the various centres of power and often transversal in nature as regards the provinces and ethnies, promoting the use of Urdu as the effective national language. The trials and tribulations of this silent struggle are quite difficult to fathom, just as it is difficult to see where it will all end. Is the fact that the MQM has abandoned its role as an ethnic network in order to try and become a political movement representing the middle class a promising indicator, or a mere incantation with no future? It must be borne in mind that what is really at stake is social change. The fact that social change can only apparently be brought about by the Pakistanis themselves, as no imported models seem operable, further underlines the country's originality. We optimistically believe that this country is not the scene of a tragedy, i.e. a bundle of insoluble contradictions, but rather, and like in the case of many other countries in the world—of a mere drama.

NOTE

1. Mario Bussagli, *L'Art du Gandhara* (Gandhara Art), Paris: Le Livre de Poche, 1996 (Italian edition 1984).

Contributors

AMÉLIE BLOM is a Ph.D. scholar in Political Science at the Institut d'Etudes Politiques de Paris where she was previously Senior Lecturer (1995-2000). She is currently Visiting and Research Fellow at the Lahore University of Management Sciences (Department of Social Sciences) where she teaches Pakistani Politics and International Relations. She has published articles on Pakistan's Kashmir policy in *Cultures et Conflits* and on Islamic parties in Pakistan in *Pakistan, carrefour de tensions régionales* edited by Christophe Jaffrelot.

GILLES DORRONSORO, Professor of Political Science, presently based in Istanbul, has done fieldwork in Afghanistan since 1988. Among his latest publications is *La révolution afghane*. He is currently working on a book about ethnicity in Turkey.

SUMIT GANGULY is Professor of Asian Studies and Government at the University of Texas at Austin. He has previously taught at James Madison College, Michigan State University and at Hunter College and the Graduate Center of the City University of New York. He has also been an Adjunct Professor of Political Science at Columbia University. Professor Ganguly has written extensively on ethnic violence, nuclear strategy and foreign policy. He has been both a Guest Scholar and a Fellow at the Woodrow Wilson International Center for Scholars in Washington, D.C. and a Visiting Fellow at the Center for International Security and Cooperation at Stanford University.

Professor Ganguly has published in the *Annals, Asian Affairs, Asian Survey*, the *Journal of Asian and African Affairs*, the *Journal of Commonwealth and Comparative Politics, Current History, Foreign Affairs, International Security*, the *Journal of Strategic Studies* and the *Washington Quarterly*. He currently serves on the editorial boards of *Asian Affairs, Asian Survey, Current History* and the *Journal of Strategic Studies*. He has recently assumed the editorship of a new social science journal focused on India, *The India Review*.

His most recent book is *The Crisis in Kashmir: Portents of War, Hopes of Peace*.

FRÉDÉRIC GRARE is Director of the Centre de Sciences Humaines, New Delhi. He holds a Ph.D. in International Relations from the Graduate

Institute of International Studies, Geneva and had previously worked for the Programme for Strategic and International Security Studies in Geneva. Dr. Grare's recent publications include: *India and ASEAN: The Politics of India's Look-East Policy* (co-edited with A. Mattoo), *India's Energy: Essays on Sustainable Development* (co-edited with P.R. Shukla and Pierre Audinet), *Islamism and Security: Political Islam and the Western World, Tajikistan: The Trials of Independence* (co-authored with Shirin Akiner and Mohammed-Reza Djalili) and *Political Islam in the Indian Subcontinent: The Jamaat-i-Islami.*

CHRISTOPHE JAFFRELOT is Director of CERI and Editor-in-Chief of *Critique Internationale*. He teaches South Asian Politics at Sciences Po (CERI).

His most recent publications are *The Hindu nationalist movement and Indian politics, 1925 to the 1990s, La démocratie en Inde–Religion, caste et politique* and *Dr. Ambedkar, leader intouchable et père de la Constitution indienne*. He has edited *L'Inde contemporaine–De 1950 à nos jours, Le Pakistan, carrefour de tensions régionales, Démocraties d'ailleurs–Démocraties et démocratisations hors d'Occident* and *Le Pakistan*. He has also co-edited with Blom Hansen, *The BJP and the Compulsions of Politics in India*.

PIERRE LAFRANCE graduated from La Sorbonne and the School for Eastern Languages and Civilisations in Paris. He is an Arabist and a student of Islamic thought by education and from experience since he spent most of his life in Muslim countries. Born in Tunis in 1932, he joined the diplomatic service in 1963 and was posted in Algeria, Libya, Iran, Afghanistan, Kuwait, Saudi Arabia, Mauritania and Pakistan. Before this last assignment, he was head of the Department for Middle Eastern and North African Affairs in his Ministry.

Having studied Urdu, fluent in Persian, and a member of NGOs working in Afghanistan, Lafrance has devoted much of his time since 1993 to Pakistani and Afghan affairs.

S.V.R. NASR is Associate Professor of Political Science at the University of San Diego. He has worked on the relationship between Islamism and politics in South Asia and published extensively on the subject. He is the author of *The Islamic Leviathan. the Jamaat Islami of Pakistan, Mawdudi and the making of Islamic Revivalism* and *The Islamic Leviathan: Islam and the making of State Power.*

JEAN-LUC RACINE is Senior Fellow, Centre for the Study of India and South Asia, School for Advanced Studies in Social Sciences, Paris. He is currently working on Indian perceptions of the world order, India's geopolitics and Indo-Pak relations. His last publication to be translated into English is *La question identitaire en Asie du Sud*.

OLIVIER ROY who has a Ph.D. in Political Science is currently Senior Researcher at CNRS. He was the head of OSCE's Mission for Tajikistan (February-October 1994). He was also Special Representative of the OSCE's Chairman in Office in Tajikistan (August 1993-February 94) and a Consultant on Afghanistan with UNOCA (1988).

He is the author of *Islam and Resistance in Afghanistan, The Lessons of the Afghan War, The Failure of Political Islam* and *The New Central Asia, The Creation of Nations*.

YUNAS SAMAD is Lecturer in Sociology in the Department of Applied Social Sciences at the University of Bradford. His publications include *A Nation in Turmoil: Nationalism and Ethnicity in Pakistan 1937-58*, and *Culture, Identity and Politics: Ethnic Minorities in Britain* (co-edited with T. Ranger and O. Stuart). He is also the Guest Editor of the special issue 'Muslims in Europe', *Innovation: European Journal of Social Sciences*, 10(4), 1998.

SAEED SHAFQAT is founder member and Chairman of the Department of Pakistan Studies established in 1973 at the Quaid-e-Azam University, Islamabad. Currently, he is Quaid-e-Azam Distinguished Professor at the School of International Affairs and Public Policy, South Asian Institute, Columbia University and Consultant, Asian Development Bank and UNDP on Democracy, Governance and Institution Building. His research articles on the culture, politics and various aspects of public policy and reform have been published in *South Asia Bulletin, Journal of South Asia and Middle Eastern Studies* and *Asian Survey*. He is the author of *Political System of Pakistan and Public Policy* and *Civil Military Relations in Pakistan*. He has also edited *Contemporary Issues in Pakistan Studies*.

IAN TALBOT is a Professor in South Asian Studies at Coventry University, where he is Director of the Centre for South Asian Studies. His publications include *Punjab and the Raj, Provincial Politics and the Pakistan Movement, Freedom's Cry. The Popular Dimension in the Pakistan Movement and Partition Experience in North-West India, Khizr Tiwana, The Punjab Unionist party and the Partition of India, Pakistan. A Modern History*, and *India and Pakistan* as well as numerous articles on South Asian history and politics. He is founding editor of the *International Journal of Punjab Studies* and is a Fellow of the Royal Historical Society.

MOHAMMAD WASEEM is the Professor and Chairman of the International Relations Department at the Quaid-e-Azam University. He is the author of *The 1993 Elections in Pakistan* and *Politics and the State in Pakistan*, *Political Conflict in Pakistan* (forthcoming), *Mohajir Nationalism in Pakistan* (forthcoming) and *Electoral Reform in Pakistan* (forthcoming).

MARIAM ABOU ZAHAB is doing Ph.D. at the Institut d'Etudes Politiques in Paris. She teaches at the South Asian Department of the Inalco and at the IEP.